# The Rise of Modern Judaism

*An Intellectual History of German Jewry 1650 – 1942*

HEINZ MOSHE GRAUPE

# The Rise of Modern Judaism

## An Intellectual History of German Jewry 1650–1942

Translated from German by JOHN ROBINSON

ROBERT E. KRIEGER PUBLISHING COMPANY
HUNTINGTON, NEW YORK
1978

Original Edition 1979

Printed and Published by
ROBERT E. KRIEGER PUBLISHING CO., INC.
645 NEW YORK AVENUE
HUNTINGTON, NEW YORK 11743

Copyright © 1979 by
ROBERT E. KRIEGER PUBLISHING CO., INC.

Printed in the United States of America

Library of Congress Cataloging in Publication Data

Graupe, Heinz Moshe.
  The rise of modern Judaism.

  Translation of Die Entstehung des modernen Judentums.
  Includes index.
  1. Judaism—Germany.   2. Judaism—History—Modern
Period, 1750-   3. Jews in Germany—History.   I. Title.
[BM316.G713  1979]          296'.09          77-9059
ISBN 0-88275-395-9

*To my wife and son*

## Foreword to the American Edition

The purpose of this book is to illustrate the rise of modern Judaism through the social and intellectual* history of the Jews in Germany. It is to my knowledge the first attempt to describe this development in its entirety. It covers three centuries up until the violent suppression of the last spark of visible Jewish spiritual-intellectual life in Germany during the Second World War**. As a background understanding of this intellectual development, the political, economic and social events of this three-century long epoch are repeatedly drawn upon, for intellectual history does not take place in a vacuum. But the real impact upon the formation of modern Judaism—its characteristic—lies in the new pattern of thought and existence.

Since the mid-seventeenth century the small German branch of Ashkenazi Jewry began to develop more and more on its own, eventually, becoming the decisive factor in the moulding of modern Judaism. In the nineteenth century it then influenced the much larger, and for a long time leading, East European branch. East European Judaism, indeed, had meanwhile been revived through the important intellectual historical phenomenon of Ḥasidism which bypassed Judaism in Germany. Yet it is directly out of the critical controversy with Ḥasidism, beginning in East European Jewry already at the start of the nineteenth century, that modern East European Judaism had emerged—influenced by and in close accord with the Jewish Enlightenment in Germany. Present-day Judaism—notably in the new centres in Israel, America and some European countries—maintained its distinctiveness through both these mainstreams of German and East European development which in the meantime have come largely to intermingle. Until about 1890 German Jewry had nevertheless been the guiding force in the modern development.

*The word "Geistesgeschichte" translated nearly always in this book as "intellectual history" is more comprehensive than any possible English rendering, since "Geist" embraces not only intellect but also mind and spirit. The translator asks the reader to bear this in mind.—See also note number 251.
**On 19 July 1942 the last institution of Jewish learning, the College for the Science of Judaism in Berlin (Hochschule für die Wissenschaft des Judentums in Berlin) was closed.

The precursors of the separate development in German Jewry appear long before the Mendelssohnian era where the cleavage between traditional and modern Judaism is usually placed. Under the cover of the rigid traditional life-style signs of loosening had begun already in the seventeenth century to penetrate the most varied circles of the Jewish population. These transformations have to be seen not as chance exceptional occurrences but as symptomatic of the self-altering attitude and inner relationship of the Jews to their life-style and environment. Thus the Jewish Enlightenment was no sudden revolutionary turning-point; it was prepared for by over a century long process.

Only a few preliminary studies for my work have come to hand. For the pre-Enlightenment period there is only Azriel Shohet's work 'Im Ḥilufe Tekufot, Reshit Hahaskalah be-Yahadut Germaniah' (English title: Beginnings of the Haskalah among German Jewry), Jerusalem, 1960 with whose interpretation of the epoch I am in general agreement—and the somewhat differently orientated books and studies by Jacob Katz. The Mendelssohnian and post-Mendelssohnian eras, on the other hand, are dealt with by Alexander Altmann, Albert Lewkowitz, Nathan Rotenstreich and Max Wiener. Monographs on these periods have been written by many others.

History, and in particular Jewish history, probably has to be written and interpreted anew in every generation—from a new perspective and with new emphasis. For the Jewish historian, after the decimation of one third of Jewry and the foundation of the State of Israel, this is especially true. Many reviewers of the first German edition of my book have to my pleasure appreciated this. In the post-war years many books have appeared especially in Germany by Jewish and non-Jewish authors who wish to show the importance of the Jews for German and Western culture. The present work differs fundamentally from this literature. It does not ask for whom the Jews were useful or important—a basically inverted antisemitic though, at all events, apologetic formulation of the question—but rather how German Jewry had come into being and what significance it is to be ascribed in Jewish history; how its particular development has decidedly shaped the rise of modern Judaism.

This book is the outcome of lectures delivered in the University of Hamburg. Their audience consisted of German students whose openness to intellectual-historical, social and political questions as well as a readiness to appreciate Judaism was to be taken for granted, but lacking knowledge of its teaching, history or problems. The same will also likely be true for many of my readers. The first two chapters, therefore, by way of introduction to the theme proper, give a brief survey of the preceding history of the Jews in Germany and an explanatory outline of the picture of traditional Judaism which was the basis of the new development. I have tried, moreover, to explain aspects like Oral Law, Talmud, Kabbalah etc. at greater length than is customary in works intended only for specialists.

That Jewish and general philosophical developments and problems come perhaps disproportionately strongly to the fore, is accounted for in the thematic of my earlier work. The close linkage of the Jewish with the German and general philosophical and cultural trends may, as I hope, facilitate the reader's understanding of Jewish reflexes and reactions. Due to the connection between the historical description of events and problems repetition has been unavoidable. This is especially the case in the two chapters "Portrayals of Jewish Self-Understanding", where I have brought together the most important witnesses of the historico-theoretical, philosophical and religious self-understanding of Judaism.

The original German edition of this book appeared in 1969 in Leibniz Verlag, Hamburg, as volume I of the Hamburg contributions to the history of the German Jews which the Institute for the History of the German Jews, Hamburg, is publishing. This Institute, founded by the Senate of the Free and Hanseatic City of Hamburg, was since 1964 built up and led by me during its first eight years. The first edition of the book has been out of print for several years. A second enlarged and revised German edition was published in 1977 by Helmut Buske Verlag, Hamburg. This First American edition differs from the 2nd German edition by numerous alterations and additions introduced by the author, mostly for the benefit of the reader who may not be conversant with the details of German history or intellectual history, and to give greater lucidity to some complicated subjects. It may therefore be looked upon as a third edition of the work.

For manifold suggestions received through discussion, correspondence and reviews of the first German edition, I am indebted to Dr H. G. Adler; to my deceased teacher Prof. Dr Hugo S. Bergmann; to Dr Solomon A. Birnbaum; to Prof. Dr Victor Ehrenberg for rectifying details on Franz Rosenzweig's relatives and friends; to Prof. Dr Hans Liebeschütz and Prof. Dr H. J. Schoeps—and last but not least to my wife for her constant and stimulating help. My son, Dr Daniel Graupe, although working in a very different field, read the English manuscript and enriched my book with many valuable suggestions, expressing hereby his deep identification with my work.

I express special thanks to the translator, Rev. John Robinson, an Irish Presbyterian clergyman, and to his wife Mrs. Muriel Robinson. Mr. Robinson, who earlier participated in my seminars at Hamburg University, undertook in close cooperation with me the difficult task of translating material, mostly new to him, with great interest and understanding.

The New York office of the Leo Baeck Institute was helpful in supplying the publisher with most illustrations included in the book.

Finally I wish to thank the publisher, Mr. Robert E. Krieger, for his interest, patience and painstaking care in the preparation of this first American edition.

*Heinz Moshe Graupe*

Hamburg, August 1978

# Transliteration of Hebrew Names and Words

The author, for the benefit of the reader, has avoided a scientific transliteration of Hebrew names and words. Biblical names e.g. are written in the form accepted in English.

To facilitate correct reading, however, he has introduced dots under the two letters "h" and "z" in cases of Hebrew letters that have no equivalent in English:

ḥ (denoting the Hebrew letter Ḥet), a strongly inflated almost guttural h, as e.g. in Shulḥan, Ḥasidism, pronounced as the German ch in doch.

ẓ (denoting the Hebrew letter Ẓadeh), pronounced ts, as in Ẓaddik, Ẓevi (pronounced Tsaddik, Tsevi).—Only exception is "Kibbutz" which is accepted in that spelling in English.

# Contents

## List of Illustrations

*Courtesy of the Leo Baeck Institute New York.

*The Rise of Modern Judaism*

*An Intellectual History of German Jewry 1650–1942*

# CHAPTER 1

## The Jews in Germany at the Close of the Middle Ages

To begin this presentation in the middle of the seventeenth century may seem in some respects arbitrary. For some of the tendencies and phenomena of which we shall hear are traceable to still earlier times. The new self-awareness, the new temper—so unlike that of the Middle Ages—that characterized the people of the Renaissance, had begun to affect Jews too.

This had not only happened in Italy where the Renaissance culture had influenced Jewish writers and scholars. The Jews of Germany also did not remain untouched by the new attitude. A man like *Josel of Rosheim*, who in the first half of the sixteenth century appeared before emperors and imperial diets as counsel for the Jews appealing for the equal rights of man, was certainly a figure who only a little earlier would have been unheard of and unthinkable.

But men like Josel of Rosheim, or the few Jewish scholars who taught Hebrew to the Christian humanists or collaborated with Christian printers, still worked initially within the framework of traditional medieval Judaism. They were merely symptoms of a change beginning to take place. These early beginnings had in fact in the sixteenth century at first been almost completely repressed. For following the expulsions of the Jews from Spain, a new Messianic mysticism in Judaism had gained ground which curbed all endeavours towards a wider outlook. Only in the course of the seventeenth century, and particularly after the Thirty Years' War, did political and social changes create the preliminary conditions for an economic and cultural de-ghettoization. Only now could those first beginnings break out into ever-widening circles and unfold their intellectual-historical efficacy.

In 1648 the Thirty Years' War came to an end. This year was also one of the most decisive in Jewish history. The uprising of the Cossacks in the Ukraine under Chmielnicki against their Polish overlords had in the same year unleashed terrible persecutions of the Jews. It was the first serious shock in a hitherto flourishing and assured Polish Jewry. After that the Jews began to migrate back to western Europe.

In the same year, 1648, in Smyrna, Sabbatai Ẓevi declared himself Messiah. The movement that was thereby set in motion agitated the entire Jewish world. In its consequences it was to shake the religious and ethical foundations of Judaism for over a century. During this time the mercantile orientated territorial states were formed in the German countries. Those modern rational administrative states gave new possibilities to the economic functions of Jews.

Out of such emotional religious shocks and political vicissitudes the first beginnings of modern Judaism arose. Consequently, to begin our real presentation with the year 1648, or at any rate with the seventeenth century of the Christian era is well justified. It was also the time during which the German branch of Ashkenazi Jewry began to sever itself from the larger Polish body.

About this time the Jews of Germany had already behind them a history of many centuries. I should like to relate this in brief outline in order to make their position at the close of the Middle Ages intelligible.

The history of the Jews in Germany may in some places extend back to Roman times, as in Cologne, Trier and Regensburg (Ratisbon).[1] This history, continuously and documentarily verifiable, begins with the Carolingians. The first Jews of Germany had probably come from the western and southern parts of France and from Italy. There were at first, it seems, few families of high-privileged merchants.[2] They had to do with transit trade with the Orient. They travelled from France (Narbonne) through the Mediterranean; and when the sea-route through the division of the Islamic empire into the feuding Caliphates of Baghdad and Cordova became too unsafe, they took the overland route across the Balkans. To the Frankish royal courts and their noblemen the Jewish merchants brought back the desired luxury articles of the old cultural centres of the Mediterranean and of the Orient. They also established industries which finished those de luxe articles, and from the outset stood in a special relationship to the royal court (commendatio), as whose agents and purveyors they worked. With the commencement of the colonisation of the Slavonic countries, Jewish merchants also played a part in the commerce of these lands newly appearing on the horizon as far

---

[1] In the year 321 the Emperor Constantine issued an edict to the decuria in Cologne concerning the exemption of Jews from municipal posts (Aronius, Regesta No. 2). Archaeological discoveries from the Roman era in Trier give indications of the presence of Jews in this period (Adolf Altmann, Das früheste Vorkommen der Juden in Deutschland, Trier 1932—The earliest appearance of Jews in Germany). In Regensburg, and probably also in Cologne, it is conjectured from the situation of the Jewish quarters in the centre of the former Roman city, that continuous Jewish settlements existed here from Roman times and beyond the epoch of mass-migration till into the Middle Ages. (Elbogen-Sterling, Geschichte der Juden in Deutschland, Frankfurt 1966, p. 14 f. History of the Jews in Germany.)

[2] Aronius No. 81-88; I.A. Agus, Urban Civilization in Pre-Crusade Europe, Vol. 1, Introduction, New York 1965.

as Russia. Here the focal point at first lay in trade with prisoner-of-war slaves.

From the beginning Jews seem to have participated in the founding of the cities of the Saxon emperors in the newly-won territories. We find Jews already at that time in Magdeburg and Merseburg, in Prague and perhaps also in Halle.[3] In these newly founded cities, as in the older centres of the Rhineland, Jews formed independent corporate bodies alongside of and on an equality with other townspeople.

Their legal and social position becomes clear from the privileges of the emperor Henry IV to the Jews of Speyer and Worms 1090.[4] The Jews of this time were farming townspeople like other town dwellers. They owned houses, fields and vineyards. The head of the Jewish community stood on a level with the mayor of the local Christian population. They had considerable autonomy in legal matters, with right of appeal to the emperor and bishop, respectively. And they enjoyed—at any rate in both the above-mentioned communities— exemption from taxes to the royal customs houses as well as the emperor's protection of life and property. In return, they for their part, were liable to certain dues.

Corresponding to the relatively favourable legal and social position of the Jews during the reign of the Franconian and Saxon emperors was a first flowering time in the intellectual life of this region, for which the name *Ashkenaz* now came into vogue in Hebrew literature, following a Biblical reference to a northern people (Gen. 10.3).

Up until now the Jews of the diaspora had been intellectually dependent upon the old centres of Jewish learning, located in the great academies of the land of Israel and Mesopotamia. Thither one had recourse for decisions on questions pertaining to the ceremonial and religious law. It was only in the tenth and eleventh centuries that the communities of North Africa, Spain and Provence freed themselves from this dependence in connection with the splitting up of the Islamic world into two separate caliphates. At that time a new independent centre sprang up in the post-Carolingian North, the old Lotharingia. In Worms, Mayence and Speyer, as well as in Troyes in the north of France, famous academies were founded. Scholars taught there whose decisions directed the life of the Ashkenazi Jews. (Two scholars of that epoch have retained their significance to the present day: Rabbenu Gershom in Mayence (dec. 1028), the first great authority in Europe, to whom, inter alia, the religious-legal directive on monogamy goes back. The other is Rashi (1040-1105), the Jewish Bible and Talmud commentator par excellence.)

This first mainly peaceful development lasted for three centuries. In 1096,

---

[3] Otto I and II placed the Jews with other citizens in Magdeburg and Merseburg under the authority of the resident Bishop (Aronius No. 129 and 132 to 134; concerning Prague: vide Germania Judaica, vol. 1 p. 270, and Halle p. 125 ff.).

[4] Aronius No. 168, 170, 171.

just six years after the privileges of Worms and Speyer, the crusaders of the First Crusade came through the Rhineland. And with one blow the privileges and the royal protection were to prove themselves brittle bulwarks.

The crusaders descended upon the communities in Worms, Mayence, Cologne and in other places. Before they undertook the long journey to combat the "infidels" in the Holy Land, they were to wipe out the infidels in their own country. And before they set out in conquest of the legendary treasures of the Orient, they were able to snatch for themselves the fortune of Jews lying within reach. The property of Jews was plundered, their houses destroyed, their people murdered. A large number of them took their own life and that of their wives and children after attempts at self-defense and at entrusting themselves to the protection of the authorities and to the help of their Christian neighbours had proved futile. Only in Speyer did Henry IV's devoted and energetic Bishop John succeed—after the first massacre—in taking strong measures and rescuing the greater part of the community. The Jews in Trier and Regensburg accepted baptism pro forma.[5] —The old relationship of trade and trust between Christians and Jews was disastrously shattered for many centuries.

Henry IV, who had been in Italy during these happenings, decided on a new orientation for his Jewish policy, since privileges obviously did not suffice to secure the protection of Jews when the emperor was not at hand. The privileges were supplemented by the inclusion of Jews into a general peace of the empire which was agreed upon by all in positions of authority. In the emperor's Peace of Mayence, in 1103, Jews are therefore mentioned alongside clerics, farmers and women. They thereby entered a number of sections of the population which were seen to be in special need of protection and whose injury constituted a breach of the peace. Punishment of breakers of the peace was incumbent not only upon the emperor, but also upon every local authority that had confirmed the emperor's peace on oath.[6]

With the inclusion of Jews in the emperor's peace, deterioration in the legal status of German Jews nevertheless set in. For whoever stood within the peace-protection of the realm, it was required of him that he should not be armed and not resort to self-protection. The right to carry a weapon was seen as a basic right of the free man. What in the case of clergy purely underlined their consecrated higher vocation, was vis-à-vis the Jews a defamatory designation. This, and the close bond of the Jews to the emperor that existed from the beginning, led after about a century's development to the new legal concept of the "Kammerknechtschaft" (court-bondage).[7]

---

[5] Cp. A. Neubauer—M. Stern, Hebräische Berichte Über die Judenverfolgungen während der Kreuzzüge (Hebrew accounts of the persecutions of Jews during the Crusades); Aronius No. 176-206.

[6] Aronius No. 260.

[7] Aronius No. 496; G. Kisch, Forschungen zur Rechts- and Sozialgeschichte der Juden in Deutschland, Zürich 1955, p. 16-90 (Research on the legal and social history of the Jews in Germany).

Servi camerae nostrae—Jews were first called this in the year 1236, when Frederick II endorsed Henry IV's Privilege of Worms and extended it to all the Jews of Germany. In support of their new status an historic legend was quoted, according to which the Roman Caesar Vespasian after the conquest of Jerusalem, instead of killing the Jewish prisoners, out of gratitude for medical help obtained  through Flavius Josephus, only made them his slaves. Now, twelve hundred years later, the Roman-German emperors, as heirs of the antique Romans, entered into those ancient rights.

Parallel to this secular constitutional-legal development there ran an ecclesiastical-legal one, according to which—as it was finally fixed by the Fourth Lateran Council—Jews were to become, as punishment for their non-recognition of Jesus, slaves of Christians. Both lines of development met in the new concept of the *Kammerknechtschaft*. If with Frederick II this was only a formal statement of the exclusive relation of the Jews to the emperor and of his exclusive fiscal law over them, this Jewish prerogative soon became literally understood as bondage. The emperor could at will interfere with the life and property of Jews.

During the struggle for the throne at the time of the Interregnum the Jewish prerogative was pawned, pledged and prostituted by the various emperors. In this way Jews fell into bondage to countless territorial lords and cities, great and small. Their earlier freedom of movement and trade in the entire territory of the realm was lost. In the "Golden Bull", Charles IV's new constitutional law of the realm, in 1356, the Jewish prerogative together with the mine and other royal prerogatives was overall transferred to the electors and later to other estates of the realm. In order to protect at least nominally the emperor's sovereignity, as well as his own prerogative to exploit the Jews, Ludovic of Bavaria had already in 1242 introduced a supplementary poll-tax on Jews, the "Golden Penny", later called the "Golden Tribute Penny". This, independently of other Jewish taxes, was to be credited direct to the royal treasury. The golden penny was followed still further by special royal taxes with every available pretext. The Jews for their part adhered to the old protective relationship to the emperor. For despite the disintegration of the central authority, this gave them a mainstay, even if a weak and very dearly purchased one.

For the emperor, the territorial rulers and the cities, Jews were only objects of exploitation and extortion, just like the mines with which in the Golden Bull the Jews were put on a level. They served as sponges which were let suck full, so that they could be squeezed out. The entire odium and hate of the broad masses, however, was turned upon the Jews, who still had to earn their money in order to pay the taxes and contributions demanded of them. In this way the realm and the territorial lords dispensed with a complicated apparatus for tax revenue. For the few Jews were easily accessible and easily compelled into paying.

Since the beginning of the eleventh century the occupational structure of

Jews had changed, too. The wholesale and transit trade had slipped from their hand. Through the Crusades it had been taken over by the Italian seaports. The Christianization of the Slavonic countries had also obstructed their trade with the East—the more so as this Christianization was widely carried out by Crusades which had no place for Jews. To them there remained only the money trade, lending in exchange for securities and interest.

Traffic in money had lain long in the hands of the monasteries and churches with whom large capitals had accumulated. But the Third and Fourth Lateran Councils (in 1179 and 1215) had terminated this activity of the Church, and over and above this had forbidden Christians to lend money for interest. These canonical precepts did not apply to Jews, who in the eyes of the church remained the only legal moneylenders. Apart from them there were of course, throughout the entire Middle Ages, the "Lombards" and the French "Cahorsins" who knew how to get round the prohibition of interest by a variety of commissions and surcharges, and whose effective rates of interest often outstripped that of the Jews. Yet, it was the Jews —everywhere recognisable—to whom the barons and territorial lords in need of money could turn when required; later, too, craftsmen in the cities. In their capacity as moneylenders Jews were pre-emptorily called into the territories and the cities. The interest rate that by modern standards was exorbitantly high was prescribed for them.[8] Through this business, not favourably looked upon by the rabbis, but patiently borne through extremity, they were able to pay their taxes. The risk, it is true, was great. For payment of debts depended very much upon the goodwill of the powerful and often violent debtor. Time and again the Jewish creditor had to consent to an extension of the period of payment. And often he lost not only his money but also his home and his life.

The precariousness of Jewish existence, through its ever increasing isolation among the population, was increased still further. The canonical decisions of the Fourth Lateran Council of 1215 were meant to prevent intercourse between Jews and Christians. Jews, already singled out from their neighbours in virtue of their different customs, festivals and holidays, were from now on also prescribed to wear special attire and marks of distinction. In pictures of the Middle Ages we find Jews made conspicuous by noticeable hats and badges. They were to be hated, mistrusted and mocked. Anyway, the person of a different faith or an unbeliever was a spectacle wrapped in mystery. He seemed to be gifted with magical powers, and it was not long until the Jew was identified with the devil.[9] Moreover his

---

[8] Cp. Stobbe, Die Juden in Deutschland während des M-A, p. 103-116 (The Jews in Germany during the Middle Ages); R. Straus, Die Juden in Wirtschaft und Gesellschaft, p. 70-75 (The Jews in Commerce and Society).

[9] Cp. Trachtenberg, The Devil and the Jews, Cleveland 1943.

occupation as moneylender, though required, was branded as unchristian and unethical. On that account one had no scruple in "taking back" from the Jew his gain and belongings by robbery or murder. Suspicion, fear and hatred of the strange looking Jew and resentment against the troublesome creditor, created a disposition towards him in which every rumour, however absurd, every circulated slander, was believed. Bloody persecutions spread avalanche-like over whole countries. Massacre, robbery and expulsions were the outcome.

Three such readily believed fabricated charges appeared in Germany from the thirteenth century onwards: the "blood-libel", the indictment of the desecration of the Host and the poisoning of the wells. Although popes and bishops condemned and prohibited these accusations, they were voiced around by the new Orders of Mendicant Friars. These preachers, coming as they did from the people, knew how to manipulate public feeling and everywhere to indulge time and again in Jew-baiting. Moreover, Jews became a pawn of inner political tensions, of the power-struggle of the guilds against the city patricians, and likewise of the struggle of the cities against the territorial lords, bishops and imperial authority.

The most long-lived of these defamations—right up to our own time—was the "blood-libel", as it is called. It was maintained that Jews required Christian blood, whether as remedy for mysterious illnesses, to which they were condemned following the crucifixion of Jesus, or for the preparation of unleavened bread for the Jewish Passover Feast. This defamation which had already been made in antiquity by Greek writers in other no less fantastic form, and which in the early Christian era was blamed upon Christians by pagans,[10] emerged for the first time in Norwich, England in the year 1144. It first appeared in Germany, in Fulda, in 1235. At that time Frederick II appointed a commission of investigation consisting of learned converts, priests and princes who exonerated the Jews from every possible guilt of ritual murder. A few years later, Pope Innocent IV did likewise, and following these many other emperors and popes. But popular superstition, strengthened by confessions wrung from the rack, was stirred up again and again. Countless are the victims who under this pretext were tortured, burnt to death or murdered.

From the thirteenth century onwards, after the Fourth Lateran Council in 1215, when the doctrine of Transubstantiation, the so called "Innocentianum", had been raised to a dogma, a new type of charge arose: that of the "desecration of the Host". Through purchase or theft, Jews had—according to this—brought consecrated wafers into their possession and pierced them with knives, whereupon the wafers had bled. Nowadays one knows that stale bakery products frequently become spotted with a reddish-

---

[10] Cp. Minucius Felix, Octavius, 9.5.

tinted fungus. In those days the reddish wafers incited the masses to murder and persecution of the Jews. In many places churches were dedicated in memory of the "wafer-miracles" and turned into places of pilgrimages in honor of the alleged ritual-murder victims. In 1298 gangs of fanatical peasants, led by a nobleman called Rindfleisch, attacked the Jewish communities in Franconia and Swabia, Bavaria and Austria. 146 communities fell to them. According to one Christian source there were 100,000 victims. From 1335 to 1338 the "Leather-arm" gangs, as they were called, rioted again in Alsace, in Franconia and Bavaria. In Deggendorf a pilgrim-church still standing today, was consecrated to the glory of the allegedly profaned Host. Even the intervention of the emperor was of no avail. In the end a compromise was made with the leader of the gangs, in which he undertook to maintain the peace for ten years. With the expiration of this period, however, the Plague of the Black Death had come (1348/49), and with it a new calumny, a new pretext and a new disaster for the Jews.

The new indictment ran that Jews had poisoned the wells, thereby causing the plague. In Germany it spread from Switzerland over Alsace and the Rhineland to every part of the empire and beyond. There began a general massacre of Jews, the "Juden-braende" (Jewish brands), as it is called. Again—as in 1096—Jews in many communities committed suicide. The slaughter extended to people in regions where the plague did not even reach, like Silesia and Prussia. Thither the Jewish massacre was brought by the ecstatic flagellant gangs whom fear of the plague had panic-stricken.

Disastrous for the Jews was the contemporaneous antagonism between patriciate and the power-thirsty guilds which in the cities reached a climax. The city councils in Strasbourg, Nuremberg and other places sought to protect the Jews. They were removed from office. And the new city-lords gave vent to their fury on the Jews, thereby ridding themselves of their creditors.

Extant "memoir"-books give report on the extent of the slaughter. Whereas "memoir"-lists of earlier persecutions still give the names of victims in detail, there is following this largest blood-bath little more than the names of the communities, who for the hallowing of the Divine Name accepted martyrdom.

Particularly obnoxious was the behaviour of Emperor Charles IV, guardian of the Jews. He managed to do business out of the death of his chamber-serfs. In the year 1348-49 he entered into agreement with several cities —Nuremberg and Frankfurt, for example—openly assigning Jewish property to them in exchange for large remittances, in the event of their owners dying for whatever reasons. These transactions constituted direct imperial licence and invitation to assassinate the Jews.

Those who had escaped murder and the "Jewish brands" fled in those days to *Poland*. Just previously, the Polish kings had called Jews into their country for setting up an urban element, and had given them favourable privileges. From Germany the refugees brought with them the old German language, dress and some customs, and have adhered to them amid their Slavonic environment right into our day.—A small number of Jews, a very small remnant, were able to conceal themselves outside the cities in the German countryside.

The cities that had just previously massacred their Jews, or banished them forever from their walls, very quickly missed the Jewish taxpayers and moneylenders. Indeed, after a very short time they began to call them back, insofar as they were able to be found. This even happened in some places, like Augsburg, in the self-same year, 1348. Within the next fifteen years, at all events, we find everywhere again small Jewish communities.

Their re-acceptance was, however, linked with new aggravated conditions. First of all the right of domicile was only granted for a few years, after the elapse of which it had to be paid for dearly again each time. In this way the cities, by not renewing their residential permits, kept the possibility open of legally re-expelling the Jews whenever desired. The right of residence, more-over, was no longer granted to communities, but to single families whose numbers were restricted. Like every social group in the city, Jews had lived all along near each other in the neighbourhood. Up till now their's was a voluntary concentrated form of settlement around synagogue, school etc., and frequently in the better and more central parts of the city in their own houses. Now, on their re-acceptance by the city, they were assigned to live in districts situated in the worst, most unwholesome and often most notori-ous quarters. Dwelling-houses belonged to the city and were let to them only for high rents. Real estate was no longer permitted them. These Jewish quarters were segregated from the rest of the city by walls and gates and only opened for specified purposes. Every city now laid down Jewish regula-tions which controlled to the minutest detail what Jews were allowed or forbidden to do and in particular what fees and taxes they had to pay.

It is worth noting that this interdiction did not break the inner life of Jews or their morale. On the contrary it strengthened it. They withdrew still more into their religion, family and community, concentrating upon the religious education of their children and the strict fulfilling of the social commandments in the care of the needy. Their flair for beauty found expression in the creating of varied objects d'art for the ornamentation of their synagogues and houses. This led to the tradition of several artistic handcrafts like silver and goldsmithery, embroidery, calligraphy and the like.

The newly founded communities of the survivors were no longer able to attain the same commercial importance as their predecessors before the Black Death. They served in even more blatant manner than previously as objects of and means to extortionery payments. The emperors of the House of Luxembourg were especially inventive in this sphere. Just as Charles IV knew how to gain from the assassination of his "chamber serfs", so too his son Wenzel devised a novel method of using Jews to bring in extra revenues. By means of an agreement drawn up in 1385 with the Swabian and Rhenish federation of cities, he resorted to open robbery of his "chamber-serfs". For a payment of 40,000 florins and the transfer to him of half the urban Jewish taxes, he ordered that a quarter of all debt owed to Jews should be cancelled, and that the remaining three-quarters was not to be paid back to the Jewish creditor but to the cities.

The cities eagerly consented to this transaction with the king, since the most important clients of Jews in those days were still the surrounding territorial lords and princes who were hostile to the cities. The latter now hoped to get them under their control by means of the promissory notes of which the Jews had been deprived. For the territorial lords and barons, as for the small debtors, the advantage of remission of a quarter of their debt was then lost, since they now got unyielding municipal councils as creditors in place of the powerless and largely forbearing Jewish ones. Yet five years later, in 1390, the wily king made a similar agreement with these lords and barons. He exempted them from their debts to Jews a second time in return for a payment that yielded the king more in fact than the payment of the cities.

Wenzel's novel liquidation of debts—called 'death-notes', because they 'erased' the debt-demands—did not only wipe out the economic existence of his Jews, but also shook the entire credit-system of his kingdom. His successors had on that account to abandon this lucrative method. Emperor Sigismund for example, adopted another course. With every possible opportunity he applied special taxes to the Jewish communities: for his coronation as king and later as emperor; for the conducting of the Councils of Constance and Basle; for the Hussite War and similar purposes.

Completely impoverished by these 'deletion of debts' and 'tax-screwing', the Jews lost their worth more and more for the municipal finance policy. They were no longer able to raise larger credits. Since they no longer showed the profit one wished to extract from them, there took place throughout the fifteenth century Jewish expulsions from almost every German city—the last from Regensburg in 1519.

Those who had been expelled from the cities were accepted by the neighbouring territorial lords. For even now the reputation of Jewish usefulness was high enough to make their acceptance look desirable to the knights of the realm and to the lesser and greater territorial lords. This resettling in the country—frequently just outside the gates of the cities which had expelled them—entailed sweeping changes in the social and economic life of the Jews. As the financial business now somewhat declined for them, they began to bring country produce to the city markets and to sell the products of city craftsmen to the peasants. In this way the Jewish retail and peddling trade arose. For the first time in centuries Jews were again associated with some branches of farming, like livestock-dealing and wine-growing

—occupations they practised in some regions throughout the centuries until the very recent past.

The 'gold and silver rush' which the discovery of America brought and the economic upheaval connected with it had bypassed the German Jews in their rural setting. The larger commercial credit and colonial enterprises now lay in the hands of Gentile firms, like Fugger, Welser, inter alia. Only when around 1600 the Portuguese Jews, the earlier 'coerced-Christians', came to Germany and Holland, did Jews again participate in the wholesale and maritime trade. In this they were slowly followed by the Ashkenazi Jews.

For those Jews outside the cities new forms of organisation took shape which corresponded to their own interests as well to those of the territorial lords. The small and scattered Jewish communities, being seldom in the position of acquiring ground for a cemetery, had to combine for this purpose. Only such a combination could also make possible support for the livelihood of rabbis and teachers. Equally, only such an association could guarantee the taxes of all its members. And it was only in these that the territorial lords were interested. Thus, there now arose everywhere 'district-Jewries' (Landjudenschaften) at whose head so-called commanders or spokesmen stood, elected by Jews and endorsed by the public authorities. The most distinguished among them during the reign of the Emperors Maximilian I and Charles V was *Josel of Rosheim* or Joselman (ca 1478-1554), the commander of Alsatian Jewry. It seems he was recognized by the Jewry of the entire realm. He was a man of great diplomatic dexterity, legal learning and personal courage. He was perhaps the first Jew to stand before emperors and princes, not as petitioner but as demander of justice whenever there had been injury. And he often won his case principally because his unselfish commitment was as much acknowledged by the authorities as by his own contemporary co-religionists.

From these commanders of the district-Jewries there emerged a new Jewish element of notables, namely, Jews who in virtue of their office had to keep in constant contact with the court and the magistracy. They were called more and more to financial-political and diplomatic tasks. As 'court-agents' and such like, they became important in the seventeenth and eighteenth centuries.

Of the large old communities there were probably only four from which the Jews had not been expelled: Frankfurt, Worms, Prague and Mayence. They were, it is true, banished from Frankfurt and Worms for a short period at the beginning of the seventeenth century, when in Frankfurt in 1614 the guilds—led by the representative of the Fettkraemer (fat dealer) corporation, Vinzenz Fettmilch and an advocate named Weitz—revolted against the council. The same happened in Worms shortly after the Frankfurt example. But now Emperor Matthew intervened. Fettmilch and Weitz were put under ban of the realm and executed in 1616. Thereupon the Jews were led back again into both cities by the imperial commissioners and the army. The imperial commissioners then publicly announced a new regulation for Jewish residence —the *Frankfurter Juden-Staettigkeit*. This differed from the old one mainly in that it was no longer limited in duration and that on this occasion it was the emperor, not the council, who had authorized it. This was probably the last time that the German emperor energetically and successfully turned imperial responsibility for Jewish protection into reality.

At the end of the sixteenth century a slow return was already taking place from the country into the cities, including cities where hitherto no Jews had lived, and partly into newly-founded cities like Altona and Fuerth. During the Thirty Years' War it stood the Jews in good stead that they lived largely in the country which did not have to suffer as much as the cities under the horrors of war.

# 2

## The Image of Traditional Judaism Around 1650

At the centre of the Jewish world in the Middle Ages was the study of the Law. Under "Law" Judaism means not only the *Written Law*, as it is handed down in the Hebrew Bible. Through century-long reading and study of the Bible in the synagogue, every sentence had been investigated, discussed and interpreted; every commandment elucidated and furnished with new directions. These interpretations, elucidations and directions, which were passed on from generation to generation and added to, were called the *Oral Law*. According to tradition this Oral law will, like Scripture itself, ultimately be traced back to the revelation to Moses at Sinai. But in contrast to the Written Law, the Oral law is not in principle considered closed, so that it can constantly be tested anew and enlarged.

For an understanding of Judaism the Hebrew term *Torah* is instructive. Torah in the strictest sense is the Pentateuch. In its wider connotation the word is used for the Written and Oral Law. Only both together constitute the entire Torah.

The meaning of the word Torah is teaching, instruction. It is no mere holy book, no mere depository of belief or groundwork of a theology. Torah includes all that. But more than this it addresses itself to the will and actions of man. It wants to mould human life and activity Godward. For this reason Torah forms the basis of Jewish education. Judaism does not fit into a picture of religion which understands under religion the passive redemption of the individual by faith (sola fide). It has on that account frequently been denied the character of a religion. In order to distinguish its religious quality from such a picture of religion it has also been called a way of life. Even "religionless Jews" have still kept this way of life in its ethical intent.

The collection of the Oral Law (*Midrash*) originally followed the Bible text. Only about the year 200 of the Christian era was the Oral Law arranged and fixed according to subject. This first collection, set out according to subjects and known as the *Mishnah*, contains juridical instructions, customs and moral teachings. During the next three centuries it formed the basis of the discussions in the academies in the land of Israel[11] and in the Babylonian Diaspora. The discussions of scholars about the sentences and passages of the Mishnah have remained preserved in catch-word-like summaries. They are called *Gemara*. The Mishnah and the Gemara together comprise the *Talmud*.[12] The Talmud which came into being in the Palestinian academies, called the *Jerusalem Talmud*—through adverse circumstances after the Roman Empire had become Christian and intolerant—could not be completed. The *Babylonian Talmud*, on the other hand, edited under more favourable conditions contains nearly all of the Mishnah-treatises. It was completed in the 6th century.

The language of the Mishnah is plain Hebrew, showing in comparison with Biblical Hebrew, many simplifications.[13] This Hebrew of the Mishnah was no artificial scholars' language. Not only the prayers, but also the "Midrash"—those juridical and homiletical collections of the Oral Law which followed the Biblical text—was Hebrew, as was in the main the later Palestinian sermon literature, also called "Midrash". Knowledge of Hebrew could, at least in Palestine, be taken for granted. Even the editor of the Mishnah, Rabbi Jehudah (ca 200), considered only two languages worthy of being spoken: Hebrew and Greek (b. Sotah 49 b; Baba Kama 83 a). In contrast to both these languages was the old colloquial language of the East, Aramaic. We already find Aramaic in the oldest parts of the Bible, and in the later books (Ezra and Daniel) it occupies a large space. For a considerable time Hebrew and Aramaic coexisted side by side. The Hebrew Bible readings in the synagogue already at the time of the second Temple were translated into Aramaic, from which the various versions of the "Targum"—the Aramaic translation of the Bible—emerged. Without ever displacing the Hebrew, Aramaic became the main everday language of the people, and finally also the medium for teaching and discussion in the academies.

---

[11] The widespread view that the Jews were completely dispossessed of their land after the destruction of Jerusalem in the year 70 is erroneous. Not only did the intellectual hegemony still persist for several centuries with Palestinian Jewry. It was still capable of mustering large uprisings, like the Bar Kokhba War against Hadrian (ca 132-135); then in the middle of the fourth century and also at the beginning of the seventh century, as well as at the time of the Arabian conquest. In the sixth century, in the region of the straits of Tiran in fact, an autonomous Jewish community existed, which fought against Romans and Arabs alike. Palestine has never been a land without Jews. Palestinian Jewry merely became for a long time peripheral and less influential on the literature and history of world Jewry. But the religious and emotional bond of the Jews to the land of their fathers, Erez Israel, never ceased.

[12] The name "Gemara" for the discussion-part of the Talmud only became generally current through the interference of Christian censorship in the 16th century, since the latter wished as far as possible to eliminate the expression "Talmud". Whereas until then Mishnah and Talmud were distinguished from each other, today we denote as Talmud the total work that consists of both Mishnah and Gemara.

[13] Modern Hebrew, as it is now spoken in Israel, goes back largely to the Hebrew of the Mishnah.

In the Talmud we find Hebrew passages from the Mishnah and other traditions cited in the name of teachers of the Mishnah which are quoted from parallel collections; whereas the discussion of these passages, the Gemara, is in Aramaic. This proximity and medley of both languages increases the difficulty of understanding the Talmud. Later rabbinic literature is substantially Hebrew interspersed with many Talmudic-Aramaic quotations, phrases and expressions.

The Talmud, and the rabbinic literature following it, took on an eminent practical significance for Judaism. The Talmud is, as stated above, a collection of discussions and investigations, an encyclopaedia whose themes embrace every aspect of life and the spirit, integrating them into its religious pattern of meaning. Alongside religious precepts and legends, transmissions of historical events and moral aphorisms of devout scholars, the essential part of the Talmud is, however, devoted to *legal* problems. It is, to be sure, no statute-book, but its juridical discussions constitute the source and collected precedents of Jewish law. Since new problems, legal and religious, arise in every generation, and since local and historical conditions likewise change, one tried, in the constant study of the Talmud and in its manifold discussions, to find whatever references one could regard as precedents and guides for new problems.—In modern states, whenever a law has become obsolete, new laws are made by Acts of Parliament or by other statutory acts. But when the law is considered as divine appointment, when it possesses the character of holiness, then a problem newly appearing, a new case, must somehow already be alluded to or discoverable in the divine law.—As a modern parallel one could point to English law. This, it is true, is secular law, possessing hundreds of laws that were created by Act of Parliament. But beside these statutory laws there is the old Common Law, the Law of Equity, which rests upon the concept of fairness. And the skill of the British lawyer today greatly depends on his ability to find cases of precedent in sometimes century-old lawsuits and verdicts which are applicable to his actual new case. So here too, is a kind of oral—an unwritten—law, based purely upon hundreds of court verdicts.—On completion of the Talmud the discussion of religious-legal problems continued in the *Responsa*-collections which contain the correspondence i.e., questions to and answers of rabbinic authors.

I should like to mention further that there have existed, and still do exist, trends in Judaism which recognise only the written law, the Torah, as binding. At the time of the Second Temple there were the Sadducees. Since the 8th century and in remnants up to the present, there were the *Karaïtes*, who were quite numerous and influential during the early centuries of the Middle Ages. The argument with them stimulated study of the Bible and the precise fixing of Biblical texts. It also led to fruitful theological-philosophical polemics. But through their rigid biblicism the Karaïtes were in religious-legal matters less pliable than Rabbinic Judaism.

Today small remnants of Karaïtes still live in the Crimea and in Egypt, from where a number recently came to settle in Israel. Until the Second World War there were several Karaïte communities in Lithuania.

The Talmud and the additional talmudic and rabbinic literature form the basis of Jewish studies. The largely intellectual preoccupation with the Talmud and its predominantly juridical questions did not, however, remain the concern of the individual specialist. On the contrary, it reached wide circles of Jewry. Not every Jew was a Talmud scholar. But everyone had, from a tender age, studied at least the rudiments of the Talmud and also endeavoured in later life to study—to "learn", as the popular expression has it—short passages of the Mishnah and Gemara. This learning was a holy religious duty, and a matter of course for everyone, like praying itself, and it found its expression in the religious way of life.

To the religious precepts and commandments handed down were added religious customs which had developed in certain places and lands. In the process of time these customs came to hold similar value to the earlier transmitted percepts. This was especially the case—as we shall see later—in Ashkenazi—i.e. German and Polish Jewry.

In order to find one's way about in the "sea of Talmud" and Talmudic literature, and especially to ascertain which of the many stated opinions in the Talmudic treatises had become legally binding, one very soon required for practical reasons compendia, law-compilations. The oldest of these compendia are really only abridgments of the Talmud itself, made by omitting the non-obligatory sections. Then in the twelfth century *Maimonides* newly arranged the entire religious law according to subjects, but in his own formulation, independent of the wording of the Talmudic discussions. In the fourteenth century *Jacob ben Asher*, whose father came from Germany and lived in Spain, compiled a similar code.

In the middle of the sixteenth century, in Palestinian Safed, a refugee from Spain, *Joseph Caro*, made a new collection of Jewish religious laws on the basis of the heretofore extant codifications. He called this code the *Shulḥan Arukh* (the "Prepared Table"). *Moses Isserles* in Cracow added supplements to the Shulḥan Arukh, having regard for the religious decisions and customs of the Ashkenazi Jews, which Joseph Caro had often omitted.

The high respect of German Jews for religious custom has a historical reason. When after the Black Death in 1349 the large majority of the Jewish communities perished, those who survived wanted to retain the custom of their fathers that had been hallowed by martyrdom. The religious custom of the place had already been recommended in Talmudic literature as worthy of attention. In Germany, and in Ashkenazi Jewry altogether, it now assumed in practice an almost similar status with the religious-legal decisions based on the Written and Oral law.

The work produced by Joseph Caro and Moses Isserles became authoritative for the religious practice of the whole of Jewry. Soon large commentaries and "commentaries on commentaries" also appeared, an entire literature which followed the Shulḥan Arukh and complemented it.

Alongside the extensive Talmudic literature, philosophy and mysticism had played an important role throughout the whole of the Middle Ages. *Philosophy*, to be sure, had been almost the monopoly first of Oriental, then of Spanish Jewry. Jewish philosophy had arisen in the tenth century under the influence of, and through discussion with, Islamic philosophy and theology as well as with the Karaïtes. Like Arabic philosophy, it included neo-Platonic and Aristotelian schools of thought. With the expulsion from Spain at the end of the fifteenth century the independent preoccupation of Jews with philosophy came to an end for about two centuries. Rational thinking took refuge in mysticism.

From the rich treasury of Spanish-Jewish philosophy almost nothing permeated to Germany. In the era before the invention of printing we hear only in quite isolated cases of German Jews being acquainted with, for example, the philosophy of a *Maimonides*, whereas the latter was well known to Christian scholastics and even to Meister Eckhart, the renowned German mystic (1260-1327). Even later involvement with philosophical questions in Ashkenazi Jewry remained something of a rarity. Independent philosophical writings of importance were not written in the Ashkenazic milieu.

What were the reasons for the break-up of the philosophical tradition and for its failure to penetrate northwards? The Jewish religious philosophers of the Middle Ages had been faced with the problem of bringing the fundamental ideas of Judaism, like the concept of God, the creation of the world, divine and human freedom into harmony with the doctrines of Aristotle, then dominating the mainstream of Arabic, Jewish and European philosophy. The concept of an active Intellect and Prime Mover, to which Aristotle's idea of God had shrunk, was difficult to combine with the religious conceptions of a personal God, who had created the world according to his will and is at work in it. Maimonides had attempted this in his "Guide for the Perplexed" at the end of the twelfth century, thereby also deeply influencing the Christian scholasticism of Albert the Great and Thomas Aquinas. Later Jewish religious philosophers of the Middle Ages faced similar problems. They all strove to preserve the intrinsic value of religion vis-à-vis philosophical formalism. This was accomplished, but not without considerable changes in interpretation and allegorizations of passages of Scripture and Oral Law.

A large section of the Jewish intelligentsia in Spain and Southern France, whom Aristotelian philosophy had influenced most, made these philosophical doctrines their own, but without the religious impulses, which had moved *Maimonides* and his followers. This led to laxity in these circles and a turning away from religion and a religious attitude to life.

The defensive struggle of the representative of Talmudic Judaism stood against these tendencies. They now saw in philosophy altogether a danger for Judaism, and in Maimonides the originator of the disintegrating world of thought. Added to this was the influence of *Jewish mysticism*, the *Kabbalah*, which for the most part stood in sharp contrast to the rationalistic evaluations of Judaism. The pursuit of philosophy was certainly not forbidden. The authority of Maimonides was too great for that. For he himself was a recognised authority in the religious legal sphere. One tried, however, to render the study of philosophy more difficult and to curtail it. Already in the thirteenth century the regulation was generally adopted that one might not study philosophical books before reaching twenty-five years of age. In this way they became virtually unknown to the majority of Jews, since after this age mostly only scholars still had time for basic studies. This restriction also hindered the spread of philosophical writings in the sphere of Ashkenazi Jewry. Even Moses Mendelssohn in the eighteenth century was only able to study Maimonides secretly and at night.

A much greater influence upon the religious thinking and practice of Jews at the close of the Middle Ages, however, was exerted by *mysticism*. Philosophy and mysticism have one thing in common: they do not appeal to the rank and file, being aristocratic disciplines. Precisely Jewish mysticism, from its inception onwards, always regarded itself as an esoteric doctrine, to be made accessible only to the chosen few. This was something it shared with every mystical movement. But the root of all mysticism lies in its close association with popular belief. It is not—like philosophy—rational reflection, but seeks a deeper hidden meaning behind the words of Scripture and the Oral Law. Thus it expresses the discovered meaning not in logical concepts but in colourful concrete images. Whereas, for example, the Jewish philosophers found the frequent anthropomorphic expressions in the Bible for the pure idea of God objectionable and unworthy, these anthropomorphic expressions formed the very concepts of mystical speculation. In this way mysticism always brings about a correlation of religion and myth, making use of an often mythological or at least esoteric language. This is indeed true of all mysticism. One needs only refer to the Oriental and Greek mysteries and to earlier Christian gnosticism, or to the strong mystical elements in Christology. Due to this close connection of mysticism with pre-religious mythical thinking, we frequently find that the official orthodoxy of every religion looks upon mystical movements with distrust. Anyway, one ought to push the mystical and gnostic elements everywhere as far as possible into the background by way of compromise. For no orthodox theology can fully dispense with these elements which are the expression of a living religiosity. In the old Christian church the radical gnostic movements were combated. Later, mystical movements were suspected as heretical and frequently persecuted. We find similar tendencies in Islam and also in Judaism.

Philosophically-minded Jewish scholars and teachers of Jewish law were mostly those circles who were disapproving of mystical movements, or at least treated them with reserve. But the remarkable thing about Jewish mysticism was just that this esoteric doctrine of individuals, through its proximity to popular belief, has exercised upon the latter and especially upon popular custom a major influence that was denied to the philosophers. There has thereby remained in official Judaism, so to speak, as it is codified for example in the "Shulḥan Arukh", a large number of traditions going back to mystical ideas.

And still something else is important: Jewish mysticism knows no unio mystica, no union and no incorporating of man into God, as both the Greek mysteries and Christian mysticism of the Middle Ages strove to attain it, or as it is expressed, for example in the Christian doctrine of the Eucharist. There always remains in Jewish mysticism the strict separation of Creator and creature. The highest to which the Jew can attain is called "the nearness of God". "The nearness of God is my good" says Psalm 73 v. 28.

Jewish mysticism from the sixteenth until the eighteenth century gained influence upon wider sections and became a decisive force in Judaism at least for a time. But it is important not to loose sight of the fact that it represented in Judaism—as also in other religions—only a secondary trend, an undercurrent. Authoritative always was rabbinic Judaism which attended to the Talmud and interpreted the Law. Decisive was the fervent piety and religiosity of the ordinary Jew, learned or unlearned, who had no need of special speculations of the mystics or of the philosophers.

From the early Talmudic period onwards Jewish mysticism largely revolved round two themes: the work of creation and the heavenly spheres, outlined in the Prophet Ezekiel's vision of the chariot. (Similarly, general philosophy and Jewish philosophy had differentiated between natural science, i.e. physics, and metaphysics.) Mysticism is concerned not so much with man as with God. It revolves round the attempt to fathom the secret of the hidden Creator of the universe, who reigns over the heavens. In the Torah—the 'Teaching'—the history of the cosmos and its Creator is seen beyond the literal sense of its passages and narratives. For everything from the beginning of time to its end should, indeed, according to an old saying, already be contained in the Torah.—In mysticism each word, each letter and each point of the Torah contains an inner meaning.

The first great work of Jewish mysticism, the *Sefer Yeẓirah* ("Book of Creation")—stemming from as early as the sixth or seventh century—deals with the ten numerals and the twenty-two letters of the Hebrew alphabet, which together are supposed to comprise the elements of creation and also of the Torah. And the painstakingness with which the Hebrew Bible-text was fixed and retained since olden times, is certainly connected with the mystic significance that was ascribed to every letter and even to every seeming error and mistake in the textual transmission and manner of writing.

In the world of ideas man is created only to fulfill the commands of the mystically interpreted Torah. Every step, every act of man contains within it a cosmic significance. Man becomes a co-worker in the completion of creation. Negatively, man upsets or thwarts the process of completion.

This function of man becomes especially clear in the movement of the "Pious of Germany", the *German Ḥasidism*, as it is called, which arose at the time of the Crusades. This movement created the ethical religious ideal of the pious man, whose piety did not express itself in the intellect or in the, so to speak, juridical fulfillment of the commandments or in the mere learning of the Torah. Neither did it express itself in ecstasy, into which the earlier and also many of the later mystics tried to transpose themselves in order to probe the divine mysteries. Piety consists in devout moral action, in turning away from the bustle of the world through penitent exercises and prayer, and in unshakable trust in God.—(Attention has been drawn to the contemporary Christian-monastic ideal, whose example has been Francis of Assisi.) The chief work of this movement is the "Book of the Pious" by Rabbi Jehuda of Regensburg, who died in 1217. This book also conveys a vivid picture of Jewish life at that time.

The German Ḥasidism of the twelfth century had its speculative foundation in the older ecstatic mysticism of the Jewish Orient. But in its effects only its religious ethical factor remained significant, and this continued in Ashkenazi Jewry for centuries. It had lasting influence upon the religious life-pattern, rites and practice of Ashkenazi Jews.—One sees here how a mysticism found its way back to non-mystical religiosity.

But with the ethical ideal of the "Pious one" there are already superstitious elements and outlooks associated with the "Pious of Germany" themselves, and even more so with the later popular tradition. These magical components belong to every popular-belief. German popular-belief in the Middle Ages teemed with it, and traces of it still affect our apparently so secularised thinking. The superstitious ideas in German Ḥasidism were often a product of the time and of the non-Jewish milieu. One recalls the illusion of the witch and the devil in popular German belief. Such influences found their Jewish legitimation in the fact that the Talmudic literature also contains a host of superstitious Oriental ideas.

The mysticism one associates with the *Kabbalah* came from Provence and developed mainly in Spain. Here in the twelfth and thirteenth centuries there were added to the Oriental mystical traditions and the influences of the old Hellenistic gnosticism also those of medieval philosophy. Then oriental and gnostic influences may have a connection with the contemporary non-Jewish movement of the Cathari, with whom the long since disappeared gnostic ideas of the Manichean religion were remarkably revivified. This sect was strongly propagated in the twelfth century in the south of

France. It was persecuted as heretical by the Catholic church and wiped out in the thirteenth century during the twenty-year Albigensian Crusade.—Its views appear to have influenced the Provençal Jews, who in part also fell victim to this Crusade.

Also neo-Platonic philosophy, as the Jewish philosopher and poet, *Ibn Gabirol*, had developed it in the eleventh century, is reflected in the Kabbalistic theory on the Being of God and creation. Thus the Kabbalah developed a doctrine of emanation, which had its parallel in neo-Platonism. But what with the philosophers is a logical process becomes in Kabbalistic mysticism a symbolic one.

The Kabbalah became the spiritual home of all those intellectuals and scholars for whom the rationalistic evaluation of Judaism through e.g. Maimonides and philosophy did not suffice. For them it was a way of religious self-understanding that sought to bring Scripture, God and the world into a unity. Kabbalah is full of intense religious ecstasy—sometimes even of a prophetic character—and at the same time of a theosophical speculation which goes into detail.

The prime work of the Kabbalah is the book *Zohar* ("Splendour"). Its pseudoepigraphic author attributed it to a scholar of the second century, Simeon ben Yoḥai. There is little doubt today, however, that it was probably largely written by a Spanish Jew of the thirteenth century, Moses de Leon.

The Zohar is written in Aramaic in the form of a mystical commentary on the Pentateuch. It contains a wealth of ideas on the origin of the world, the Being of God, and it seeks to fathom the hidden meaning of every occurrence and commandment. Alongside semi-intelligible sentences it contains many profound thoughts and sublime prayer-passages which it attributes to the old teachers of the Talmudic era.

The catastrophe of the Jews in Spain produced a cleavage in the spreading influence of the Kabbalah on almost the whole of Jewry of that time, and altered the direction of its mystical speculation. The expulsion from Spain in 1492 had reawakened with unprecedented intensity longing for the Messianic redemption. By emerging from an esoteric theosophy of individuals to a mysticism that sought to bring in the Messianic kingdom, the Kabbalah gained a hitherto undreamed of influence upon the Jewish masses—not only upon the refugees from Spain but also upon the Jews in the Balkans, in Italy, Poland and Germany.

The small town of Safed in Palestine where a circle of Spanish Kabbalists had settled, became the centre of this new Kabbalah. To them belonged, among others, Joseph Caro, author of the "Shulḥan Arukh". The central figure of this circle in the second half of the sixteenth century was *Isaac Luria*.

Luria who was born in 1534 in Jerusalem and lived to be only 38 years old, had for years led the life of a hermit, confining himself to the study of the Zohar, and of the Kabbalah which he was later fundamentally to change.

In Safed, his place of activity during the last years of his life, a circle of disciples gathered around him. The fascination that doubtlessly emanated from him is scarcely imaginable. Even his contemporaries considered him a holy one. He himself bequeathed no writings, but his pupils wrote down his sayings and mystical actions in detail. In this way he became a legendary figure in his own lifetime. Through his followers his teaching was immediately spread abroad in the Jewry of that time.

The new Lurianic Kabbalah centred round the problem of redemption. In its theory of creation the Infinite (Hebrew "Ein Sof") has contracted to a point, in order to create and give room to the world. From this point an immense light proceeds that penetrates the spheres and breaks them to pieces. In Lurianic language this is called the shivering of the vessels, of the spheres. These fragments now find themselves in space and have to be collected again, i.e. redeemed. This collecting and reassembling of the fragmented vessels is man's task in the world.—Two analogies are drawn here: through the scattered vessel fragments, parts of the divine light, God himself has, so to speak, gone into exile, and likewise Israel is scattered in exile. When the divine fragments and the fragmented people of Israel have been successfully gathered together, the unity of God will be restored and redemption for Israel and the world will come.

This new cosmic messianic theory exercised a magnetic influence on the Jews. It encroached upon their attitude to life and way of living for generations. For everyone could share in the task of bringing about the restoration of heaven and earth—called "Tikkun". Through asceticism and penitance, fasting and prayer, one wanted to play one's part in this work and hasten its completion. Through this objective of being allowed to assist in the redemption of God, the world and Israel, the Kabbalah became more than a mere mystical absorption in theories, letters and numbers, as it perhaps seemed from the outside. The Kabbalah, particularly in this last Lurianic expression, embraced God and the world, the creation of nature and man, law, sin and atonement and finally the Messianic redemption.

In the Lurianic Kabbalah the concept of redemption had taken on an entirely new direction and been enlarged. In traditional messianic belief the redemption of Israel was the precondition, the first act of the redemption of mankind. In the Lurianic interpretation redemption is the goal, the restoration of the broken perfection of the cosmos. The historic redemption of Israel is the activating factor, but it is, so to speak, only a natural implication of this further goal, the redemption of creation. The person of the Messiah becomes relatively uninteresting.

Such a messiah, who distinguished himself neither in character nor by deeds, who became possible only in virture of the situation, because he appeared in a time of catastrophe, was *Sabbatai Zevi*.

Here I should like to interrupt my brief summary of Jewish mysticism, for the movement beginning with Sabbatai Zevi is already closely linked with the presentation of the beginnings of modern Judaism.

The presentation of the main themes of Jewish intellectual life has to be supplemented with some remarks about the nature of Jewish education and literature in the Middle Ages, especially in Germany. With the Jews, education had never been the monopoly of certain groups, as in the Middle Ages it was with non-Jews—confined to clergy, poet-barons and a few others. "Learning" —to know and to understand the commandments of Holy Scripture—was taken as holy duty which was incumbent upon every Jew. Already at a tender age children were introduced to the elementary attainments of reading and writing, to the prayers and weekly portion of Scripture read in the synagogue every Sabbath. There they learned Scripture with the commentary of Rashi who thereby introduced them to the language and thought world of the Oral Law. The latter itself still belonged only in its simpler part, the Mishnah, to the elementary instruction, which already in the pre-Christian era in the land of Israel was obligatory for rich and poor.[14] Higher instruction, the introduction to the discussions of the Talmud and to rabbinic literature, was made possible for all who were capable. The pride of every larger community was the maintenance of an academy and its students. Only in the fourteenth century were rabbis given professional status as salaried officials of the community. Till then it was virtually forbidden and considered unworthy to accept money for teaching. That is the reason why the rabbis till then, and often later, still had another means of livelihood.

The basis of the higher learning was the Talmud together with the com- mentary of Rashi.[15] *Rashi* (1040-1105), this scholarly winegrower from Troyes, who had studied at the Rhenish academies, was not only a great commentator. He had a distinct pedagogic and philological aptitude, and one might say that our present-day Talmud-text is based upon his version.

The school of Rashi was continued by his grandsons. These and their pupils in Northern France and in Germany composed supplements to the commentaries, in which questions left open by Rashi were clarified, and new problems and cases of law added. The authors of the "supplements" (in Hebrew "Tosafot") are known as the "Tosafists". Their activity extends to

---

[14] The High Priest, Joshua ben Gamla, had already around the year 64 B.C. introduced obligatory school attendance for children over five years.

[15] The name is an acronym of Rabbi Shimon ben Yizhak.

The commentaries of Rashi are, by the way, like most works of rabbinic literature, not printed in Hebrew square characters but in a type similar to the curve that is called after its most popular example, the "Rashi script".

Through his commentaries on the Pentateuch Rashi also influenced the Christian exegesis of the Middle Ages, especially that of Nicolas de Lyra (1270-1340), an influential Christian Bible com- mentator, from whom Luther took his own slight knowledge of rabbinical Bible interpretation.

the end of the thirteenth century. Many of them were already influenced by the "Pious of Germany" Movement, from whose circles a mystical-ascetic ethical literature developed.

From the twelfth century originated the *Book of the Pious* by Rabbi Juda ben Samuel in Regensburg, and the book *Rokeah* ("Unguent-Mixer") by Rabbi Elazar Rokeah from Worms who derives his name from this work. In both these books the intellectual position of the generation of the Crusades and of the life of the Jews at this time is reflected. At the same time there began the first attempts towards a historical literature in the preserved Hebrew Chronicles of the Crusades, and a religious poetry that has in part as its theme the martyrdom of the perished communities. Sections of this poetry were included in the prayer-book.—Besides the aforementioned "Supplements" printed in the Talmud editions, the Tosafists have also left behind responsa and codified collections.

The catastrophe of the Black Death (1348/49) brought to an end this rich intellectual life. The dominant factor of the intellectual activity in the next hundred years went over at first from the Rhineland to Austria, which had been less affected by the massacre of the years 1348-49. That, despite the social and spiritual decay and the persecutions in those days, Jews were still able to acquire an all-round education, is evidenced by the figure of Rabbi *Lipmann Muehlhausen* (ca 1400), who knew Latin and the New Testament and also the Spanish-Jewish religious philosophers.[16]

A great number of those who survived had found acceptance in Poland, where there soon arose a new intellectual centre of Ashkenazi Jewry. From the sixteenth century onwards there were academies there, which developed their own method of Talmud-study as well as a rich literature, upon which the smaller Jewry in Germany became more and more dependent.

---

[16] Cp. his polemical "Sefer ha-Nizahon", which was translated into Latin in the seventeenth century.

# 3

## *Signs of Loosening of Traditional Bonds in the Seventeenth Century*

Perhaps the most decisive social change resulting from the expulsion of Jews from the cities, was their renewed stronger contact with the non-Jewish world. In their urban ghettos Jews had been almost hermetically sealed-off from every contact with the rest of the population. Non-Jews only knew them from the inflammatory sermons and pamphlets now being spread everywhere through printing—ornamented with horrible and provocative wood-cuts—telling of alleged ritual murder or desecration of the Host. Or they knew them from the rumors of fabulous Jewish wealth and possessions. Burghers and handworkers came into personal contact with Jews only in the unpleasant cases of having to borrow money from them. And this contributed to their now seeing them as personal enemies.

The cities had indeed expelled the Jews, but mostly allowed them to visit their markets—in exchange, of course, for special taxes. Expelled Jews therefore often settled in the country in the vicinity of their old places of residence, where they were gladly accepted by the territorial lords. But even there agriculture and ownership of land were denied them. On this account they turned again with renewed intensity to trading. Already in the cities, where they had been confined solely to money-lending, they had to be allowed a certain share in trade. Non-redeemed pawned articles had to be re-sold for money. This limited branch of business with mostly second-hand articles had also aroused opposition from the city-merchants' and craftsmen's guilds, since these goods had to be cheaper than newly-manufactured ones. Trading, which earlier had been a sideline of money transactions, now became the main livelihood of Jews in the country, and it was no longer restricted to the sale of pawned and used articles. It extended to the selling of agricultural products to the townspeople, to livestock and wine-trade and the sale of urban handwork-products to the peasants. Despite the considerable benefit that countrypeople thereby gained from Jews, their distorted image due to the inflammatory preaching persisted unaltered there too. And the relation of peasants to Jews, brought about by hostility and suspicion, manifested itself in various outrages and humiliations.

The Thirty Years' War marked a turning-point for future development, also for Jews. The Peace Treaty of Westphalia in 1648 confirmed the extension of the Jewish prerogative to all the territorial authorities, also to those who had not heretofore expressly received this right from the realm.[17] After the war the territorial-rulers had to build up their destroyed territories by new methods. The slogan of the time was to stimulate trade and commerce and bring capital to the land. And with their new economic policy the princes sought to enforce their absolute sovereignty. To realize this a civil service was created which was dependent only on the prince who administered the territories without consideration of the local representatives of the 'estates'. In the struggle against these local representatives—the rural aristocracy, the cities and the guilds—the princes relied on the new civil service and newly organised army. In order to carry out the mercantile economic policy, the territorial lords now also drew upon Jews, who were the only group outside the feudal system and rigid medieval order of guilds, having never been accepted into them. Jews now became for the princes an important element in the expansion of trade, due to their extended family and business relationships to other territories.

The Jews who had been called upon by the reigning princes and their officials, represented, of course, only a small thin upper layer of Jewry. It was this same section which, as leaders and representatives of the territorial Jewries, already had to cultivate constant relations with the court and the authorities. They now received official titles as court-factors, court-agents and the like. Besides financial and commercial responsibilities, they were also entrusted with diplomatic assignments and had, as war commissioners, to see to the equipping and supplying of the armies. They were in fact occasionally raised to a status similar to that of the nobility. And sometimes they became a kind of factotum for the princes, even in their private matters.

These *court-Jews* were, for better or worse, dependent on the person of the territorial lord. They were hated by the opposing remnants of the feudal system, the lesser aristocracy and the cities, and by the common people. Through change of sovereign, through suddenly aroused disfavour, or even through the mere attempt of the territorial lord to avoid payment of his debts, Jews sometimes had to forfeit their lives—like Suess Oppenheimer in Wuerttemberg—or suffer long years of confinement and the loss of their property. It was, as one would say, dangerous to lend money to great rulers. Christian merchants and bankers mostly fought shy of this risk; whereas

---

[17]The police order of the realm of 1548 had already established in principle the extension of the Jewish prerogative.

Jews could not always avoid it, or saw therein the only possibility of showing initiative or acquiring influence and wealth.

To carry out their tasks, court-Jews and their numerous agents and employees retained the right of residence—even in places which for long had tolerated no Jews within their walls. In dress and custom they had to adapt to the court circles and their high office.

The new active economic-political functions assigned to Jews in the emerging territorial state, gradually brought ever more extended social strata into contact with the cultural influences of the time. Even in the Middle Ages there were always Jews who had connections with the royal courts and who possessed a more or less ample secular education. But what earlier were exceptions now spread to wider circles, at least in Germany. Not only were there hundreds of territorial lords; the number of Jews employed by them and their officials was also quite large, since each of these court-Jews required numerous additional assistants. Thus it was not only the thin upper-stratum which was obliged to acquire a knowledge of the written and spoken language of the employers—and in part also foreign languages, particularly French, at that time the everyday speech of refined society.

Out of this there developed a freer relationship with the Christian milieu. Jews were able to speak with certain circles of the Christian population, with officials and part of the intelligentsia on a more or less equal footing.

The lowest section of the Jewish population bore a certain resemblance to the corresponding Christian one. The so-called *beggar Jews*, i.e. Jews who had no right of settlement in a community or territory, since they could pay neither the necessary protection fees nor the corresponding taxes, were hunted from one territory to the next. In their conditions of life they barely differed from Christian vagrants, peasants who had become landless, impoverished townspeople and discharged soldiers—marauders as they were called—people who roamed about the country, especially after the Thirty Years' War. These groups—Christian and Jewish alike—cared little about law or right. We hear again and again of thefts committed by beggar Jews, even in the houses of their co-religionists; also of gangs, made up of Christians and Jews. The thieves' cant, the so-called "Rotwelsch", had at that time absorbed a number of Hebrew expressions.

The majority of Jews, of course, who neither belonged to the court Jew circles and their assistants, nor to the proletariat of beggar Jews, were at first little affected by contemporary influences. They lived—when accepted into a community—in relatively greater security now than at the close of the Middle Ages, since they had in general no sudden expulsions to fear. More and more they made a living by trading in small goods, or more precisely, by peddling from door to door, since in most cases, due to the resistance of the guilds, especially the small shopkeepers, they were not allowed to keep open stores in most places. Pawnbroking still played an important role, but was no longer the sole possibility of livelihood for the

Jewish population. Money-changing became an important activity for them because of the endless variety of coins in circulation in the realm. They also traded in precious stones, furs and other de luxe articles. And this trade again brought many Jews into touch with the court-nobility and with the rich city merchants. On the other hand, all skilled occupations were, now as earlier, forbidden them, due to the resistance of the guilds, with the exception of those which had to meet the needs of the Jewish community, e.g. ritual slaughter etc. Also in branches of handwork not controlled by the guilds and mostly engaged in the manufacture of luxury articles do we find Jews in great number. Embroidery in silver and gold, the making of lace for uniforms, engraving of signet rings and such like, were occupations that lay almost exclusively in Jewish hands. And these occupations naturally involved trade with their products.

Of great significance for the commercial activities of Jews were the various trade-fairs, which took place at fixed times in several cities. These fairs offered Jews an opportunity not only of buying and selling foreign goods, but also for the opening up of wider business connections and contacts with Jewish communities in every part of Germany, in Poland, Russia, Hungary and other countries. The territorial rulers were glad to see their Jewish businessmen visiting the fairs, since the marketing of their country's products was thereby promoted. Fairs often took place in areas where for centuries Jews had no longer been permitted, as in Breslau and Leipzig.[18] From such fair-visits Jewish settlements developed again in these places in the course of time.

Many Jews, therefore, by nature of their occupation, were almost continually travelling. Even country Jews, whose quota of customers was too small, were obliged to peddle their wares from village to village. This in its turn involved constant contact with non-Jews, so that now even the Jewish middle-classes, who as such were rather conservative and set in their ways, were not quite able to resist the influences from outside. Thus, more and more the general culture of the time and its language penetrated wider strata of Jewry.

Since the early Middle Ages Jews had spoken the German language, but in their progressive isolation it had remained static with them at the level of Middle High German, and not kept pace with the living language-development of the environment. Instead, it had undergone a development of its own by absorbing many Hebrew words and constructions—and in Eastern Europe Slavonic elements—to form what is known as the 'Yiddish' language. But through growing contact with the non-Jewish population in commercial intercourse and travel, ever more Jews had now to acquire the spoken and written word of their surroundings. This applied especially to the many

---

[18] Leipzig Fair-Lists for the years 1668-1764 registered 81,937 Jews, who in duties alone paid out 719,661 talers. Cf. EJ (German, X, column 761; Elbogen p. 142.

clerks, 'servants' of the businessmen, who had to deal with their business and official correspondence. And in this role they imbibed a large part of the surrounding culture. These clerks formed a secular class of intelligentsia, which created a social basis for the later Enlightenment, especially since after some time they often made themselves independent, entering into the circles of businessmen and indeed of the court Jews.—Even Moses Mendelssohn belonged to this group of commercial servants.

Mastering the German tongue—spoken and written—had certainly at first been understood only as a business necessity. In private correspondence and inter-Jewish business transactions the Hebrew curve-script remained in use for correspondence in the German language until well into the nineteenth century. Heinrich Heine, for example, still wrote to his mother using Hebrew letters.

The beginnings of a secular general education spread increasingly, especially since many Jews now had their children given secular instruction mostly by Christian teachers. Thus we read in the memoirs of *Glueckel of Hameln*, a Jewish middle-class woman in Hamburg, that her step-sister was by chance able to protect her father from financial loss through her knowledge of French and that, already in the mid-seventeenth century, she played the harpsichord.—Then in the eighteenth century secular books, travel-literature and even novels in German and French found their way into Jewish households, but above all newspapers, then coming into fashion. How widespread this was, is seen from the fact that it was discussed in contemporary rabbinical responsa as to whether such reading was allowed on the Sabbath. About this time we also hear complaints from rabbis that parents were having their children instructed in French, dancing and music, while neglecting their Jewish and religious education.

Jewish school education at this time was in a sorry state. Time and again it was lamented that primary teachers were incompetent and unreliable. These teachers were mostly former students and graduates of the Talmudic academies in Poland who lacked the general knowledge then required in Germany. Besides, children were now already failing to understand the slavonized East-Yiddish of their teachers.

The seventeenth century was also the time of the great upheavals in natural science. Copernicus, Galileo, Kepler and later Newton had fundamentally altered the picture of the universe, giving scholars material that led to a century of excited and fruitful argumentative discussions, until finally around 1700 the "New Science" was universally able to win through. The new thinking also infiltrated the Jewish fold. To the circle of Tycho Brahe and Johannes Kepler in Prague there already belonged a Jewish scholar, *David Gans*, who made astronomical calculations for them. Gans was probably the first Jew in Germany to give a Hebrew portrayal of world history.

The medical profession among Jews has been a tradition going back to antiquity. It was one of the very few occupations in which Jews were tolerated, but they were mostly restricted to treating fellow-Jews—although Jewish doctors already appeared in the Middle Ages as personal physicians to princes and church dignitaries. Many of them combined the profession of medical doctor with that of rabbi. Their training frequently relied upon the extensive Hebrew-medical literature alongside practical medical experience that often passed from father to son. Thus there exist numerous translations in Hebrew, Arabic and Latin, through which Jewish physicians passed on the medicine of classical antiquity to the Middle Ages. In addition, independent works by Jews sprang up, as e.g. those of Maimonides, which in Latin translation influenced medieval medicine.

Meanwhile it had become necessary for physicians to have a university education. If Jewish physicians did not want to appear in the eyes of their colleagues or of the public authorities as quacks, they, too, had to have a university education. At first they could only obtain this in Italy. Since the early Middle Ages Jews had been admitted there as students—at some universities even as teachers—first at Salerno, later at Padua. Padua was for a long time the centre for Jewish medical students from many countries.

In the seventeenth century Dutch universities also opened their doors to Jewish students. The first to do so in Germany was the University of Frankfurt-on-the-Oder in 1678. In fact, the first two Jewish students at Frankfurt received a scholarship from the Great Elector. One of them, *Tobias Cohn* (1652-1729), later wrote a Hebrew encyclopaedic textbook on every branch of the natural sciences, which became the source of natural scientific knowledge for several generations of Jews. What is interesting is the motivation he gives for publishing his work. In Frankfurt he had often been reproached by Christian students to the effect that Jews were uneducated in every branch of the sciences and that this was a sign of their inferiority. In order to refute this charge, he made a vow then to spread scientific learning among his fellow-Jews. To be able to graduate as a Jew, Tobias had to leave Frankfurt for Padua. He became court-physician to five successive sultans in Turkey and towards the end of his life went to Jerusalem.

Following Frankfurt-on-the-Oder, other Protestant universities such as Heidelberg, Duisburg, Halle and Koenigsberg enrolled Jews; whereas with Catholic universities it took considerably longer, in Vienna till 1787. The first award of a doctor's degree to a Jew in Germany took place again in Frankfurt-on-the-Oder. There in 1721, a Prague Jew, Moses Solomon Gumperz, who had already qualified at Prague university, was awarded a doctorate.

In the seventeenth and well into the eighteenth century the basis of Jewish education in Germany was—as in times past—religious literature, especially Talmud and rabbinic literature. Those engaged in any branch of the sciences approached it from this basis. Their representatives were therefore rabbis or those with a rabbinic training. We find also in Germany in every generation rabbis with many-sided scientific interests, also outside the religious-legal sphere.

Physicians at this time, whose training, as we saw, was transferred to the universities, also came from these circles of rabbinic scholars. Some practised —as in earlier times, and in isolated cases even today—both professions.

Since the Talmudic era, mathematics and astronomy were held in high esteem. Knowledge of them was required to calculate the Jewish calendar. This is why many rabbinical authorities more or less thoroughly occupied themselves with both these sciences. Here I should like to highlight Joseph del Medigo (1581-1655) and David Gans to whose work I have already referred. Rafael Levi (dec. 1779) of Hanover may also be mentioned. He was a personal pupil of Leibniz and already before Mendelssohn had published mathematical writings in German.

Hebrew philology remained neglected until the Enlightenment. Since the sixteenth century it had become the domain of Christian Hebraists. Only one Jewish Hebrew grammarian may be mentioned: Solomon Hanau, who belonged to the first half of the eighteenth century.

In relation to philosophy the mistrust fostered by the Kabbalists still held sway. Only a few rabbis concerned themselves with it. The knowledge of Hebrew philosophical literature, however, like that of Maimonides, Juda Halevi and especially that of the popular Joseph Albo from the fifteenth century, was more widespread in their circles than one might have thought.

We saw how contacts of the most varied sections of Jewry with their non-Jewish environment had become closer. The widening of the horizon and of the picture of the world also affected the traditional style of living. The increasing laxity in adherence to the religious traditions was censured in many documents of the day. It is deplored that Jews are spending their leisure time playing cards or smoking tobacco instead of devoting this time to study; that they are holding banquets and carousals without proper religious occasion; that Jews together with non-Jews get drunk in public-houses; that the sanctifying of the Sabbath is being neglected. The time-honoured separation of the sexes is being no longer strictly observed; groups of young men and maidens are going together on outings and dancing with one another. Not only are the rules of traditional propriety being broken; forbidden sexual intercourse and its consequences is also reported. The customs of the environment with their greater freedom but also with their greater dangers are infiltrating the Jewish world. How widespread these surrounding influences were—as well as a certain laxity in the observance of Sabbath laws—already before 1700, is illustrated by the community regulations of Altona and Wandsbek in 1686 and 1687, respectively.[19] Already

---

[19] Cp. § 34 of the Altona rules and § 89 of the Wandsbek rules, respectively, in the edition of H. M. Graupe.

at that time one had to prohibit the visiting of non-Jewish saloons, of fencing schools and of the theatre on the Sabbath and on holidays. Women were forbidden to attend the opera even on weekdays. In Wandsbek, however, they might do so in the company of their husbands. In 1714 even men were forbidden to visit the opera. One may not, of course, draw conclusions from the seaport of Hamburg for the rest of Germany, much less, for Poland or Lithuania. However, the wealthy Portuguese Jews in Hamburg were probably illustrative of some socially ambitious Ashkenazi Jews.

All this had its effect on community life and discipline. The authority of the community committees and of the rabbis received many a shock. Heretofore mostly well-to-do people had stood at the head of the communities. That was unavoidable because of their manifold financial responsibilities to the public authorities. But hitherto one saw to it that it was educated men of integrity who represented the community. Now it happened increasingly often that the nouveau riche uneducated Jews gained control over the communities and misused this position of power—often with the encouragement of the public authorities. Rabbis sometimes fell into unworthy dependence on community heads. Frequently wealthy Jews, especially from the circles of court Jews, tried—with the help of their protectors—to evade paying their share towards the community upkeep or to free themselves from the jurisdiction of the rabbinic courts. Quarrels among Jews were in many cases brought before non-Jewish courts—something that earlier would have been unthinkable and that also often would have infringed community privileges. Many public authorities encouraged such attempts. Others refused to do so, since they were interested in the orderly functioning of the community authorities, who relieved them from many police and administrative tasks, mainly in the sphere of tax-raising.

These signs of slackening in the traditional way of life were brought about by outside impingements through closer contact with the environmental and cultural surroundings. But the inner shocks within Judaism equally contributed to these slackenings, which especially in their after-effects were to threaten the traditional religious and ethical foundations of Judaism.

In my brief portrayal of the Kabbalah we saw how the experience of the expulsion of the Jews from Spain impelled Jewish mysticism to an imminent expectation of the Messiah. In 1648 a similar shock came over Ashkenazi Jewry in Poland, whose remnants after the Chmielnicki-persecutions clung to the belief that the coming of the Messiah must now be near.

This actualization of the Messianic expectation had its climax in the appearance of Sabbatai Ẓevi. The abrupt failure of this movement plunged the whole of Judaism into a century-long serious crisis.

The effects of these inner shocks particularly in Germany reinforced the tendencies that were working from outside. For this reason I should like to discuss briefly the occurrences in Poland and the development of the Sabbatai Ẓevi movement. Then, in the following chapter, the special problem of the Marranos will be highlighted, which likewise contributed to the loosening tendencies.

After the Black Death and its subsequent persecutions the number of Jews in Germany had dwindled. Their economic state of affairs had collapsed and their spiritual life was stagnating. In *Poland* on the other hand, a new intellectual and numerically strong centre of Ashkenazi Jewry had been able to develop. The status of Mayence, Worms and Regensburg now passed over to the communities of Cracow and Brody, Lublin, Vilna and Poznan.

The Jewish communities in Poland formed—stronger than in Germany— a particular ethnic-linguistic, social and religious group. They represented on the whole the urban-industrial element in the Polish community. Trade and commerce lay in their hands, since at first no corresponding social strata in the Polish population were ready for these functions. Jews possessed an extensive autonomy for the regulating of their own affairs and for their representation vis-à-vis the local and central political bodies. Tightly organised communities established themselves early in the more important cities, which had a hinterland of many smaller localities belonging to them. Since the beginning of the seventeenth century heads of the communities and some of the eminent rabbis used to meet at the Spring Fair in Lublin to deliberate on matters of more than local importance, to settle differences between communities and to make decisions on complicated law-cases. From these meetings in Lublin and soon also at the Autumn Fairs in Jaroslav there arose the Central Organisation of Polish Jewry, the *Council of Four Lands* (Poland, White Russia, Volhynia and Lithuania, or rather—after Lithuania withdrew in the seventeenth century—Great and Little Poland, Russia and Volhynia). In this council there sat the representatives of the community associations and six rabbis as supreme judges.

The bi-annual assembly of the "Council of Four Lands" had binding legislative and administrative functions for all Polish Jews. They stipulated, inter alia the quota of taxes falling to each community. Their rabbinical members comprised the court of last instance for the local Jewish jurisdiction. Their authority was recognised and upheld by the government. Rabbinical decisions of the Court of the Council of Four Lands were authoritative also for the Jews in Germany.

The council of Four Lands represented the autonomy of Polish Jewry for about 200 years. Only within the setting of the last attempt at a reform of state and administration in Poland before the partition of the country, was it dissolved in 1764.

Since the sixteenth century Polish Jewry had produced a line of distinguished Talmud scholars, as e.g. the already mentioned Moses Isserles. More important even than these personalities was Talmudic education, which at no time earlier had spread to such an extent or penetrated so wide circles. Even relatively small communities of about fifty families took pride in main-

taining an academy, a Yeshiva, as it is called, at which a recognised scholar
would introduce younger students to Talmudic literature. These students
in their turn gave instructions to classes of boys. By this means and through
the custom of providing the upkeep of students by free board—placed on
each household in turn—direct contact with higher rabbinical learning and
its representatives reached every home. The general standard of Jewish
knowledge and its accompanying moral niveau, especially in Lithuania and
Poland proper, became thereby an unusually high one. Everyone set his pride
in acquiring a rabbinic training for himself, or in having his son "learn", or in
seeing his daughter married to a rabbi or scholar.—The later modern "Science
of Judaism" in Germany has never been able to strike such roots among the
people. It always remained a matter for specialists.

The Jews in Poland made up the urban element as craftsmen and merchants. But just like the small territorial lords in Germany, the quite independent Polish nobility sought to attract Jews into their service. We find
them therefore everywhere in the country as leaseholders of mills and
brandy-monopolies of the nobility, and in association with this as inn-
keepers. But, above all, they became administrators of the estates and wood-
lands of the nobles, agents who had to extract taxes from the farmers for the
landed nobility.

Through this connection with the Polish nobility, Jews were drawn into
all the tensions existing between these noble estate-owners and their peasant-
serfs. They stood "between hammer and anvil", especially in the *Ukraine*
which the Poles had conquered. The hatred of the Cossacks, who had become oppressed and enslaved serfs, levelled itself against the Polish nobility
for both social and national reasons, and over and above that because of
religious antagonism between Roman Catholic Poles and Greek Orthodox
Ukrainians. This hatred was directed against the Jews in even stronger
measure, since they were not only nationally different from the Ukrainians
but were also for them the embodiment of the "unbelievers". They were,
in addition, the ever visible representatives of the Polish oppressors, while
the Polish nobles and magnates were leading a high life in the capital cities
far away from their Ukrainian estates.

In 1648 a large-scale insurrection of the Ukrainian Cossacks broke out
against Polish domination. Their leader was Ataman *Chmielnicki.* The
uprising was protracted in several upsurges over a period of eight years. The
Ukrainian Cossacks obtained help from the Tartars and later from the
Russians, who were interested in winning back the Ukraine. Even Karl X of
Sweden marched into Poland.

The insurgent Cossacks advanced over the entire Polish kingdom as far
as Lithuania, venting their accumulated hatred, their lust for blood and
plunder primarily upon the Jews. Chmielnicki still knew how to stir up their
hate by noising abroad that the Cossacks had been sold as slaves by the Poles
to the Jews. Thus began the massacring, robbing and torturing of all Jews,

the destruction of the Jewish communities in their path. It was the cruellest and biggest blood-bath that had befallen Jewry since the time of the Black Death. And now also, as then, the Jews accepted martyrdom and rejected every deliverance through baptism. In the Ukraine no Jews remained alive. Even the besieged Polish population turned over their Jewish neighbours to the murdering hordes, in the hope of being able to save their own skin. The number of victims of the Cossack uprisings is quoted at several hundred thousand, and that of the plundered and destroyed communities at between 300 and 700.

In these assaults several thousand Jews had the 'good fortune' to fall into the hands of the Tartars. For the latter were more interested in a ransom than in the death of their prey. Thus these Jews were later released through communities in Turkey and Italy with the help of Jews from other lands.

At that time there began the first migration back to western Europe of those who had fled centuries ago to Poland and Lithuania. We hear of refugees in Hamburg and Amsterdam, in Constantinople, Egypt and Italy, and of the help and support they received everywhere from resident Jews.

In the years that followed, accounts from eyewitnesses of the Cossack massacres appeared. The most important one comes from a Volhynian, Rabbi *Nathan Hanover*, who published it in 1653 under the name of *Yewen Mezula*. His report only covers the first three years of the Cossack uprising. It shows a remarkable knowledge of its inner Polish background, political motives and causes, ending in the belief that this doom, which had stricken Polish Jewry, is part of the End-catastrophe which is immediately to precede the advent of the Messiah.

The expulsion of the Jews from Spain had given the Kabbalah a new Messianic emphasis. Isaac Luria had, as we saw, extended the concept of the redemption of Israel to the whole cosmos, the near realisation of which depends upon the active cooperation of each individual.

With the Ashkenazi Jews, the mystically founded custom and religious ethical teaching had—even from the times of the "Pious of Germany"—the predominance over mystical speculation. Even the Lurianic Kabbalah in its German and Polish expression laid special stress on the importance of action and asceticism, of ethical stirring into action. The standard work of this Lurianic Kabbalah in the Ashkenazi sphere is the religious compendium, *Shne Luhoth ha-Brith* (The Two Tables of the Covenant) of *Isaiah Horowitz* (1555-1630). Horowitz, a native of Prague, was for a long time rabbi in Poland and later in Frankfurt-on-Main. He spent his last years in the Holy Land in Safed, Isaac Luria's place of activity and his book—the last great work of the Jewish Middle Ages—became the most popular book of the Lurianic Kabbalah. He created a synthesis of religious law and Lurianic mysticism. His influence directed generations of Jews, learned and unlearned. Fasts, asceticism, prayer and a host of old and new practices commended in this work were intended to hasten and bring about the Messianic redemption. This work dominated the life style of Jews, especially in Poland, until the rise of Ḥasidism.

Sephardic and Ashkenazi Jewry were thus prepared for a messianic turning-point. The frightful suffering of the Cossack persecutions gave the kindling spark, especially as some Kabbalists had already calculated the appearance of the Messiah for 1648–the year they began.

The person of the Messiah had already been divested of its importance through the Lurianic Kabbalah. The Jews throughout the world clung to the first-comer promising them an end to their sufferings and the Messianic realisation.

In 1648 a young Kabbalist of Smyrna (Turkey), named *Sabbatai Ẓevi* claimed before his friends to be the promised Messiah, announcing the year 1666 as the inauguration of the Messianic era. At first the community in Smyrna took steps against him. He had to leave the city, and for a period of years nothing was heard of him, till in 1665 he appeared again in public.

Already in his youth Sabbatai Ẓevi had gained the reputation of an ascetic who lived completely in the Kabbalah. He suffered from deep depressions which alternated with outbreaks of exalted enthusiasm. In these conditions he did unusual deeds which violated the religious law. These, referred to in Sabbatian literature as "strange deeds", were apparently regarded by himself as sacramental acts. While he otherwise let himself be driven by the course of events, and no memorable words of his (as for example the "master-words" of Jesus) are handed down, these deeds became, as Scholem stresses,[20] Sabbatai Ẓevi's essential contribution to the later theory of his followers. His perhaps unconscious example bestowed on their conscious antinomian, indeed unethical actions, a basic and sacramental sanctification. They were reinterpreted into "fulfillment of the law through sin".

Sabbatai Ẓevi had meanwhile found a helper who had perhaps induced him to make his renewed public appearance. It was the then twenty-years-old Nathan of Gaza in Palestine. He became Sabbatai Ẓevi's Elijah–who according to tradition is to be the forerunner and herald of the Messiah– and at the same time his Paul, the really first significant propagandist and theoretician of the movement.

The news of the appearance of the Messiah spread like wildfire through the entire Jewish world–ready to clutch at every straw of hope. Everywhere preparations were made for the approaching return to the Holy Land. A rapture of expectation and joy laid hold of Jewish communities throughout the world. Copious gifts flowed to Ẓevi from every quarter, enabling him to make a princely appearance. The recognition he found was universal. Even Spinoza, who was consulted, saw no reason to doubt the possibility of the

---

[20] Scholem, Major Trends in Jewish Mysticism, p. 293 ff.

restoration of a Jewish kingdom. News of the appearance of the Jewish Messiah even penetrated non-Jewish circles. Only a few rabbis, like Jacob Sasportas in Hamburg, remained sceptical. In the end Sabbatai Zevi had to proceed to actions, for he had announced he would move on Constantinople and dethrone the Sultan, in order with this act to begin his messianic reign. On his arrival in Turkey he was arrested, but still kept court in prison for the faithful flocking to him from every corner. The Sultan then gave him the alternative of converting to Islam or being executed as a rebel. Sabbatai Zevi, who possibly—and almost understandably—was at that time in one of his states of depression, chose conversion. He received a Mohammedan name and a pension, living then a further nineteen years as semi-prisoner.

The hopes that Sabbatai Zevi had engendered collapsed. His apostasy disillusioned the great majority of Jews throughout the world. But the number of those who clung to their Messianic hope, and whom even the betrayal of Sabbatai Zevi did not shake, was considerable. Indeed there developed therefrom a particular Sabbatian theory, which found justification for this act of the master. As already intimated, Sabbatai Zevi appeared in this theory as an embodiment of the holy sinner, who was instrumental in restoring the broken harmony of the cosmos by his "strange deeds", the most terrible of which was his apostasy. The Lurianic Kabbalah was given a new interpretation that suited Sabbatai Zevi's living example. It was not sufficient to gather in the fragments of the cosmos. The gatherer himself must go into the broken vessels, in order from within to make them ready for the restoration and restructuring. Thus, for the sake of the work of redemption, Sabbatai Zevi had to accept Islam, and this fact was seen as a direct confirmation of his Messianic task.

The whole concept of such a feigned-conversion must have appeared plausible to a large section of the Marranos, the conversos who fled from Spain in face of the Inquisition. It was for many of them a rehabilitation of their forebearers' forced-baptism and an easing of the great qualms of conscience, under which they had suffered through forced conversion. A large number of Sabbatians came from these Marrano circles. But the sect of Sabbatai Zevi-believers also had its followers in Ashkenazi Jewry, continuing to live in small secret conventicles till well into the eighteenth century.

The principal spokesmen of Sabbatian theology after Nathan of Gaza were the Portuguese Marrano Abraham Cardozo (circa 1630-1706) and Nehemiah Hayun (circa 1650-1730). They developed a strange concept of the Trinity. In its concept of God, classical Gnosticism had distinguished between the highest God and the Creator of matter, the Demiurge, who with his creation of the world had brought evil into it. This Demiurge was for Gnosticism the God of the hated people of Israel and of the Old Testament. The Sabbatians took up this concept, but reversed the value-relation between these two parts of God. Ein Sof, the unknowable and eternal God, is for them a mere abstraction, while the God of Israel is the living God of religion. To both of these was now added the Presence of God—in Hebrew the "Shekhina". The figure of Sabbatai Zevi somehow became incarnated in the Shekhina, as that of the Messiah waiting for his return.

If the dualistic theology of Gnosticism had always been combated by Judaism, even within the hitherto existing Kabbalah, so the new, indeed, now trinitarian doctrine of the Sabbatians had to be regarded as heretical. This new doctrine of God moreover strongly resembled the Christian conception. And when in fact Sabbatian circles were being persecuted by the Jewish communities, they sometimes turned to the Christian authorities for protection on the grounds that they were being persecuted for teaching the doctrine of the Trinity. Many Sabbatians actually converted to Christianity from the end of the seventeenth century onwards, a step for which they had certainly been prepared by Sabbatian theology.

Only a very small group had followed Sabbatai Zevi into Islam. There, the *Doenmehs* as they were called, nevertheless retained a certain connection with the Sabbatians who remained Jewish. This sect, residing largely in Salonica and Adrianople, still numbered by the outbreak of World War I about ten thousand members. After the exchange of population between Greece and Turkey in 1924 the Doenmehs emigrated to Turkey where they quickly assimilated. Their present-day number is therefore unknown.

The large majority of Sabbatians, however, who remained true to their Messiah stayed within the framework of Judaism. There were actually among them important rabbis and scholars, who of course only covertly risked letting their Sabbatian way of thinking shimmer through into their Kabbalistic writings—often going unnoticed by their contemporaries.

Beside these moderate Sabbatians, however, who had remained within rabbinic Judaism and the traditional Jewish way of life, there also sprang up radical antinomian groups. Their theory was that not only Sabbatai Zevi must have taken sin upon himself, but that the same was incumbent upon his followers. For only by the taking sin upon oneself, can the redemption and restoration of the shattered cosmos be brought about. The Torah and the Ten Commandments, the Jewish religious and ethical law have been set aside through the appearance of the messiah, Sabbatai Zevi. One may now sin with impunity—indeed, this is a touchstone of true belief. In effect this nihilistic tendency expressed itself in a practised sexual libertinism in the Sabbatian conventicles. These radical circles thereby set themself in contrast to the religious and moral views of Judaism and provoked strong counter-measures.

In the mid-eighteenth century the nihilistic tendencies of Sabbatianism reached a final dangerous flare-up in the *Frankist* movement, so called after its founder *Jacob Frank*. This young Sabbatian had come from his Podolian homeland to Salonica, where he became attached to the Doenmehs. On his return he claimed to be an incarnation of Sabbatai Zevi. He preached the anullment of the Law and found enthusiastic followers. When the community heads and rabbis of Polish Jewry banned the Frankist movement, the latter turned to the Polish bishop of Lemberg (Lvov), who organised a religious disputation between the Frankists and some rabbis. The disputation, entirely following the medieval tradition, ended with the condemnation of the Talmud and the burning of several thousands copies. In order to prove the credibility of their Trinitarian conviction, Frank then joined the Catholic church with several hundred of his followers. This group, however, retained further its sectarian identity and its relations with the Frankists who did not convert. Jacob Frank was revered by them as a holy master. For this reason he was imprisoned by the church authorities in Czenstochowa. Only after thirteen years, at the time of the first division of Poland, was he set free by the Russians. With his daughter and some supporters he emigrated to Moravia and later to Offenbach near Frankfurt, where the Prince of Isenburg—who inclined towards mysticism—placed a castle at his disposal. Here he kept court with the financial support of his followers from Moravia and Poland. After his death his daughter Eva remained the head of the movement. She died in 1816.

In East-European Jewry these signs of ethical disintegration were finally overcome, despite the quite wide circles which had here for a time been affected by them. But these circles were easily dissociated from the Jewish communities; some of them like the Frankists even leaving the fold.

It was different in Germany, where the signs of loosening caused by social conditions were now strengthened by the nihilistic ideas of Sabbatianism. However, Sabbatian influences may have only been restricted to very small groups and secret circles as they existed in Prague, Hamburg and other places.[21]

---

[21] Gershom Scholem points out connections between Sabbatian circles and the Enlightenment and the Reform Movement existing at the beginning of the nineteenth century. Cp. Scholem, op. cit. p. 304, 319 f.

## *The Marranos*

In my presentation of the Lurianic Kabbalah and the Sabbatian Movement I have on several occasions referred to the influence of the refugees from the Iberian peninsula. Spanish Jewry had had its greatest efflorescence during the period of Arab rule in Spain—lasting for about eight centuries, despite oppression and persecution by the Moslem rulers and masses. At that time there arose an extraordinarily rich Arabic-Jewish culture bearing fruit in every sphere of intellectual life—in philosophy, poetry, philology, mathemathics, medicine, astronomy, Talmudic and Bible study.

The Iberian peninsula was called in Hebrew *Sepharad* after the name of a region mentioned in the Bible (Obadiah 20). The Sephardic Jews still today comprise the second major branch of Jewry next to Ashkenazi Jewry. For after their expulsion from Spain the Sephardic refugees left their cultural mark and synagogal rite upon the Jewish communities in the then largely Turkish Mediterranean countries, in North Africa, the Balkans and from the Near East to as far as India. Consequently all the Jews of these countries from that time on are considered Sephardic Jews.

The Jews in Moslem Spain spoke and wrote their scholarly writings in Arabic, but they composed in Hebrew, although influenced by Arabian poetry in their use of metre. The most famous of these Hebrew poets were *Judah Halevi* (ca 1080-1145) and *Solomon Ibn Gabirol* (ca 1021-1058), from whom—apart from religious and secular songs—philosophical works have come down. Judah Halevi is, above all, author of one of the most significant and popular presentations of the religion of Judaism in his book *Kuzari*, which has as its background the conversion of the rulers of the Khazars to Judaism in the eighth century.[22]

---

[22] The Khazars lived in the Crimea and Southern Russia between the Black and Caspian Seas. It was probably mainly the court and the nobility who converted to Judaism. Their rule, however, only lasted a few centuries. Under the pressure of the Byzantine kingdom on the one hand, and of the Russians on the other, they fell victim to the Russians of Kiev during the eleventh century.

Ibn Gabirol is the author of a neo-Platonic work. This work has been known to Christian scholastics from the early Middle Ages onwards in a Latin translation under the title of *Fons Vitae* (The Well of Life) attributed to a certain Avicebron or Avicebrol, who was thought to have been an Arab. Only in the last century were Hebrew extracts found, enabling the scholar Solomon Munk to identify the author with the religious poet Ibn Gabirol.

The most significant and universal personality to emerge from Spanish Jewry was Moses ben Maimon, *Maimonides*, also called "Rambam"—the acronym of *R*abbi *M*oses *b*en *M*aimon. Born in Spain, he lived in the twelfth century—mainly in Fostat near Cairo in Egypt—as physician and medical writer. I have already spoken of him as codifier of Jewish religious law and author of the principle work on Jewish religious philosophy *Guide for the Perplexed*. His work as physician and medical writer has also been mentioned.

In Spain there raged for many centuries the conflict between the Muslim Arabs and the Christian successors of the Visigoths, who were pushed towards the north of the country and founded the later Spanish states. The social position of Jews in both parts of the country was for a long time quite good, though legal restrictions and outbreaks of persecution were not uncommon. Jewish statesmen served the Caliphs of Cordova and Arab princes. Somewhat later they also held similar positions in the Christian states, where the Arabs had slowly been dispossessed.

Here in the course of the fourteenth century a serious setback befell the Jews. The struggle against the Arabic states was for the Christian Spaniards a religious war. It grew out of the especially fanatical form of Spanish Catholicism which turned more and more against the unbelieving Jews to undermine their position. Their cultural achievements in this Christian period, however, were still considerable. Spanish Judaism became the centre for the development of speculative mysticism, the Kabbalah. In mathematics and astronomy Spanish Jews also distinguished themselves. Their achievements in this sphere decidedly advanced Spanish and Portuguese navigation, and made possible the discoveries of a Columbus and other Spanish and Portuguese seafarers. *Levi ben Gerson* (or *Gersonides*), who was renowned as a philosopher, invented the Jacob's-staff, or Astrolabe. By commission of a Spanish king, a Jew compiled astronomical tables which—after their patron—were called Alphonsinic tables.

In the fourteenth century, after a succession of serious Jewish-persecutions, the most cruel one in 1391, wide circles of Spanish Jewry saved their lives by means of baptism, which for most of them was a baptism in name only. Through this a tragedy began, which was to have consequences for several centuries. For these "New Christians"—who were largely very well-to-do and educated and who viewed their conversion as a temporary rescue measure—social perspectives and possibilities again opened up, which for them as Jews had for a long time been unattainable. The highest posts in army, church and state now stood open to them. Almost the entire nobility of Spain became related to them by marriage. Where they had previously often been leading merchants, manufacturers and financial advisers of kings, so now they could be all this within Spanish society and not as unbelieving outsiders. That the disfranchised of yesterday should suddenly be the influential of today, now aroused the suspicion, envy and hate of the religiously fanaticized population. The once so coveted conversion of the Jews appeared to society to have been a "gift of the Greeks". For one had not eliminated the unpleasant rival by baptism. On the contrary, one had given him still greater possibilities. Moreover, the covert adherence to Judaism of most of the New Christians rendered the victory of faith into a Pyrrhic victory. This popular frame of mind vented itself, under the slightest pretext, in bloody outbreaks against the *Marranos*, as the New Christians were now called.

After sustained efforts, Ferdinand and Isabella of Spain succeeded in initiating the Inquisition, which developed into a powerful institution against all heretics, but chiefly against the Marranos. The first Auto da Fé—the burning of a heretic to death in public—took place in the year 1481. Their stakes were to burn in Europe till the end of the eighteenth century. The Spanish Inquisition became a national institution independent of the Papal See, that, with the seizure of the possessions of the condemned, brought in an enormous sum of money to the Crown and to the Spanish church. Material interests stood open and shameless behind the religious mask.

In order to make every connection between the New Christians and their former co-religionists impossible, all Jews were banished from Spain in 1492. Over a hundred thousands had to sell their property and belongings for a trifling sum or leave it behind. Derided and persecuted, they sought refuge in other countries. They went to Italy, to the Moslem countries, to the Balkans and a large section went to nearby Portugal.

In Portugal they soon experienced a similar fate to that in Spain. At first their children were snatched from them and forceably baptised, and subsequently the expulsion of all Jews from the country was decreed. This decree revealed itself as deception. The Jews, concentrated in Lisbon for their shipment out of the country, were imprisoned, starved, tormented and finally notwithstanding violently baptised. Seven or eight Jews were loaded on to a ship and banished.

The Inquisition had been introduced into Spain after most of the Marranos had already undergone forced baptism about a century earlier, so that their descendants did not nominally pass for forced-Christians and could therefore be placed under the Inquisition. The situation in Portugal was different. For that reason the popes declined for decades to agree to introducing the Inquisition there. And the conversos themselves sought by every means to prevent this. They declared openly that they were Jews. They intervened with popes, the curia and the Portuguese court—naturally with huge bribes. But the Inquisition gained the victory.—Only a section of Marranos succeeded in the course of the next hundred years in leaving the country by legal and illegal means.[23]

In Portugal, as in Spain, the Marranos were soon cut off from living contact with Jews and Judaism. They were suspected of judaising from the beginning, and lived under constant observation on the part of the Inquisition and its informers. An instructional pamphlet propagated by the Inquisition set out 37 points according to which one could recognise secret sympathising with Judaism. To possess or even look over Hebrew books was perilous. The practice of religious regulations and customs, of Sabbath rest and dietary laws, was made impossible—even in the most intimate circles of the family.

The second and third generation of Marranos remaining in Spain and Portugal already did not know any Hebrew. In place of the Hebrew Bible they resorted to the Latin, and in place of Hebrew prayers the Latin Psalter —augmented by a few Spanish forms of prayer—entered their secret worship. Rudimentary Judaism, to which they still clung amid the greatest dangers and bloodshed of the Inquisition, was more and more interlaced with Christian ideas. Many Marrano families had one of their sons study theology, in order later to have a confessor-father in the family whom they could trust and naturally, also, in order outwardly to manifest their orthodoxy. But by these means, too, strong Christian influences entered their Jewish faith.

Throughout the entire seventeenth—and indeed eighteenth—century the Marranos tried to flee the Iberian peninsula, in order that they might again freely confess their Judaism. This faith of theirs—built upon the words of Moses and the prophets—had now taken on for them an ideal configuration. But the prosaic Judaism that they then found abroad was not able to live up to these ideals.

The Marranos had meanwhile become accustomed to applying Christian standards to the religious law. For many of them the picture of the Pharisee which the New Testament had painted, had determined their view of Rabbinic Judaism, and their opposition was levelled against this and its outward expressions. On the other hand, the communities—especially those in Amsterdam, Hamburg and London—already formed by the first Marranos, had introduced a very austere community-discipline. This discipline was possibly an echo of the rigorous Spanish-Catholic example. One had to force it upon the newcomers, without considering how far they had meanwhile departed from living Judaism. As a result there were time and again individual tragedies, especially among those enthusiastic newcomers, who could

---

[23] Like the refugees from Germany who brought the German language with them to Poland, so the Jews driven from Spain likewise brought the Spanish language into their new countries of residence. Ladino (or Spaniolic) became their everyday speech in the Balkans and the Mediterranean. Today it is still widely spoken by Sefardic Jews. The Marranos who fled somewhat later from Portugal and who went to Holland, England and North-Germany, retained Portuguese for a further three centuries, at least for translations of the Prayer-book and official functions of the community.

not adapt to the prevailing rigour. Out of the by no means slight number of such cases, two names became generally well-known: Uriel da Costa and Baruch Spinoza.

*Uriel da Costa* (1590-1647) who fled from Portugal to Amsterdam, published several works in which he disputed the validity of the Oral Law and Rabbinic tradition. The Jews of Amsterdam were not willing to let their community be endangered by an unrealistic young enthusiast, who did not in the least take into account the development of post-Biblical Judaism. He was put under a ban and had to flee to Hamburg for some years. On returning to Amsterdam he was moved to recant. In his upright way he soon came into conflict again with the religious law, and approached more and more a sort of deistic religion, which rejected all historical religions as the work of man. After a second and degrading ban, which completely isolated him, he committed suicide.

The most significant of the Marrano opponents of traditional Judaism is *Baruch Spinoza* (1632-1677). In contrast to Uriel da Costa he was born and brought up in Amsterdam. The psychological difficulties confronting da Costa and many Marrano newcomers did not really apply to Spinoza. His opposition, however, was much more deep-seated, and on a different level. Da Costa wanted simply to restore the ideal Biblical Judaism present in his mind. He felt himself a Jew among Jews. For Spinoza, on the other hand, ever since he began philosophising, Judaism was no longer the focal point of his thinking. He tends in his doctrine of God, in his relation to nature and in his political writings towards a much more universal system.

His approach to Judaism was only from the outside. Jewish religious philosophy of the Middle Ages may have influenced him; the Bible may serve him as material; but from early youth on they were no longer the framework of his thinking. I should like to explore briefly the ideas of this thinker, because I believe his philosophy stands in direct contrast to the fundamental concepts of Jewish doctrine.

Since Galileo modern sciences have been founded upon the fundamental and underlying hypothesis that natural phenomena are to be understood in terms of logical-mathematical relations. Mechanical occurrences and movements of the heavenly bodies have thus to be represented by mathematical relations and be similarly calculated.

The range of this fundamental law of the natural sciences will be left here undiscussed. However, it could perhaps be said that only with the natural sciences of the nineteenth century, e.g. with Laplace, has this law been interpreted in a rigidly deterministic way. Newton himself, to whom the mechanistic interpretation of classical physics is generally attributed, still allowed a large range for the free arbitrary activity of God. This is especially shown in Newton's controversy with Leibniz, contained in the Clarke-

Leibniz correspondence. Leibniz appears in this as advocate of determinism, while Newton and Clarke represent here a more religious interpretation of nature. But since the time of Galileo and Newton right into present day quantum physics, one thing has remained the hallmark of the natural-scientific method: natural phenomena should in principle be presented mathematically, and translated into numbers and equations. Reality is reduced to quantities, to numerical relationships. Even the probabilistic relations of quantum physics mathematically determine the physical behavior via probability quantities.

Aristotelian metaphysics, on the other hand, deduces the attributes of being from a supreme divine principle. Not numerical relations or quantities, but rather qualities are the material with which Aristotle and medieval philosophy concern themselves.

The Aristotelian schools differ in detail among themselves, as to whether the divine principle opposes matter which is likewise eternal and only formed by the divine principle, or whether this matter itself is regarded as having originated from God. For the supreme forming Principle is considered from the outset to have a share in Being. In Scholasticism God is thus called Ens-Realissimum—the most real Being.

Spinoza attempts now to apply the new fundamental law of the natural sciences to philosophy. With him—as with Aristotle—everything has to be deduced from a supreme principle. But his deduction is not teleologically directed to the definition of reality. It is rather a logical-causal-deduction. His real world-picture is thereby construed parallel to that of the medieval Aristotelians. He is, one could say, a scholastic, but with a new and in principle different method. Spinoza proceeds from infinite substance, which is at the same time infinite reality. The infinite divine substance possesses an infinite number of modes, or forms of phenomena, of which admittedly only two are known to us: thought and extension. The one is, so to speak, the intellectual principle, the other, the physical world. The Ens-Realissimum of the Christian scholastics thus became an identity. For thought and the conceptual contents of the world of phenomena are both united in the divine substance—as he once expressed it: *deus sive natura*—which are thus interchangeable, identical terms. The world is thought of as immanent in God.

Much has been written on the possible influences which formed Spinoza's philosophy. We know he had a good knowledge of the Jewish-Spanish philosophy of the Middle Ages, especially of Maimonides and Ḥasdai Crescas. And it is certainly against these Jewish religious philosophers that he—without mentioning their names—polemizes. Reference has also been made to the influence of the Italian natural-philisophy of the Renaissance. And Spinoza's close connection with *Descartes* is always rightly emphasised.

Descartes is accepted as the real father of modern philosophy, which takes the thinking subject as its starting point. His sentence is well-known: *cogito ergo sum*—"I think, and that means I am". And from the thinking subject, of which man first becomes conscious, Descartes infers a supreme divine Intelligence to whom Being must likewise be attributed.

Spinoza really proceeds in the opposite direction by placing Descartes' last inference at the beginning and by reversing the accentuation. Not thought, not the process of thought, but rather infinite Being stands for him in the foreground, while thinking is only one of the modes of inference drawn from Being. Descartes finds Being through thought; Spinoza thought through Being.

Descartes was also an important mathematician, the founder of co-ordinate arithmetic. Because of this he was himself an active mediator, one of the creators of the new combination of the mathematical sciences and philosophy. Spinoza on the other hand, was neither a mathematician nor a natural-scientist. True, he took over from Descartes as stimulus the methodical combination of these new sciences with philosophy. But he transfers the logical-mathematical method somewhat schematically to his philosophy. He wishes to investigate the actions and drives of man, as though they were geometrical figures. In his *Ethics* he gives the basis of his teaching concerning the infinite, all-embracing divine substance. But when Spinoza comes to the action of man—his teaching runs into a certain discrepancy. What is commonly called ethics—the teaching concerning the action of man —stands in an unresolved inconsistency with the intended geometrical method. Thus we find with Spinoza two things: on the one hand he develops an ethic without good and evil, value-free and leaving no room for the will—either of God or man. In this respect there is for Spinoza only one difference, namely that between truth and falsehood, or as he calls it, adequate and inadequate knowledge. On the other hand, however, man should indeed, by means of his knowledge overcome his drives and passions and find a direct intuitive relation with divine Being. Spinoza calls this intuitive relation *amor dei intellectualis*—the intellectual love for God—in which man feels himself part of the eternal divine substance. In this way there comes into his other-wise so arid system of logical propositions and inferences a mystical-religious strain. Spinoza's own life also reflects this duality of intellectualism and mystical world-feeling.

Through his teaching that made God and creation into one, leaving no room for the will of man or for a ruling God, Spinoza had placed himself outside the tradition of Judaism. When the synagogue of Amsterdam imposed a ban on him in 1656, excommunicating him from the Jewish community, that was really only the consequence of Spinoza's attitude—an attitude he had repeatedly expressed and which at that time he had already begun to set down in writing. If the ban and exclusion from the Jewish community did not upset his mental balance, as was the case with da Costa, they may have been responsible for his increasing estrangement from Judaism which ultimately degenerated into hatred. His outspoken pantheistic religiosity, however, also hindered his conversion to Christianity.

Spinoza's hostile attitude to Jews and Judaism finds expression in his *Theological-Political Treatise*. This was a political work favouring the policy of Jan de Witt, who was on friendly terms with him and stood at the head of the Dutch republic. De Witt was trying to carry through a policy dictated purely by the interests of the state, a kind of state-totalitarianism. He found his main opponents in the preachers and clergy of the churches and sects, with whom the popular House of Orange had formed an alliance. This coalition soon led to de Witt's fall.

In his treatise Spinoza tries to justify de Witt's politics through the Bible. With this work he became the precursor of modern Biblical criticism. But this was not the purpose of his writing. He wanted rather to safeguard the authority of the state against ecclesiastical claims and influences. For Spinoza the Christian preachers who rose against de Witt correspond to the Biblical prophets. The prophets are for him not God-inspired personalities who vis-à-vis king and people insist upon the unconditionality of the divine demands. Instead, they are in his eyes phantasts and even enemies of the state who are seeking to undermine those in authority. The validity of Biblical law is altogether restricted to the boundaries of the Jewish land and to the Jews then living there. There, and at that time it was binding as state-law, whereas today it can in no way claim validity. It has lost its validity both for the Jews of today, and—even more so—for Christian clergy and politicians who appeal to it. Indeed each individual has the right to think what he will, for the thoughts of man are free and uncontrollable. Likewise, everyone has the right to give free expression to his thoughts and to believe concerning God and religion whatever his knowledge of God directs. Not the prophets and not Dutch preachers, but only the authority of the day has the right to decide what should be *done* in the state, especially as to which kind of religious services and practices may be allowed in the land. Thus Spinoza goes back to the idea of the *cuius regio, eius religio*—whoever owns the land decides its religion—that principle of religious peace of the sixteenth century which in Spinoza's time had already long become obsolete.

Spinoza's ideas have had no direct consequences in Judaism. His philosophy was really rediscovered outside Judaism in the 1770s during the time of the pre-Romantics. Friedrich Heinrich Jacobi became the—one might say—involuntary initiator of his revival, through his discussion with Moses Mendelssohn about Spinozist utterances by Lessing. Herder, Goethe, Fichte, Schleiermacher were all strongly influenced by the ideas of Spinoza. And the philosophy of German Idealism, especially Schelling's so-called "Philosophy of Identity", is unthinkable without him. Thus Spinoza became a significant factor in general intellectual history.

The remarkable juxtaposition of cool logical intellectualism and a thoroughly emotional feeling of the All in the philosophy of Spinoza has exerted a great attraction since the Romantic era until our own day. It became the philosophy of generations of intellectuals. It expressed the intellectual position of determinist romantic natural philosophy, as did the equally deterministic natural science of the nineteenth century. However at the same time it retained in the amor intellectualis an element which met irrational needs.

It is only in modern times that Spinoza has occasionally influenced Jewish circles (e.g. Moses Hess, Constantin Brunner). But religious Judaism in all its trends has always found him strange and rejected him.

In the earlier period there was probably only one occasion when a Jewish scholar has been suspected of Spinozism which at that time was tantamount to sympathizing with atheistic lines of thought. This was the Sephardic Chief Rabbi in London, *David Nieto* (1654-1728) from Venice. He had studied medicine in Padua and acquired a wide general education. Having completed his studies he served at first in Leghorn as physician and rabbi, publishing astronomical, mathematical and philosophical writings in Spanish and in Hebrew. He was an important apologist of Judaism with regard to both, Christianity and the Sabbatian movement. Nieto had widely-ramifying scientific correspondence and personal communication with well-known Christian scholars of his day. He was called to London in 1701 as Chief Rabbi of the Sephardic community there, where he remained until his death.

In 1703 Nieto preached a sermon in London in which he inveighed against the misuses of the word "nature". The term "nature" in the popular colloquial usage of his contemporaries, had come to mean something midway between the divine Creator and the world. One was ascribing to nature what is to be ascribed to God, who according to Jewish tradition is the Creator of nature and all of its phenomena. Unfortunately, Nieto used for nature in this context—by which one really meant God—the expression *natura naturande*, which was reminiscent of Spinoza.[24]

This sermon, and a booklet published by Nieto in the following year on the same theme, created great unrest in his congregation. Only the advocacy of the greatest rabbinic authority of his time, that of the Ḥakham Ẓevi of Altona, cleared him of the suspicion of Spinozism.

---

[24] cf. Jakob J. Petuchowski, The Theology of Hakham David Nieto, New York 1954 and Responsum No. 18 of Ḥakham Ẓevi.

# The Pre-Enlightenment in Germany

We saw how various phenomena had combined, which led imperceptibly to a loosening of the medieval world of Jewish life: the closer contact of wide circles and classes with the world around them, its language and culture, the shocks sustained by Polish Jewry and the collapse of the Messianic hope of Sabbatianism.

It is worth noting that the popular-piety of the Jews in Germany had at first absorbed these influences to an astonishing degree. The memoirs of *Glueckel of Hameln*, mentioned earlier, illustrate the latter point. This Hamburg lady, born about 1646, was a Jewish middle-class woman, who after the death of her husband carried on and consolidated his business, and at the same time brought up and educated her large family and eventually saw them married. From her memoirs, written in Yiddish, we gather that she and her circles had been affected by the loosening of many traditional bonds. For a woman of her time she possessed a remarkable education, though she does not refer to this and mentions only once the language and musical ability of her elder step-sister. She travelled to fairs etc., and through the marriage of her children came into closer relations with court-Jew circles and was conversant with the politics of the day. But how little the world-openness of this woman impaired her simple faith is seen from the way she overcame the deep disappointment following the collapse of the Sabbatian messianic hope. She writes: "because of our sins" redemption has not yet come.

The obvious proximity of the traditional attitude of life and of an unaffected acceptance of contemporary culture was characteristic of the majority of Jews in Germany even into the mid-nineteenth century. Jewish learning and the Jewish way of life had still preponderance over the values and attitudes accepted from their time and surroundings. The Jewish aspect long remained the determinative factor. However, a certain balance developed between the Jewish and the surrounding culture. Only at the end of the eighteenth century did the influences of the environment—as we shall see—gain the upper hand in the hierarchy of values, at least in the upper sections of society.

Just as the Jews in Germany gradually began to participate in their cultural environment, so an interest in Jewish literature and in Jews themselves had begun in small groups of Christian scholars. This interest still had its roots in the Renaissance, when a revival of the classical age, its language and culture was aspired to. The humanist scholars of the Renaissance had reformed Latin style. Abandoning medieval silver Latin they returned to Cicero and Virgil. The Greek language had been newly discovered in the West when after the fall of Constantinople in 1453, Greek scholars came to Italy. In these circles an interest in Hebrew also grew up, in which one saw at that time the original language of mankind.

The centre of these endeavours had been the Platonic Academy in Florence. There Platonic philosophy and mysticism were renewed and given preference over Scholastic Aristotelianism by *Pico della Mirandola* and his circle. There one also aspired to the primeval wisdom, believed hidden in the original language of Hebrew and to be found in the Kabbalah—the more so since one had noticed certain similarities between neo-Platonic and Jewish mysticism. The mystical tendency characteristic of the neo-Platonic natural-philosophy of the sixteenth century also looked for confirmation in the Kabbalistic primeval wisdom. This search was the leitmotiv of the preoccupation with "Hebrew truth" which meant involvement with the Hebrew language and Rabbinic literature. A good example and representative of this school of thought was *Johannes Reuchlin* (1455-1522). By his testimony on the Talmud against the defamations of the baptized Pfefferkorn and the Dominicans of Cologne, Reuchlin brought the latent antagonism between medieval Aristotelian scholasticism and humanist thought into open collision. The world of learning at that time was split in a quarrel lasting several years, in which Reuchlin was supported by every well-disposed humanist.

It was not only Renaissance philosophy that influenced the revival of Hebrew studies, as begun in Germany by Reuchlin and Pellican and continued in Basle by Sebastian Muenster. The Reformation had pushed the principle of Scripture into the foreground of theological thinking in its Protestant orientations, which necessarily involved an intensified preoccupation with the Jewish Bible in its original language. *Luther* had translated the Bible into German, and for this purpose had had to learn Hebrew. His passing benevolent attitude to Jews, expressed in his pamphlet *Dass Jesus ein Geborener Jude gewesen*, ("Jesus was born a Jew"), very soon turned into most vehement and boorish hate when his expectation of the conversion of the Jews did not materialise. Following his lead, the Lutheran clergy by and large assumed the same role for centuries in relation to Jews in the Protestant part of Germany which, in the Catholic part, itinerant preachers and religious orders long fulfilled.

Despite their hostility to Judaism and its representatives, however, Protestant clergy of all persuasions were in any case obliged to learn at least some Hebrew, in order to understand the 'Old Testament'. With a number of Christian scholars this interest spread to post-Biblical Hebrew literature. Hence, despite the polemical and missionary tendency inherent in their writings, they had remarkable achievements in some fields. Hebrew Lexicography and grammar, in fact, remained for a long time a monopoly of Christian scholars, as was Biblical scholarship almost till the present day. The seventeenth century in particular saw some important achievements of Christian Hebraists, such as the translation of the Mishnah into Latin by the Dutchman Surenhuys, the lexical works of Johannes Buxtorf senior, the Latin translation of Maimonides' "Guide for the Perplexed" by Buxtorf's son, the critical Biblical writings of the French monk Richard Simon and the Kabbalistic writings of Knorr von Rosenroth. Following them in the eighteenth century were the bibliographer Johann Christoph Wolf of Hamburg and the two Michaelis's in Halle and Goettingen.—Preoccupation with Rabbinic literature had far-reaching consequences in intellectual history. The protagonists of natural law—Grotius, Selden, inter alia—refer to the juridical concepts of Rabbinic Judaism, in order to establish valid human rights for all men.

Besides these scholarly achievements and supplementing them was a literature on Judaism of a different kind, giving information about Jews and their customs. In these writings description and polemics combine. *Johann Jacob Schudt* published his *Juedische Merkuerdigkeiten* (Jewish Curiosities), where he gives a detailed description of the customs he observed among the Jews in Frankfurt. He reports on their religious services, community-organization, legal status and history, and indeed printed two complete comedies which the Frankfurt-Jews had presented at their carnival-like Purim Festival. This work has become an important source for the cultural history of the Jews at the beginning of the eighteenth century.

Similar to Schudt's work, but perhaps more systematic and scholarly, is the Protestant Theologian *Johann Christian Bodenschatz's* book, that appeared about thirty years later in 1748. Bodenschatz gives an accurate unbiased description of Jewish customs—illustrated with many etchings— as he had come to know them from his Jewish contemporaries in Franconia. His book is also an important source of information about Jewish life in Germany around the mid-eighteenth century.

A Professor in Altdorf, *Johann Christian Wagenseil*, had collected Jewish polemical writings against Christianity, translated them into Latin and published them with a detailed refutation under the title *Tela Ignea Satanae* (Fiery Darts of Satan). Wagenseil was a scholar with a great knowledge in the field of Rabbinic literature, which he of course approached as critic and as apologist of Christianity. He sharply criticised the 'Blood Accusation' and other defamations against Judaism and the Jews.

In contrast to him was *Johann Andreas Eisenmenger* in Heidelberg. In his book *Entdecktes Judentum* (Discovered Judaism), he unscrupulously made out as true facts all the lies and slanders levelled against the Jews in the course of centuries—poisoning of the wells, ritual murder and the rest. By means of quotations completely torn from their context which he selected from the Talmud and other rabbinic literature, and from which he drew the most absurd conclusions, he sought to substantiate all the accusations. His work breathes the crassest hatred of Jews and became arsenal for later anti-semitic writings. The Jews of Vienna, under the leadership of the court Jew *Samuel Oppenheimer*, were anxious to prevent the publication of this inflammatory work. Eisenmenger himself was prepared to destroy his book for a payment of thirty thousand thalers. Since he refused the offer of half the sum, Oppenheimer secured by imperial edict the seizure of the already printed copies. But after Eisenmenger's death the book appeared with permission of the Prussian King Frederick I in Koenigsberg which lay outside the Roman-German realm and the jurisdiction of the Emperor.

The interest of Christian scholars, however, was not confined to the language, literature and tradition of the Jews. Alongside venomous polemics, like those of Eisenmenger, we find in all the afore-mentioned scholars a tendency, through controversy and argument towards promoting the conversion of Jews to Christianity. This missionary tendency through voluminous scholarly books has scarcely been able to make an impression on Jews. It passed them by, all the more so as, being in German or Latin, these writings could be read by very few.

Another and novel form of mission to the Jews at the end of the seventeenth and in the eighteenth century had, on the other hand, met with a certain success. Under the influence of Pietism the method of missionaries had altered. They no longer proclaimed in reproving tone the obduracy and blindness of Jews in relation to Christian doctrines. They tried rather through friendliness and participation in their life to win their trust. This new attitude was for many Jews unusual, and the human interest was gratefully received by many, even by those who had no intention whatever of converting. The new missionary method had already been introduced in Hamburg in the seventeenth century by Esdras Edzardi (1629-1708), who was himself not a proselyte as one sometimes reads.[25] He and his son, who together also set up a residential home for converts, are said to have baptized hundreds of Jews. In 1728 Professor *Callenberg* (1694-1760) established an Institutum Judaicum in Halle for the training of missionaries. Callenberg sent his co-workers right across Germany. He saw to the occupational re-education of his converts and to their integration into the Christian community. He pub-

---

[25] He was a clergyman's son and pupil of Buxtorf senior. He learned Rabbinics from the Portuguese Rabbi de Lara of Hamburg. The fund for proselytes in Hamburg that Edzardi founded was only dissolved by the national-socialists in 1942.

lished the reports of his emissaries in several booklets, which are culturo-historically very interesting.

Who then were the Jews, who became objects of this new missionary activity? A large contingent came from the circles of the *beggar-Jews*, who, without right of residence in a community, wandered through the country and accepted the advantages baptism offered them. It even happened that they accepted baptism several times in different places—for the sake of material benefits.

Another group of Jews at this time, however, were also emotionally prepared to convert to Christianity. These were former Sabbatians, whose world had been shattered by the collapse of their hopes. As already mentioned, their Sabbatian theology had familiarized them with Trinitarian concepts. They had only to change the person of the Messiah. These one-time Sabbatians were in many cases students of the Talmud who, coming from Poland, sought out a wretched subsistence as primary-teachers in Germany. Some of these baptised persons soon became literarily active. Azriel Shohet has published a list of more than twenty such baptised literators, whose books for the most part came from the press of the Callenberg Institute. Some of them became lecturers in Hebrew at various universities, as for example Johannes Kemper in Upsala and Karl Anton in Helmstedt.

On the other hand, there were scattered individual Gentile seekers after God, who—mostly in Amsterdam—converted to Judaism. The best-known among them became Moses Germanus, previously called Johannes Spaeth. He was originally Catholic, actually monk for a time, then Protestant and pupil of Spener and finally a Jew.

The influence of the new secular scientific culture could not bypass the rabbis of the time. Some knowledge of mathematics had to a certain extent belonged to the curriculum of the traditional scholars. Also the combining of the medical and Rabbinic profession in the seventeenth and eighteenth centuries goes back to old traditions. Physicians with rabbinical education, however, had now already studied at universities, where knowledge of Latin was a basic requirement. We find such university educated rabbis more often in Portuguese-Sephardic communities or in Italy and in isolated cases also in Germany. In addition to the already mentioned Joseph del Medigo and the Londoner David Nieto, I whould like to give prominence to the name of *Solomon Fuerst*, Rabbi of Koenigsberg, who in 1712 became the first Jew to matriculate at that University.

However, also outside the precincts of University education we meet, at the beginning of the eighteenth century, more and more frequently rabbis with versatile language ability, with knowledge of new philosophical trends, of the New Testament and the movements in contemporary Christianity. We hear of personal relations and correspondence between Jewish and Christian scholars. Christian Hebraists had Jewish teachers. Professors and clergy turned to rabbis for advice on questions of Rabbinic literature and language. *Joseph Stadthagen*, Rabbi in Stadthagen, kept in touch with professors of the small university of Rinteln near his residence. In 1704 he had to hold a religious discussion with a baptised Jew at the Electoral Court in Hanover in the presence of George the Elector (later King of England) and his mother Sophia the Electoress, patroness of Leibniz. Here he met his former acquaintance from Rinteln, the theologian *Gerhard Molanus*, who together with Leibniz had had discussions regarding union between the Catholic and the Lutheran Reformed Church. Stadthagen has left behind a report, from which it incidentally emerges that he spoke and read French and knew the New Testament. Noteworthy is Stadthagen's reserved attitude to the Zohar which he said he did not understand. For an era, when the Kabbalah so strongly influenced Jewish thought, this attitude of a rabbi is at all events unusual.

Rabbis *David Oppenheimer* and *Jonathan Eybeschuetz*, both in Prague, had had relations with the Catholic clergy there. David Oppenheimer became especially well-known as a book collector. He built up a Hebrew library, the most famous and extensive of its day, which he later transferred to Hanover to safeguard it from ecclesiastical censure in Prague. In Hanover it was used by the bibliographer Wolf of Hamburg. Then it lay for sale in Hamburg for decades without finding a buyer. Only in 1829 was the Oppenheimer library acquired by the Bodleian in Oxford.

*Zevi Ashkenazi*, known as *Ḥakham Zevi* (1658-1718), stalwart defender of the strictest Jewish religious observance, and the most significant religious-legal authority of his time, knew eight languages, including Latin and Greek, and had a considerable secular education. He was the protagonist of Rabbinic Judaism against the Sabbatians.

His no less significant contemporary, *Ḥayim Yaïr Bacharach* (1639-1702) pursued, as he himself said, philosophy and the secular sciences. But he abandoned them in view of their many conflicting schools of thought and the impossibility of obtaining real knowledge from them. Bacharach introduced a new method of Talmud study. He saw the Talmudic problems in their inter-relatedness and in their historical context, thereby approaching the methodology of modern scholarship. Thus he stood in contrast to the dominant dialectical method of the Talmud study of his time which rated pure sagacity higher than systematic understanding. For this reason he has been called a pioneer of the modern 'Science of Judaism'.

At the beginning of the eighteenth century attempts began to be made to overcome the dangers and damages which had arisen as a result of the manifold shocks Jewry had experienced. We find complaints of contemporaries in the moral sermons and responsa of various scholars. But some Jews refused to be content with complaining and looked for positive ways of changing the threatening situation. The cause of moral and religious decline was seen in the false practice of the traditional educational system. A simple country Jew in the Hessian village of Hergershausen, *Aaron Hergershausen* (ca. 1709), was of the opinion that the instruction of children would have to begin with their mother tongue, in order to awaken early their religious sensibility and understanding. He therefore made a Yiddish translation of the Prayer-Book, which he called *Die Liebliche Tefillah* ('The Lovely Prayer'). About 1749 in Celle, a wealthy scholarly Jew, *Isaac Wetzlar*, laboured for a reform of the Jewish educational system. He desired, most of all, a restriction of the one-sided study of the Talmud in favour of better instruction in the Bible and in the moral teachings of Jewish literature. He left behind a book, *Liebesbrief* (The Love-letter) which is only preserved in manuscript.

These attempts at change and reform were prompted neither by schismatic or assimilatory tendencies. Nor were they inspired by the ideas of contemporary religious rationalism, like the later pedagogic undertakings of the Enlightenment. They were the expression of the concern of pious Jews in view of the religious and moral decline, but they faded away without effect in their time. The "Lovely Tefilla" was prohibited by the rabbis of Hessen. Only in 1830 was a copy of it found in the attic of a Hessian synagogue. And Wetzlar's book wasn't even printed.

More far-reaching was the impact made by the Hebrew press of Jessnitz in Anhalt. The Princes of Anhalt, especially the well-known 'old Dessauer', organizer of the Prussian army, had attracted Jews to Anhalt about the same time of their readmission to Brandenburg. The community of Dessau soon obtained a certain importance, since it was the nearest Jewish community and burial-place for visitors to the Leipzig fair. In Dessau during the 1730s *David Fraenkel* (1704-1762), who had strong scholarly leanings, served as rabbi. He was author of an authoritative commentary on the Jerusalem Talmud and was the teacher of Moses Mendelssohn first in Dessau and later in Berlin to where he was called in 1743. The court-Jew family of Dessau, relatives of the rabbi, founded a Hebrew printing press in neighbouring Jessnitz, where several important works were printed or reprinted which had in part been inaccessible for centuries. Here, among others, the aforementioned natural science textbook by Tobias Cohn was reprinted in 1721.[26] Most important, however, was the reprinting of Maimonides' 'Guide for the Perplexed'. This principal work of Jewish religious philosophy which Maimonides published in the twelfth century, had only been printed once in the sixteenth century in Sabionetta. It was subsequently unobtainable for almost two hundred years, since,—as was indicated—engagement with philosophy had been restrained during this time. The reprint of 1742 in the village of Jessnitz, which renewed the interest and study of Jewish philos-

---

[26] It was first printed in Venice in 1707.

ophy, was thus a significant event for intellectual history. It was from this edition that Mendelssohn and Solomon Maimon learned philosophy.

These books, however, reached only relatively small circles. Most of the community heads and rabbis were still caught up in the old spirit, which regarded with suspicion any interest in philosophy, natural science or history.

# CHAPTER 6

# Breakthrough to Enlightenment

In the preceding chapters I have discussed events and phenomena which began to slacken the traditional religiously defined life style of the Jews of the Middle Ages. This life style had just previously been definitively codified, as it seemed, in the *Shulḥan Arukh* and in its commentaries. Only in 1649 had the popular work of Isaiah Horowitz *The Two Tables of the Covenant* appeared, linking the religious law with the Lurianic Kabbalah, which through penitence and asceticism wanted to hasten the coming of the Messianic kingdom. These frames and ideas held sway in the, so to speak, official Judaism of the day. The inner segregation of Judaism in relation to religious and intellectual trends and events in the world at large had reached its climax.[27]

The earlier described signs of slackening emerged paradoxically against the background of this Lurianic rabbinic world of thought. In fact in 1700 they were no longer exceptions but had gradually penetrated into every strata of the Jewish population in Germany.

But both in business circles, as with Glueckel of Hameln and also with the learned rabbis and diffident education reformers, the new influences only attained *decorative significance*. These influences had indeed changed the outward life of Jews and became to a certain extent part of their daily life. But the new and outside influences were unconsciously and quite naturally absorbed without reflection. The spiritual ghetto for the Jews in Germany was doubtlessly broken. Yet it was only the walls of this seclusion that had fallen. What was previously protected by these walls had not yet or had only slightly been touched. Their way of thinking and perspective still remained those of the Jewish tradition.

When for example Ḥakham Ẓevi defended David Nieto against the charge of Spinozism, he did not take his arguments from current philosophy but from Jehuda Halevi, the Spanish-Jewish poet and philosopher of the twelfth

---

[27] Cp. Jacob Katz, Exclusiveness and Tolerance, Oxford 1961, Chapters 11 and 12.

century. Jonathan Eybeschuetz referred to Descartes, was familiar with Copernicus and Newton's theory of gravity and used expressions of the theory of natural law and of modern philosophy. He polemized against arguments of deistic textual criticism of miracles and morality in the Bible. But his own thinking was not yet determined by it. Men like Nieto and Eybeschuetz, Oppenheimer and Stadthagen were proud of knowing some Latin, of having read foreign theological and historical books and of numbering Christian scholars among their acquaintances. Such knowledge and relationships raised their prestige in their communities, which were already beginning to desire this from their rabbis.[28] The personal attitude of the rabbis with a secular education, however, remained determined by the Lurianic Kabbalah.[29]

In the second third of the eighteenth century, however, a substantial change took place. What for the generation around 1700 was still "ornament" or "showpiece", something that was taken over from contemporary culture naturally and without reflection into one's own life style—that became the starting-point of the reflection from which Judaism was now regarded.

This change was at first unconscious. By those who brought it about, it was not at all experienced as something new. On the contrary, the first great figure of the Jewish Enlightenment, *Jacob Emden*, considered himself custodian of the strictest observance and orthodoxy and was reckoned as such by his contemporaries. Even Mendelssohn thought of himself as an "arrant" Jew ("Stockjude").

The new attitude had its parallel in Jewish intellectual history. When Gaon Saadia in the tenth century wished to differentiate Judaism from the Karaïtes and Islamic theology, he employed the methods of the Arabian philosophy of his day. His successors, the medieval Jewish religious philosophers, tried to see how far their Judaism harmonized with neo-Platonism and the Aristotelian schools of thought and to what extent it differed from them. They did not want to justify Judaism by means of contemporary thought, as one might expect. None of them needed at that time to do so. They wished rather to contribute to Jewish self-understanding. Their outlook had remained Jewish. But it was now perceived in the intellectual trends of the time which reflected their own concept of Judaism.

The dangers of the Sabbatian heresy had now taken the place of the Karaïtes, and the theology and philosophy of the Enlightenment that of Plato and Aristotle. The Saadia of the Jewish Enlightenment of the eighteenth century, the man who—it seems to me—was the first to express this

---

[28] When Jonathan Eybeschuetz was applying for the rabbinical post in Metz, he enumerated in detail all his knowledge of foreign scholarship. Cp. Shohet, p. 199.

[29] Joseph Stadthagen may be an exception. At any rate he shows in the Hanoverian religious discussion an unusual reserve towards the *Zohar*, whose utterances he dismisses as "Geschwänk" ('idle talk') declaring that he does not understand them.

new attitude was Jacob ben Zevi, called—following his brief activity as rabbi in Emden—*Jacob Emden*. Such a description precisely of this man may seem at first paradoxical. It would also be directly opposed to his own self-understanding. For Jacob Emden felt himself too much a lone and solitary champion of the strictest rabbinic tradition, an opponent of every ideological and practical deviation, for the idea to have come to him that he could be pointsman of a new era in Judaism. He is a Jewish scholar about whose life and work we are especially well informed. He not only left behind a large number of books, polemical writings and pamphlets, responsa and commentary works. He also wrote a comprehensive autobiography[30] which represents an important source for his own life-history and that of his time, especially for the Jews in Hamburg.

Jacob Emden was born in Altona in 1697. His father was Ḥakham Zevi Ashkenazi—mentioned earlier—who was for many years rabbi there, where a small academy was founded for him, and subsequently rabbi of the "Three Communities" of Altona-Hamburg-Wandsbek. Jacob (*ben* Zevi) Emden, known by his acronym as "Ya'abez", was the pupil of his father. He felt himself in everything to be his spiritual heir, his father being for him an implicit example. For this reason he begins his autobiography with the biography of his father, in which he has erected a memorial to Ḥakham Zevi in a manner that a son has seldom done. He sought throughout his life to emulate his father and his work, especially to continue his struggle against the Sabbatians.

Jacob Emden was highly sensitive to every remark in print or daily life which seemed to him a deflection from traditional biblical rabbinic Judaism. Yet at the same time he himself had acquired—mostly self-taught—an astonishing general education. He had learned by himself Latin and Dutch and probably also English. He possessed a good general knowledge of contemporary trends and opinions and of the scientific discoveries of the day. He describes his urge to know and to comprehend everything. Especially developed were his historical insight and critical faculty. Also known to him were the Jewish philosophers and—even when he mentions no names—the philosophy and Christian theology of his time. But for all his interest he declined to penetrate deeper into the surrounding culture. He acknowledged only those academic subjects which had a general human usefulness, like medicine, astronomy, geography, mathematics and history. According to him, one should appropriate so much from the outside store of knowledge as is necessary for life among other people, in order to be able to join in conversation and—this is for him the Jewish point of view—if necessary to reply to attacks or objections.

The ideal of general education that he thereby developed is, as I see it, similar to that of "L'homme d'esprit" of the court society and of the higher

---

[30] Megillat Sefer, edit. by David Kahana, 1897. Reprint New York, 1956.

middle classes of the eighteenth century. Much of his knowledge he may
have gained from reading the daily press, for he was a keen newspaper
reader.[31] He was suspicious of philosophy and condemned the reprinting
of Maimonides' "Guide" in Jessnitz. Indeed, it was hard for him to believe
that a religious legal authority like Maimonides could have written the
"Guide for the Perplexed", though in a response (No. 14) he conceded that a
scholar like Maimonides very well may have occupied himself with logic and
philosophy. However, later generations lacked his depth and that is why
according to Emden pre-occupation with such subjects should justifiably
be rendered more difficult. For in the pursuit of philosophy and its consequences he saw dangers comparable to the theology of the Sabbatians,
namely, the undermining of the traditional Jewish way of life. Yet at the
centre of his own theology he pays Maimonides almost hymnic homage,
expressly setting the "Guide for the Perplexed" in contrast to the errors of
Maimonides' successors (Birat Migdal Oz 54b), and he himself bases his own
religious interpretation on the philosophers Saadia, Maimonides and Albo.

Jacob Emden showed a marked striving for personal independence—
this too an inheritance from his father. He did not want to be bound to
or dependent on anyone, notably on wealthy community heads. Only once
did he give in to accept a rabbinical post—in Emden—after which he was
later named. But as he soon came into conflict with the community council
he stayed in that post only five years. At that time he vowed never again
to take on office. From Emden he moved in 1733 to his native city of
Altona where he lived as a private scholar and died in 1776. The Altona
community allowed him to hold a private religious service in his house. But
his gruffness and personal inflexibility caused him to remain isolated here
too. In fact he soon quarrelled with the old devotees of his father. His following therefore comprised only the few who attended his private synagogue. For a long time he did not do well financially, for he was not at all
suited to business life. His attempts to work in business were a series of
disappointments described at length in his autobiography. Only when the
Danish authorities gave him permission to open a printing shop did his
position improve. As one of the first productions of his printing press, he
published between 1741 and 1748 an edition of the Prayer Book in several
annotated volumes. This "Siddur Ya'abez" became a success and retained
a decisive influence on the modern scholarly Prayer Book editions of the
nineteenth century by Wolf Heidenheim and in particular by Seligman Baer.

In the year 1750 the rabbinate of the "Three Communities" became
vacant and Rabbi Jonathan Eybeschuetz of Metz was elected chief rabbi.
Soon there began a conflict between Jacob Emden and the new rabbi which

---

[31] In responsum no. 162 he deals with the question whether the reading of newspapers is permissible
on the Sabbath. He affirms it in principle but advises business people against it, since they naturally
contain financial reports, through the reading of which the Sabbath rest command would be transgressed.

dragged on for years, overshadowing the real significance of Jacob Emden for Jewish intellectual history. This quarrel between two of the most important scholars of the day was to have serious consequences for the intellectual-spiritual life of German Jewry. I should therefore like to consider this more fully. It is worth noting that not only in the eighteenth century was Jewry split into followers of Eybeschuetz and of Emden. Even today—and despite a certain consensus in favour of Emden—this dispute cannot be discussed, so it seems, without taking sides.

*Jonathan Eybeschuetz* (1690-1764) was one of the most prominent Talmud scholars of his time. He was a man of captivating personality and an outstanding speaker. Already in his very early years he directed the famous academy in Prague where he exerted a great attraction on the students. Over the years he is said to have had more than twenty thousand students, who always remained attached to him. As already mentioned, he possessed a comprehensive education. He had contacts with the Catholic clergy of Prague and held the office of censor for Hebrew literature.

In 1742, at the time of the first Silesian War, when Prussia together with France fought against Maria Theresia of Austria (who also ruled over Prague), Eybeschuetz received a call as rabbi to Metz. Although he only moved there in 1744, the suspicion of the Austrian authorities had already been aroused through his negotiations with the French community. Eybeschuetz was later forbidden to return to Austria for the rest of his life, and the entire community of Prague fell under suspicion of having sided with the country's enemies. In the middle of winter 1744 the Jews were expelled from Prague.

Eybeschuetz only remained in Metz a few years, accepting at the end of 1750 a call to be Chief rabbi of the Three Communities of Altona-Hamburg-Wandsbek.

In his youth Eybeschuetz had contacts with Sabbatian circles, which had one of their main centres in Bohemia-Moravia. A Kabbalistic work with strong Sabbatian tendencies that appeared anonymously was attributed to him. And following an investigation against Sabbatians in Mannheim in the year 1725 Eybeschuetz was deeply incriminated. At the same time, Eybeschuetz was the initiator of a ban, which some rabbis in Prague had published against the supporters of Sabbatai Zevi in 1725. He himself later repeatedly quoted this fact as proof of always having been an opponent of Sabbatianism.

Rumours of Eybeschuetz's Sabbatian past had been known to Jacob Emden. At first their mutual relationship remained thoroughly correct. Eybeschuetz in fact strove hard to win over the famous scholar. But six months had not elapsed before an open conflict broke out between them.

In Altona childbed fever was rife, costing great loss of life. According to the custom of the day, pregnant women requested from the chief rabbi amulets for their protection. These believedly contained mysterious protective formulae taken from the practical Kabbalah which only someone

experienced in Kabbalah could decipher by rearranging the letters according
to certain rules. Eybeschuetz had already distributed such amulets in Metz
and was now continuing to do so in Hamburg. One of these was brought to
Jacob Emden, who found in it a clear allusion to Sabbatai Ẓevi. Word soon
got around that the private scholar, Jacob Emden, suspected the chief rabbi
of the Three Communities, Jonathan Eybeschuetz, of Sabbatianism. Sum-
moned before the community council, Emden declared emphatically that
the writer of the amulet was a Sabbatian and that the chief rabbi who had
distributed them would have to clear himself of the suspicion of having
known about their heretical contents. This request was rejected by the
community council, who, charging Emden with a ban, forbade attendance
of his private synagogue and placed a watch before his home to secure the
ban's enforcement. Thereupon Jacob Emden in his house-synagogue proclaimed a counter-ban on Eybeschuetz and the community council, obtaining written support for his charge from well-known rabbis. Eybeschuetz
swore he was no Sabbatian, declaring that the amulets referred to were in-
correctly interpreted by Emden, who (he maintained) had insufficient knowledge of the Kabbalah. Parties and opposing parties emerged, Eybeschuetz
setting his numerous followers—some of whom had meanwhile come to
hold important rabbinic posts mainly in Poland—against Emden's supporters.
In Eybeschuetz's favour is the fact that these former pupil followers were
behind him, though Eybeschuetz in correspondence with one of them had
expressed dualistic ideas. Although he distinguishes these from the views of
the Sabbatians Cardozo and Ḥayun, they are thoroughly heterodox-gnostic.
Against him is also the fact—apart from the content of the amulets—that the
Frankist movement which emerged in the 'fifties, cites him as an authority.[32]

Emden had to flee to Amsterdam for a considerable period as he was
personally threatened. From there he continued the struggle with pamphlets,
neither too particular in choice of language nor material, casting suspicion
on every action of Eybeschuetz and on his personal life. In choice and tone
of expression—as in the pamphlets published by his party—Eybeschuetz was
more than a match for his opponent. Ban and counter-ban were pronounced,
so that in the end nearly every Jew in Germany and Poland, as supporter of
one side or the other, was under some ban or another. The dispute extended
to Holland, Italy, Turkey and Palestine. Even the Hamburg and Danish
authorities became involved. At the end of it all, Eybeschuetz in fact remained chief rabbi, but it was a victory neither for him nor for Emden, who
through royal rescript was soon able to return to Altona.

The dispute was, however, a defeat for the reputation of Judaism. Above
all, this six-year long dispute had shaken the prestige of the rabbis and community discipline in Germany. Wide circles turned aside from the squabbling

[32] Investigations of Perelmutter: R. Jonathan Eybeschuetz and his relation to Sabbatianism (R.Y.E.
w'Yaḥasso el Hashabta'ut) Tel Aviv, 1942, proved that Eybeschuetz not only in his youth, but also in
his later works held Sabbatian or at any rate dualistic trains of thought.

rabbis, turning with greater freedom towards the current tendencies of the Enlightenment.

In the amulet dispute Jacob Emden appeared as a stubborn, fanatical and quarrelsome heresy hunter, and this picture of him is preserved in the historical accounts. But this strife, in my opinion, has obscured Emden's real intellectual-historical importance. For as critic and theologian he is the linking figure between the Middle Ages and the Enlightenment. His attitude to Kabbalah had been up till then the usual one for a rabbi of his time. Without being a real expert in this sphere—something his opponent Eybeschuetz always cast up to him—Emden had made use of Kabbalistic concepts in the commentary to his Prayer Book and other writings. For indeed in scholarly circles the influence of the Lurianic Kabbalah was still a living one. But in the course of his struggle against the Sabbatian heresy his critique switched over to the "Zohar", the basic work of the Kabbalah. The "Zohar" was considered holy, being placed almost on a level with Bible and Talmus. Jacob Emden found that at least a large part of this book could not—as was assumed by tradition—have originated from Simeon bar Yoḥai, a sage of the Mishnah, but was a later pseudograph.

Doubt as to the authenticity and holiness of the "Zohar" had already been expressed earlier, more often up till the fifteenth century, whereas only now and again afterwards. Jacob Emden was the first authoritative rabbi to join these opponents. He emphasized that by questioning the "Zohar's" authenticity one does not cease to be a pious Jew.[32a]

Emden's Zohar critique, however, was not a chance incidence of a polemicist, nor was it a tactical move in the struggle against the supporters of Sabbatai Ẓevi. It is related to his interpretation of religion which unconsciously had been strongly influenced by contemporary Enlightenment-theology.

Emden had already developed his *theology* in the 'forties. The concept of God is for him not a postulate of belief but a postulate of reason, and therefore accessible to all men and of necessity to be acknowledged by all. That to which understanding obliges us, thereto is no commandment required, and what understanding rejects cannot be commanded to be believed. Even apparent faith-commandments of the Bible, like the confession of God's Oneness: "Hear, O Israel", or the opening of the Decalogue: "I am the Eternal, thy God"—which are in fact included among the commandments—must be viewed as rational statements. The special feature of Judaism is not the universal recognition of God's existence, but the revelation to Israel which manifests itself in the commandments. Revelation complements and confirms universay natural religion.[33]

---

[32a] Cp. Emden's 'Mitpaḥat Sefarim', Altona 1768.

[33] Cp. Birat Migdal Oz (3rd part of Emden's Prayer-book commentary), 1748, p. 46b.

*Moses Mendelssohn* took over this Emdenian theology almost word for word, developing it thirty years later in his *Jerusalem*. Here Mendelssohn identifies Judaism with the religion of reason, confining revelation to the revealed Law which applies only to Israel. Mendelssohn came to his interpretation of religion from the same premises. He could certainly have arrived at it without Emden. But it is very likely that he knew Emden's theological views, for these had already in 1748 been developed in Emden's commentary to the Prayer Book, then in wide circulation. He honoured Jacob Emden, corresponded with him and saw in him his teacher. And his agreement with him may have facilitated him in the formulation of his own religious philosophy.

After Emden's death in 1776, Salomo Dubno—the close co-worker with Mendelssohn—wrote a Hebraic elegy, showing how much the Enlightenment circle felt bound to Jacob Emden, probably as the only one among the older generation of rabbis. Extracts from Emden's autobiography were first published in this circle's Hebrew periodical "Hame'assef".

Jacob Emden was the first to introduce elements of Enlightenment thinking into Jewish theology. That is his importance in intellectual history.

Many religious-philosophical outlooks and emphases have, of course, changed in later generations. But the reservedness to or rejection of mysticism which set in with Emden's critique of the Zohar—and adopted by the Enlightenment—affected German Jewry for more than a hundred and fifty years. It impressed itself upon their intellectual and spiritual habitus from Orthodoxy to Reform. This attitude of mind is to blame for the disappearance of such an important branch of Jewish religious life and thought as mysticism from Jewish consciousness in Germany, and therefore responsible for impoverishing and narrowing the religious conception of German Jews and wide strata of world Jewry. It was pressed to a one-sided rationalism, facilitating perhaps in this way indifference and apostasy. Only with the commencement of our own century did an interest in the religious valency of mysticism begin again, but essentially from a historical or folklore point of view.

Alongside the self-willed and argumentative personality of Jacob Emden, other figures of pre-Mendelssohnian Enlightenment appear insignificant. His somewhat younger contemporaries, who like him reflected the general intellectual climate of the Enlightenment, are today almost forgotten. Two of them, however, Israel Zamosć and Aaron Gumperz, are—largely due to their biographical association with Mendelssohn—well known. A third, Mordecai Gumpel Shnaber-Levison, was perhaps more important, but lived too late for his contribution to be felt in face of the new trends of the Mendelssohnian era.

*Israel Zamosć* (circa 1700-1772) was a Polish Talmud scholar, teacher at the Yeshivah in Zamosć, and already engaged there with astronomy, mathematics and philosophy. In 1742 he came to Berlin, where a circle of young

Jewish intellectuals gathered around him, among whom were Gumperz and
Mendelssohn. The young Mendelssohn learned mathematics and logic from
him. In this circle the books of the Bible were read and discussed, at that
time something quite unusual in view of the then predominant occupation
with Talmud, rabbinic and kabbalistic literature.[34] Zamość later returned
to Poland and died in Brody.

It is noteworthy that Zamość was acquainted with the new scientific
tendencies while still living in Poland. There, besides mathematical works
he wrote a book openly criticising the tenability of many astronomical
and cosmological assertions of Talmudic literature. It was not in Frederician
Berlin that he first became an Enlightener. East European Judaism, too, had
not remained untouched by the intellectual movements of the new era. Yet
their influences did not grip wider circles, not even scholars, as was the case
in Germany. The social preconditions for the spread of these influences did
not exist in Poland, since in the Jewish mass-settlements the loosening
tendency brought about by interlacement with the non-Jewish environment
was missing. But one may recall that Joseph Del Medigo lived and worked
for several years in Lithuania; that Nathan Hanover possessed remarkable
insight into contemporary history and Polish politics. And somewhat later
Solomon Maimon was already an Enlightener when he left Lithuania.

In background and walk of life *Aaron Gumperz*, also called Emerich
(1723-1768), was very different from Zamość—later his teacher. He came
from a rich court Jew family, the Gumperz' of Cleve, who had great influence on the Brandenburg-Prussian court. The young gifted wealthy Jew of
wide literary and natural scientific education stood in close contact with
literary and academic circles in Berlin. He was introduced to the President
of the Prussian Academy, Maupertuis, and to Frederick the Great's friend,
the Marquis d'Argens, both of whom he served as a kind of honorary secretary. In Frankfurt-on-Oder in 1751 he obtained a doctorate of medicine,
though did not practise as a physician.—"Satisfied with the desired title
and living in comfortable prosperity he continued his earlier sociable contact
with the literary circles of Berlin at greater leisure and handled part of the
correspondence of the gentlemen of the academy . . . For the young promising
writers he was pleasant company in the coffee-houses and in their clubs . . .
Among Jews he was the first in a series of those lovers of art and science
for whom familiarity with their new manifestations and association with
their main representatives signified the enhancement of their existence".[35]

This made him a new phenomenon in the Jewish world. There had always
been Jewish scholars with a rabbinic training, and sometimes with great

[34] Cf. A. Shohet, p. 329 note 196.
[35] J. Eschelbacher, Die Anfänge allgemeiner Bildung unter den deutschen Juden vor Mendelssohn,
p. 175. (The beginnings of general education among the Jews before Mendelssohn.)

authority, who did not practise the profession of rabbi but pursued "learning" for its own sake. Gumperz was perhaps the first Jew who now sought this "learning" principally in the surrounding culture. His books, however—written during the last years of his short life—were composed in Hebrew. On the medieval Bible commentary of Ibn Ezra on the "Five Scrolls" he published a commentary (*Megalleh Sod*, Hamburg 1765), to which he appended a brief "Essay on the Sciences" (Ma'amar Hamada). In this he gave a concise outline of mathematics, natural science and philosophy.—Gumperz had great influence on the development of Mendelssohn, who was six years his junior.

*Mordecai Gumpel Shnaber-Levison* (1741-1797) was a younger contemporary of Moses Mendelssohn. Intellectually-historically, however, he still belonged to the pre-Mendelssohnian Enlightenment.

Shnaber-Levison[36] was an important physician and author of several medical works in English and German. His life-history is full of adventurous features. As a young man in Breslau he fell under suspicion of murder and spent some months in detention. In 1770 he went to London, where he stayed for ten years. There he became pupil of the brothers Hunter, famous physicians of the day, and later physician himself to the General Medical Asylum of the Duke of Portland. The community of the Great Synagogue in London forbade him entry in 1775—apparently due to rumours about the Breslau contingency. In 1779 he came to know the Swedish alchemist Nordenskjöld, travelling with him the following year to Stockholm. After a few weeks he received from King Gustav III of Sweden the title of Professor for a project for the founding of a dispensary modelled on the pattern of his London Institute. Shortly afterwards again in London he is said to have challenged an Earl of Schaumburg to a duel. In the autumn he came once again to Stockholm but very soon had to leave the country hastily—perhaps in connection with this duel challenge. After a brief stay in his native city of Berlin he lived as physician from 1782 until his death in Hamburg, where he had become physician to the Swedish legation. Here, in addition to his practice, he published popular medical journals and manufactured chocolate. On the one hand an academically respected—and in the sphere of social medicine a pioneering—doctor, and on the other hand an adventurous man of the world, he was out of place among his Jewish contemporaries. His restless life was not altogether foreign to the general spirit of the age.

As is well known, a proneness to mysticism and mystery accompanied

---

[36] Regarding Shnaber-Levison cp. Schoeps, ZRGG IV, 1952, the present author's essay in the Bulletin of the LBI, vol. 5. Tel-Aviv 1962, and Moshe Pelli in Jewish Quarterly Review, Vol. 64 (1973/74) p. 289-313.

the rationalistic feature of the eighteenth century. At that time the Free-mason Lodges—which many well known men of the Enlightenment joined—came into being, and the Order of the Rosicrucians; and figures like Swedenborg, Cagliostro and St. Martin appeared on the scene. Even pietism, with its religious individualism, belongs to this setting. Jewish adventurers, too, knew how to make use of these trends as bearers of sup-posedly Kabbalistic or Oriental mysteries. Well known was the great uncle of Heinrich Heine, Simon van Geldern, and the London miracle-man, "Dr." Falk.

Yet the same time-stream also produced men like Hamann, Lavater, Herder, F. H. Jacobi, who despite their close contacts with Enlightenment circles, formed a transition from Enlightenment to Romanticism. Shnaber-Levison should be seen in this general context.

This physician and man of the world was, at the same time, quite an independent religious thinker, who even here took a different path from that of contemporary Jewish Enlightenment intellectuals. Though as con-tributor to the Hebrew journal "Hameassef" he had connections with these circles too.

Shortly after emigrating to England he published in Hebrew in 1771 his "Dissertation on the Law and Sciences" (*Ma'amar Hatorah we-Haḥokhmah*) which gives a broad encyclopaedic presentation of the sciences. For the derivation of these he applies, for the first time in Hebrew literature, the entire apparatus of the sensuous teaching regarding the faculties of the soul, which the Enlightenment since Locke and his followers had developed. For him Torah and science belong together and are complementary. Learning and research are expressly commanded to the Jew.

In his main work, the "Principle of Torah" (*Yessod Hatorah*), Shnaber-Levison recasts the widely held teaching of the Enlightenment on eternal truths—as opposed to historical truths—into a theocentric theology. He distinguishes between truth and belief. Truth applies only to God, who is timeless, eternal. Everything else, including God's works and his command-ments, exists in time, being dependent on change and purpose. They are related to divine truth only through belief in God, the Creator. In this work he takes his arguments from Jewish medieval philosophy and modern philos-ophy, his examples being drawn largely from medicine and psychology. Yet he seeks to support his arguments with Talmudic passages and quota-tions from Kabbalistic literature.

In this attempt to harmonize philosophy and science with the Kabbalah he is following rabbinic theology of the pre-Mendelssohnian period. For the Mendelssohn-Enlightenment-circle, which had no understanding for a philosophy of faith, he was therefore an outsider and very soon forgotten.

Shnaber-Levison's only direct influence was on the Jewish nineteenth century outsider, *Solomon Ludwig Steinheim*, whom I shall discuss later. Shnaber-Levison's interpretation of the subordination of the commandments to time and creation influenced the later Reform movement, but one would only hesitatingly regard him as a precursor of it.[37] He seems to me a link connecting the Enlightenment with the older rabbinic theological tradition. Yet at the same time he goes beyond the Enlightenment by following certain post-Enlightenment trends.

These four figures—Jacob Emden, Zamosć, Gumperz and Shnaber-Levison —already approached their Judaism from the presuppositions of the non-Jewish intellectual and religious trends. They are no longer precursors of the Enlightenment, which itself breaks through in them—unconsciously but with far-reaching consequences in Jacob Emden, then openly in Zamosć and Aaron Gumperz and in independent and—for his generation—incomprehensible fashion, in Shnaber-Levison.

---

[37] See, however, the essay by M. Pelli mentioned above.

# CHAPTER 7

# Moses Mendelssohn

Moses Mendelssohn was the first modern Jew to participate in the general culture of his time not as a mere onlooker but actively helping to shape it as one of its leading protagonists. That was his epochal significance. He became thereby for his younger contemporaries and for posterity a symbol of the Jewish Enlightenment, of the era of assimilation and emancipation of German and West-European Jewry. For his numerous opponents, on the other hand, he symbolized apostasy and the progressive demolition of the traditional Jewish way of life.

With Mendelssohn and the circle that had gathered round him in Berlin there began in German Jewry a new approach to Judaism as well as to the surrounding world. Yet this did not only signify a turning-point for the Jews. Since Mendelssohn and due to him Judaism became a factor in general culture again. This factor has been often too readily overlooked down to our day. But its relevance can no longer be ignored or denied.

Mendelssohn's lasting impact was made possible through several particularly favourable circumstances. These had their roots in the philosophy of the Enlightenment, which formed a new image of religion and a new ideal of humanity. And it led to the rise of a new social group, whose aim was the spreading of these ideals.

The new *concept of the religion of the Enlightenment*, the religion of reason, had rendered God, freedom and immortality as metaphysical and provable truths independent from the dogmatic limitations of the historical religions. This religion of reason, however, had also changed the *concept of man*: the faculty of understanding shared by everyone has as its assumption the equality of all men.

Added to this was a new *social formation*: a quite small widely scattered stratum of people, who no longer fitted into the class and professional categories of the groups into which they were born. These were men of nobility with scholarly leanings, and members of the now more prominent middle class whose social and economic possibilities had afforded them a

71

comprehensive education and training. A number of them had gone into civil service posts. Others lived with varying fortune as writers, critics and beaux esprits. These circles were joined by scholars, especially mathematicians and natural scientists from the universities and outside them. Common to all of them was their awareness of comprising an intellectual élite and being instrumental in the spreading and realisation of the ideas of the Enlightenment. Through this common striving they felt bound to each other in various open alliances and societies. They met in coffee-houses and worked together on certain review magazines and journals. Many joined the freemason lodges. They all knew one another personally or through widely ramified correspondence. This circle of intellectuals and their relations to each other created a new social element.

This new intellectual élite, assessing man purely on his ability and co-operation in the common aims of the Enlightenment, could not allow distinction according to class or creed. It was therefore almost quite natural that individual Jews found acceptance in these circles.

Pre-conditions for such an affiliation were created on the Jewish side too. We have already seen with Jacob Emden that the Enlightenment's view of religion could be fully combined with a Judaism of the strictest observance. The concept of the equality of all men, moreover, had not only its roots in the Bible but entirely corresponded to the commended Jewish watchword of the seventeenth century—and again in the case of Jacob Emden in particular —"to live with our fellow-men".[38] This commendation had largely contributed to secular education, knowledge and languages finding access to wide Jewish circles. Yet there was still no question of an active participation of Jews in the cultural or social life of their surroundings. Even Jewish physicians with a university training behind them still remained constricted in way of life and milieu to Jewish circles. Connections with non-Jews, numerous as they were, remained functionally defined—by business intercourse, dealings with the authorities, medical treatment, scholarly contacts with or instruction to Christian scholars in Hebrew and rabbinic subjects, inter alia. Even the circles of court Jews who had largely adapted to the court surroundings remained fully within Jewish society. There existed as yet no stratum of society that was prepared to recognize Jews as of equal status or to amalgamate. Only the new élite of Enlighteners, who themselves stood as individual intellectuals outside the existing social groupings, represented for the first time a social group, an entire stratum, which accepted Jews as persons without demanding of them the denial of their religion. To this group like-minded Jews were able to assimilate. They wanted no longer simply to acquire non-Jewish knowledge that was still regarded by them as foreign; it was through such knowledge that they felt themselves to have something in common with its non-Jewish representatives. 'The

[38] 'Lih'yot me'orav im habriyot', Jacob Emden in Megillat Sefer, p. 94.

conscious membership of this group of Enlighteners' was 'changed into a social one'.[39] This had been the case with Aron Gumperz and now also with Moses Mendelssohn. Both began to live in two entirely distinct spheres of consciousness. They remained strictly believing Jews, yet at the same time —and almost apart from their Jewishness—participating in all the endeavours of the Enlightenment circle. Gumperz did this in a passive manner, while Mendelssohn became an exceptionally active participant in the cultural strivings of his time.

*For the new age that dawned with Mendelssohn it is indicative that he wrote in German.* Jacob Emden and Gumperz himself, who was so well integrated into the Enlightenment circle, had written their works in Hebrew. The later Gumpel Shnaber-Levison actually wrote his medical books in English and German. But he composed his religious writings in Hebrew as a matter of course. Mendelssohn and his followers had quite understandably a different public in view, namely educated Germans. And with this they took a decisive step for which there was no turning back. From now on Jews began to take part in general culture, becoming members and representatives of German and European intellectual history.[40]

Even when Mendelssohn and his friends wrote in Hebrew, it was no longer Hebrew of the living rabbinic tradition. This rabbinic Hebrew of the responsa, the commentaries and mysticism, was interspersed with Aramaic reminiscences from the Talmud, the Zohar and the Prayer-book, and often degenerated through ignorance and neglect of grammar and philology. Long before Mendelssohn efforts were made to restore Hebrew grammar to its place. It was lamented and felt as a shame that the study of Hebrew philology had become a domain of Christian scholars. In the first half of the eighteenth century a competent grammarian appeared in the person of *Solomon Hanau*, who as teacher of Wessely helped perhaps to influence the new style. This new style now approached the classical Hebrew of the Bible. Just as the humanists of the Renaissance had spurned medieval Latin, taking instead the classical Latin of Cicero and Horace as their model, so in the Mendelssohnian circle there grew up an artifical and affected pseudo-biblical Hebrew. And just as the Latin of the Renaissance in style, choice of words and classical

---

[39] Katz, *Die Entstehung der Assimilation der Juden in Deutschland* (Jewish Assimilation in Germany), p. 43, Reprinted in *Emancipation and Assimilation* p. 237.

[40] The Jewish Renaissance Platonic scholar *Leone Ebreo* (Judah ben Isaac Abarbanel, dec. 1535), had already written *Dialoghi di Amore* in Italian. A generation later, *Judah ben Isaac Sommo* (or de Sommi), composed Italian poems and dramas for the Italian court in Mantua, also producing them on the stage. But neither work had any Jewish-historical after-effects. The same is true of the *Historia dei Riti Ebraici* by the Venetian rabbi, *Leon de Modena* (1571-1648) publ. in 1637—a presentation of Jewish customs intended for non-Jews. It was ordered for the court of James I and thus very soon translated into English. On the other hand, there were numerous Jewish writings in the 17th and 18th century in Portuguese and Spanish written for a Jewish public—descendants of the Marranos in Amsterdam, London and Hamburg.

associations—even when dealing with theological themes—represented a break with traditional ecclesiastical language, so the new Hebrew, despite its reliance on Biblical language, inaugurated a *secularisation of language.*

The choice of German and of Hebrew itself was a declaration of war on Yiddish—the Judeo-German colloquial speech written and spoken in every stratum of Jewry. Not until the nineteenth century in eastern Europe did Yiddish become a literary language. Hitherto only popular reading material was published in Yiddish in western and eastern Europe, intended for the non-rabbinically-educated classes and for women. Yiddish adaptations of popular German books, sagas and novels appeared, as did collections of Jewish legends retold from Talmud and Midrash; popular summaries of religious precepts and translations of the Bible and the Prayer-book. Yiddish was despisedly called 'Weiber-Deutsch' ('old wives' German). Scholarly literature and correspondence had always remained in Hebrew.

This traditional despising of Yiddish influenced Mendelssohn and his friends. They viewed it as a corrupted and ugly jargon, unworthy of an educated person and making Jewish participation in their cultural surroundings the more difficult. Within a few decades Yiddish actually died out in German Jewry apart from isolated expressions and phrases. With its disappearance many emotional values were lost, mutual understanding between German and East-European Jews hindered and their estrangement increased.

The biographical outline of Mendelssohn's life is well known. He came as a youth of fourteen from Dessau to Berlin in 1743. Rabbi David Fraenkel—his teacher in Dessau—had just previously been called to Berlin and Mendelssohn followed him there to continue "learning" from him. After six difficult years of study and hunger he became private tutor and then book-keeper in the house of a Jewish silk manufacturer. During his first years in Berlin Maimonides' newly printed *Guide for the Perplexed* came into his hands which he studiously read in secret at night.

Already in the early years of his stay in Berlin he came into touch with a circle of Jewish intellectuals, who helped him acquire the rudiments of Latin and Greek, French and English. These friends also directed him to the writings of modern philosophy, which—with his slight knowledge of language—he worked through with difficulty. Locke, Wolff and Shaftesbury particularly attracted him. His uphill path of self-learning—besides philosophy he also studied mathematics and literature—made him realise the importance of easing the transition to the surrounding culture for Jewish youth through systematic general school-education. Perhaps the roots of his later popular educational endeavours are to be found here.

Among his friends were Israel Zamosć, Dr Kisch, a physician from Prague who taught him Latin, and especially Aaron Gumperz. The latter introduced him to modern philosophy and arranged tuition for him in classics. Of greatest consequence was his introducing him to *Lessing*, through whom he came to know the publisher and writer *Nicolai*. His acquaintance with Lessing quickly developed from a partnership at chess into a lifelong friendship.

Mendelssohn must have impressed these non-Jewish acquaintances like a strange exotic prodigy and caused them to review their opinion of Jews. The small hunchbacked Jewish youth, who outwardly and in his traditional Jewish life style fitted the picture of a Jew as one met him in the streets and markets of Berlin, fascinated them not only by his penetrating mind but especially by his intellectual and human integrity, his understanding and judgement in things of philosophic and literary taste. His contemporaries were soon referring to him as the Jewish Socrates and the Jewish Plato. Already in a letter of 1754 Lessing called him the future Spinoza, who would, however, avoid his errors. It was Mendelssohn—according to widespread opinion—whom he was later to memorialize in his *Nathan der Weise* (Nathan the Wise). Next to Lambert, *Kant* rated him the highest among all his contemporary philosophers. He presented him with a copy of his *Kritik der Reinen Vernunft* (Critique of Pure Reason). When Mendelssohn visited Königsberg on business in 1777 he came to know Kant personally. An eye-witness describes how one day an elderly deformed Jew appeared at a course of Kant's lectures to the amazement of his students, seeking a place and silently accepting their teasing. When at the close of the lecture this stranger was recognized by Kant with joyful surprise and great respect, the students formed a guard of honor for both scholars on their way out.

It was Lessing who introduced Mendelssohn to the public by publishing without his knowledge, albeit anonymously, a manuscript he had given him to read. Mendelssohn became one of the principal co-workers of the *Bibliothek der schönen Wissenschaften* (Library of belles lettres) and its later continuation, *Briefe, die neueste Literatur betreffend* (Letters concerning the newest Literature), both published by Nicolai. In these periodicals he wrote several essays on aesthetics, a philosophical discipline among whose co-founders he is regarded. In 1763 Mendelssohn entered an essay competition set by the Berlin Academy and with his contribution *Über die Evidenz der Metaphysischen Wissenschaften* (On the evidence of the metaphysical sciences) took first prize over Immanuel Kant.

The best-known of his writings are the *Phaedon*, a dialogue on the immortality of the soul—based on Plato's Phaedo—and *Morgenstunden* (Morning Hours) in which he deals with philosophical proofs of God after the manner of the Leibniz/Wolffian philosophy.

As already stressed at the beginning of this chapter, Mendelssohn's uniqueness lay from the start in addressing himself to the general public through his literary and philosophical activity. He had begun to write in German as a matter of course. True, Spinoza had also written—in Latin—for the world of learning. However, for him this had happened as a conscious withdrawal from his Jewish ties which his pantheistic religiosity had severed. With Mendelssohn this was not the case. Perhaps it was the mere accident of

Lessing's having published his young Jewish friend's essay that Mendelssohn continued to write German and contribute to literary and philosophical themes. Perhaps at first he was not aware of the new and revolutionary in what he was doing. Yet on no account did his close association with Judaism and Jewish people slacken. Already in his younger years—probably in 1758—he had tried to found a Hebrew periodical. All his life he kept in close touch with the Jewish community in Berlin which honoured him as one of its most respected members and exempted him from payment of community tax when he received the Academy prize. He also stood in close contact with important rabbis and scholars of the day. Alongside extensive correspondence with non-Jewish scholars he kept up a wide Hebrew correspondence. In self-understanding and attitude to life he was an orthodox Jew. His labours outside Jewish circles were seen—perhaps this is also an innovation—not as disloyalty but as an honour for the whole of Judaism.

Yet in all this Mendelssohn did not differ at first—or for many years—from other enlightened ortho-practising Jews of the type of Aaron Gumperz or Gumpel Shnaber-Levison. With all of them their Jewishness was strictly separated from their membership of non-Jewish intellectual and scholarly circles. This dichotomy of the spheres of life was only obscured in that they comprised two sides of one and the same personality. In Mendelssohn's personality in particular both spheres found a happy sympathetic and almost natural harmony.

It was not till quite late in the year 1769, that Mendelssohn was brought into a situation where, unexpectedly and involuntarily, he had to become defender and representative of Judaism.

One of his correspondents was the Swiss theologian and writer *Johann Caspar Lavater*, who had once visited him in Berlin. In 1769 Lavater had translated a treatise by the Genevan scholar Bonnet: *La Palingénésie philosophique ou Idées sur l'état passé et sur l'état futur des êtres vivants*, with the German title *Untersuchungen der Beweise des Christentum* (Investigations of the Proofs of Christianity) and published it with an open letter to Mendelssohn. In his dedicatory preface he urged Mendelssohn "to refute the treatise, or if he found the proofs correct to do what prudence, love of truth and honesty bade him to, what a Socrates would have done, had he read this treatise and found it irrefutable".[41] Mendelssohn was thus challenged to defend his faith before the Christian world.

Mendelssohn replied to Lavater in public too. He pointed out that he had always previously avoided public discussions on questions of faith; that this was due in part to the suppressed legal and social position of Jews, who

---

[41] Moses Mendelssohn, *Schriften zur Philosophie, Ästhetik and Apologetik* (Writings on Philosophy, Aesthetics and Apologetics), ed. Moritz Brasch, Leipzig, 1881, p. XXXXVI. I quote this edition which is today the most easily accessible (Reprint 1968).

in most countries were merely tolerated and not even allowed to enter others, such as Lavater's home canton of Zürich; that every disputation or argument with the prevailing religion could entail serious consequences for them. (Mendelssohn himself had applied for permission from the Berlin consistory to answer Lavater, and received it immediately.) Judaism, moreover, did not engage in mission but was rather the "inheritance of the house of Jacob", being essentially confined to Jews by birth. Furthermore, the inducement to missionary activity did not arise, since according to the Jewish view all righteous people have a share in blessedness. From his earliest youth he had examined the teachings of his religion. Only in this regard did he concern himself with philosophy and science. And the result of his investigation had convinced him of the truth of the religion of his fathers. "If I were convinced in my heart of the truth of another, it would only be the most abject baseness of inner conviction, to withhold one's allegiance to the truth".[42] As far as Bonnet's proofs were concerned, every religion could be defended by them and not just Christianity.

Lavater wrote once again, and there was a subsequent reply from Mendelssohn. Bonnet also joined in the dispute. There ensued an exchange of letters with the Crown Prince of Brunswick, only printed later, and a published quarrel in which the Goettingen physicist and philosopher *Lichtenberg* alone intervened on Mendelssohn's behalf. In his *Timorus*, Lichtenberg ridiculed Lavater and the methods of mission to Jews. Mendelssohn's other non-Jewish friends, however, expressed themselves only in private letters, remaining silent in public on Lavater's challenge. It appeared they were separating man and Jew in Mendelssohn.

This attitude is explainable only by the nature of the Enlightenment in Germany which from the beginning was shaped by religious problems. Whereas the French branch of the Enlightenment soon took up the struggle against the Catholic Church—something often leading to criticism of Christianity and to atheistic materialism—the English branch and in its train the German Enlightenment, were much more theological. It sought to rationalize matters of Christian belief and thereby generalize them. Both English deism and the Leibniz-Wolffian religion of reason were rationalistic new, or reductive, interpretations of the doctrines of Christianity into theological ethics. In this way it was always quite naturally assumed by them that Christianity represented the religion of reason. Even Kant and Hegel shared this view. Herein lay the psychological reason why Lavater could never understand that an enlightened man and adherent of the religion of reason like Mendelssohn was not really a Christian at heart whom one had only to encourage openly to acknowledge this.

This exclusive claim of Christianity to be the basis of the religion of reason probably accounted for the silence of Mendelssohn's non-Jewish

[42] Letter to Lavater of 12.12.1769.

friends. All of them, including Lessing, consciously or unconsciously could not free themselves from the prevailing opinion. Lessing at that time was already occupied with the publication of the Reimarus Fragments, and perhaps on that account did not wish prematurely to enter the theological thunderstorm zone. But he too, despite the apparent relativism of the ring parable in *Nathan*, remained altogether fettered to the view of the exclusive primacy of Christianity. Even in his *Erziehung des Menschengeschlechts* (Education of the Human Race) in which the concept of the development of history was perhaps first applied to the historical religions—as didactic steps towards the religion of reason—the objective is only a new enlightened 'gospel'. That is for Lessing no accidental choice of language.

It was from this consensus of his contemporaries that Mendelssohn the Jew departed. He came from without and not from the latent basic Christian disposition of the Enlighteners. Thus he was—perhaps the only one among them—in a position of treating really seriously both the rational and emotional claims of the Enlightenment. He had not only taken over the new conception of man according to the Enlightenment, but had himself helped to shape it. And he brought to the religion of reason a universal human character. Even two years earlier, when he wrote the *Phaedon*, the supraconfessional character of the religion of reason seemed to Mendelssohn to be established. Now Lavater's challenge taught him that for his contemporaries the religion of reason was merely an expression or consequence of Christianity.

In view of this attitude he now seriously had to re-examine the relation of Judaism to, and the extent of its agreement with, this religion of reason. From his Jewish presuppositions this examination must have been easier for Mendelssohn than for the Christian theologians of the Enlightenment. The latter must often have led them to forced reinterpretations in order to make out of Christianity and its myth of redemption a rational optimistic doctrine of reason and morals. Mendelssohn, on the other hand, needed no such reinterpretations when he desired to find in his ancestral faith a religion of reason. We shall see in our outline of Mendelssohn's religious philosophy how he did this. It was not first in his *Jerusalem*, however, but already earlier in his replies to Lavater and in the correspondence with the Crown Prince of Brunswick and Bonnet that he elevated the generally despised, even if unknown, *Judaism to the status of partner in the philosophical and theological discussion*. This had been least expected from Mendelssohn, and the outcome was mistrustful astonishment and incomprehension. Mendelssohn had overstepped the limit Christians were willing to go in their understanding of Judaism.

The controversy with Lavater marked a turning-point in Mendelssohn's life. It had above all seriously impaired his health. The period of his intellectual creativity was, as he complained, terminated, at least regarding his receptiveness to new philosophical ideas. For a long time he was as though maimed, incapable of reading or thinking things through—a condition that tormented him terribly and which recurred intermittently until his death.[43] From now on he devoted whatever remaining strength he had to his Jewish brethren. Only towards the end of his life was he once more drawn into controversy when, after Lessing's death *Friedrich Heinrich Jacobi* spoke of his secret Spinozism, Mendelssohn felt obliged to defend his dead friend. It was in connection with this dispute that he compiled in 1785 his philosophical views in *Morgenstunden* (Morning Hours).

In his new overriding Jewish activity, however, the accent had shifted. Before 1770 his Jewish and his philosophical literary activity lay, as it were, on two distinct levels. This is not to say he had ever previously shirked specific Jewish tasks. He had published Hebrew commentary works and German translations of occasional synagogue sermons and prayers. But now he and his friends—almost inevitably—applied the values of the surrounding culture to the Jews, their customs and way of life, and even to the Jewish religion. The aims they set for their educational strivings for Jews were the values of their environment, the ideal of the well-mannered reasonable man of the Enlightenment. Compared with these, traditional Jewish values appeared to them more and more inferior. When Mendelssohn himself speaks of his translation of the Pentateuch as the "first step towards culture", this seems to us absurd, coming from one so conversant with Jewish culture, but it illustrates the new attitude. The later continuing process of assimilation and self-surrender had begun in this generation. Mendelssohn felt himself so much a Jew and almost representative of Judaism in and against the surrounding world, that for him the tension between Judaism and the culture of the environment did not seem to exist. In everything we hear about and read by him the happy harmony of his personality comes continually to the fore. But he was the first—perhaps unconsciously and unintentionally— to introduce the new system of values which led to a depreciation of the content of Judaism. On the other hand, he is perhaps an example to us all in that he showed how one can hold one's own as a conscious Jew in the modern world. But already amongst his followers in the next generation the equipoise and synthesis of both elements disappeared, and the Jewish factor faded more and more.

Mendelssohn's labours in education for Jews culminated in his *translation of the Pentateuch* into German. It appeared in 1780, printed at first in Hebrew characters. He published it together with an appendaged Hebrew commentary compiled mainly by several co-workers. With this translation of the Pentateuch Mendelssohn became the teacher of the German language for the Jews, not only for those of his own country but for many in Eastern Europe too. Of course, some German rabbis and many in Eastern Europe as well saw in this translation a dangerous innovation, because it was written

---

[43] Regarding Mendelssohn's illness, however, compare A. Altmann, Mendelssohn, p. 268-271.

in literary German and not as in earlier translations in Yiddish, almost considered a sacred language in those days.[44]

Of the books of the Bible translated by Mendelssohn himself that of the Psalms became especially famous. It was published from the beginning in both Hebrew and German characters.

This translation of Pentateuch and Psalms into German would, Mendelssohn hoped, contribute to breaking down the wall of partition between Jews and their Christian neighbours and eliminating anti-Jewish prejudice. For Mendelssohn believed prejudice had its chief cause in the other colloquial language of the Jews, the normally spoken Yiddish (Judeo-German). Whereas if Jews were to become accustomed to pure German as their everyday speech, psychological opposition to them would disappear and with it, in time, legal restrictions too. As a result of his efforts there was founded in Berlin a *Jüdische Freischule*, the first Jewish Free School in Germany where, besides traditional Jewish subjects, German in particular was taught, as well as the fundamentals of a general secular education. Similar free schools soon grew up in many Jewish communities in Germany. Their purpose was to give poor children a general education, which those of well-to-do parents were already usually receiving from private tutors.

Mendelssohn's guiding principle was, as he once said, to use either German or Hebrew, but not a mixed language. As already mentioned, he called for a purification of Hebrew style and grammar. Accordingly he and some of his closest colleagues and disciples are regarded as precursors of modern secularized Hebrew. The later development of this renewed Hebrew, however, discarded the close literal imitation of biblical Hebrew cultivated by the Mendelssohn circle. Instead, the clear simple language of the Mishnah and much of the rabbinic Hebrew was taken as its guideline.

Mendelssohn also strove for improvements in the legal position of Jews. Since his voice was listened to in the Christian world, people turned to him when Jewish communities were threatened by danger, as e.g. in Switzerland, Dresden and Alsace. Under his influence the Prussian ministerial councillor, *Dohm*, wrote a treatise *Ueber die buergerliche Verbesserung der Juden* (On the Civil Improvement of the Jews) in 1781. This book, of which a second part appeared two years later, awakened great general interest, making wide sections of the public more conscious of the question of Jewish emancipation. The Edicts of Tolerance of Joseph II were perhaps the first constitutionally legal response to the Dohmian theses.

In the Middle Ages the various religions had determined their respective cultures. Judaism had likewise formed its own cultural complex, embracing in its religious structure the entire intellectual-spiritual life of the Jews.

---

[44] A ban on this translation has, by the way—contrary to widespread opinion—never been declared.

Modern European civilisation having freed itself from these religious ties, destroyed the earlier unity between culture and religion. Mendelssohn was perhaps—disregarding Spinoza—the first Jew to accept their modern separation. He thought he was acting perfectly within the framework of tradition and on its behalf. But in reality he was a child of his time, thinking in its thought-forms. For him—and even more for succeeding generations—the Jewish sphere of life was essentially confined to religious life in the stricter sense. All other intellectual areas, and that included philosophy, had withdrawn from the religious framework. Not just for Mendelssohn but also for his Jewish and non-Jewish contemporaries and followers religious philosophy could now be dealt with quite generally and without regard to a particular religion. It was only in the year of his death in 1786 that Mendelssohn summarized his general philosophy—and with it his philosophy of religion —in *Morgenstunden oder Untersuchungen über das Dasein Gottes* (Morning Hours or Investigations on the Existence of God). Kant regarded this book as the significant conclusion of a philosophical position he thought he had overcome in his own philosophy. Yet through the work *Jerusalem oder Ueber religioese Macht und Judentum* (Jerusalem or on Religious Power and Judaism), which appeared in 1783, Mendelssohn became the first modern Jewish philosopher of religion.

The distinction between general religious doctrine and the special quality of Judaism we first noticed in Jacob Emden. Similarly, Mendelssohn distinguished in Judaism two components, its doctrinal part, identical with the natural religion of reason and therefore lacking a special Jewish content, and the religious Law, revealed at Mt. Sinai, which adds to the general doctrine the Jewish quality.

The first component Mendelssohn deduces from the premises of his own metaphysical outlook. The religion of reason is accessible and common to all men, to every sensible thinking person. It claims general recognition and validity. It teaches nothing which does not agree with the general religion of reason—a pointed allusion to Christian dogmatics.

This fundamental approach of Mendelssohn exercised a fascinating influence on his Jewish followers, reaching far into our own day. It heightened the self-awareness of many generations of Jews. On the other hand it brought about the dilution and gradual dissolution of the Jewish 'substance'. It led to the blurring of a specific Jewish quality in matters of religion, since this quality appeared more and more superfluous.

Mendelssohn himself, however, did not remain static in his mere identification of Judaism with the religion of reason. He was far too much a Jew, intimately rooted in Jewish tradition and Jewish intellectual life. He sought to incorporate this tradition, especially religious law, into his presentation of Judaism, achieving this by a new interpretation and limitation of the concept of revelation. Mendelssohn wrote "I do not believe that human reason is incapable of perceiving those eternal truths which are indispensable to human happiness and that God had therefore to reveal these truths in a supernatural manner".[45] And "miracles and extraordinary signs are, according to Judaism, no proof for or against the truths of reason".[46] Revelation is, therefore, not necessary to uphold the religion of reason, since its content—the concepts of God, his providence, goodness and the immortality of the soul—are accessible to human reason, to everyone. Mendelssohn can therefore write: "Among all the precepts and ordinances of the Mosaic Law there is no single injunction saying, 'Thou shalt believe or not believe.' Rather they all say 'Thou shalt do or not do.' Belief is not commanded, for it accepts no orders other than those coming by way of conviction. All the commandments of the divine Law are directed to the will, to the energy of man. . . ." And "where the eternal truths of religion are concerned it is not spoken of as believing but as discerning and knowing. That you may know that the Eternal is the true God and apart from him there is no other". "Know, therefore, and take to heart that the Lord alone is God in heaven above and on earth below; there is none else".[47]

Revelation for Mendelssohn, therefore, is confined to that which a Jew is assigned to do. For him, Judaism is not revealed doctrine but *revealed Law*, since Jewish doctrine, as he stressed, doesn't require revelation, although its concepts are dispersed in the Torah and Holy Scripture. The Law—the commandments—on the other hand, had its source in revelation. It is not demonstrable by reason, but it guides the life and the actions of the Jew. The Law is binding and unalterable. Jews could not shirk its fulfillment, unless God himself were to annul it through a similar solemn revelation like that at Mount Sinai.

It has been thought paradoxical that Mendelssohn, "the confirmed rationalist, when he wanted to state his case by means of philosophy, for religion, for Judaism, retained only the non-rational elements".[48] I do not think this is quite correct. For even these non-rationalist elements, viz. the revealed Law, are drawn again by Mendelssohn into the primacy of reason. He stresses just this: "All the Biblical laws refer to, or are based upon, eternal truths of reason or else, reminding us of them, they induce us to reflect on them, so that our rabbis rightly say: 'The laws and doctrines act reciprocally, as do body and soul' ".[49]

This quotation shows that Mendelssohn tried to achieve a balance or interrelatedness between these two components in his presentation of

---

[45] *Jerusalem*, Brasch, vol. 2, p. 423.

[46] *Jerusalem*, p. 429.

[47] *Jerusalem*, p. 430, Deut. 4, VV 35 & 39.

[48] Fritz Bamberger, *Mendelssohn's Begriffe vom Judentum*, (Mendelssohn's Conceptions of Judaism), *Korrespondenzblatt d.Akademie d.Wissenschaft d.Jundentums*, 1929, p. 17. (Reprint in K. Wilhelm, Wissenschaft des Judentums, pp. 521-536.)

[49] *Jerusalem*, p. 430.

Judaism. Yet, it was here, that the main tenet of Enlightenment philosophy impeded him, from which he could not free himself and which resulted in an over-emphasizing of reason at the expense of revelation. Mendelssohn's younger friends and disciples—as we shall see in Chapter 10—soon abandoned this uneasy balance. They sundered the doctrines and commandments which he had sought to fuse, retaining Judaism's share in the religion of reason and undervaluing the essential practical Jewish element—partly for emancipatory political reasons. Despite subsequent correctives, gained from historical perspective and from the efforts of some philosophers of religion, this abandonment (of Mendelssohn's position) had ruinous consequences, reaching into our own day. These consequences—such as apostasy, indifference and decline in Jewish education and lifestyle—indirectly go back to Mendelssohn's divisioning of Judaism into two elements.

Mendelssohn, however, persisted in his attempt to fuse both elements. In their union lay for him the specific task of Jewry to be a living witness to the religion of reason by steadfast and continued adherence to the revealed Law. The Jews are for him a kind of alliance of genuine theists, who are and must remain bound together through this Law "so long as polytheism, anthropomorphism and religious usurpation dominate the globe".[50] In 'Jerusalem' he says that the Jews were chosen by Providence "to be a priestly nation, i.e. a nation which through its constitution and institutions, through its laws and actions and throughout the vicissitudes of destiny was always to point to wholesome, unadultered notions of God and his attributes, continually teaching, preaching and seeking to maintain these notions among the nations through its mere existence".[51]

This last passage of Mendelssohn's also had a long-lasting effect on later times. For it created the concept, dominating the entire nineteenth century, of the *mission of Judaism*—not a mission which promotes Judaism, but which Judaism itself presents through its existence in the world. This concept was developed particularly in Reform Judaism, where it was to take the place of adherence to the Law, and provide a substitute for traditional national roots. (Even *Moses Hess*—the early theorist of Zionism—like the reformers held firmly to the idea of mission, transforming it into a demand for exemplificary social conduct.)

In his dispute with Friedrich Heinrich Jacobi over Lessing's attitude to Spinoza, Mendelssohn himself had had to take issue with intellectual trends foreign to the philosophy of the Enlightenment and to his own thought. He surmised Kant's epoch-making significance—coining the expression "the all-crushing Kant"—but to his regret he was now physically incapable of 'digesting' him.

---

[50] Letter to Herz Homberg dated Sept. 22, 1783.
[51] *Jerusalem*, p. 450.

Apart from Jewish tradition and the Enlightenment, new influences were already affecting the generation of his younger friends and disciples. Strivings towards civil emancipation and assimilation were gaining momentum. The influence of Kantian philosophy—so decisive for Jewish intellectual life in Germany—was coming to the fore. Soon the direct natural relation to Judaism was frequently replaced by a historical, historicized relation. To many Jewish intellectuals Judaism became a mere subject for specialists. It ceased to be a decisive factor in their own life. All these new influences in their positive and negative aspects merged to form the image of modern Judaism.

Before we turn to the new epoch that began with Mendelssohn's followers, I should like first to describe the legal and social position which preceded the era of emancipation. Also the great movement of Ḥasidism in Eastern Europe will at least have to be sketched, since this movement made—outside the development in German Jewry—its own vital contribution to the total picture of modern Judaism.

# The Social and Legal Position of the Jews in Germany in the Eighteenth Century

The modern concept of the state, as it first found expression in the seventeenth and eighteenth centuries in the form of sovereign absolutism, shared a common origin with the Enlightenment. Both were elements in that breaking away with the Renaissance from the hierarchically organized medieval idea of society. The one historical line of thought led from Macchiavelli via Hobbes and Spinoza, later to Hegel and to a modern myth of the state, to the concept of the all powerful state which pushes aside all other principles of order. Even the church in the era of the counter-reformation in both camps, Catholic and Protestant, applied the same concepts to the ecclesiastical sphere and organisation: papal centralism with its executive organ —the new Jesuit Order—and similarly the Anglican and Lutheran Landeskirchen (national churches) with their sovereigns as heads. The other historical line of thought, that of the Enlightenment, on the other hand, influenced by the revolutionary Free Church movements in Germany, Holland and England as well as by the democratic individualism of Locke and Rousseau, was guided by the idea of natural right.

The binding link between these two contrasting lines was often represented by the higher civil service, in whose personalities both tendencies frequently overlapped. They had, in part, close personal contact with Enlightenment circles, bringing natural right points of view into state legislation, as for example the compilers of the general Prussian common law did at the end of the eighteenth century.

Apart from such overlappings, however, the absolutist state was far removed from the humanitarian and social ideal of the Enlightenment. The courtly society of rococo loved of course to dally in an imaginary and sentimental arcadia of the fashionable pastoral poetry. But apart from this enthusiasm for nature and the customs of simple folk, the boundaries of station and rank were strictly observed. Also in the society of the eighteenth century the class-like structure, which defined one's place and standing according to origin and occupation, remained unchanged. The absolute state had in fact evolved in its struggle against the class organisation of society as it came down from the Middle Ages. But this struggle was only directed against political rights and privileges, which the various class groups in the state claimed. In relation to the ruler there were only to be subjects. His sovereign will alone was to decide what was right. With regard to him the conventional rights and prerogatives of the nobility, cities, guilds and corporations were to be invalidated. This levelling was thought of and carried out merely as a political levelling, namely, in relation to subject and ruler. But it did not affect the validity of the traditional class structure itself. Through his army and officials, dependent on him alone and no longer on local authorities, and likewise through the new mercantile economic policy, the ruler tried to enforce his sole authority. By means of these three factors he was able to break the resistance of the estate representatives, achieve a uniform administration and undermine economically impeding forms of production and organisation. To this end he now made use of the Jews, who stood outside the guild-controlled economic structure.

On the other hand, however, the state consciously made use of the existing class structure for its own purposes. The nobility were diverted to a military career through which—as well as through the various offices at court—they were directly bound to the person of the ruler. The educated upper middle-class was largely absorbed into the civil service. In the hierarchy of public administration, consisting of numerous titles and ranks, this upper middle-class was able to attain influence and social prestige. The ordinary middle-class of artisans and urban traders was compensated for the loss of former monopoly positions by giving them the honour of being purveyors to the court and leaving in their hands certain rights of quality and market control. The state seemed thoroughly interested in the multiplicity of class differences —following the principle of "divide et impera".

Into this class-like state controlled structure Jews, too, were incorporated. They were not looked upon as a special class, but denoted in the seventeenth and eighteenth centuries as a "nation" and described themselves as such. The concept "nation" at that time had not yet the emotional and political overtones which the word was subsequently to acquire from the Romantic era onwards. It had still nothing to do with the later popular concept. One spoke e.g. in Hamburg of Jews of the 'Portuguese' or of the 'hochdeutsche' nation. "The eighteenth century used the term 'nation' as a category for ethnographic units with precise characteristics acquired from experience".[52] These characteristics were of a linguistic and religious nature, depicting a

---

[52] *Die Entstehung der Judenassimilation in Deutschland und deren Ideologie* (Diss.) Frankfurt 1935, p. 14. Reprinted in Katz: Emancipation and Assimilation. Studies in Modern Jewish History, Farnborough, 1972, p. 208.

different kind of life-style based on religious law. Secondary features were the different kinds of dress, in particular the style of beard.

Under this special category the legal position of Jews was regulated, based as in the Middle Ages on privileges bestowed by the territorial ruler. Jews were thereby in principle not so different from other groups and social strata, since rights and privileges still formed the basis of the social structure. There was not one right applicable to all. Difference consisted rather in the form and content of these privileges. The privileges of Jews constituted a legal relationship of protection. Their recipients became Danish, Anhaltian, Prussian etc. 'protected subjects' (Schutzverwandte), but they did not become direct subjects like other citizens. In their civic duties the *Schutzverwandte* did have something in common with other subjects and were at times even placed in the same category. But as it applied to Jews, the expression 'privileges' was a euphemism. It did not mean, in the modern sense, a prerogative or special right. A privilege should, of course, govern the rights and legal position of any given group. But in contrast to the privileges which Gentile professional groups and classes enjoyed–privileges procuring them real legal patronages and preferences–Jewish privileges were a juridically formulated restriction of rights. They gave a minimum –protection against brute force, and a limited right of residence–but demanded from Jews a maximum with regard to payments, and frequently involved the most humiliating interference in their private and communal life by curtailing their professional and trading activities. The protective relation, moreover, was often temporarily limited. With every change on the throne, privileges had to be newly confirmed–this usually going hand in hand with a deterioration in the prior state of affairs–and repurchased at a higher price.

The Jews' protection in the territorial states was a derivative of royal protection in the Middle Ages. In the Peace of Westphalia of 1648, this *Judenregal* had been officially bestowed on all the estates of the Empire. (Only in relation to the free cities did the imperial influence in this sphere remain noticeably significant. This influence still prevailed e.g. in 1710 in Hamburg in the Jewish regulation imposed by an imperial commission.) However, the concept of *Kammerknechtschaft*, (court-bondage), long associated with the royal connection, seemed gradually to recede, except in the theological anti-Jewish argument. Already since the sixteenth century was the old Roman legal conception (of the pre-Christian imperial era) of civic rights coming to the fore again, also in relation to Jews.[53] Together with ideas similar in tendency to that of natural right they led–at least in the administration of the protective relationship through the civil service and through many of the rulers themselves–to a liberalization that would

---

[53] Selma Stern, *Josel von Rosheim* p. 197.

previously have been unthinkable. Thus the actual enforcement of oppressive restrictions was in many cases milder and more elastic than the wording of the privileges would have lead one to expect. The communities and individual Jews, on the other hand, became dangerously dependent upon the insight, goodwill and corruptibility of public officials.

The new privileges and Jewish regulations (Judenreglements) in the various countries of the Empire had many features in common. They were frequently given—especially at the beginning—to Jews specified by name. And where they did not apply to individuals but to entire communities or to territorial Jewries (Landjudenschaften), the number of those taken under protection was mostly restricted to the so-called 'escorted' Jews. Where no numerical restrictions were specified, as was the case in Altona, an applicant had to produce a certificate of good conduct from the Jewish community in question together with its consent for his acceptance. Protection entailed payments of protection money from the individuals temselves or a lump sum from the community, collected from its members. The amount of real protection money, though in many cases not so high, was frequently increased by special taxes under the most varied nomenclature —often developing from occasional payments into permanent taxations that became oppressively burdensome on the communities.[54]

Matters of religious practice and community autonomy, of jurisdiction and freedom of trade, were settled quite diversely. The modern state meddled in the inner affairs of its subjects at all levels of society more powerfully than had been customary or possible in the Middle Ages. Control of trade and traffic was frequently followed through to the smallest detail. State interference and control took on special forms with regard to Jews who were numerically few and dependent for their entire livelihood on the state.

Whereas earlier the free practice of religion had probably always been granted to Jews, it was now in many cases severely limited. There were prohibitions against holding public religious services and having synagogues, against sounding the Shofar-horn at the festival of New Year and singing during divine service, inter alia. In some areas Jews were only allowed to conduct their services in private houses, with a limited number of participants as though in secret. Such prohibitions existed, for example, in Vienna (till 1811) and Hamburg. In neighbouring Danish Altona, on the other hand, Jews enjoyed religious freedom and had open synagogues, graveyards and Talmud schools. And in Hamburg the above prohibitions in this harsh form existed only on paper. They were meant to calm the orthodox-Lutheran 'clerical ministry' and the city's representatives, while the council and admin-

---

[54] In Prussia Jewish parents whose son or daughter married were obliged to purchase rejected porcelain from the Berlin china manufactory which they could only resell abroad at great loss.—In Altona there was the *don gratuit*, which developed from an occasional freely given queen's dowry gift into a permanent tax.

istration silently tolerated the by-passing of prohibitions, in order to check an economically undesirable drift of Jews into the more liberal Danish region.

Great differences also existed in the scope Jews were given for the regulating of their own community affairs. The jurisdiction of the rabbinical courts was for the most part limited to ritual and ceremonial matters, from which cases of marriage, divorce and inheritance were sometimes excluded. In fact the most important means of community discipline at that time, the various kinds of exclusion and excommunication, were often made dependent on state approval. Only in few territories were the rabbinical courts—which functioned according to Talmudic law and procedure—given jurisdiction in civil matters, at least at a first juridical level. Again it was the Danish policy towards Jews that was the most liberal. The jurisdiction of the Altona rabbinate extended over most of Schleswig-Holstein. The majority and wealthiest of the Jews living in Hamburg belonged to the Jewish community of Altona, and were therefore Danish protected Jews. Consequently the jurisdiction of the Altona rabbinate over Jews in Hamburg was for Denmark a major political issue in its quarrel with Hamburg, whose status as an imperial free city the Danes had never really recognized.[55] This jurisdiction was jealously guarded till well into the nineteenth century, until the dissolution of the Three Communities' Federation in 1811, and the Hamburg Senate had to reconcile itself to it.—In the former Danish provinces, the jurisdiction of the Altona rabbinate in matters of civil law came to an end only in 1863, with the emancipation of the Jews of Schleswig-Holstein.

In Prussia civil law-suits of Jews were likewise entrusted to rabbinical courts. If they came before the state court in cases of large sums of money or appeals, their cases were tried on the basis of Jewish law. In order to give Gentile judges a survey of this, the chief rabbi, *Hirschel Levin*, was commissioned to draw up a digest of Jewish law. For its preparation he engaged the help of Moses Mendelssohn. The collection appeared as *Ritualgesetze der Juden* (Ritual Laws of the Jews) in 1778. A similar collection including not only Jewish but also Prussian law concerning Jews was published by the Prussian official, Terlinden, in 1804.

Favourable privileges existed in those regions where rulers, for reasons of their trading policy or with a view to populating newly-founded towns, were interested in attracting Jews. That was for example the case in Mannheim and Karlsruhe, in Brandenburg under the Great Elector and Frederick I, in Glueckstadt for Portuguese Jews and in Altona.

As in Glueckstadt and Altona—established as competitive ports vis-a-vis Hamburg—so the Jews in Fuerth owed their special position to the political dispute between two territorial rulers. Fuerth was claimed both by the

---

Margrave of Ansbach and by the Bishop of Bamberg. Already at the beginning of the sixteenth century the rulers of Ansbach attracted Jews to Fuerth, descendents of those expelled from the imperial city of Nueremberg in 1499. They were followed by Jews who lived under the protection of Bamberg and who soon gained the numerical superiority. Like the rest of the inhabitants of Fuerth, Jews also benefitted from this quarrel of the two rulers, each of whom strove to outdo the other by offering better privileges. Fuerth developed into one of the most important Jewish communities in Germany. It was probably the only place where Jews enjoyed corporate urban civic rights, being able since 1719 to delegate two representatives to the municipal council. Fuerth, whose hinterland comprised the many small communities in the various Franconian territories of present-day Bavaria, became the principal community of southern Germany. It also became the seat of one of the most respected rabbinates in Germany. Here, an important Talmud academy was founded and a large Hebrew printing house.

Of the new developments in public, economic, political and intellectual life, the old imperial cities were least affected. Here medieval clannishness continued to hold sway. Most of these cities had banished their Jews in the fifteenth and sixteenth centuries. Where, due to imperial intervention, they were allowed to remain, as in Frankfurt and Worms, they stood under the old *Staettigkeit* (municipal regulations). In Frankfurt there still existed into the nineteenth century the dreadful ghetto of the Jewish alley, outside which no Jew was allowed to reside. In the new communities, on the other hand, Jews lived amidst the Christian population, where at the most a few streets were forbidden to them. (In practice, however, they congregated mostly near the synagogue.) The Frankfurt Staettigkeit regulated the commercial activity of Jews in detail, so as to preclude all conceivable competition with Gentile craftsmen and businessmen. If, in spite of this, Frankfurt in the eighteenth century still remained the most famous and—probably next to the Three Communities of Altona-Hamburg-Wandsbek on the Elbe —largest Jewish community, the reason for this lay in the commercial importance of the city. Here was the financial centre of the realm. The medieval exclusion of the Frankfurt Jews from every other commercial activity had driven them—as in centuries past—directly into the money and finance business. The imperial urban Frankfurt Jews especially, living since 1617 again under direct protection of the emperor, served the imperial court and its finances in Vienna.

In contrast to the broadminded mercantile economic policy in the seventeenth century, the eighteenth century saw more and more the new physiocratic tendencies. Public and administrative uniformity—typical of the new idea of the state—had meanwhile gained acceptance. Now the centralist state was also to be made economically autarchic. From promoting interterritorial trade the states now switched over to furthering agriculture and industry, called in those days 'manufactures'. All this affected the new policy with regard to Jews, as the development in Brandenburg-Prussia showed most clearly.

If earlier Jews under the Great Elector still enjoyed a wide measure of free trade, so now trading was no longer at all favourably looked upon. Restrictions on the opening of Jewish stores were again introduced. Trans-territorial trading by Jews was considerably curtailed. On the other hand, Jews who opened factories and manufactures, received state support. Frederick William I, with his deep religious antipathy to Jews, took on the task of reducing their number as much as possible. In the year 1730 he introduced a new Jewish law, the *General Reglement*, which set Prussian Jewry both organisationally and legally on a new basis. In place of the method, still applied by the Great Elector, of personal protective letters for individual Jews or those in various provincial areas, this new law treated all Jews in the Prussian states as a single entity. This law represented a substantial worsening of the previous state of affairs. A major point in this new regulation was to limit the number of Jews in the Prussian states, and to prevent the natural growth of families by giving the right of residence only to the first-born children of protected Jews. For the second and third-born this right of residence had to be bought with especially high and progressively rising payments.

The restrictive Jewish policy of Frederick the Great in his *Revidiertes General-Judenreglement* (Revised General Jewish Regulations) of 1750 went still further. This law of the so-called enlightened king was perhaps the worst document in the development of the Jewish legal position to date. The restrictions that Frederick William I had, so to speak, hesitatingly introduced in constant struggle with his frequently liberal high officials, were now elaborated and systematised.

First of all Jewry was divided into six classes. The top class comprised (since 1762) the *General-Privilegierte* (generally privileged), the richest Jews. Their rights were regulated again through a specially granted personal privilege. They had the same rights as Gentile merchants; they could settle anywhere, acquire real estate and—most important of all—bequeath their privilege to all their children. To this class, however, belonged only very few families. They were probably largely identical with the earlier court-agents.

The second class, that of ordinary protected Jews, possessed a sovereign privilege too. But they were just allowed to reside in the district specified in their privilege, and could bequeath this right only to one child. The right of residence of the first child was, moreover, only possible with the voucher of a thousand talers; but there was no legal entitlement to settle a second or third child, although their settlement could be granted by special permission in each case where they possessed a thousand talers.

To the third class belonged the extraordinary protected Jews, such as physicians, dentists, painters, artists, i.e. more or less the professions. Their privilege was not inheritable.

These first three classes were together responsible for the payment of Jewish taxes and dues. Whenever a protected Jew wished to emigrate, great difficulties were set in his way both by the state—not only in Prussia—and by his community, since with his going an important taxpayer was lost. He had therefore to pay a special emigration tax, and was often obliged even from his new residence to help defray the liabilities of his former dwelling-place for several years.

The fourth class comprised public servants like rabbis, community officials, etc. They were not permitted to engage in any trade or business, and their privilege held good only for their term in office.

The fifth group comprised the so-called 'tolerated' Jews. These consisted of the non-settled children of protected Jews, those of extraordinary protected Jews and of community officials. None of these had the right to marry within their own group, and little prospect of marrying at all in Prussia. Nor were they allowed to pursue a trade or business of their own, but depended on the patronage of the paternal family.

The sixth class was made up of private domestic servants, who were not allowed to marry and were tolerated only for the duration of their employment. Clerical and office employees of protected Jews also counted as private domestic servants. Moses Mendelssohn was counted as such until in 1763 he received the right of an extraordinary protected Jew. Outside these six classes were those completely without rights like the persecuted beggar-Jews, who were unwanted in the state.

Frederick William I had initiated the prohibitions which confronted Jewish young people—who mostly came from large families—with the choice of never marrying and setting up home, or of emigrating. Frederick the Great developed these restrictions and made them more stringent still, and other states very soon learned from them and followed suit. In the countries of the Bohemian monarchy for example there was the *Familiants-Law*, renewed in 1797, i.e. more than fifteen years after the so-called *Patents of Tolerance*. According to this law Jewish families in Bohemia, Moravia and Austria-Silesia were not allowed to exceed a given number. Thus a Jew could only marry whenever a number became free for him through the death of another married Jew. A similar law was introduced in Bavaria after the Napoleonic war.

The attitude towards Jews in the absolute state of the eighteenth century, moreover, was solely determined by the political and commerical benefit they effected. In the political sphere this consisted in their procuring public credit and organising supplies and equipment for the army, in their inter-territorial Jewish family connections and—as we saw in the case of Altona—in making use of Jews to bring direct political pressure to bear on other states. Economic benefit was brought about by the expansion of trade and industry, export of the country's products and direct income to the state treasury through revenues gained from the activities of Jews and from their special taxes. This profit for the state treasury was considerable. To give one example: in 1705 the Jews of Berlin—about 120 families—paid in excise, i.e. inland duty, 117,437 talers, whereas the non-Jewish population of Berlin in the same year paid altogether only 43,865 talers in excise.[56] Indeed, it was usual for the state treasury to claim half the fines imposed by the community on Jews for not attending synagogue or for irreverent behaviour at divine service, etc., as well as half of those imposed by rabbinical courts. This was also one of the reasons why public administration in many territories supported the authority of community committees and rabbinical courts.

In order that these substantial sums might be raised, the economic scope of Jews, despite all restrictions, had to be proportionately enlarged. Large-scale commercial activity, however, was only possible for court-agents, to whom the 'general privileged' Jews in Prussia corresponded. Some Jews in trouble of importing certain goods. It was really only in these wealthy Jews that the states were interested. They supported them against their com- the states were really interested. They supported them against their com- munities or else the latter were made dependent on them. The rich Jew was —as Lessing in his *Nathan* says—by no means the better Jew, but for the purposes of the state he was the more useful. All other Jews were tolerated as a necessary evil and everywhere hampered. The large majority of pro- tected Jews were engaged in trading in merchandise. They kept mostly to peddling, since the urban merchants' guilds knew how to prevent Jews in most places from offering their wares for sale in open stalls. They remained confined to markets, fairs and itinerant selling. Very many, whose capital and credit possibilities did not suffice for trading in goods, earned their bread through broking or by spotting occasional business.

There were, in addition, a few guild-free handicrafts which were partially carried on in small family undertakings. Alongside was the traditional auxiliary occupation—largely looked after by the women—of lending on pawns. But from all actual handicrafts Jews were excluded. The guilds— their worst opponents for centuries—cut them off from access to all handi- crafts, which at that time represented the most important occupation of the middle classes. (Only in Silesia and Bohemia did some branches have Jewish handicraft workers, who in Bohemia were organized in several Jewish guilds.) Jews were completely excluded from agriculture. Ownership of town property was often permitted them in the eighteenth century—sometimes under the proviso that it was formally registered in the name of a Chris- tian. In Prussia in 1705 Jews were not even allowed to live in the country- side. Frederick the Great turned down an application to lease a dairy- farm to a Jew for a trial period, on the grounds that Jews were tolerated

---

[56] Elbogen-Sterling, p. 142.

only for the sake of trade and manufactures, while agriculture was reserved for non-Jews.[57]

Poor Jews in the communities who had no possibility of self-employment, not even as junk-dealers or middle-men, had to work as employees in the houses or firms of other Jews. Exclusion from craftsmanship and agriculture and confinement to trading, finance and to the few manufacturing enterprises had made the occupational and social position of Jews an unnatural one. What prejudice, envy and public economic policy had bred was perversely cast in their teeth as due to their depravity and deficiency.

While the aforementioned groups of Jews still managed to earn their living, the position of those with no right of settlement in a community or of those who had lost this right, was a miserable one. They included the bankrupt, for example, who, within the unstable economic life of Jews that was dependent on so many contingencies, were quite numerous. And they included the wandering beggar-Jews from abroad, especially from Poland. Among them were students of the Talmud, a kind of academic proletariat trying to find a livelihood as child-teachers or beadles in the synagogue. Where they succeeded, their situation was secure for a while. Otherwise they too became beggar-Jews, hunted from place to place. And the communities secluded themselves from them, as they posed a political and economic burden. They lived from begging, charity and chance free meals, and in night-shelters for aimless wanderers. From this group came many of the baptised, who then confronted Christian missionaries, like *Callenberg*, with major social problems. Some beggar-Jews joined up with non-Jewish vagrants and deserters, forming gangs of thieves and robbers. Remnants of such gangs still existed at the turn of the nineteenth century.[58] In his autobiography *Solomon Maimon* has given us an insight into the situation of these beggar-Jews.

In spite of their slight number in relation to the large majority of Jewish community residents,[59] beggar-Jews not only helped to create the popular misconceptions regarding Jews, but also influenced the deliberations and misgivings directed against Jewish emancipation by scholars and public officials right into the nineteenth century. Nothing was done to facilitate their social integration, for they were considered—together with all Jews—as incorrigible and therefore a hazard.

From this attitude towards Jews, nurtured by fear of these poorest of the poor—the products of most inhuman restrictions on occupation, residency and marriage—there runs a direct line to modern antisemitism.

---

[57] B. Koenig, *Annalen der Juden in den preussischen Staaten.* (Annals of the Jews in the Prussian States), (1790) reprinted Berlin, 1912, p. 297.

[58] Cf. R. Glanz, Geschichte des niederen juedischen Volkes in Deutschland (History of the Jewish poor in Germany) New York, 1968.

[59] Shohet, p. 17 ff.

# CHAPTER 9

# Ḥasidism

In the same epoch in which the described slackenings among the small German Jewry developed, leading ultimately to the Enlightenment, the position of the Jews in Poland had also greatly changed after the major Cossack uprising led by Chmielnicki.

The development in Poland—the large centre of Ashkenazi Jewry—took different directions and had different sociological conditions from those in Germany. There it took the path of convergence towards the language and educational resources of the environment, whereas in Poland it led to greater seclusion and isolation from its surroundings. The attitude of the Polish population in all its strata had undergone a change towards Jews. With the growing national consciousness of the Poles, the rise of a Polish urban middle-class and a very nationally-minded Catholic Church, Jews began to be regarded as a national enemy. In Germany, as in Poland, they differed from the surrounding world in religion, custom and dress. But in Poland this difference was the more intensified in that they were already marked off from their Slavonic and Lithuanian neighbours by their completely foreign everyday speech—the Yiddish-German—brought with them from Germany. They were ousted out of their occupations and economic functions for whose sake they were once called to Poland, or they were at least limited in the practice of them in both town and country. In addition, there was the position of power regained by the Catholic clergy in Poland. In the sixteenth century a large section of the Polish nobility had been won over for the ideas of the Reformation. The most varied Protestant groups and sects—among them the Socinians—found support in many residences of the nobility. Against this diversity the homogeneous Catholic Church regained predominance in the seventeenth and especially in the eighteenth century, soon embodying the national Polish character against Russian Orthodoxy and Prussian Protestantism. The clergy struck an especially sharp course against the Jews. This was probably connected with the fight against Protestant—notably Unitarian—heretics. The people were repeatedly incited against Jews through accusations of ritual murder and other charges. Assaults, plunderings and riotings, especially by pupils of the clerical colleges and by students—the so-called *Schueler-gelauf* (Students run amok)—became every-day occurrences.

The increasing deterioration of the economic and political situation of Jews in Poland had serious consequences for their mental attitude. The outward framework was still intact. The "Council of Four Lands"—the central organisation composed of representatives from the major communities with its administrative and rabbinical machinery—still existed till 1764. During the sixteenth century and first decades of the seventeenth, scholars of the highest repute—personalities of a high human niveau—were teaching in the Polish academies. With their significant commentary and codification works they had achieved distinction and authority, making Poland a centre of Talmud study. But now, after the great physical and psychical caesura brought about by the Cossack uprising, a certain decline had set in. The best minds went abroad, later to become famous in German communities. Only at the close of the epoch, in the second half of the eighteenth century, was there to be found here again an important representative of rabbinic Judaism: Rabbi *Elijah ben Solomon* in Vilna, Lithuania, called the *Gaon of Vilna*.

In the more urban north of Poland, in Lithuania and the so-called Great Poland with its main city of Poznan, the great tradition of Polish Judaism —with its widespread Talmudic erudition and the aspiration of all circles towards it—had been still largely preserved. Here a family, be it ever so rich, was really only considered distinguished if it had scholars to boast of. Here rabbinical authority and community discipline still remained intact.

The position was different in the southern part of Poland, in Podolia, the Ukraine, Volhynia and Galicia. There the great masses of impoverished Jews existed in small communities or were scattered over the country. They lived in constant struggle for their daily bread in hostile surroundings. A few well-to-do notables governed the communities together with rabbis to whom they were mostly related. These rabbis lived in the ascetic spirit of the Lurianic Kabbalah which, after the Chmielnicki persecutions and the collapse of the Sabbatian-Messianic dream, had grown all the stronger. Their ascetic piety and, on the other hand, their legal formalism, had become foreign to ordinary Jews. People living perpetually on the edge of starvation could no longer see any point in asceticism and had neither time nor ability to study the Talmud regularly. Thus among the simple Jews in the southern provinces of Poland there smouldered an animosity against scholars and the Judaism they embodied. Such a phenomenon, a socially-conditioned animosity against scholars and learning, is a rare occurrence in Jewish history. Similar occurrences are found only in the first and second Christian centuries among the simple country folk of Galilee, the circles from which Jesus of Nazareth and his disciples came and which still 150 years later caused difficulties for the scholars of Tiberias.—Among these embittered uneducated Jews of southern Poland, whose misery and depressed intellectual niveau made them impervious to rational argumentation, Sabbatianism smouldered in its antinomian forms. Here in Podolia and Volhynia the Frankist movement arose. Practical Kabbalah and superstition held sway; popular miracle-men appeared on the scene. Perhaps nowhere else in Judaism was there such a seething of emotional powers.

These tensions, however, did not lead to schism, but to a renewal of religious Judaism in eastern Europe. This renewal did not change Judaism but the people whom it took hold of.

A man from among the people, *Israel ben Eliezer*, called the *Ba'al Shem Tov*—Master of the Divine (Good) Name—abbreviated Besht (1700-1762), created a religious movement known as *Ḥasidism. Ḥasiduth* means piety, a piety that met the needs of a simple people.

Since the expulsion of the Jews from Spain and especially from the time of the activity of Isaac Luria and his disciples in Safed, the Kabbalah had become a mysticism of redemption, seeking to compel the coming of the Messiah and the kingdom of God through asceticism and penitence. Rabbinic Judaism very soon adapted this mysticism and ascetism to its own legal formalism. For the character of Kabbalah—perhaps like every mysticism being intellectualistic—resembled this formalism even in its ecstatic expressions. The old principle of Oral Law ruled unchallenged, namely that an ignorant person could not be pious, that only the study of the simple and the hidden mystical meaning of the Divine Word leads to right action.

The teaching of Ḥasidism was likewise based on concepts and terminology of the Lurianic Kabbalah, but clothed here in popular easily-remembered language. In particular the relationship between God and man, giving cosmic significance to every word and deed and impregnating the fulness of creation with diffused divine sparks, are Lurianic ideas which permeate in manifold form the sayings and symbolic actions of the Ba'al Shem and his disciples. What stands at the centre of Ḥasidism, however, is not theory but direct religious experience, which binds the simple man of prayer and all his daily work to his Creator. Prayer is the act of union between creature and Creator. "Godwardness", ecstatic enthusiasm and dedication of body and will are the three pillars of Ḥasidic prayer. Each human task, each deed done in such a spirit is service to God which—'like the cobbler and his awl'—binds the higher with the lower. Rhythmic—often unusual—movements, melodies and dances gave the prayer of the Ḥasidim an ecstatic character. Reflection, knowledge and law receded into the background.

The Ba'al Shem brought joy into the dreary life of the Jews again. Asceticism and learning were replaced by prayer that came from the heart. And in place of grief and a sense of sin the Ba'al Shem taught joy in God's creation and love to every created thing. God will be served with gladness.

Ḥasidism was a revolt against the intellectualisation of religion and the sombre yoke under which it then seemed confined. No longer could only the few learned be considered pious.

The Ba'al Shem and his disciples lived among their simple followers— handworkers, carters and water-carriers. They knew their worries and shared their sorrows. And very soon their every step, word and deed, their very melodies, were transformed into a source of innumerable legends.

Even within the lifetime of Israel Ba'al Shem Ḥasidism was beginning to become institutionalized. Despite its devaluation of "learning" and study, the movement since its inception had not been antinomian. In this respect Ḥasidism differed from the Sabbatian groups and the contemporaneous Frankists. Among the first significant disciples of the Ba'al Shem were already to be found members of the rabbinically educated class who created the first Ḥasidic literature and theory of Ḥasidism. The Ḥasidic groups had adopted the Lurianic order of prayer with its formulations drawn from the Sefardic rite and grafted onto the conventional Ashkenazi one. This mixed rite, the *Nussaḥ Sefarad* as it is called, distinguishes still today the Ḥasidic from the common Ashkenazi prayer-book, as it remained in usage in Germany, for instance.

The altered prayer-book with its ritual peculiarities, notably the joyful ecstatic and rather excited kind of religious service, marked the difference between the Ḥasidim and other Jews of Poland. Added to this was a remark- able and otherwise strange phenomenon in Judaism. The human ideal of Ḥasidism was the *Ẓaddik*, the perfect righteous man who stood in a direct primal relationship to God. Obviously not every Ḥasid was capable of at- taining this ideal. Most of them simply had to content themselves by vener- ably following such a truly inspired man and seeking thereby to obtain religious and spiritual satisfaction. The *Ẓaddik* came to be—even in the case of Israel Ba'al Shem—a charismatic personality.

The immediate disciples of the Ba'al Shem and their disciples were at first revered as *Ẓaddikim*. This charismatic function then became hereditary in the families of the descendants of the Ba'al Shem and of his disciples. The Ẓaddik came to be regarded as an inspired human mediator between God and other Jews, special power being ascribed to his prayer and intercession in the heavenly spheres. The generous contributions of their adherents enabled the Ẓaddikim to keep court, as it were. Each word and action of theirs was considered full of meaning. Their every word of counsel that proved useful, every reassurance that helped a sick person, came to be seen as a miracle.

Ḥasidism soon embraced large masses of believing followers, spreading within decades from southern Poland (the Northern Rumania of today) over the greater part of Jewry in eastern Europe. But it took a remarkable separate development when it tried to gain a foothold in Lithuania and White Russia. Here, where social conditions were better, it was confronted by a much broader section rooted in Talmudic learning. The leader of the Ḥasidic movement in White Russia, *Shne'ur Zalman* (1747-1812), was himself an eminent scholar with wide Jewish and general education. He founded an intellectual branch of Ḥasidism based on "wisdom, insight and knowledge", the so-called *"Ḥabad"* Ḥasidism (after the acronym of the three Hebrew words: *ḥokhmah, binah, da'at*). Here the enthusiasm of original Ḥasidism was recast into a psychological mysticism, which held that through withdrawal into one's inner self the knowledge of God may be found.

Of all branches of the Ḥasidic movement the *Ḥabad* group has remained the most vitally alive. It did not go along with the others in their belief in the miraculous. It transformed its Ẓaddik—from the family of Shneur Zalman —from being a mediator and wonderman into a teacher and hereditary leader of the movement. Even today Ḥabad-Ḥasidism maintain teaching centres in America, Israel and England which appeal to some modern Jews. They have, in fact, in recent years been able to infiltrate circles of Sefardic Jewry in North Africa. Shne'ur Zalman composed a Ḥasidic adaptation of the *Shulḥan Arukh*, and wrote a mystical-philosophical book, *Tania*. In our own century this Ḥabad circle produced the distinguished Chief Rabbi of Israel, *Abraham Isaac Kook* (1865-1935), the last great mystic in Judaism who had a strong influence on the beginnings of the Zionist settlement—notably on the otherwise so *a*religious workers.

It was inevitable, of course, that Ḥasidism aroused the opposition of leading rabbis and community heads. The various mystical movements at the beginning had not yet been differentiated, and the struggle against the Sabbatian Frankists stood at first in the foreground. Real resistance, therefore, only began when the movement encroached on Lithuania. The battle-cry went out from Vilna to the other large centres. The spiritual leader of the conflict was one of the most prominent scholars of rabbinic Judaism, the already mentioned *Elijah ben Solomon* in Vilna, called the *Gaon of Vilna* (1720-1797).

The Gaon of Vilna lived ascetically and withdrawn from life, having never occupied rabbinical office. He embodied the old tradition of Ashkenazi Judaism with its synthesis of mystical piety and learning. In his own way he was a renewer of rabbinic Judaism. He reformed the study of the Talmud by combating the use of mere acumen regarding it, especially prevalent in Lithuania and Poland. He laid special emphasis on the otherwise neglected Jerusalem Talmud for which he wrote marginal notes. He also occupied himself with mathematics and philosophy. His influence, handed down by important disciples, extends to the present day.

Supported by the Gaon's explicit approval the rabbis and community heads of Vilna, Brody and other centres tried to call a halt to the advance of Ḥasidism. These "opponents", *Mitnagdim*, as the Ḥasidim named them, saw in the minimizing of scholarly study a danger for the continuity of Judaism. They disapproved of their departure from the Ashkenazi prayer-book. The behaviour of the Ḥasidim at divine worship and in public, their ecstatic singing and dancing, seemed to them a contradiction of the dignity of prayer, as was also the stimulation of ecstasy through their customary use of alcohol. Finally, the function of the Ẓaddik as mediator between people and God and the dubious charismatic nature of the institution had to be rejected.

The struggle began in the 'seventies of the eighteenth century and lasted for decades. In fact the Mitnagdim called for the intervention of the Russian government, which took the Ḥabad leader Shneur Zalman into custody for a prolonged period. In the long run, however, the triumphal advance of Ḥasidism could not seriously be stopped.

But even Ḥasidism ultimately made its peace with rabbinism. Many of its leaders from among the first Ẓaddikim and especially the later ones—were themselves rabbinic authorities. But while rabbinic "mitnagdish" Judaism in Lithuania and Russia kept more or less open to the Enlightenment and to secular education, Ḥasidism very soon grew to be the most reactionary element in Judaism, hostile to every innovation.

Judaism in Germany and western Europe remained remarkably unaffected by Ḥasidism. In Germany the rejection of, or reservedness towards, mysticism inaugerated by Jacob Emden and adopted by the Berlin Enlightenment held sway. Ḥasidism was not able even to penetrate the provinces of Poland —West Prussia and Poznan—which became Prussian only after the divisioning of Poland.

The attempt has occasionally been made to parallel Ḥasidism with Pietism, especially with Zinzendorf who was born and died in the same years as the Ba'al Shem. I do not think such a parallel can be drawn, no more than one may seriously compare the Ḥabad-ideology with the Romantic philosophy of German Idealism. The common factors would be purely coincidental, like the founding of the older pre-Zinzendorfian pietism on feeling and *practica pia*. A parallel with Zinzendorf's basically non-mystical Lutherism seems to me quite inappropriate. Pietism has neither known an institution like "Ẓaddikim" nor desired mass-appeal.

For Jewish *Geistesgeschichte* Ḥasidism is rather a *parallel development to the Enlightenment*. Like the latter it brought slackening and stir into Judaism.

# CHAPTER 10

# The Disciples of Mendelssohn

In Berlin Mendelssohn had become the focal point of a circle of Jewish intellectuals who determined—in part during Mendelssohn's own lifetime —the direction of the coming intellectual-historical, political and social development in German Jewry. The active centre of this circle was the younger members, the real disciples, who continued and transformed the Mendelssohnian ideas. Beside this circle of disciples was a group of friends and co-workers from Mendelssohn's own generation who were also close to him in their unbroken Jewish way of life. Two rabbinic scholars from Poland, Solomon Dubno and Isaac Satanov, belonged to this group.

*Solomon Dubno* (1738-1813) was for some time tutor to Mendelssohn's eldest son Joseph, the only one of his children who remained true to Judaism. Dubno was an expert in masoretic studies, a grammarian, Hebrew poet and bibliophile. It was he who persuaded Mendelssohn to publish his translation of the Pentateuch, originally intended for his children's instruction. Dubno had started writing a Hebrew commentary to this translation using the most important traditional Hebrew Bible commentaries. In 1778 he published—for the purpose of gaining subscribers—a prospectus with samples of translation and commentary. But while he was still working on the commentary to Genesis, he abruptly left Berlin, apparently startled by the unexpected opposition the undertaking met within rabbinic circles. He afterwards lived in Frankfurt and Amsterdam, where he made a living by lending books from his own valuable library and as teacher of Hebrew. His lasting significance lies in his encouraging the publication of the Mendelssohnian Pentateuch translation and in his later influence upon Wolf Heidenheim, who lived in Roedelheim as book-printer, masoretic scholar and literary historian of the Prayer Book.

More interesting than important was the somewhat controversial figure of *Isaac Satanov* (1733-1804). He represented the later not uncommon type of Jewish intellectual from eastern Europe, a mixture of strict adherence to the Law and great rabbinic knowledge, radical freethinking ideas and leanings towards the Kabbalah, a secularist in the garb of an eighteenth century Polish Jew. He was a Hebrew poet and grammarian, natural scientist and philosopher. As head of the printing press attached to the Jewish Free School in Berlin, he published works of ancient Hebrew writers with interpolated additions of his own. He was a master of biblical style. A collection of proverbs which he put in the mouth of the biblical singer, Asaph, was at first taken by his contemporaries for a rediscovered book of the Bible. Due to his doubtful method of working he was called a plagiarist, though in his case not one who turned out the works of others in his own name, but his own under the name of others. Indeed he published a list of all the books he "re-edited". He wrote a Hebrew commentary on the second and third parts of Maimonides' "Guide for the Perplexed", published in the Free School Press (Solomon Maimon had written a commentary on the first part).

Satanov was a brilliant sardonic scholar suited to the mentality of the wealthy "general-privileged" of Berlin and of the younger Mendelssohnian circle. His relation to Mendelssohn himself was probably only slight.

Rabbi *Hirschel Levin* (Zevi Hirsch ben Aryeh Loew)[60] (1721-1800) of Berlin had also only a slight connection with Mendelssohn and his friends. Following rabbinical posts in London, Halberstadt and Mannheim, he became chief rabbi in Berlin in 1772 and thereby the first representative Prussian rabbi. It seems to me significant that in the decisive years of Mendelssohn's Jewish activity the Berlin rabbinate was occupied by a man, who was understanding and well disposed to him. Hirschel Levin was in a way the connecting link between the older Emdenian Enlightenment and the Mendelssohnian circle.—On being directed by the government to publish a digest of the civil legal 'Ritualgesetze der Juden' (Ritual Laws of the Jews) for use in the Prussian courts, Levin worked in close connection with Mendelssohn. He was probably its real author and editor, whereas Mendelssohn was more responsible for its German style.[61] Yet despite this cooperation, the priority of the surrounding culture, which was coming increasingly more to the fore with the Mendelssohnians, separated the rabbi from them. Levin also tried unsuccessfully to get Wessely removed from Berlin.

Naphtali Hirz (or Hartwig) *Wessely* (1725-1805) belonged to the second— the culturally politically active—circle of Mendelssohn's friends, though he was actually somewhat older than Mendelssohn. Son of a Danish court Jew and himself a banker, he became the assumed representative of the literary interested wealthy Jews of Berlin, though his Jewish scholarship distinguished him from them. In his youth he was pupil of the grammarian Solomon

---

[60] He was a grandson of Hakham Zevi and nephew of Jacob Emden.

[61] Cf. Moritz Stern, *Beitraege zur Geschichte der juedischen Gemeinde zu Berlin, Heft 4: Die Anfaenge von Hirschel Loebels Berliner Rabbinat*, Berlin 1931. (Contributions to the history of the Jewish community in Berlin, No. 4: The Beginnings of Hirschel Loebel's Rabbinate in Berlin.)

Hanau and of Eybeschuetz. He came to be the first master of biblical styled Hebrew poetry in Germany. Following the model of Klopstock's "Messiah" he composed among other poems "Shirei Tiferet", an epic on the life of Moses. He wrote a commentary on Solomon's Proverbs and on the "Sayings of the Fathers" as well as various grammatical works.

Wessely was probably the first to introduce the Enlightenment's concept of man into Hebrew literature and to call for the reshaping of education in accordance with this view of man. How easily this led to a devaluation of the traditional Jewish view of man soon became apparent.

Like Mendelssohn, Wessely was not only an outwardly pious Jew who strictly observed the religious law. He thought of himself as such and was considered thus by the leading rabbis of his day. Two of his later principal opponents, Ezekiel Landau of Prague and David Tevele of Lissa, approved writings of his. The last mentioned specifically praised Wessely's rationalism, recommending him as an example for youth.[62] However, his emotional poetic nature was very soon to disturb the unstable equilibrium between his piety and his enlightened views. He was stirred into active involvement by the new regulations for Jewish education which the Josephian Edicts of Tolerance stipulated and the majority of Austrian Jews rejected.

In 1781 *Emperor Joseph II* had begun to issue the so-called *Toleranzedikte* (Edicts of Tolerance) for the non-Catholic population including the Jews. These laws were a typical product of enlightened absolutism, intending forcibly to bring about a levelling of class, of national and cultural differences as well as a standardisation of the country's inhabitants. What seemed to be progressive in these edicts of tolerance, as far as they affected the Jews, were certain relaxations of their occupational restrictions such as the removal of body-tax levied on them since the Middle Ages, access to public schools and universities and adoption of permanent surnames. Restrictive measures separating Jews from other Austrian citizens were to be gradually phased out. The Patents of Tolerance were on this account known as the first emancipatory laws.

From the very start, however, a number of alleviations were in practice or through contradictory regulations rendered invalid. Thus the holding and cultivation of land by Jews was encouraged without making the necessary land available. But where Jews had lived on the land for centuries, in Galicia which had just become Austrian, their acting as leaseholders or licensed publicans was now forbidden. Several tens of thousands of leaseholders, now without a livelihood, were deported with their families to Poland. The acquirement of skilled trades was to be promoted, but the trained could not become masters of their trade. Apprenticeships with Gentile masters were scarcely to be found. Only the setting up of manufac-

---

[62] Levin, *Aus dem juedischen Kulturkampf* (Out of the Jewish cultural struggle), JJLG XII. 1917, p. 177, Note 4.

tories—even in areas otherwise forbidden to Jews—and the wholesale trade were encouraged. Hence in practice—just as in the past—only rich Jews came to benefit from these reliefs, except that earlier such reliefs were not trimmed with "tolerance". Moreover, as mentioned earlier (Chapter 8), restrictions on even the number of Jews that existed in many parts of the Austrian empire had not been removed. The jurisdiction of rabbis in matters of marriage and divorce was curtailed. Permission to marry was made dependent on an examination in German. The openly declared intention of the emperor was to make the Jews into "useful" subjects, but thereby to let them dwindle away as a distinct group. This intention also lay behind the *educational reform*, which the Patents of Tolerance demanded. Jews were to found schools—*Normalschulen* (normal schools)—giving instruction in the German language and training in skilled crafts and other useful occupations, or else they were to be allowed to attend Gentile schools.

Mendelssohn's attitude to the aims and demands of the Austrian laws was reserved. He suspected that dejudaization, or "religious integration"[63] as he called it, really lay behind the façade of toleration. He feared that harm could ensue from rash and forceful advance.

In contrast to him, his friends and disciples saw in the Edicts of Tolerance the dawn of a new era of legal and cultural integration of Jews into the state. Shortly after the appearance of these laws Wessely published a pamphlet, "Divrei Shalom ve-Emet" (Words of Peace and Truth), in which he drafted an educational programme for the planned *Normalschulen*.

As we saw, the first Jewish men of the Enlightenment had already attached great importance to familiarity with languages, social manners and secular knowledge. Acquaintance with them would make it easier for the Jew "to live with other people". In other words, the range of secular knowledge within the framework of the Jewish scale of values was determined from a mere utilitarian viewpoint. With Jacob Emden, for example, such knowledge had a purely marginal character. So much should be appropriated as was necessary to be informed in the ways of the world and to be able to form one's own judgement. But this general information should not be too deep or far-reaching and must remain entirely subordinate to the Jewish ideal of education—the pursuit of Torah.

In Wessely's educational programme, on the other hand, these humanities had their own intrinsic value. They should no longer be merely desirable or utilitarian complements of religious knowledge, but rather stand alongside it on an equal footing. Indeed they had a certain priority in relation to religious knowledge, since without the humanities a proper understanding of religion would not be attainable. The Enlightenment's concept of the religion of reason—in contrast to the specific characteristics of individual churches and religious groups—was applied here by Wessely to Jewish education,

[63] Letters to Herz Homberg of 9.22.1783, 10.4.1783, 3.1.1784.

following most likely the ideas of contemporary educational reformers like Basedow and the Philantropinists. Wessely distinguished between "law of man" and "law of God". Under the first he lists language and grammar of Hebrew and German, social behaviour and good manners. The second comprises knowledge of the Bible, religious precepts and—for the specially gifted—of Talmud and rabbinic literature. Instruction should begin with the law concerning man, rising by grades to the law of God. Without such social knowledge a Talmud scholar dishonours his profession in the eyes of the outside world and is not, as it were, a rounded personality.

Wessely's radicalism evoked the opposition of several prominent rabbis of the day: Ezekiel Landau of Prague, the Gaon of Vilna and notably Wessely's former supporter, Rabbi David Tevele of Lissa. Tevele, who was no "Winkelrabbiner" (obscure rabbi)—as the biased Graetz called him—but a scholar open to the new endeavours, took particular offence at the unhappy separation Wessely seemed to make between being man and being Jew—as though a pious Jew truly observing God's commandments was not precisely thereby displaying the highest humanity.[64] Besides repudiating this devaluating distinction the rabbinic leaders also objected to the "step-motherly" treatment of Talmud study in Wessely's curriculum, which took from it its traditional general educative character, virtually reserving it for the professional training of future rabbis. In three further circular letters Wessely himself toned down his first radical attitude. He realised he had gone too far in his excessive enthusiasm, especially since he personally by no means agreed with the conclusions the younger members of the Mendelssohn circle drew from his first circular regarding the practical work of education.

Since, unlike Mendelssohn, Wessely wrote in Hebrew, his was a particularly strong intellectual influence that radiated upon Italian and East European Jewry. He became the model of a great many poets and writers soon to emerge in Italy, Austria, Galicia, Poland and Russia where they became bearers and spreaders of the Hebrew Enlightenment, the *Haskalah* as it is called. In choosing Hebrew they wrote again—unlike Mendelssohn and most of the enlighteners of the Berlin circle—only for Jews. But their aim was the spread of contemporary culture and its ideas and values among Jews, at least among a Hebrew educated élite. This enlightenment was largely coupled with a sharp critique, irony and satire vis-à-vis traditional Judaism and its institutions. The main object of the derision of these men of enlightenment was largely focused on the Ḥasidim with their unusual customs.

The practical implementation of the Josephian educational reforms was consigned to *Herz Homberg* by the Austrian government in 1784. Homberg (1749-1841), a native of Bohemia, was a Talmud student in Prague who came to pedagogy through the influence of Rousseau's "Émile". As successor to Dubno he was tutor to Mendelssohn's son Joseph for three

[64] Cf. Louis Levin, op. cit., p. 187.

years and later continued to correspond with Mendelssohn himself.

Through his over-zealous striving towards enlightenment Homberg did not succeed in putting through the new educational principles among the Jews of Bohemia and Galicia. What he saw in their opposition was not their justified concern for the continuation of tradition but only superstition and fanaticism. He identified himself completely with the denationalisation policy of the Austrian government, even though the latter took coercive economic measures which left many thousands of Jewish families out of work.

Homberg alas was not the man of integrity to have inspired enthusiasm for the new cultural aims. He was accused of nepotism and corruption and an enquiry was brought against him, all of which led to the discrediting for decades of even the positive ideas of the Enlightenment among the large Jewry of Galicia. Supervision over the Jewish *Normalschulen* was taken from him and the schools themselves dissolved in 1806.

Homberg lived afterwards in Vienna and Prague as censor, lecturer in Jewish ethics and author of several school-books on Jewish religion and Hebrew. His books on religion were widely circulated in his lifetime, since Jewish marriage candidates had to be examined on them. In spite of his radicalism he gained the approval for two of his books from Rabbi Mordecai Benet of Nikolsburg, a rabbinical authority at the beginning of the nineteenth century, for relations between enlighteners and enlightened rabbis of the old school in this period of transition were still quite fluid.

Among the younger men around Mendelssohn were the philosopher, physician and psychologist *Marcus Herz*, *David Friedlaender* the first politician of the emancipation, and the Hebraist *Isaac Euchel*, all of whom—apart from Moses Mendelssohn's charisma—*Immanuel Kant* had influenced. Kant also decisively influenced *Solomon Maimon* and *Lazarus Bendavid*. I shall be discussing all of them in connection with Kant and his influence on the Jews.

For the *younger Mendelssohn circle* only the identification of Judaism with the religion of reason had survived the Mendelssohnian synthesis of the religion of reason and revealed Law (dealt with in Chapter 7). The remnant of revealed religion, namely the revealed Law, to which Mendelssohn had clung, had been relinquished by them, and with it commitment to the religious-legal precepts. They saw in them mere outdatedness and superstition impeding the realization of full legal and social integration and therefore to be opposed. This struggle was levelled with increasing vehemence against the representatives of tradition—the rabbis and the Talmudic scholarship they embodied. What with Wessely were still carefully argued didactic considerations, became with the later Homberg and especially with the educationalist and head for many years of the Berlin Jewish Free School, Lazarus Bendavid, a systematic hostile attitude to Talmud and tradition. The *standard of values* of these circles, of Bendavid, for example, or David Friedlaender, had now fully become that of the *environment*. Their sense of Jewish values had reached zero. Their Jewish activity was limited to educational reforms and to the struggle for civil equality. For the mess of pottage of desired emancipation one was prepared to surrender all the values which Jewish individuality and its life style implied. The very word "Jewish" seemed objectionable and the attempt was made to replace it with that of "Israelite" or "Mosaic".

The achieving of equal rights became the life task of *David Friedlaender* (1750-1834). On the death of Frederick the Great in 1786, Friedlaender, in his capacity of 'General Deputy' of Prussian Jewry, stood at the centre of fruitless negotiations, lasting for years, with the Prussian Government. In 1793 he rejected, on behalf of the Jewish delegates, the government's proposal to change the Frederician General Reglement of 1750 as inadequate. However, now he was prepared in his disappointment over the still protracted delay in granting civil equality to take the despairing step of relinquishing the Jewish identity. In this frame of mind he sent a circular letter in 1799 to Provost Teller, a Berlin Enlightenment-theologian. In this letter he made, in the name of several Jewish heads of families, a remarkable suggestion, that if equality of rights could not be otherwise obtained, his party would be ready formally to convert to Christianity. This step, however, should be subject to the qualification that his circle would not be obliged to accept the dogma of Christian belief. Friedlaender thereby basically suggested founding—together with Teller and other Enlightenment theologians, whose Christianity he considered as much diluted as his own Judaism—a new church of the religion of reason out of Christians and Jews. The "blindness to religious values"[65] vis-à-vis both Judaism and Christianity expressed in Friedlaender's proposal was all the more awkward and anachronistic, as the new dominant Romantic intellectual position had long since moved away from the ideals of the Enlightenment. The proposal provoked a series of printed objections, among them one from Schleiermacher. Teller felt obliged flatly to reject the suggestion.

Nevertheless, a baptismal movement now got under way among quite wide circles of "arrived" and "enlightened" Jews—without the reservations the honest Friedlaender still considered necessary. Friedlaender himself remained a Jew and a leading representative of his co-religionists and of the Jewish community in Berlin during the subsequent negotiations on emancipation. He also took an active part in efforts to reform the synagogue service, which seemed to him a necessary consequence of the equal citizenship at last formally attained in 1812.[66] However, even Mendelssohn's own

---

[65] Cf. Schoeps, 'Geschichte der Juedischen Religionsphilosophie in der Neuzeit', (History of Jewish religious philosophy in modern times), 1935, footnote p. 41.—Cf. Ellen Littmann, ZGJD VI., 1936, pp. 92-112 on Friedlaender's circular letter to Provost Teller.

[66] Immediately after the Edict of Emancipation of March 11, 1812, Friedlaender wrote a memorandum which was circulated among the Prussian communities and sent to the king, to Lord-chancellor Hardenberg and to the director of the department of education and religion, Schuckmann. In this memorandum Friedlaender called for reform of the synagogue service, dispensing with both Hebrew

children with the exception of his eldest son Joseph and all his grandchildren had, like many others of their generation, converted to Christianity. These conversions precisely from the circles of the rich, educated and socially ambitious Jews, were justified by them through the idea of the universal religion of reason. And was not the religion of reason common to the various confessions of faith, and their peculiar historical expressions relatively incidental? Why then should Jewish adherents of the religion of reason further distinguish themselves from its Christian adherents, thereby forming an artificial cleft between themselves and other decent fellow-citizens? This in a manner was how Mendelssohn's son Abraham argued with his children.[67] As a child of nine he had lost his father and did not have the advantage of growing up under his influence.

The equilibrium between the religion of reason, identified with the doctrines of Judaism, and revealed Law, the religious precepts that Mendelssohn had taught and lived out (see Chapter 7), was abandoned by his younger disciples. For them there only remained his identification of Judaism with the religion of reason. At best, the special character and individuality of Judaism confined itself to being, in Mendelssohn's phrase, "the fellowship of genuine theists". As for the rest, everything potentially separating Jews from their fellow-citizens should, they held, be avoided and cut out in order to pave the way for fuller civil and legal equality.

This pragmatic attitude—so often leading one eventually out of Judaism—was personified in Friedlaender and Bendavid. But side by side with these pragmatists was another trend that had likewise arisen from the curtailment of the religious law in this generation and from which, as I like to call it, a new *theological* interest developed. It was an outcome of educational reform, which, since the founding of the Jewish Free School in Berlin, its sister institutions and the Austrian "normal schools", was one of the main pursuits of the enlighteners. 'Religion' in these schools had become a special subject of instruction. It was never taught as such in the traditional Jewish system of education. Formerly the Jewish child, through gradual introduction to biblical and talmudic sources as well as through the Torah-orientated way of life in the home, had from an early age quite naturally imbibed the principles and religious obligations of his religion. Now, through the increasing introduction of secular subjects and the curtailment of Jewish ones, a new pedagogic situation had arisen. The Bible, moreover, was mostly taught in Mendelssohn's translation and only in excerpts in Hebrew. Instruction in Talmud and rabbinic literature—if it appeared in the syllabus at all—

---

as the language of prayer—save a few passages—and the messianic hope which no longer suited the age of achieved emancipation. The memorandum is printed in Moritz Stern's 'Beitraege zur Geschichte der Juedischen Gemeinde zu Berlin', Heft 6, Berlin 1934. (Contributions to the History of the Jewish Community in Berlin, No. 6.)

[67] Hensel, Die Familie Mendelssohn, 1908, vol. I, p. 111 ff.

was reserved for a few chosen pupils and soon disappeared entirely from the curriculum. All that remained of Hebrew in the course of time was the ability to read it and a scanty understanding of several main prayers.

As replacement for the primary Jewish sources which had receded into the background and at the same time in order to acquaint the pupil to some extent with his faith, textbooks on the Jewish religion were printed for use in the new schools. Many of these imitated the question and answer form of the Christian catechisms.[68] They endeavoured to summarize the Jewish religion in a way understandable to young people. Herz Homberg was notably active in this sphere. Most of these textbooks followed Maimonides' Thirteen Articles of Faith contained in the Prayer Book or else the "Principles" of Joseph Albo of the fourteenth century. Despite this common traditional basis, the various textbooks diverged considerably from one another according to the radical or conservative sentiments of their authors.[69] For the first time in the history of Jewish thought the doctrinal element in Judaism—theology—began to move into the foreground, while the revealed Law which guides and regulates human action withdrew.

What had developed here out of the new provisions of instruction was a clear break with Mendelssohn's position. This position had expressly denied an independent Jewish doctrine standing alongside the universal religion of reason. Despite the accepted rationalism of the Enlightenment, pains were now taken to stress precisely the religious singularity of Judaism. With these new educational reforms an entirely new attitude emerged which in its turn influenced nineteenth century Reform Judaism into our own day.

Apart from this school-book literature there were during the Mendelssohnian era (1780-1820) to my knowledge only two attempts made to present Jewish teaching outside the thought-schemata of the religion of reason. The first—the theocentric theology developed by Mordecai Gumpel Shnaber-Levison in his commentary work 'Yessod Hatorah' (the book appeared in 1792)—has already been considered in Chapter 6. And then in the same year the Berlin writer *Saul Ascher* (1767-1822) published a remarkable book under the title: 'Leviathan oder Ueber Religion in Ruecksicht des Judentums' (Leviathan or On Religion with regard to Judaism). Here in direct contrast to Mendelssohn a substantiation of Judaism as religious doctrine is attempted.[70]

---

[68] Cf. Jacob J. Petuchowski: Manuals and Catechisms of the Jewish Religion in the early Period of Emancipation, in: Studies in 19th Century Jewish Intellectual History, edited by Alexander Altmann, Harvard Univ. Press, 1964, pp. 47-64.

[69] As already mentioned, Rabbi Mordecai Benet of Nikolsburg approved the printing of Homberg's textbook and himself composed one which his son later published. The textbooks of Solomon Plessner —one of the first German preachers and admirer of Wessely—as well as many others breathe a strongly traditional spirit.

[70] Cf. Ellen Littmann: Saul Ascher, First Theorist of Progressive Judaism, in Yearbook V, 1960 of the Leo Baeck-Institute, pp. 107-121. cf. also Schoeps pp. 45-46.

Ascher, too, proceeds from concepts of Enlightenment thinking, from the idea of happiness as the highest good for man and human society. But in his own characteristic terminology Ascher distinguishes between "regulative" and "constituted" religion—wording somewhat reminiscent of Kant's distinction between regulative and constitutive principles.[71] The "regulative" religion of Ascher is what is generally known as the religion of reason. Ascher, however, in sharp contrast to Mendelssohn, does not identify this religion of reason with the doctrine of Judaism. Religion of reason is bound up with human thought and—therefore being subjective—cannot reach the degree of certainty which "constituted"—revealed—religion does. The content of constituted religion is its religious doctrine, dogma. Hence, revelation, according to Ascher and in contrast to Mendelssohn, is not limited to revealed law, the precepts. Jewish *doctrine* itself is the centre of revelation, religious law only a part of it. The religion of reason in comparison with religious doctrine can only have a subjective claim to truth according to Ascher—since for him belief not only stands in contrast to reason but is superior to it as expression of an objective truth. Likewise religious law, i.e. the sociological constituted form of doctrine in comparison with religious doctrine, has only a derivative subjective character. And just as Gumpel Shnaber-Levison contrasts the objective eternal truth of God with the time-limited divine commandments, so we see a quite similar line of thought in Saul Ascher. With Ascher, indeed, the emancipatory aspect again comes into the foreground. For him Judaism requires a reformation in order to become part of the new social realities and endeavours. This reformation has, for all that, to be guided by the doctrinal content of Judaism. Ascher summed this up—in Maimonidean fashion—in *fourteen* articles of faith. But reformation for Ascher is not antinomian in character. The intention is not to abrogate the Law as Bendavid and Friedlaender wished to do. With him the law has a purely symbolic character. How he envisaged its reformation is left unanswered. It is known that he criticized and ridiculed reforms of the synagogue service which he lived to witness, notably the introduction of the organ. He saw in them only outward frippery borrowed from Christianity.

Ascher's "Leviathan" and programme have certainly only symptomatic importance in the history of thought. His ideas, like those of Shnaber-Levison, foundered alongside the prevailing trend of the Mendelssohnian school. Bendavid said of Ascher that a "cod" is not a Leviathan! Friedlaender maintained he offended the memory of Mendelssohn.

Ascher was influenced by contemporary philosophical discussions and probably read Kant. The influence of Friedrich Heinrich Jacobi, however,

---

[71] Kant, Critique of Pure Reason, second ed., pp. 210-11, 450 ff.

seems to me to be more strongly in evidence.[72] Jacobi's quarrel with Fichte, Schelling and the Romantics has perhaps its counterpart in Ascher, when he later became publicist, in his polemics against "Germanomania" and romantic Teutomania. His book *Germanomania* was burnt at the students' associations' Wartburg Festival in 1819.

In his activity as publicist and journalist Ascher developed more and more into a cosmopolitan supporter of Napoleon and the French Revolution. He clung to these ideas even at the beginning of the Restoration after the Napoleonic wars. His aversion to the prevailing nationalist orientated Romanticism may have reverted him to more rationalist views as far as his religious outlook and attitude towards Judaism was concerned. But his position in *Leviathan*—the product of his youth—with its demand for reform in virtue of the priority of belief, he probably never entirely gave up, even when he later desired to have the revealed religions, Judaism and Christianity, raised to a cosmopolitan universal religion. As far as we know he kept aloof from Jewish life at the beginning of the nineteenth century. He appears to have led the life of a cynical and sceptical eccentric according to Heine's description in his *Harzreise* (Journey to the Harz Mountains). Zunz, who came to know him in 1818, wrote of him: "Saul Ascher, a man of queer views, enemy of excessive enthusiasm, opponent of the Germanomaniacs; his moral character is not highly estimated".[73] By the new generation of the historically conscious *Wissenschaft des Judentums* (literally 'Science' of Judaism) he was considered only as a curiosity. He anticipated many ideas of the later moderate Reform movement but remained unknown to the movement itself, having influenced it neither directly nor indirectly.

Much closer to the popular educational endeavours of the Mendelssohn circle was the undertaking by some younger people for the *revival of the Hebrew language* and literature that emanated from Koenigsberg and Berlin and found its continuity in Dessau, Altona and other places. Under the direct patronage of Wessely and co-operation of Mendelssohn, a "Society of Friends of the Hebrew Language" was founded in 1783 by a student and a tutor in Koenigsberg. The student was the Kantian disciple *Isaac Euchel* and the tutor was his friend *Mendel Bresselau*. In 1784 they began to publish a Hebrew periodical, the *Ha-Me'assef* (which can be translated both as "gatherer" or as "rear-guard"). Its purpose was to cultivate the Hebrew language and introduce readers of Hebrew to world literature and to Jewish

---

[72] He was certainly not influenced by Schleiermacher, as has been assumed. Schleiermacher's 'Reden ueber die Religion' (Discourses on Religion) only appeared in 1799, whereas Jacobi's 'David Hume ueber den Glauben' (David Hume on Belief) was already in print in 1787. Ascher's 'Primat der Offenbarung' (Priority of Revelation) was later taken up more methodically by S. L. Steinheim.

[73] Letter to S. M. Ehrenberg of 1.1.1819. Cf. Glatzer: Zunz. Jude, Deutscher, Europaer (Zunz, Jew, German, European), Tuebingen 1964 p. 96.

and general problems of the time. The circle of contributors—the *Me'assfim* —included Hebrew writers from many countries. Together with original contributions of Hebrew poetry, translations from German and from world literature were published as well as literary essays, biographies of eminent Jews, as e.g. a biography of Mendelssohn by Euchel and parts of Jacob Emden's autobiography, etc. Apart from some interruptions the magazine ran on for ten years of publication.

After its termination in 1797 it re-appeared from 1809 to 1811 as the *New Hame'assef* under the editorship of Shalom Cohen. But the German language had taken so strongly among the Jews in Germany with the simultaneous decline of Hebrew that there was no longer any place for a Hebrew magazine. Shalom Cohen moved to Vienna where—with its strong Galician and Polish hinterland—he renewed the periodical under the altered title *Bikkurei Ha'ittim* (First fruits of the Times), reprinting in it between 1820-1831 selections of the old *Me'assef*, as well as new poetical and scientific essays by some of the first pioneers of the Wissenschaft of Judaism who wrote in Hebrew. The *Me'assef* found its final sequel in a magazine called *Kerem Ḥemed* (Vineyard of Delight) which strengthened the Judaic-scientific tendency. Under the editorship of S. L. Goldenberg and later Senior Sachs the 'Kerem Ḥemed' appeared between 1833 and 1856 for reasons of censorship in the form of mutual correspondence of its contributors.

The *Me'assef* periodical and those succeeding it became the champions and pioneers of the Enlightenment and later of the Wissenschaft of Judaism and of modern Hebrew literature among East European Jewry. Originating in Germany and Austria, these periodicals developed into the literary reservoir of the Haskalah movement, the Hebrew Enlightenment in eastern Europe. Since the seventeenth century several sporadic attempts had been made to publish Hebrew magazines, among them one by the young Moses Mendelssohn, *Kohelet Mussar* (Preacher of Morals) in 1758 which saw only two issues. Yet *Ha-Me'assef* and its successors represented the first Hebrew periodical that was not only of long standing but also made a very great intellectual-historical impact on the shaping of modern Judaism. Through the revival of the Hebrew language, these periodicals brought together the Enlightenment-factor and the later increasingly important national element.

# CHAPTER 11

# Kant and Judaism

Among the younger members of the Mendelssohn circle were several from Koenigsberg who as disciples or acquaintances stood in personal contact with *Immanuel Kant*. Kant's influence with them stood alongside or took the place of Mendelssohn's influence.

Beyond these personal relationships, the Kantian philosophy influenced the self-understanding of Judaism in the nineteenth century down to our own time. The after-effects of the Kantian ideas extended to generations of educated Jews even further afield than Germany. Kant's ethical rigorism was found to be congenial to Judaism.[74]

The impact Kant had upon Jews and Judaism was unquestionably more profound and decisive than his influence on non-Jewish Germany and Europe. Here, within Kant's lifetime, the Kantian philosophy was superseded by "German Idealism" and the philosophies of Fichte, Schelling and Hegel. Later on in the nineteenth century Kant was for a long time only a highly respected name with no real influence on philosophical developments or on intellectual life in general. Here Hegel, Feuerbach, Marx and Schopenhauer predominated, as did later Nietzsche and Comte, John Stuart Mill and Spencer. Only in the last third of the nineteenth century was Kant rediscovered, significantly by the Jewish philosophers Otto Liebmann and Hermann Cohen, giving rise to the various neo-Kantian schools of thought, in particular the Marburg school established by Cohen and his non-Jewish colleague Paul Natorp.

The deeply felt "inner connections of Kantian philosophy to Judaism"[75] may seem astonishing and even paradoxical, when one considers the picture

---

[74] Similarly *Friedrich Schiller* with his ethical pathos and ideas of freedom was for many Jews—and especially for Jewish youth in Eastern Europe—the German writer par excellence who was early and often translated into Hebrew.

[75] So runs the title of an essay by Hermann Cohen (1910) in his 'Juedische Schriften' (Jewish Writings), vol. 1 p. 284-305, Berlin, 1924. For the entire complex of Kant's relationship to Judaism cf. the lecture of Julius Guttmann, 'Kant und das Judentum' (Kant and Judaism), Leipzig 1908, and more

of Judaism Kant himself depicts in his writings on religion. He had a peculiarly ambivalent relationship to Jews and Judaism. With him there exist side by side friendly—in the case of Marcus Herz affectionate—relationships to individual Jews, solicitude for Jewish students and crude anti-Jewish utterances in several letters.[76] Similarly, Kant's hostile delineation of Judaism within the systematic motifs of his philosophy of religion is like a bypath continuing the thread of contemporary Enlightenment-theology, which Kant's critical philosophy really surmounted and abandoned. It is therefore well to go into the question of religion in Kant's work more fully.

Kant had grappled with the question of religion from early youth, but his approach to it has always been conflicting. Criticism of religion and of its outward expressions stands alongside a certain kind of theology—a deistic devaluation of revelation to a mere historic instance—side by side with the theistic affirmation of a Creator God and Ruler of the world. Since his schooldays in the pietistic 'Fridericianum' school Kant had a deep resentment against all religious practice. In his eyes it was sham and false pretence. Prayer, as he tried to show in a short essay, is only hypocrisy; for whoever is found praying feels ashamed as though caught doing something reprehensible.[77] Yet he can refer to God as "something distinct from the world".[78]

Both these decisive elements in Kant's prior understanding of religion: the deistic element of the Enlightenment and that of theistic theology shimmer through the methodical framework of his system. But here both undergo a fundamental change. Through the critical transposition of both elements Kant became the real originator of the *philosophy of religion*.[79]

The question of religion, as far as theology left it for philosophy to deal with it, had until then—notably in the philosophy of the Enlightenment, e.g. with Leibniz, Wolff and Mendelssohn—been the real theme of metaphysics. By means of his critique of the proofs of God and his doctrine of the antinomies, Kant stripped metaphysics of its foundation, contending its right to secure "eternal truths" through deductive thinking. For him metaphysics has to be replaced by a new philosophic discipline, the philosophy of religion. The status of the latter, it is true, remains not only with Kant, but in the entire subsequent history of philosophy, a manifest or at any rate latent problem.

recently of Nathan Rotenstreich in his book "The Recurring Pattern", London 1963, pp. 23-44. The present author's essay 'Kant und das Judentum' (Kant and Judaism) in the ZRGG, vol. 13, 1961, pp. 308-333 also deals with Jewish Kantianism.

[76] Cf. Kant's letter of 3.28.1794 to Reinhold on Maimon, or his earlier letter to him of 5.12.1789 regarding a copper engraving of Kant by a baptized Jewish artist.

[77] Vom Gebet (On Prayer) Werke vol. VIII in edition by Vorlaender, p. 169 ff.

[78] Critique of Pure Reason, 2nd ed. p. 724.

[79] This expression only appears after Kant. He himself speaks of 'philosophische Religionslehre' (philosophical doctrine of religion)—the original title of his 'Religion innerhalb der Grenzen der bloßen Vernunft' (Religion within the Limits of Reason alone).

Kant's systematic treatment of the question of religion is closely linked with the basic tendencies of his critical method. His well-known sentence in the preface to the second edition of his 'Critique of Pure Reason': "I have found it necessary to set knowledge aside in order to make room for faith"[80] gives an entire programme of the critical method in its proceeding from the phenomenal world of appearance to the noumenal. The philosophy of the Enlightenment—and of Mendelssohn perhaps most directly—had just previously affirmed the demonstrability of metaphysical objects, i.e. their knowability; whereas Kant had clearly shown the limits of comprehending them. They could "at best be matters of belief. . . . They are ideas whose objective reality cannot be guaranteed".[81] Such ideas whose connection a religion renders possible, are God, freedom and immortality.[82]

These concepts of religion, reduced to borderline concepts, continued to be a constant ferment in Kant's thought. That which cannot be objectively secured he tried to secure in "practical reason", in ethics. With Kant the latter becomes the systematic bearer of the ideas, of every surplus denoted by him as "noumena", which he then again correctly calls "metaphysics", i.e. the "metaphysics of morals". Ethics proceeding from the autonomy of the human will give systematic room to the bases of the doctrine of religion. God, freedom and immortality become "postulates" for the possibility of ethical realisation.[83] The concept of God for Kant always remained linked to morality, even when God is referred to as Creator and Author of the world.[84] He is "moral Author"—or "moral Ruler of the world".[85] "Religion is the acknowledging of all duties as divine commands".[86]

The concept of God thereby preserves its indefiniteness, its borderline character, since our statements can never exceed analogies, never go beyond "as-though" statements. The idea of God is on one occasion expressly termed "symbolic".[87] Indeed, the basic concepts of religion cannot be demonstrated as the philosophy of the Enlightenment had believed. But the concepts of religion do not thereby become transcendent vis-à-vis reason. They are not unknowable chimerae. As border-concepts they retain rather their relation to thought. This is what Kant denoted by his characteristic term "transcendental" in contradistinction to "transcendent". Without this relation those border concepts would "fall into meaninglessness".[88] Thus for Kant, the question of religion becomes a clamp coupling the various

[80] Critique of Pure Reason, 2nd ed. p. XXX.
[81] Critique of Judgement, 2nd ed. p. 459. Cf. Critique of Pure Reason p.512.
[82] Critique of Judgement, p. 467.
[83] Critique of Practical Reason, Pt. I 2nd Main Section IV-VI pp. 22-134 of 2nd ed.
[84] Critique of Pure Reason, p. 839.
[85] Religion within the Limits of Reason alone, p. 91 ff., 117 ff. 130.
[86] loc. cit. p. 142.
[87] Critique of Judgement, p. 257.
[88] 'Opus posthumum', vol. XXI of the Academy edition, p. 74 ff.

parts of his system. From ethics as centre it turns back in the 'Critique of Pure Reason' and reaches over into the teleology of his 'Critique of Judgement'.

This picture of the Kantian philosophy of religion that we have reconstructed from his systematic writings, the three Critiques, does not at all seem to tally with his actual writings on religion, where one would naturally assume his philosophy of religion to be found.

In these writings too—in the "Religion within the Limits of Reason alone", and in the "Conflict of the Faculties"—Kant takes his point of departure from his ethics as the systematic locus of the question of religion. However, now the starting point is not the borderline character of religious statements —such as the doctrine of the postulates, which is the climax of Kant's ethics—but rather the autonomy of the will, with which his moral philosophy begins. Only those actions of man can be called moral which proceed from his autonomous will—a will guided by the sole intention of coming into harmony with a general law that applies to all men. A will governed from outside—be it even adherence to a divine command—is for Kant heteronomous. Therefore, any action arising from it can no longer be called moral.

Kant, who in his systematic thought surmounted and unrooted the philosophy of the Enlightenment and hereby its teaching regarding religion, picks up again in his writings on religion, in somewhat altered form, the thought-schemata of contemporaneous Enlightenment theologians. For morality based on the rational principle of autonomy requires no outward justification for right action, although that "which results from this right conduct of ours...cannot possibly be a matter of indifference to reason".[89] This goal towards which one strives is "the idea of a highest good in the world, for whose possibility we must postulate a higher, moral, most holy and omnipotent Being".[90] "Morality thus leads inevitably to religion, through which morality extends itself to the idea of a powerful moral lawgiver outside of man, whose will comprises the ultimate purpose of creation which at the same time can and should be mankind's ultimate purpose".[91] This new substantiation of natural religion or religion of reason—both expressions are used by Kant—connects his philosophical doctrine of religion in terminology and in content again with the philosophy of the Enlightenment. And just as in the latter, so here he contrasts the historical religions with the universal religion of reason. This contrast is now reinforced by the pair of opposites: autonomy and heteronomy. The historical religions as heteronomous religions, are therefore deprived of morality. The model example of an historical religion for Kant is *Judaism*, whose essential character he sees in its subordination to a divine law. Christianity, while stemming

---

[89] Religion within the Limits of Reason alone, preface to 1st ed. p. 4.
[90] loc. cit. pp. 4-5.
[91] loc. cit. pp. 5-6.

from Judaism, has in its diversion from the religious law still a share in natural religion and morality. Only when Christianity—according to Kant—manifests itself in ecclesiasticism and dogmatism is it likewise "sham" and "religious fantasy" like other historical religions.

With this philosophical wording Kant now outlines his picture of Judaism. This picture goes back to Spinoza. It dominated English and German Enlightenment theology, having its seeming authentic Jewish confirmation in Mendelssohn's *Jerusalem* which appeared a few years earlier.

Kant writes: "The Jewish faith . . . is an embodiment of mere statutory laws, upon which a political constitution was established. . . . . Judaism is really not a religion at all but purely an alliance of people who, since they belonged to a particular stock, formed themselves into a commonwealth under purely political laws". God is respected "merely as an earthly regent who makes absolutely no claims upon, and no appeals to, conscience. . . . Although the Ten Commandments . . . are to the eye of reason valid as ethical commands, yet in that legislation they are not so given as to induce obedience by laying demands upon moral disposition, but are plainly directed only to outer observance. . . . For a God who wants mere adherence to such commands, for which no improved moral disposition is required, is after all not really the moral Being whose concept we need for a religion". The prophets are only prophesying priests. "They had, as leaders of the people, burdened their constitution with so many ecclesiastical and consequent civil encumbrances that their state became completely unfit to exist for itself".[92]

This view of Judaism—appalling to Jewish ears—influenced Schleiermacher, Hegel, David Friedrich Strauss and others up to the present. It probably shapes the image of Judaism in wide circles even today. According to these statements it would appear as though Kant had never read the story of Creation, the Prophets or the Psalms, to say nothing of Jewish prayers, when he so sharply reproaches Judaism for want of religion, morals and inner piety. This is all the more astonishing when one considers Kant's other writings of the same period. For in his historical and ethical-philosophical writings of the same time he refers approvingly to Old Testament passages and ideas.[93]

This inconsistency and onesidedness of the Kantian argumentation, expressed in his "Religion within the Limits of Reason alone" and in "Conflict

---

[92] The above main passages on Kant's picture of Judaism are to be found in "Religion within the Limits of Pure Reason alone", pp. 116-118 and in "Conflict of the Faculties", p. 79-80, 131-132.

[93] 'Mutmaßlicher Anfang der Menschheitsgeschichte' (The Conjectural Beginning of the History of Mankind), 1786; 'Ueber das Mißlingen aller philosophischen Versuche in der Theodizee' (On the Futility of all philosophical attempts at a Theodicy) 1791. In this latter book, Job as a man of "uprightness of heart" is contrasted with his friends, who embody "the religion of currying favour". In the Critique of Judgement p. 124 he says in praise: "Perhaps there is no more sublime passage in the Jewish Book of the Law as the commandment 'Thou shalt not make unto thee any graven image' . . . The very same is true of the conception of the moral law". Hence, moral law plays an important role in Judaism after all.

of the Faculties", is explained by the religious political nature of these writings. They arose out of Kant's struggle against Prussian theological censorship, the regime of the Woellnerian Edicts on religion under Frederick William II, in the course of which Kant himself was reprimanded. He wanted to highlight the agreement of his ethical belief with Christianity in his polemics against ecclesiastical orthodoxy. Judaism served him in this connection only as a foil. He 'punched' the Jews and meant the ruling Prussian orthodoxy—"the dreadful voice of orthodoxy", as he calls it.[94]

However, when we follow up the reinterpretations of Christian-dogmatic conceptions, which Kant undertakes in his writings on religion in order to arrive at his interpretation of Christianity as "natural religion", we find remarkable inner relations and parallels to the basic theological conceptions of Judaism.[95] Original sin and the Fall of man, so fundamental to Christianity while absent in Judaism, are eliminated. The possibility of "the restoration of the original disposition towards goodness",[96] repentance and the ethical responsibility of man, which play such a central role in Judaism, are emphasized.[97] The divinity of Jesus is carefully dropped. He is mostly called "Teacher of the Gospel", and as "Son of God" is purely "representative of mankind".[98] Kantian religion thus tends in the direction of Judaism while at the same time considerably distancing itself from specific Christian-theological conceptions.[99]

This rather detailed presentation of Kant's philosophy of religion and his attitude to Judaism seemed necessary to me in order to indicate his influence upon both Jews and the modern Jewish philosophy of religion.

The powerful new influence emanating from contact with Kant and his philosophy had at first a disintegrating impact on his contemporaries, the first *Jewish Kantians*. It was probably this influence which for them ultimately destroyed the Mendelssohnian equilibrium between the religion of reason and revealed Law.

In Koenigsberg Kant had come into contact with Jews—mostly students —apparently quite early on. The Jewish element among his students must have been quite large. For when Kant first became Rector in 1786, among the nineteen signatories of his students, who presented him with a eulogistic poem, four were Jews.[100] Letters of commendation which Kant gave to some of his Jewish students reveal an accurate personal knowledge of them.

---

[94] Religion within the Limits of Reason alone, p. 121.
[95] See especially Cohen's and Guttman's Essays mentioned in footnote 75.
[96] Religion within . . . p. 40 ff. (General Observation).
[97] loc. cit. p. 46 ff.
[98] loc. cit. p. 54 ff.
[99] In this connection the difference between a living religion—like Judaism—and Kant's essentially philosophically orientated teaching should not, of course, be overlooked.
[100] Academy edition, vol. XII p. 406.

Among the younger members of the Mendelssohn circle was, as already mentioned, a group from Koenigsberg which was influenced by Kant. David Friedlaender—not really a disciple but an acquaintance—need not be discussed again. Kant remained in contact with him even after Friedlaender moved to Berlin in 1770.

Of Kant's Jewish students two achieved special significance: *Isaac Euchel* in Jewish intellectual history and *Marcus Herz* in intellectual history in general. Euchel's part in founding the *Ha-me'assef* has already been mentioned. Kant had applied on his behalf for a lectureship in Hebrew in the philosophical faculty, just at the time he became Rector. He himself as Rector then had to sign the letter of rejection to his Jewish pupil.[101a]

To none of his disciples, Jewish and non-Jewish alike, nor to any of his numerous correspondents, had Kant so close a relationship as to *Marcus Herz*. When in 1770 Kant became Professor of Philosophy in Koenigsberg, he named the twenty-one year old Jewish medical student Herz as respondent[101b] for the defence of the theses of his "inaugural dissertation", which formed the first expression of Kant's later critical philosophy. Herz then lived in Berlin as physician and medical writer. In his work he loved, as he once wrote to Kant, "strolling about in the borderlands of philosophy and medicine" (letter of 2.27.1786). Already in 1778, three years before the publication of the Critique of Pure Reason, Herz gave lectures on Kant's philosophy to the élite of Berlin of that time, including the Cabinet Minister von Zedlitz. He died in 1803 at the age of only fifty-six. His wife Henrietta was the center of attention of the first Berlin Salon. More important than Herz' own philosophical significance—which Kant entirely over-estimated —was, for the history of philosophy, the personal relationship between them. Marcus Herz—much the younger—was one of Kant's few personal friends, and this friendship deepened with the passage of years despite the geographical distance separating them. Cassirer has noticed the increasing cordiality of salutations in Kant's letters to Herz.[102] We can follow in this correspondence the growth of Kant's critical philosophy. We see how from an originally planned book on the limits of sensuousness and reason the "Critique of Pure Reason" came into being, the title of which first appears in a famous letter to Herz at the end of 1773. To none of his many correspondents does Kant give himself so directly and without the barriers of ceremonial politeness. From Koenigsberg he sought out his medical advice both for himself and even for friends, while entrusting Herz with the respon-

---

[101a]Academy-edition, vol. XII, "Official Correspondence" p. 426 ff.(Kant's letter to the Faculty of Philosophy of 3.20.1786—and p. 429 Kant's latter as Rector to Euchel of 5.24.1786).

[101b]It was a rule at all universities that candidates for higher grades or professorships had to defend their theses in public, choosing for this task as respondent (i.e. advocate) one of their students.

[102]Vide E. Cassirer, 'Kant's Leben und Lehre' (Kant's Life and Teaching) vol. X, p. 130 of Cassirer's edition of Kant.

sibility for the printing and binding of the "Critique" and for the distribution of complimentary copies.

However, despite this close personal relationship, Herz, who had formed a close link with Mendelssohn in Berlin, was more a philosopher of the Enlightenment, more Mendelssohnian than Kantian. He once said to Solomon Maimon that he really did not understand Kant's Critique of Pure Reason.[103] Herz translated the missive to Cromwell of the Amsterdam rabbi Manasseh Ben Israel "Defence of the Jews"—prefaced by Mendelssohn—which was instrumental in the resettlement of Jews in England. Although sharing in the endeavours of the Mendelssohn circle now and again, Herz was apparently estranged from Jewish custom. He received the title of Professor of Philosophy in 1787.

Herz' friend *Lazarus Bendavid*, mentioned in the previous chapter, though not a student of Kant was one of his keenest followers. He lectured on Kant in Vienna and Berlin and was so full of Kantian ideas that he took over Kant's distorted view of Judaism, making the struggle against "the shameful senseless ceremonial law" his life task in his Jewish activity.[104]

The attitude of *Solomon Maimon* (1754-1800) was different. This fruitful critic and continuer of Kant, as is well known, deeply influenced Fichte, and many of his methodical ideas were later freshly developed in Cohen's neo-Kantianism. He became important for logic by introducing a logical calculus of his own.

Maimon too considered himself outside the religious and legal obligations of Judaism. As philosopher he thought he was entitled to be above them. But he had the highest respect for rabbinic ethical teaching. He took his surname from Maimonides, the great Jewish philosopher of the Middle Ages. In his autobiography he gives a comprehensive presentation of Maimonides' principal work and wrote—according to Kantian and his own philosophy—a Hebrew commentary on the first part of "Guide for the Perplexed".[105] In the 'Berlinische Monatsschrift'—organ of the enlighteners in Berlin—to which Kant contributed many articles, he published an essay (1789) 'Probe rabbinischer Philosophie' (Sample of Rabbinic Philosophy).[106]

Solomon Seligmann *Pappenheim* (1740-1814) was not a follower or continuer of Kant but his opponent. Member of the Breslau Rabbinical Court, Pappenheim was one of the first rabbis to publish philosophical

[103] Solomon Maimon, 'Geschichte des eigenen Lebens' (History of his own Life), ed. by K.P. Moritz, Berlin, 1792, p. 254.

[104] Cf. Bendavid's essay 'Etwas zur Charakteristik der Juden' (On Jewish Characteristics), 1793, Cf. also Lewkowitz, p. 67.

[105] This commentary *Giv'at Hamoreh* was printed along with the edition of Maimonides' "Guide for the Perplexed" published by Euchel (Berlin 1798). N. Rotenstreich and Hugo Bergmann published Maimon's commentary separately in 1965 in Jerusalem without the text of the "Guide". The commentary on the second and third parts of the 'Guide' was written by Isaac Satanov.

[106] Cf. also Noah J. Jacob's 'Solomon Maimon's Relation to Judaism', Yearbook VIII of the Leo Baeck Institute, London, 1963 p. 177 ff.

works in the German language.[107] He was concerned with the 'speculative dilemma' of the existence of God in which he defended the ontological proof of God's existence. Another of his writings gives a theological slant to the problem of time, according to which time is the hall-mark—the distinctive feature—of all creation.—Although Pappenheim's German philosophical works are today forgotten, his influence as a Hebrew poet has been more lasting. Taking Edward Young's "Night Thoughts" as his model, he composed a four-part poetical work *Arba Kossot* (Four Goblets), which appeared in 1790 and was successively reprinted for decades. He also published polemical writings in the strict orthodox spirit against the early efforts at Reform.

The older among Kant's Jewish followers like Bendavid, Herz and Maimon had, as we saw, taken over Kant's description of Judaism as a religion of statutory law. They had reinterpreted Judaism as a mere doctrine of ethics, which beyond its strict monotheism retained little that was specifically Jewish.

The volatilization of religion into a pure ethic was one of the forms in which the Kantian influence found expression in the life and life-style of many Jews. It also fitted in with the tendencies of the Jewish struggle for emancipation in minimizing the differences between Jewish and Gentile citizens. In this form the rigorism of the Kantian ethic—felt congenial to Judaism—influenced many generations of Jews. Until the nineteenth century this influence is difficult to verify literarily for those gripped by it were not writers but mostly business people, doctors and lawyers unaccustomed to reflecting their life style in writing.

In the nineteenth—the "historical"—century Kant's influence on the Jews changed. The historical perspective now coming into fashion began to affect the attitude towards Jewish tradition. The religious law—for Kant the essential and rigid factor in Judaism—became itself, especially with the Jewish reform-theologians, a historical factor subject to development,[108] as will be seen later. But with this, the negative Kantian delineation of Judaism was shaken. The opportunity was now given to reach a new evolutionary appreciation of the concept of Law in Judaism. The Jewish philosophy of religion could now orientate itself towards the Kantian systematic philosophy in general and not just towards his ethics.

This attitude did not manifest itself in the first pioneers of the Wissenschaft of Judaism. Not until the middle of the century do we meet in *Manuel Joel*, lecturer at the Breslau Rabbinical Seminary, a convinced Kantian, who

---

[107] Pappenheim had a predecessor in this in the Regensburg rabbi, Isaac Alexander (ca. 1722-ca. 1800). Cf. M. Kayserling in MGJW vol. XVI (1868) p. 161 ff.

On Pappenheim cf. J. L. Landau, "Short lectures on Modern Hebrew Literature", London 1938, p. 83 ff., and H.-J. Schoeps, 'Geschichte der jüdischen Religionsphilosophie in der Neuzeit' (History of the Jewish Philosophy of Religion in Modern Times), Berlin 1935, p. 61 ff. note.

[108] On this matter comp. especially N. Rotenstreich, loc. cit. p. 41 ff.

applied the new historical approach to his own religious and philosophical-historical works. It also found expression in his activity as a moderately conservative rabbi in Breslau.

At the end of the century the well-known *Voelkerpsychologe* (proponent of a psychology of nations), *Moritz Lazarus*, tried to make the Kantian concept of autonomy into the basis of an "ethic of Judaism". The synthesis of Kant and Judaism finally culminated in the comprehensive Jewish philosophy of religion of *Hermann Cohen*.

A different and quite individual approach was taken by *Solomon Ludwig Steinheim*, who arrived at his supernatural doctrine of revelation from the theoretical and not the ethical motifs of Kant.

As recently as 1925, *Franz Rosenzweig* wrote indignantly that we made our spiritual Jewishness dependent on whether we could be Kantians.[109] *Julius Guttmann*, the historian of Jewish philosophy, and *Leo Baeck*, the last significant representative and leader of German Jewry, belonged to these Jewish Kantians—so important was the role of Kantian philosophical analysis, not Kant's own attitude, to the understanding of Judaism up to our time.

[109] 'Die Bauleute' (The Builders), Philo Verlag, Berlin 1925. Cf. Rosenzweig, 'Kleine Schriften' (Minor Writings), p. 103 ff.

# CHAPTER 12

## *Revolution and Restoration*

The disciples of Mendelssohn were contemporaries of that turbulent era during which the entire political, social and cultural structure of Europe was transformed in the aftermath of the French Revolution, the revolutionary wars and of the new restorative order. For the Jews it was the beginning of their struggles for civil emancipation. The rapid succession of outward events with their political changes affected in a similarly rapid manner the life style and mental attitude of Jews.

I have tried to show that the Jews of central and western Europe did not enter the whirl of this epoch of revolution entirely unprepared. The view that they had to make up, so to speak, in one generation for that which had taken several generations to bring about[110] in the non-Jewish world, certainly needs correcting. The great mass of contemporary Gentile artisans, townspeople and peasants had hardly participated in the process that led to the Enlightenment and its concept of man and society. The upheaval had come even more suddenly perhaps for these people than for the broad strata of Jews, whom the loosening of the traditional Jewish way of life had already affected.

These loosenings, however, now took on a galloping intensity. Outward events and catchwords became for the generation between 1790 and 1820 the leading and often sole criterion of Jewish orientation. For equality and brotherhood seemed attainable and claimable only if Jews adapted to the majority among whom they lived—in way of life, customs, language and in the very forms of their religious service. Such adaptation was already the requirement of the Tolerance Laws of Joseph II and of the later Prussian legislation. It was likewise called for by the revolutionaries of the French National Assembly and by Napoleon. Behind the seductive slogans pro-

---

[110] See e.g. Max Wiener, 'Juedische Religion im Zeitalter der Emanzipation' (Jewish Religion in the Age of Emancipation), Berlin, 1933.—On the civil integration of Jews see Jacob Toury, Prolegomena to the Acceptance of Jews to German Citizenry (Hebrew), Tel Aviv, 1972.

claiming a homogeneous brotherly national people, propagated both by
the Revolution and the enlightened absolutism in Austria and Prussia, lay
the frequently undisguised intention of letting the Jews disappear as Jews
among their fellow-citizens. Behind it—in secularised form—stood the old
Christian theological view that Judaism was a relic of a past age which in
the Christian and now modern world no longer had any right to exist.

Many Jewish spokesmen of that time were prepared to accept the demand
for assimilation and adaptation as a precondition of civil equality. We saw
this in the case of Bendavid and Friedlaender. But while they both nevertheless adhered to the religious individuality of Judaism, though ready if
need be, to *confessionalize* it, others proceeded to total self-surrender
through baptism. That equality of rights means the same rights for a minority in recognition of its singularity was appreciated at that time neither by
Jews nor Gentiles.

Seldom did so clear an interplay of ideas and events become evident, or
conversely of events and their intellectual consequences, as in the era of
Revolution and Restoration. The ideas of the Enlightenment had till then
been the common bond of only an élite of writers, scholars and officials
who stood as a "neutral society" outside or above the traditional class order.

At the end of the eighteenth century these ideas were to become a political
force. In the French Revolution of 1789 they had gained mastery over one
of the leading nations of Europe. Beginning from France they conquered
—partly through the revolutionary armies, partly through the beacon-like
French example—the European continent.[111]

But the path from the Declaration of Human and Civil Rights via the
French National Assembly in August 1789 until the application of the new
principles to Jews was at first strewn with obstacles. It took a further two
years before citizens' rights were granted to French Jews as a whole. The

[111] Already about a hundred years previously, concepts of natural right and freedom of conscience
had attained political importance in several North-American colonies. In the constitution of South
Carolina which was formulated with the assistance of Locke in 1669, freedom of conscience was also
guaranteed to Jews, heathen and dissenters, though in most other colonies only given to the various
Christian denominations. The American Declaration of Human Rights of 1776 preceded the French.
Yet we may disregard this historical priority of the USA in our context. Those events still lay at
that time outside the European scene and may scarcely have influenced the events in Europe. We may
not disarrange perspectives or confuse the small remote USA of 1776 or 1789 with that present day
world power. Moreover, the declaratory regulations of the Union's Constitution were often limited
by the constitutions of individual states and even by those constitutions drawn up during or after the
War of Independence. In Maryland, for example, Jews could be voted into public office only in 1826
after long parliamentary struggles. In New Hampshire the last restrictions against non-Protestants
only disappeared in 1877. The proclaimed equality was granted to negro slaves only after the Civil
War. Equal rights for negroes is still being fought for today. Even Moses Mendelssohn concluded his
*Jerusalem* with the pessimistic remark: "Alas! we hear in the Congress debates in America the old
song strike up again of a dominating religion." This was written in 1783 some years after the "Bill of
Rights"—a sign as to how careful we have to be in assessing the influence of the American Revolution
on European events.

advocates of equality, Mirabeau—who had come to know Mendelssohn and Dohm in Berlin and already in 1787 achieved prominence with a book on Mendelssohn and Jewish emancipation—the Abbé Grégoire, Clermont Tonnerre[112] and Robespierre were faced with a strong anti-Jewish opposition. This opposition was led by delegates from Alsace[113] who knew how to thwart implementation of the announced principles under ever new pretexts and threats of popular risings. The civil equality of Jews was first adopted on the 27 September 1791, two days before the dissolution of the First National Assembly, and became law in November.

The civil equality of rights finally obtained was borne through Europe by the revolutionary armies and implemented in those countries dependent on or conquered by France: Holland and Switzerland, the new kingdom of Westphalia, the Rhineland and the Hanseatic cities temporarily annexed to France. This equality also penetrated to some extent, though hesitantly, the Confederation of Rhenish States. But in France itself it received a serious setback under *Napoleon*.

The equality of rights for Jews brought about through the French Revolution began to be restricted by Napoleon by means of special laws. In 1806 he called a meeting of Jewish notables in Paris in order to bring the French Jews to a major surrender of their Jewish identity through a combination of intimidation and apparent imperial benevolence. The *Assembly of Notables* was furnished with twelve questions. These questions concerned in part the relation of Jewish law, notably matrimonial law, to the provisions of the French Civil Code and in part the religious regulations pertaining to the economic activity of Jews, particularly on the matter of charging interest. Having deliberated for several months, the Assembly of Notables answered the questions entirely as the government had intended. They were under the clear impression that continuation of citizens' rights for Jews—possibly even their rights of residence and livelihood—would depend on a satisfactory reply to the questions. Most members of the assembly, moreover, were suffused by the spirit of self-surrender—which in the post-Mendelssohn era was widespread in western Europe—combined with a special desire to evince their loyalty and patriotism. Consequently they sometimes gave in their answers more than was expected of them, by declaring e.g. that the Jews of France were now simply Frenchmen of Jewish religion; that a Jewish nation no longer existed and that accordingly foreign Jews were now for them mere

[112] From him comes the sentence: "To the Jews as a nation, nothing; to the Jews as individuals, everything" (Session of 12.23.1789)—a sentence illustrating again the constant tendency even among liberal friends of Jews to couple equality with adaptation and abandonment of individuality.

[113] The majority of Jews in France, estimated about fifty thousand at that time, lived in Alsace-Lorraine. A second major group lived in the former papal districts around Avignon and about three thousand "Portuguese" in Bordeaux with its semi-legal branch community in Paris. Jews lived therefore merely in the peripheral regions, which only with the passage of time had fallen to France. They had been banished from the French ancestral countries in 1394.

foreigners. To other questions careful diplomatic answers were given, as for example regarding mixed marriages. The latter were recognised as valid under civil law but could not receive religious consecration.

Napoleon was satisfied with the decisions of the Assembly of Notables, but wanted to give it additional religious sanction. He resumed the old institution of the *Sanhedrin* (Synhedrion) that had existed at the time of the Second Temple, having been in its time the highest tribunal of religious and legal jurisdiction.

In 1806 Napoleon announced the convocation of a new Sanhédrin in Paris. Like the old Sanhedrin the new one had seventy-one members, who came mostly from France and the countries she ruled.

The "Sanhedrin" assembled in February 1807 with great pomp. Since its only function consisted in confirming the decisions of the Assembly of Notables of the previous year, it had only a few sittings. Hence, after confirmation of all the answers it was immediately dissolved.

Although only delegates from France and countries under French influence participated in the Sanhedrin, Napoleon's gain in prestige was very far-reaching among Jews. When he visited Poland for the founding of the Grand Duchy of Warsaw he was enthusiastically received by the Polish Jews, although they knew neither the political purpose of convoking the Sanhedrin nor that of its decisions.

What is interesting, however, is that the decisions of the Sanhedrin did not only represent an act of Napoleonic national policy. Some of these decisions also expressed the honest opinion of many enlightened Jews. They formed, so to speak, the "Magna Charta" of the later reformatory efforts in Germany and were explicitly sanctioned at the first Assembly of Rabbis in Brunswick in 1844.

The Jews of France were then thanked for their submissiveness through the notorious *Décret Infâme*, which Napoleon enacted about a year after the Sanhedrin "show". In this edict the freedom of movement of Jews was withdrawn for a period of ten years, their occupational activity made dependent on references of good character, which they had to obtain from the largely anti-Jewish local authorities in Alsace, and regulations of a similar nature stipulated.

The restrictions of the Décret Infâme affected in the main the Jews of Alsace and in general the German Départements of France including those annexed by Napoleon. Here they remained in force for decades even after the collapse of French rule, although the ten-year period to which Napoleon limited his decree had long since expired. Until 1848, for example, Jews from the Rhineland needed a character reference from the local authority before entering business or a profession. In the restored Bourbon kingdom of France, on the other hand, that otherwise had the name of being extremely reactionary, the French Jews had in 1818 again become citizens enjoying equal rights. In the kingdom of Westphalia, the most important Napoleonic satellite country, the edict was not introduced at all, although the other part of the Napoleonic reorganisation of Jewish life, the Consistorial Constitution, was adopted.

The *Consistorial Constitution*, that new pattern of organisation of Jews enacted soon after the great Sanhedrin "show" and on the same day as the Décret Infâme, disbanded the local communities. The intention was to strike at the heart of Jewish life and fragment it. In place of the community a consistoire, namely, a regional representation of Jewry, was established in every Département exceeding two thousand Jews. The consistories were composed of a *Grandrabbin*, and where necessary, of an additional rabbi, and of three lay members chosen by twenty-five notables named by the authorities. A central consistory in Paris supervised the regional bodies. The task of the consistories—apart from responsibility for the synagogue service and religious education—was to carry out Sanhedrial decisions. In addition, compliance of Jews with military service was to be supervised. Only with Napoleon III was a democratic system of voting for the consistories introduced.

Although the consistories were intended to be an instrument in the supervisory policy of the government and to destroy the community organisation of the Jewish population, in practice they adopted the tasks of the former communities. Since the separation of Church and State in France in 1905, the French Jews have retained the consistorial constitution as a voluntary administrative institution till the present day—a sign that it has stood the test and met the collective, organisational, social and religious needs of the Jewish population.

Events in France gave renewed stimulus to the emancipatory tendencies in those countries that formed the great coalition against France during the revolutionary wars.

In *Austria*, it is true, after the Edicts of Tolerance of Joseph II, the trend rather was retrogressive. The ambiguity of Joseph's Jewish policy—taking with one hand what the other gave or linking its advantages to impossible preconditions—has already been described. It was the first European country to introduce military service (1787) for Jews—a measure that met with resistance not only in the non-Jewish population and in the army. The Jews of Bohemia and Galicia saw in this step the aim of forceably diverting young people from the practice of religious duties and customs, making way for apostasy from their paternal religion.

In 1797 a *Juden-systemal Patent* for Bohemia, Moravia and Austrian-Silesia was enacted, incorporating inter alia the regulations of a former law, the *Familiantengesetz* (Familiants Law) of 1726. In this law the number of Jews permitted to live in each part of the country was again laid down. A Jew could only marry and raise a family when a number became free for him through the death of another and when he passed an examination in the

German language. Under Joseph's successors till 1848 these worsening trends increased even if there were sporadic movements in the opposite direction. After 1810, for example, a Jew in Austria could become an army officer.

In *Prussia* immediately after the death of Frederick the Great, Jews tried to obtain a revision of the legislation, replacing the General Reglement of 1750. The new monarch, Frederick William II, had raised hopes of this just after his accession to the throne. In the same year he abolished the body tax, the porcelain tax and the collective liability of Jews in cases of theft and bankruptcy. But the negotiations of the representatives of the Jews with a royal commission was protracted for six years till 1793. The final draft agreement drawn up by the government satisfied the Jewish representatives so little that they had the courage to turn it down, preferring instead to abide by the old regulation. The equality the Revolution had brought to the Jews in France gave moral support to their Prussian brethren.

A few years later deliberations on a liberalisation of Jewish policy were again resumed in the departments of government. A glance at the development in France must have shown pro-Enlightenment officials that also in Prussia—the country of Mendelssohn—a change of policy towards the Jews could not be postponed. Due to the divisioning of Poland, however, great masses of Jews had come under Prussian rule, posing a serious new problem for the authorities, since the slackening in Jewish life-style—long since taken root in Germany—and the Enlightenment had barely spread to Poland with the different social structure of its Jewish population. But the entire problem-complex was now set in motion. From the circles of enlightened bureaucracy there emerged a number of books on the Jewish question. *Johann Balthasar Koenig* published in 1790 his 'Annalen der Juden in den preussischen Staaten' (Annals of the Jews in the Prussian States) which is also important as source material. In 1804 *Terlinden* printed his compilation of the legal position of Jews in Prussia and of Jewish law.[114] On the other side, a wave of anti-Jewish literature appeared, which again called forth refutations from Jewish and non-Jewish quarters alike.

The national crisis brought on by the defeat of the Prussians at Jena and Auerstaedt in 1806 did not seriously affect preoccupation with the Jewish problem. On the contrary, this problem now apparently became much simpler as the Polish territories were for the greater part taken again from Prussia. The new city regulations of the Baron von Stein in 1808, establishing communal self-administration, gave the Prussian Jews municipal citizens' rights and thereby the right to vote in, and be voted for, municipal bodies. As a result, David Friedlaender and Abraham Mendelssohn—son of Moses and father of the composer Felix Mendelssohn-Bartholdy—became

---

[114] R. F. Terlinden, 'Grundsaetze des Judenrechts nach den Gesetzen fuer die preussischen Staaten' (Principles of Jewish law according to the laws of the Prussian states), Halle 1804. Terlinden was a government official in Hamm.

the first Jewish city-councilors in Berlin. After the liberal *Hardenberg* became Chancellor of State (Prime Minister), the formulation of the new laws affecting Jews was soon completed. On March 11, 1812, the *Edict ueber die buergerlichen Verhaeltnisse der Juden in den preussischen Staaten* (Edict on the civil status of Jews in the Prussian States) was issued, declaring the Jews of Prussia citizens of that state. They had to adopt permanent surnames and use the German language in business transactions. They could take up residence wherever they wished, acquire land, practise the teaching profession and serve on local boards. They could trade without restriction and were exempted from all special taxes. This of course entailed paying general taxes and fulfilling the duties of a citizen including military service. The special jurisdiction of rabbis and the Jewish bench, on the other hand, was terminated. The question as to whether Jews could be admitted to public or state posts was to be reserved for future attention. During the later period of reaction some of the stipulations of the Prussian Edict were withdrawn, as for example admission to academic and other teaching posts. The points postponed for future ruling remained indefinite for decades, such as eligibility for the civil service. Yet, by and large, the Prussian Edict of Emancipation was for a long time pace-setting and certainly the most liberal in Germany.

In these years before the wars of liberation against Napoleon the legal position of Jews was revised not only in Prussia but also in other German countries. The most far-reaching was the regulation in Baden where the Jewish religion was recognised as one of the three official faiths. Jews were granted citizenship of the country but, remarkably, still not local civil rights. Other German states like Bavaria, for example, took the very opposite line of granting local civil rights but not state citizenship.

Jews too were gripped by the wave of patriotic enthusiasm of the wars of liberation. They rallied in great numbers to the flags, received the Iron Cross and promotion to rank of officer. Yet hardly was the war over and Napoleon exiled to St. Helena when the Jews, who together with their Christian fellow-citizens had just previously fought with enthusiastic public approval, were relegated again to their old position.

Soldiers returning home felt the first blow. Ex-servicemen had been promised employment in the civil service by the Prussian king. Jews were again excluded from this. Even holders of the Iron Cross were not admitted, since, as the Prussian Minister of Justice put it, "the suspicion of a lack of morality is not refuted by temporary bravery."[115] But when a Jew converted to Christianity he was to become entitled to all the privileges of Christian subjects. Thus a premium was quite openly put on perfidy and lack of

---

[115] I. Freund, 'Emancipation der Juden in Preussen' (Emancipation of the Jews in Prussia), Berlin, 1912, vol. II, p. 466.

character, as though precisely lack of loyalty to the Jewish faith proved a moral quality. The validity of the Emancipatory Law of 1812 was confined to the territory that remained Prussian after the defeat of Jena. Furthermore, the Edict itself was undermined by later royal *Cabinet-Ordres*. The provision in the Edict for teaching and academic posts was annulled in 1822. It was proposed that the choice of taking Christian forenames should be forbidden. There even ensued a direct interference in religious liberty by prohibiting sermons in German and any change in the synagogue service.

The behaviour of the Prussian authorities, notably that of the king, was disappointing and humiliating. And the conduct of the Free Hanseatic Cities, of the Free City of Frankfurt and of other states, was a crude regression into old attitudes.

The future civil status of Jews in all the states of the German Confederation was to be regulated at the *Congress of Vienna*.[116] With the consent of Hardenberg and Metternich, *Wilhelm von Humboldt* had submitted a draft of a German Constitution. It included the sentence: "Those professing the Jewish faith will, so long as they take upon themselves the performance of all civil duties, be granted corresponding civil rights". The Humboldt draft did not win acceptance in the debates of the Congress on this paragraph— later article 16 of the Act of Confederation. Only a recommendation was accepted which ran: ". . . to consider how in as unanimous a manner as possible the civil standing of those professing the Jewish faith in Germany is to be effected and in particular how they may be ensured the enjoyment of citizens' rights in return for the assumption of all civic obligations. In any case they will until then receive the rights already granted *in* the confederate states". With this the status quo created by the French had at any rate been retained. This already accepted wording appeared unwarrantable to the Free Cities. They pressed their viewpoint upon the Editorial Commission and in the subsequent published minutes of the Confederation Act of June 8, 1816 the little word "in" had been substituted for with the word "*by*". The Jews, however, had not received equality of rights *by* the federated states of Hamburg, Luebeck, Frankfurt or Bremen, but by the French, so that these states had legal ground for depriving Jews again of their rights.

The years of occupation and war had meanwhile created a serious economic crisis. The population, having expected economic recovery and political reforms to follow victory, made the Jews—as ever— scapegoats for their disappointments. Moreover, patriotic enthusiasm was now pursuing a fierce nationalism. At the same time discussion of the Jewish question had produced an anti-Jewish political literature. Best known were the writings of a Berlin historian, Ruehs, and a frightful piece of writing by the noted philosopher Fries in Heidelberg, who already at that time was calling for

---

[116] Cf. S. Baron, 'Die Judenfrage auf dem Wiener Kongress' (The Jewish question at the Congress of Vienna). Vienna and Berlin, 1920.

the physical wiping out of the Jews root and branch. After the murder of the poet Kotzebue by the student Sand, the students' association had been prohibited. The hatred against Metternich, who was responsible for this prohibition, was in a remarkable way also in this case deflected onto the Jews. It was argued, that the Jewish bankers in their capacity as creditors of the Austrian government, were partly to blame for Metternich's policy. In Wuerzburg student unrest and riots broke out against the Jewish population, spreading like wildfire over a great many cities such as Heidelberg, Frankfurt and Hamburg. After the student battlecry: "Hep! Hep![117] Jud verreck" (Hep, Hep, death to the Jews!), these riots have been called the Hep-hep disorders.

The national policy towards Jews coming from the spirit of the Enlightenment—irrespective of whether it was liberal, as in France and in the Prussia of Hardenberg and Humboldt, or whether it stemmed from the mentality of benevolent absolutism as in Austria—had one thing in common: the new state no longer wanted to tolerate special separate groups. It had succeeded in the course of the eighteenth century in its struggle against the estates and guild bodies. Now these same Jews, having served the state as one of the instruments in the undermining of the old framework of society, remained the only single group to be harshly differentiated from the rest of the population. In dress, language and way of life they seemed a backward element. Proffered improvement in their legal status was therefore coupled with educational measures, as they were called. This was done in the selfish interest of the state, which wanted to make this group disappear by adapting to the majority. Legal concession was coupled with cultural adaptation. However, when Jews underwent baptism they automatically received equality, as well as premiums of a tangible kind.

The character and function of the Jewish communities themselves underwent a fundamental change in the era of emancipation. The communities in the eighteenth century had still quite a large measure of autonomy that was actually encouraged and supported by the governments. Even though the elected community heads had to be confirmed by the authorities, the latter entrusted them with the distribution of taxes among their members. Assistance to the poor, care of the sick and education lay in the communities' hands. Community discipline, and control of inner Jewish legal matters in particular, had been left to the communities and rabbinical courts. This included matrimonial and hereditary rights, together with some limited civil legal cases and petty offences such as insults, brawls, violations of community discipline and the like.

Even where the *civil-legal jurisdiction* was formally reserved for the public courts, Jews preferred to bring their frequent business differences before

---

[117] This anti-Jewish rallying cry was then said to be formed as an acronym of *Hierosolyma est perdita* ("Jerusalem is lost").

Jewish bodies. Already in the Talmudic era it was considered objectionable to turn to outside courts with their sometimes religious and morally doubtful legal principles and procedures. With the Jewish court one was sure of getting justice quickly without long-winded and abstruse formalities and according to familiar legal principles. The enforceability of judgements could mostly be secured under warning or application of a ban.

Fear of the ban and therefore of community discipline had, as a result of the general slackenings, lost their socially compelling power—and with it the authority of the rabbinical courts had declined. Jews, on the other hand, precisely in virtue of the juridical functions of the rabbis, formed that secluded and distinct corporate entity within the state which stood in contrast to the social ideal of the Enlightenment. For this reason all the emancipatory laws aimed at dissolving the special character of the Jewish communities and making them into pure religious organisations. No matter how varied in method and principle the emancipative legislation of the German states and those beyond were, they all had this point in common: abolition of the disciplinary and juridical power of the rabbis and community heads. Education—even in those places where there were special Jewish schools—was now incorporated into the state educational system, including teacher-training and in some countries even the training and appointment of rabbis. This diminution of Jewish autonomy was meant to contribute to the fragmentation of Jewry and especially to its disappearance as a special group.

It is interesting that this upheaval in broad circles of Jewry in Germany and western Europe was not experienced as a coercive measure. Instead it was accepted and welcomed by Jewry in all its trends, including the conservative and orthodox, so much had the striving after participation in the surrounding culture and after civil equality overshadowed every other aspect.

Nothing is perhaps more characteristic of the new attitude than the astonishing ease with which the representatives and guardians of the unbroken tradition, the orthodox circles, relinquished their rabbinical jurisdiction. Only the Altona Chief Rabbinate still retained civil jurisdiction of first instance until 1863, the year Jewish emancipation came into effect in Holstein and Schleswig. Nevertheless in orthodox circles everywhere it still often remained the practice in matters of dispute to consult a rabbi or Jewish arbitrator who adjudicated according to Jewish law. But this was now entirely an act of voluntary jurisdiction and no longer a compulsory religious or social injunction.

This silent relinquishing by Jewish *Orthodoxy* of its own religiously founded jurisdiction was a much more drastic sign of assimilation than for example the contemporaneous changes in the synagogue service of the Reform movement. Here one quarter of the codified religious law in the *Shulḥan*

*Arukh* was de facto dropped,[118] namely, that part representing the corner-stone of the old autonomy.

Meanwhile in general intellectual life the Enlightenment had been super-seded by new trends. Rousseau was already combining enlightenment-tendencies with a utopian romantic call for the return to nature. All Europe became enraptured with songs appearing under the name of Ossian, a leg-endary Scottish bard. In Germany the intellectual world of Lessing and Mendelssohn, of Lichtenberg, Haller and Kant was taken over by a new movement. With the young Goethe, Herder and others of this circle a new intellectual attitude made its presence felt, beginning as *Sturm und Drang* (Storm and Stress) and leading into Romanticism. No longer was reason the measure of all things. The full development of the individual personality was now the ideal. It encouraged the bypassing of conventional values and moral judgements. "Genius" claimed its own right to some extent beyond good and evil.

Added to this were two further tendencies. From the élite-concept of En-lightenment circles there arose in England the Order of Freemasons. Into the ritual of their Order—surrounded from the beginning with the mantle of exclusiveness and secrecy—mystical ideas very soon intruded. These twined round the deistic-enlightenment heart of the Order's principles, in many cases eventually obscuring it. Hebrew words and Kabbalistic expressions found their way into the vocabulary of the Freemasons—and even more so into that of the Rosicrucians—heightening the aura of the incomprehensible and mysterious. Mysticism itself, which Swedenborg represented in Sweden, St. Martin in France and Hamann in Germany, found new followers. And cosmopolitanism—prevalent for so long and expressed in the Latin of the Church and of the enlightened world of learning and in the French of the court circles—was supplanted by concepts of nationalism. The Middle Ages, hitherto considered as a barbaric past, was rediscovered. Bookshops were full of novels on chivalry. Goethe wrote his *Goetz*. The concept of individ-ualism was personified in personages of national antiquity. Besides this was the sense of mission of the French revolutionary army, intent on spreading freedom, equality and brotherhood with the edge of the sword—thereby establishing the national pride of France, *la Grande Nation*.

As a reaction to this there developed in the occupied or conquered coun-tries a self-styled nationalism that was not only anti-French but very soon became hostile to everything foreign. This new nationalism, called "German-

---

[118] Following Jacob ben Asher's model in the fourteenth century, Joseph Caro had classified the *Shulḥan Arukh* into four parts: daily duties, order of prayer, Sabbath and Holy Day prayers (*Oraḥ Ḥayim*); dietary laws and provisions for ritual slaughter (*Yoreh Deah*); marriage and divorce law (*Even Ha'Eser*); civil-law (*Ḥoshen Mishpat*)—the part now becoming irrelevant.

omania" by Saul Ascher, was especially anti-Jewish, since Jews—always the easiest target—appeared as the most conspicuous beneficiaries of the hated French revolutionary ideas in virtue of the improvement in their civil status. This nationalism now replaced the liberal catchwords of the revolution with the *Volksgeist* (national spirit), that seemingly manifested itself in the fixed social order of the past, with its ancient laws and customs. The political restoration in the years after the fall of Napoleon took root in this soil. It had for a long time stifled the first beginnings of a patriotic freedom-movement, which wanted to translate into political reality the liberal tendencies of the Enlightenment. In Prussia Hardenberg and Wilhelm von Humboldt succumbed to court circles and to the "Holy Alliance", which had been founded by Czar Alexander II, Metternich and European reaction in order to build a Europe of emphatically Christian states.

The transition from the ideas of the Enlightenment to this Romanticism was, for all that, quite fluid. Much as Kant, for example, had unmasked and destroyed the self-certainty of Enlightenment-philosophy, he still belongs in his scientific as in his political ideas to the Enlightenment and its rational method. The same would be said of Solomon Maimon. Fichte, however, was already taking over from Maimon the subjective interpretation of Kant and passing it on to Schelling and Hegel—the real philosophers of Romanticism. Herder's introduction of the principle of evolutionary development and of national character influenced both the Historical School of Jurisprudence and the historiography of the nineteenth century, whereas Schiller, for example, stands closer as historian and poet to the way of thinking of the Enlightenment.

A new generation, meanwhile, had also arisen among the Jews. This second generation after Mendelssohn, the sons and daughters of his disciples who had been brought up in the values of German culture, were soon captivated by the new trends of German literature. This was especially true of women, the daughters of well-to-do Jewish families. In place of a Jewish education, which in the case of girls had been generally neglected, and in place of the atmosphere of a Jewish family, they had received a purely secular and in particular aesthetic education. Literary circles formed themselves around some of these female personalities. The young poets, philosophers and theologians, the men of genius, as well as members of the aristocracy and royal house frequented their *salons*. In these neutral Jewish homes outside the social barriers and demarcations of rank, circles could meet which otherwise never came socially together. They filled "the gaps of the missing upper middle class".[119]

The difference between the generations is well illustrated in the case of *Marcus Herz* and his wife Henrietta, who was about seventeen years his

---

[119] Cf. Sigmar Ginsburg, 'Die zweite Generation der Juden nach M. Mendelssohn' (The second Generation of Jews after M. Mendelssohn). In the Bulletin of the LBI No. 2, Tel Aviv, 1958, pp. 62-72.

junior. Here two generations and two intellectual attitudes met. The circle
of the Jewish medical doctor, Herz, comprised the friends and disciples of
Mendelssohn and Kant, e.g. Friedlaender, the Minister von Zedlitz, Biester,
Kiesewetter and the contributors to the 'Berlinische Monatsschrift' (Berlin
monthly magazine). The circle of *Henrietta Herz* included the brothers
Humboldt, Novalis and Jean Paul, Schlegel and Schleiermacher. Here Dorothy
Mendelssohn came to know Friedrich Schlegel for whose sake she left her
husband. She became Protestant and married Schlegel, the literary oracle of
the younger generation, later converting with him to Catholicism. Henrietta
Herz was of a less passionate nature than her friend Dorothy. She had a
strong sense for the essential traits of the new literary and intellectual
movement. She was bound to her friends by veneration for Goethe. The
Goethe-cult of the Romantic intelligentsia found one of its first centres in
her Salon. She formed a lifelong friendship with Schleiermacher and was
baptized under his influence in 1817—though she waited till after the death
of her mother before taking this step. Her husband had already died in 1803.

Perhaps the most important of these Jewesses, at any rate the most active,
was *Rahel Levin*, a gifted letter writer and author. She married the much
younger diplomat *Varnhagen*, converting at this time to Christianity. She
was probably the only one of these women whose Jewish consciousness remained alert and who described herself a leaf torn off from the Jewish tree.

The Berlin Salons—to which the Viennese Salon of the Berlin-born Fanny
Arnstein also belonged and which the diplomats of the Congress of Vienna
visited—with their cult of the beautiful and the sentimental had brought a
new element into Jewish life. Their aesthetically orientated life-style affected
a wider stratum of the Jewish middle class. People wanted to show off their
education and taste to the world around—something that certainly did not
always happen in the most dexterous manner and often provoked ridicule
and criticism. In the salon circles and among its fellow-travellers this trend
was bound up with an increasing indifference to, and negation of, the values
of Judaism. People sought the path to the great—or seemingly great—world,
seeking excitement in its culture and wealth. One knew nothing more of
the treasures of one's own past or of the culture of the fathers and no longer
wanted to know them. They were regarded as coarse, backward and "barbar-
ian". Most of those who left Judaism at that time trimmed opportunistic
inducements with their new "christliness" which the Christian world and
governments rewarded in many ways with honours and aristocratic titles,
official positions and professorships. Not everyone was as honest as *Heinrich
Heine* when he called conversion the "*Entrée Billet* into European culture".

The aesthetic lifestyle which began with the Goethe-veneration of the
Jewish salons found its continuation up to our day in many Jewish literati
and writers, who had lost their connection with Judaism even though they
were not baptized.

Alongside this trend, however, which often led out of Judaism, was a positive Jewish trend existing from the beginning and in later times. This trend had also originated in the Enlightenment. But it was orientated since Mendelssohn's day towards the ethical ideals of Lessing, Kant and Schiller, and remained more closely linked to the spirit and tradition of Judaism. It decisively directed Jewish intellectual history in the nineteenth and twentieth century.

Once before in Jewish history there had been a similarly fruitful encounter of two cultural streams, when in the flowering period of Spanish Jewry Jewish and Arabian culture met. Now German Judaism was to become a phenomenon of special stamp, through the meeting of Jewish tradition with a branch of German culture to which the Jews felt special affinity: German Classicism. However, their identifying this latter with the whole of German culture, proved later to be a tragic misunderstanding. The most important intellectual historical example of this meeting was the influence of Kant on Jewish thinking—treated in the previous chapter—which then reinfluenced German intellectual life through Maimon, Hermann Cohen and others.

# CHAPTER 13

## *The New Historical Consciousness*

The struggle for equality absorbed the interest and energy of the Jews in Germany for decades. In face of this struggle everything else receded into the background. Even cultural concerns were nearly always dominated from the standpoint as to whether and how far they were conducive to the attainment of full equality. The reversal in values, already begun in Mendelssohn's day, was now expressed in a way that was sometimes grotesque. The ideal to which the German Jews now aspired was almost considered to be nothing more than the cultural and intellectual values of the non-Jewish environment and its social conventions. One wanted, as was repeatedly said, to prove oneself worthy of acceptance in state and society. And one was therefore prepared to give up not only the Jewish language, customs and outward garb but also the very content of Jewish life. Many at that time took the ultimate step towards adaptation by chosing baptism, in order thereby as they believed to surmount every social limitation and prejudice. And many now retained only nominal links with Judaism. They no longer knew it, its history or culture. However, the vast majority still clung to the Jewish way of life, notably in the communities of Poznan, southern Germany and in the rural areas as a whole. These orthodox Jews already differed from the generation of their fathers and, for example, from east European Jews in that the written and spoken German language as well as secular knowledge had become normal and natural for them.[120] Jewish education slowly retreated into the background in these circles too. What began to disappear in this generation during the first decades of the nineteenth century I should like to call a Jewish *historical consciousness*.

This situation caused concern among a small group of Jews in Berlin recruited mostly from Jewish university students there, who had come

[120] Cf. J. Toury, 'Die politischen Orientierungen der Juden in Deutschland von Jena bis Weimar', (The Political Orientations of the Jews in Germany from Jena to Weimar), Tuebingen 1966. See also Toury's article in the Bulletin of the L.B.I., Year 8, 1965.

137

under the influence of Romanticism in the years following the Wars of Liberation (1813-1815). They had become familiar with the new trend of seeking a historical reason for every cultural phenomenon. At that time the so-called historical-law school had drawn attention to the popular and historical background of jurisprudence. Friedrich August Wolf and August Boekh had created the modern classical philology by linking the history of literature to the study of language and grammar. Etymology began to dominate the whole of linguistics. All knowledge and learning were regarded as essentially historical. This approach was general, dominating not only the humanities but also the natural sciences. One recalls Goethe's natural scientific theories, for example, and how through Hegel the philosophy of history became a main aspect of German Idealism.

The young Jews who in 1819 formed themselves into a *Verein fuer Cultur und Wissenschaft der Juden* (Society for Jewish Culture and Learning), called in brief *Culturverein*, hoped to bring about the renewal of Judaism by interpreting it as a historical phenomenon and making it into a subject of *historical* research. We saw how in the post-Mendelssohnian generation many viewed Judaism as something onerous, unlovely and antiquated, whereas general culture seemed to promise freedom and beauty and correspond to their modern needs. The Culturverein's programme was to bring back the knowledge of Jewish history and culture into wide circles of Jews and to teach them to understand their Judaism as a part of general culture and not as something outside and opposed to it. The aim was, as we would say today, a cultural-political one. The society planned to influence Jewish educational matters, to establish schools and seminaries and by means of lectures to provide for adult education. But the only outcome of this broadly based programme was a high school course in which young members of the society gave instruction. Social reforms were also on the programme, through which Jewish youth was to be diverted from trade into more practical occupations.

For the realisation of these long-term aims, however, the association's members were too few and their financial resources, the means of students, too limited. Membership consisted of a small circle in Berlin, a still smaller group in Hamburg and some few individuals in other places. Its chairman was *Eduard Gans*, its secretary *Leopold Zunz*. *Heinrich Heine* was a member for a while. Heine's friend Moses Moser and also the Hamburg educationalist *Immanuel Wohlwill* were important members. It was in this society that the phrase *Wissenschaft des Judentums* (literally translated: 'Science' of Judaism) was first coined. This expression which was later to denote a new academic discipline derived apparently from Gans. It appeared also in the title *Zeitschrift fuer die Wissenschaft des Judentums* (Periodical for the Wissenschaft of Judaism), published by the association and appearing under the editorship of Zunz from 1822-1823. In an important programmatic essay Wohlwill attempted to define the tasks and scope of this new branch of learning, while Leopold Zunz laid the foundations for it in his lifework.

The enthusiasm of the young members of the Culturverein, however, very soon collided with the harsh reality of the policy of the restoration which was virtually trying to undo Jewish emancipation. The society's chairman *Eduard Gans*, a disciple of Hegel and a highly gifted jurist, had applied for an appointment at the University of Berlin, for, as a result of the Edict of Emancipation of 1812, academic posts were now also open to Jews. His application was turned down by the university authorities, where-upon he turned to the government with the support of Chancellor Hardenberg who was well known to his family. But even Hardenberg was unable to secure Gans' appointment against the minister in charge, von Altenstein, who justified the refusal with a very tortuous legal interpretation. According to the Edict of 1812 the holding of academic posts by Jews was indeed not precluded, he argued. However, another paragraph of the same edict said that the holding of state and public positions by Jews was to be subject to a later regulation. The task of a university lecturer was to educate future officials, judges, etc. Hence, it was impossible for anyone to teach disciplines which he himself could not practise. Since neither Gans nor Hardenberg agreed with this specious argument, Altenstein succeeded in obtaining from the king in 1822 a special Cabinet-Ordre, a "Lex Gans" so to speak, which now officially excluded Jews from holding academic posts in Prussia. The departments of government advised Gans to look for another occupation in which he could employ his talents, offering him meanwhile a stipendium which he accepted. This made his position as chairman of the *Culturverein* morally untenable, as he had allowed himself as it were to be bought by the government. He resigned and soon after, in 1824, the Society was dissolved.

Gans' attempts to find an academic post outside Prussia also failed and they exhausted both his morale and financial means. He was eventually baptized in Paris in 1825, whereupon he was immediately made Professor Extraordinary in Berlin and four years later full Professor. Heinrich Heine, writing on Gans' behaviour, said: "His defection was all the more distasteful as he had played the role of an agitator (against the baptismal movement) and taken on certain duties of chairman".

The ignominious collapse of their ideals and hopes shatteringly affected most members of this circle. Some of them, like Heinrich Heine, accepted baptism. Some, fully despairing of life, committed suicide, or fell ill and died very young. Others emigrated to the USA. Wohlwill tried to found a free religious congregation in Hamburg and in Kiel—attempts which failed. He later became director of the Jewish school in Seesen but he too died early in life.[121] These young people of the *Culturverein* had been an intel-lectual vanguard morally worn out because they wanted to realise the ideals

---

[121] Cf. Reissner, Rebellious Dilemma. The Case Histories of Eduard Gans and some of his Partisans in Yearbook II of the Leo Baeck Institute, London, 1957.

of an emancipation for which the political preconditions and the psychological readiness in the world around were not yet ripe.

The only one to survive the collapse of these hopes and efforts was *Leopold Zunz*, who clung to the Wissenschaft, or literally, science of Judaism. It expressed in characteristic fashion the new historical awareness, which typified modern Judaism in its various and often contrary forms. What the post-Mendelssohnian generations lost by adapting to the surrounding world at any price, became again an intellectual-historical force. The Jewish past was once more found worthy of interest. This sometimes began as an antiquarian interest—as it did with the young *Zunz* and still more intensely in the case of *Steinschneider*. But soon Jewish history became a value that was affirmed and for which one felt responsible.

In the following chapters we shall pursue the various streams which the Wissenschaft of Judaism linked up with the religious Renaissance movements of Reform and of Neo-Orthodoxy and later with the politico-social development in Jewry. Here I should like to elucidate the new *concept of history* that arose with the Wissenschaft of Judaism.

There are interpretations which see Judaism as an extra or supra-historical phenomenon. In his "Stern der Erloesung" (Star of Redemption) for example, *Franz Rosenzweig* gives an eloquent description of this view. He contrasts the "one people on earth"—as Israel is called in a liturgical poem —with the nations which are engulfed in the fluctuations of history; and Judaism with Christianity, which is 'always on the way'. (This assertion, it seems to me, is also reversible: Judaism awaiting the Messiah, could be said to be 'on the way'; whereas Christianity, whose Messiah has come, has arrived, as it were, being at the goal of history or standing outside it. One sees, how ambiguous and dangerous such formulations are.)

One of the earliest pioneers of the Wissenschaft of Judaism in Galicia, *Nachman Krochmal*, sought in a similar way to apply the Hegelian idea of flowering, maturing and dying away, to the analogy and difference between the nations and Israel. Judaism too, knows this threefold dialectic in its history. But whereas the other nations succumb to this process, thereby terminating their role in history, in the case of Israel there ensues with every decline a new beginning. Its history, following Krochmal, reflects the eternal inherent movement of the Divine world-spirit.

The interpretation of extra-temporality also appears with the great historian *Simon Dubnow* in a secularised form. Here it becomes an omnipresent temporality. Dubnow called his presentation of Jewish history *"World-History of the Jewish People"*. The title is based on his belief that Jewish history has a share in every historical epoch from antiquity till the present and in every geographical region on earth.

These reflections on Jewish history, interesting as they are, should not distract us from our investigation of the idea of history in the Wissenschaft of Judaism and its relation to both *the interpretation of history in Jewish tradition* and to modern historical scholarship.

By certain characteristics constantly recurring in the sources we can recognise the approach of traditional Jewish learning to history.[122] A strong historical consciousness already existed in the Pentateuch. In the revelation at Sinai, which called Judaism and Jewry into being, God says, "I am the Eternal, who led thee out of Egypt . . ." Earlier still He had revealed himself to Moses in the midst of the burning bush as the God of Abraham, Isaac and of Jacob. This historic reference to the patriarchs occurs repeatedly in the Bible and in the Prayer book. Entire books of the Bible are historiographic. World history, not just the history of the Jewish people, is reflected in the biblical account of Creation and in the prophets. Hermann Cohen called the prophets the originators of the concept of "world history."

It would apparently be more difficult to ascertain a historical consciousness in the Talmudic era. It has often been observed that Talmudic literature is lacking in descriptions of historical events. We would know virtually nothing from Talmud or Midrash on the Maccabean uprising, for example, were it not for the Apocryphal books of the Maccabees and Josephus Flavius. This silence may be due to the later antagonism of the Pharisaic party to the Hasmonean Dynasty. But it is more difficult to understand when the Bar-Kokhba-Revolt (132-135) is sometimes confused a century later with the Jewish War, which ended with the destruction of the Temple in the year 70. It seems almost that some events lingering in the memory were thought worth reporting, but that the time and connection of the events were a matter of indifference to the reporter. We find often too that events, conditions and problems of the present are clothed in Biblical references; or conversely, that Biblical events are applied to the present.[123] This would seem to suggest a certain attitude to history. Present happenings are projected into a selection of past events determined by the interests of the present.—The same is true with regard to the future.

Since the prophets the Jewish concept of history has been keyed to the future. The dynamic nature of the Jewish religion points to the future, assigning the Jew the task of developing the world towards God's kingdom.[124] But this kingdom of God is not—as in apocalypticism, for example, and thence in Christianity—an eschatological meta-historical concept, but rather a concept within history. True, it is not known when the kingdom will

---

[122] Hardly any preliminary studies exist on the traditional Jewish interpretation of history, especially as it appears in the midrashic compilations. Glatzer's 'Untersuchungen zur Geschichtslehre der Tannaiten—Ein Beitrag zur Religionsgeschichte' (Investigations on the Tannaite Doctrine of History—a Contribution to the History of Religion), Berlin 1933, still remains basic.

[123] The identification of Edom with Rome, Bileam with Jesus, inter alia, belongs in this connection even if political caution may have often required the use of code words.

[124] Glatzer calls it the "activation of history", op. cit. p. 32 ff.

come. But its coming partially depends upon the will and involvement of men. The future can therefore become the present at any time, though not in the sense that in the natural lapse of time the "not-yet" becomes "now" and is then at once "no more". This goal of history in the traditional interpretation is not reached unassisted as a natural process but when human responsiveness meets divine expectation.[125] The present is the plane of projection. It finds its confirmation in the events of the past and its goal in the messianic concept of the future. The accent is always on the present. Such a notion of history in its supra-temporal tendency does not negate history. It is rather the expression of an intense awareness of time and history.

The difference between the traditional Jewish view of history and the modern view developed especially in the nineteenth century may be illuminated by a quotation. *Friedrich Schiller* concluded his inaugural lecture as professor of history at Jena in 1789 with the following words: "Every preceding age—without knowing or achieving it—has exerted itself to bring about our human century. Every treasure is ours which diligence and genius, reason and experience, in the long history of the world, have at last accomplished". Here too, the past is applied to the present and considered from the standpoint of the present. Yet this apparent similarity reveals the difference that separates modern history—and its derivative, the Wissenschaft of Judaism—from the old Jewish view of history. The new approach is to see history as a process, as *development*. This process leads into and culminates in the present. But for the actual present, for the reflecting historian, the previous ages are past and gone. They have fulfilled their task of bringing about the present and now a new relation exists between them—that of *distance*.[126] What is missing here is the inclusion of the past in the present, whereby the Jewish scholars of the old school held past and present actively together. *Development and distance* came to be criteria in the modern historian's view of history and method of working.

With the adoption of these two factors and their application to the heritage of Judaism and to the history of Jewry, the new Wissenschaft of Judaism came into being. By adopting the approach and method of historical research—even when it was not really concerned with historical, but with philological, exegetical or philosophical questions—the Wissenschaft of Judaism stepped outside the framework of traditional Jewish scholarship. The new aspects from which Judaism and its past were from then on con-

---

[125] There is a legend that Rabbi Joshua ben Levi (ca 260) met the Messiah among a group of beggars at the gates of Rome. To his question as to when he would appear Rabbi Joshua received the answer: "Today". When Joshua later expressed his disappointment, it was pointed out to him that what was meant was: "Today, if ye would but hearken to his voice!" (Psalm 95,7–Cf. Yalkut on this verse).

[126] The future is also part of the process of time. The concept of "distance" applies to it as well, since no scientific assertions can be made regarding the future (although this has sometimes been attempted, as in the case of Marx and Spengler). Through this agnostic attitude to the future, the concept of history in modern historiography is in principal non-teleological.

sidered, i.e. the concepts of distance and development, were soon to prove
themselves very fruitful. Modern Judaism, in all its tendencies and nuances,
has received vital impulses from the Wissenschaft of Judaism. What was
often lost in the immediacy between past and future and in religious simplicity was replaced by a new positive awareness of history. And this critical
awareness of history raised the old questions with new intensity.

In 1817 *Leopold Zunz*, then only twenty-three years old, succinctly formulated the concept of distance: "here the entire literature of the Jews in its
widest sense is seen as a subject for research, without having to worry whether
its entire content can or should be normative for our own judgements".[127]

That is the exact reversal of the previous relation to the past. The latter
has now become the subject of research. Before this the past belonged, as
it were, to the investigating person himself. It was part of him. The old
Jewish scholar felt himself to be a link in the traditional chain to which he
—like the events of the past—belonged, and from which he could make a
real valid decision for his present age. The modern historian, on the other
hand, approaches this material—the events—from without. He is no longer
a part of the chain of tradition. The concept of distance is expressed in the
above Zunzian words in almost classical form.

The conept of distance, however, was more than a mere academic approach. It had become the hallmark of the age of emancipation, the expression of the actual intellectual situation. In face of all the new, the enticing
and the glittering that the surrounding world, society and economy offered
the Jew in unknown possibilities, one no longer knew what to do with the
ghetto garb of the old Judaism. We find in that generation—in the letters
of the young *Abraham Geiger* to his friend *Josef Dernburg*, for example—
a rejection of traditional Judaism bordering on nihilism and self-hatred.[128]
In the autobiographical parts of his 'Offenbarungslehre' (Doctrine of Revelation) *Solomon Ludwig Steinheim* tells how he "was repelled, like so many
of my contemporaries by the old ceremonial of the synagogue".[129] *Heine*
spoke of the "incurable sickness of Judaism". Distance from Judaism was an
emotional condition, when and even before it became a scientific approach.

This basically emotional and pre-scientific awareness of distance was supplemented by the concept of *historical development*. This was the second step
taken by the young scholars. With the young Zunz, as we have seen, the legacy of the past became the subject-matter of research without being concerned
about its significance for the present. For the somewhat younger *Abraham
Geiger* the past, indeed, continued to be the subject of research, the attitude

---

[127] Zunz, 'Etwas zur rabbinischan Literatur' (Something on Rabbinic Literature), Collected Works,
1875, Vol. I, p. 5, footnote.
[128] Cf. Geiger, 'Nachgelass. Schriften' (Posthum. Works) vol. V, p. 27 ff.
[129] S. L. Steinheim, 'Die Offenbarung nach dem Lehrbegriff der Synagoge' (Revelation according to
the Doctrine of the Synagogue), vol. II, p. 201 ff and passim.

of distance remained. However, his concern was how tradition, the inheritance of the past, could become fruitful for the Jew's attitude to his own time. Tradition itself was no longer merely past and finished, but rather became dynamic again and was brought into the *process of development*.[130]

For the representatives of the Wissenschaft of Judaism, the concept of development itself—subject as it is to the most varied influences—is difficult to define. But common to all modern Jewish scholars was the insight into the process-character of historical becoming. Yet at one point the process of development is limited: the Wissenschaft of Judaism abides by the concept of a *goal of history* for the Jews and for all mankind.

By setting a goal to historical development, which is geared to the future, the Wissenschaft of Judaism approached again the old Jewish doctrine of history regarding the "days of the Messiah".[131] It thereby took over a pronounced theological and teleological motif into its basic concepts. Messianism links the new discipline with traditional Jewish scholarship. And as with the latter so the Wissenschaft of Judaism remains linked also with the Enlightenment's and Kant's doctrine of history. Their messianism is messianism in "cosmopolitan perspective". It believes, as does Lessing, in an "Education of the Human Race", and like Immanuel Kant in the actual "realisability" of perpetual peace.[132]

With the theologically motivated retention of a goal of history the Wissenschaft of Judaism clearly distinguishes itself from the historico-theoretical tendencies of general history. These tendencies were agnostic regarding the future and thereby non-teleological. The same applies to the prevailing philosophies of history of that epoch.

In the case of *Herder*, for example, history is a cosmological process.[133] Being the evolutionary development of an organic constitution, it is part of natural history. Man has his place in this process as an intermediate being (Mittelwesen) between animal and an unknown higher rung. His intellect also is a product of genetic development. "Humanity", the development of which Herder assigns to man as task, is the unfolding of his talents that are furthered or hindered by climatic and geographical conditions. Herder's influence on his contemporaries and on Romanticism—largely

---

[130] Cf. Rotenstreich, Vol. I, p. 92 ff.

[131] This Messianic idea, indeed, takes up only part of the traditional teaching. In it the concept of a personal Messiah, the son of David, gives way to the idea of the "days of the Messiah", the Messianic era. This conception is also traditional. But now the universal nature of the Messianic idea is emphasised. The national, or as one said then, the political side of the Messianic belief received renewed emphasis in Zionism.

[132] Cf. Kant's "Ideen zu einer allgemeinen Geschichte in weltbürgerlicher Absicht" (Ideas on a General History in Cosmopolitan Perspective) and "Traktat zum ewigen Frieden" (Treatise on Perpetual Peace); Lessing's "Erziehung des Menschengeschlechts" (Education of the Human Race).

[133] Herder, "Ideen zur Philosophie der Geschichte der Menschheit" (Ideas on the Philosophy of the History of Mankind), 1784 to 1791.

inaugurated by him—was powerful. Through him the concept of organic connections, the unity of nature and mental development, entered into the intellectual consciousness of the nineteenth century.

With *Wilhelm von Humboldt*[134] a characteristic concept of idea took the place of a goal of history. Ideas "are not brought into history, but rather constitute the very essence of history". They "emerge from the fulness of events themselves . . . and do not have to be lent to history as something extra". Humboldt's idea is immanent in history, not as for Kant regulative with a teleological task.[135] The goal is really history itself. "From the human perspective . . . all history is only the development of an idea, and in the idea there exist simultaneously the activating power and the goal".[136]

Finally, *Hegel* made history into a process within the divine world-spirit. If with Spinoza God and nature are equated, for Hegel God is a threefold identity of Idea, Nature and Spirit.[137] "World history is the representation of the absolute Divine Spirit".[138] This process unfolds both in a logical-dialectical and an ever alternating organic life triad of blossom, fruit and decay among the spirits of peoples (*Volksgeister*). But this process leads virtually to nothing, for "the general aspect of philosophical world-history . . . is spirit, which is eternally with itself and for which there is no past".[139] And one could add that for it there is no future. Here the real meaning of all history is lost, for not only has it no goal, but not even, as with Herder, a purposeful perpetual process. It remains a movement within, as it seems, an eternally reposing World-spirit.[140] This process ends again, according to Hegel, in Being. Being and Becoming are identical for Hegel. Characteristic of him is the exclusion of ethics from history. If with Kant history is a part of morality—since the moral ideal should be realised in it—with Hegel history is rooted in Being of which the World-spirit is only one form of expression.

Now we may sum up the interrelations and differences between the concepts of history in the Wissenschaft of Judaism, in traditional Jewish histori-

---

[134] Wilhelm von Humboldt, "Ueber die Aufgaben des Geschichtsschreibers" (On the Tasks of the Historiographer), Selected Phil. Writings, ed. by Joh. Schubert, 1910, p. 89 and 91.

[135] Cf. op. cit. p. 60: "Philosophy prescribes a goal to events . . . disturbs and falsifies every free notion of the characteristic influence of powers. Teleological history never reaches the living truth of world destiny".

[136] Op. cit. p. 98.

[137] Hegel, "Die Vernunft in der Geschichte" (Reason in History) ed. by Georg Lasson, 2nd Edition, 1921, Philos. Bibliotek, p. 30.

[138] Op. cit. p. 52.

[139] Op. cit. p. 177.

[140] There is no inconsistency here in the great influence which Hegel's dialectical method, the dialectical movement of cultures, has exercised on historians, theologians and social scientists. With *Marx* this method is again teleologically directed, though his classless society expresses more the old messianic nature of Utopian socialism than it represents Hegelianism. A different teleological application of the Hegelian dialectical process is perhaps August Comte's Doctrine of Hierarchies.

osophy and in those of the philosophies of history prevailing among 19th
century historians.

The dividing line between these conceptions lies in the question of whether
history has a *goal*, or whether it is just a meaningless chain of events.

*The traditional Jewish conception of history* is teleological. It recognizes
a goal—the kingdom of heaven and the days of the Messiah.

*Nineteenth century philosophy of history*, in contrast, is non-teleological.
As we have seen, with Herder human history is purely a branch of natural
history. Humboldt also uses the word goal (Ziel). But for him the goal is
history itself, an immanent goal emerging from historical events. Humboldt
actually called (cf. note 135) teleological history a falsification of history.
We don't need to repeat Hegel's position, who excludes not only the future
but even the past from history by converting history to the status of an
—although  dialectical—inside-movement  within  the  divine  World-Spirit.

*In the Wissenschaft of Judaism the conception of history* is somewhat
in between. On the one hand it was deeply influenced by the philosophical
conceptions of the time, from which it really originated.—We shall later find
this influence when dealing with Zunz, Krochmal, Graetz.—On the other
hand, on the central point of a goal of history the Wissenschaft of Judaism
holds firm to the traditional Jewish view (and that of Kant, whose attitude
is a kind of secularization of the Jewish concept of the kingdom of heaven).
Here, as will be shown, Zunz gives an instructive example (see Chapter 14).
There is, however, a difference between the modern scholar of the Wissenschaft of Judaism and the traditional rabbi. The modern scholar views the
Jewish past from the outside, as subject of his research, even if he himself
might be a traditionally orthodox Jew (as were e.g. scholars like Rapoport,
Abraham  Berliner  and  even  Samson  Raphael  Hirsch).  The  traditionalist
scholar considers himself a mere link in the long chain of Jewish scholars,
and hence a link in the process he is viewing. On each page of the Talmud
the reader will find passages of the Bible, the old sages in the text of the
Talmud, then in the text's margins Rashi, Tosaphists and other commenta-
tors. Every new and subsequent reader becomes, as it were, a further link
in this chain. He is, so to speak, a contemporary of the scholars of past
centuries, continuing the discussion with them. This illustration, originally
due to Franz Rosenzweig, may serve to explain the difference between the
traditional scholar and the modern Jewish historian.

# CHAPTER 14

## The 'Wissenschaft' of Judaism

The *Wissenschaft of Judaism* had adopted the new approach to history. The not very fortunate name—"Science"[140a] of Judaism—originated in the *Culturverein*. Its real programmatic document, however, was a booklet of Leopold Zunz already published in 1818, 'Etwas ueber die rabbinische Literatur' (Something on Rabbinic Literature), as Zunz then termed the new discipline.

*Leopold Lippmann Zunz* (1794-1886),[141] born in Detmold, was educated in the Samson Free School in Wolfenbuettel and studied in Berlin. During his long life—he lived to be ninety-two years old—he himself built up a large part of the Wissenschaft of Judaism which today is still based upon his work and insight. Zunz approached the subject from classical philology, being particularly influenced by his teacher August Boekh. He considered the Wissenschaft of Judaism to be a branch of classical studies just as Greek is. His real field of work, however, was not the biblical period or antique Judaism but the history of medieval Jewish literature. Only in his first and probably most important work, "Die Gottesdienstlichen Vortraege der Juden"[142] (The Synagogal Sermons of the Jews) does he touch on the late period of Antiquity, dealing with the history and arrangement of midrashic compilations and their significance for the Jewish sermon, whose develop-

---

[140a]The term "science" in English is usually limited to natural sciences. Besides, "Science of Judaism" might suggest associations with "Christian Science". Therefore, the author prefers The German term "Wissenschaft" that includes the humanities and avoids misunderstandings.

[141]On Zunz cf. L. Wallach, 'Liberty and Letters—The Thoughts of Leopold Zunz', London 1959, and the two volumes of letters edited and introduced by N.N. Glatzer 'Leopold and Adelheid Zunz, An Account in Letters 1815-1885', London 1958, and 'Leopold Zunz, Jude, Deutscher, Europaeer' (Leopold Zunz, Jew, German, European), Tuebingen 1964. Both volumes contain the personal correspondence of Zunz with his teacher S. M. Ehrenberg in Wolfenbuettel, the Ehrenberg family and personal friends. Little of Zunz's important scholarly correspondence has been published.

[142]The work appeared in 1832. In the Hebrew edition of 1947 Ḥanokh Albeck brought it up to date with additional notes and comments.

ment he traces through the Middle Ages to his own day. Zunz never concerned himself with modern Jewish history. The titles of his subsequent
writings are: "Zur Geschichte und Literatur" (On History and Literature)
1845; "Synagogale Poesie des Mittelalters" (Synagogal Poetry of the Middle
Ages) 1855; "Der Ritus des Synagogalen Gottesdienstes geschichtlich ent-
wickelt" (The Rite of the Synagogue Service historically developed) 1859;
Literaturgeschichte der synagogalen Poesie" (Literary History of Synagogal
Poetry) 1865. Besides this he wrote a large number of essays and articles
for encyclopaedias—like Brockhaus and Ersch/Gruber—expert reports and
lectures. These smaller works were collected during his lifetime into three
volumes of the "Gesammelte Schriften" (Collected Writings) in 1875 and
1876. In collaboration with others he edited a new Bible translation (1838),
and gave lectures to small groups, having preached in his younger years[143]
(1820-1822) in the Reformed Synagogue in the house of the banker Jacob
Herz Beer. His zeal for an inner reform of Judaism, revealed in his letters
and sermons of the years of the "Culturverein" and during his office as
preacher, very quickly clashed with Jewish reality. The rich satisfied at-
tenders at those synagogue services were only interested in an outwardly
embellished and comfortable form of Judaism. Zunz was dismissed. He
despaired of being able to help the Jews. After the break-up of the Culturverein he immersed himself in his work on the elucidation of the Jewish
past. Judaism became for him more and more a branch of classical studies.
He lived in straitened circumstances for decades, and was everywhere offensive with his marked sense of independence and refusal to compromise.
For eight years he edited the "Haude und Spenersche Zeitung" a Berlin
paper, and for a short while was director of the Jewish community school in
Berlin. Once again for a few months he was preacher in a somewhat reformed congregation in Prague, being private teacher and free lance writer
in between. By commission of the Berlin community he wrote an essay on
"Die Namen der Juden" (Jewish Names) in 1836 in order to oppose an
intended official prohibition of the use of so-called Christian forenames.
Finally in 1840, after being long since recognised as leading scholar, he
became director of the Jewish Teacher Training College in Berlin. It was the
only Jewish public position he occupied for a considerable time. On his
retirement in 1850 he received a pension. Having almost despaired of the
Jews in their lack of understanding for the scholarly illumination of their
past, his second disappointment came with the unwillingness of the authorities and German universities to recognise the Wissenschaft of Judaism as
an academic subject.

The official Jewry of the community leaders of his day appreciated

---

[143] Cf. Alexander Altmann, Zur Fruehgeschichte der juedischen Predigt in Deutschland. Leopold
Zunz als Prediger (On the Early History of the Jewish Sermon in Germany. Leopold Zunz as Preacher).
Yearbook VI, LBI, London, 1961.

the value and usefulness of historico-scientific argumentation only when it had to do with civil equality. For expertise on things like Jewish forenames, circumcision, inter alia, Zunz was good enough. But that the famous David Oppenheimer Library was allowed to go to Oxford for a mere pittance and the important library of the Hamburg Jewish scholar and bibliographer, Ḥayyim Michael, to the British Museum, made him despair and aroused his sarcastic scorn for the wealthy Jews of Germany.

The universities—in a decision to which Ranke added his signature—and the Prussian Ministry refused Zunz's application for a university post in 1843 and again even after the Revolution of 1848. Minister Ladenburg, answering him on December 4 of that year, wrote that a professorship "founded with the twin concept of intellectually supporting and strengthening Jewish life in its particularity and in its estranging laws and customs would contradict the intention of the new freedom aimed at levelling glaring differences. It would be a . . . misuse of the University".[144] Clearly one can stifle undesired intellectual trends and even academic disciplines in the name of freedom.[145]

While other contemporary scholars were now advocating the creation of their own Jewish theological faculties (as e.g., Geiger, Ludwig Philippson, Meir Isler) and while this idea was being realised in the founding of the Jewish-Theological Seminary in Breslau, Zunz remained uncompromisingly faithful to his demand. He saw in such establishments the danger of an intellectual inbreeding and threatening clericalism, which could only be avoided through incorporation within the framework of the university. As late as 1872 he declined a call to the Berlin Hochschule fuer die Wissenschaft des Judentums—founded meanwhile by Geiger and Steinthal—on grounds of principle, not, as one might assume, because of advanced age.

Zunz gave expression to his dynamic personality by throwing himself passionately into the political proceedings of the day. He followed the French Revolution of 1830, the Revolution in Germany and the Polish uprisings of 1848 and the reaction, the liberation of Italy and subsequent conquest of Rome in 1870 and the accompanying hope and despair of all these events with religious-messianic enthusiasm. He linked both the religious and political future of the Jews with the political liberation of the peoples of Europe.[146]

Zunz saw in the civil integration of Jews into the political scene a part of the messianic task. The Jews, he believed, would be able to participate again in real history only within the framework of national liberation move-

[144] See Glatzer's Leopold Zunz, Jude, Deutscher, Europaer, p. 42.
[145] The decision very clearly expresses the tendency—apparently in the name of liberalism and universal equality—to contest Judaism's right to its own existence.
[146] Zunz delivered the funeral oration for those fallen during the revolutionary riots in March, 1848. He was elector, chairman or committee member of political societies, gave political lectures, joined the progressive party.

ments. This is why the revolutionary and political events of his day have had
for Zunz a naive religious and messianic accent. After the liberation of Rome
he expected—in an essay entitled "Erloesungsjahre" (Years of Deliverance),
alluding to Isaiah 11.8,9—an era "when the children of freedom shall play
over the dens of reigning cobras, and Europe, delivered from infallible
papacy, shall be filled with the knowledge of God".[147] Zunz's was not a
secularized messianism superseded by mere belief in progress. It was linked
with contemporary happenings yet religious. The events of his time seemed
to him to authenticate the kingdom of freedom and the knowledge of God.
The latent theological motifs of the Wissenschaft of Judaism clearly come
to the fore with this mocker and hater of theologians of every religion.

*Moritz Steinschneider*[148] (1816-1907) was very similar to Zunz in character and in approach to the Wissenschaft of Judaism. Like him Steinschneider
grew more and more into a sarcastic oddity about whom many anecdotes
have been handed down. But he lacks the other's religious messianic élan.
He was really an agnostic, influenced more than Zunz by the concept of
distance. For him Judaism was something completed, without a future,
and now deserving "a decent burial". And the task of the Wissenschaft of
Judaism was to do just that. Even more than Zunz, Steinschneider was a
"notekeeper", as Graetz once called the former.[149] His large library catalogues
like his Hebraica catalogue of the Bodleian in Oxford and his catalogues of
Hebrew manuscripts in Leyden, Munich, Hamburg and Berlin were epoch-
making. For a long time he was director of the Jewish Girl's School in Berlin
and assistant at the Prussian State Library.

Steinschneider's special interest was devoted to those points of inter-
section where the contribution of Jews to general science and culture came
to expression. He therefore gave his attention to those medieval Jewish
translators, who made Greek and Arab culture accessible to the Jewish and
Christian Middle Ages. He wrote about Jewish mathematicians and scientists,
composed several concise accounts of Jewish literature and intellectual
history and published a host of contributions in the multi-volume "Zeitschrift
fuer Hebraeische Bibliographie" as well as for various encyclopaediae.

Belonging to Zunz's generation were some scholars who wrote in Hebrew,
most of whom worked outside Germany. *Samuel Judah Rapoport* (1790-
1867) in Brody (Galicia) and later chief rabbi in Prague, was the first to research and correct the biographies of several Jewish scholars of the early
Middle Ages.

[147] Zunz, Gesammelte Schriften, Vol. III, p. 231. Cf. Glatzer, op. cit., pp. 50-61.
[148] Cf. Kurt Wilhelm in Bulletin of the LBI, No. 1, 1957, p. 35 ff.—After Steinschneider's death,
H. Malter planned an edition of his brief scattered writings, of which only the first volume, a biographical appreciation, appeared in 1925.
[149] Graetz, Geschichte der Juden (History of the Jews), Vol. V, Foreword p. VI: "Dr. Zunz's more
confusing than enlightening note-lumber and arid nomenclature have furthered my work but little."

*Nachman Krochmal* (1785-1840), also of Brody, worked in a similar sphere to that of Rapoport. As philosopher of the history of Judaism, his influence is lasting in his Hebrew work "Guide for the Perplexed of our Time", at his request published posthumously by Zunz in 1851.

To the first generation of these Judaic scholars there also belong the German Jews: Isaac Markus Jost, Julius Fuerst and Solomon Munk.

*Isaac Markus Jost* (1793-1866) in his youth was a friend of Zunz, and like him educated at the Samson School in Wolfenbuettel. He taught for a considerable time, first in Berlin, later at the Philanthropin in Frankfurt. Even prior to Graetz he wrote a scientific Jewish history in several versions[150] which is again receiving attention today. He was by disposition a disciple of the generation of the Enlightenment. Graetz said of Jost that he disliked excitement both in life and in history.

*Julius Fuerst* (1805-1873) was the only Jew and representative of Judaic studies in the first half of the nineteenth century who could teach in a German university—in Leipzig—though only as an unsalaried lecturer. On his twenty-fifth anniversary as private lecturer in 1864 he received the honorary title of Professor. His bibliographic handbook "Bibliotheca Judaica" is still made use of today, as is also his history of the Karaïtes. He published philological works and was editor of a Jewish weekly paper, the "Orient", which had a scholarly supplement "Das Literaturblatt des Orients".

*Solomon Munk* (1803-1867), due to the hopelessness of finding a suitable position in Prussia, had gone to Paris where, having been tutor in the home of Rothschild, he became librarian to the National Library. Munk was a distinguished orientalist. He discovered in the Paris library a manuscript containing Hebrew excerpts from a philosophical work by the famous poet Solomon Ibn Gabirol and found out, that these excerpts were identical with a book in Latin known in the Middle Ages as "Fons Vitae"—attributed to an otherwise unknown Arab writer Avicebron or Avicebrol. Munk identified this obviously corrupted name with Ibn Gabirol, thereby establishing the Jewish origin of a work influential on Christian scholastic philosophy.

Munk's most important achievement, however, was the publication of the original Arabic version—written in Hebrew characters—of Maimonides' "Guide for the Perplexed". By combining the original Arabic text with a French translation and comments, he created the first scholarly edition of this standard work of Jewish religious philosophy, which till then had only been known in Latin and Hebrew translation. He accompanied Adolphe

---

[150] Jost, Geschichte der Israeliten seit der Zeit der Makkabaeer bis auf unsere Tage (History of the Israelites from the Maccabees till the present day), in nine volumes, Berlin 1820-28; Geschichte des Israelitischen Volkes ... fuer Wissenschaftlich-Gebildete Leser (History of the Israelite People ... for educated readers) 2 vols., Berlin 1832; Neuere Geschichte der Israeliten (A Modern History of the Israelites), Berlin 1846-47; Geschichte des Judentums und seiner Sekten (History of Judaism and its Sects), 3 vols., Leipzig 1857-59.

Crémieux and Moses Montefiore to Egypt at the time of the charge of ritual murder in Damascus (1840) where, through his fluent Arabic, he played a considerable role in clearing the case and saving the Jews.

One of the most prominent and certainly one of the most interesting scholars of this generation was *Samuel David Luzzato* (1800-1865) in Padua (Italy). He wrote philosophical, historical, poetic and religious-philosophical works in Hebrew and some in Italian. He lectured at the first modern Rabbinic college, the Collegio Rabbinico in Padua, founded in 1829, 25 years before the first academic college for rabbis in Germany.

Luzatto opposed a rationalist approach to Judaism and to religion in general. For him the Hellenic and the Hebraic spirit—Atticism and Abrahamism—were opposites. He therefore rejected attempts of philosophers, especially of Maimonides, to harmonize Judaism and philosophy. In contrast to eudemonic and rationalist moral philosophy and to Kant's ethics he placed "compassion" at the centre of his ethical views. He differed from the Romantics in that he did not construe the past, which for him needed no mystic halo. He was a Jewish scholar still within the unbroken chain of Jewish tradition, for whom modern culture and academic methods were only the means of furthering and understanding that tradition. His model was Judah Halevi, the twelfth century Spanish Hebrew poet and critic of philosophy, the first scholarly edition of whose poems he published.

A phenomenon sui generis, Luzzatto was as much removed from the cool distance towards Jewish tradition—represented by Zunz, Steinschneider and Jost—as he was from the concept of evolutionary development employed by Geiger and the theologians of Reform.

This latter group around Geiger was dedicated to exploring the Jewish past with an eye to the needs of the Jewish present. They were not sceptics of the future of Judaism, but its affirmers. For their efforts they found analogies and justification in Jewish history. History became the medium of their relation to Judaism. In it they sought an answer to the question of how one could remain a Jew; of what Jewish religion could achieve and give to a generation for whom living tradition was largely broken, because it had become strange and unknown. They strove to re-form the Jewish religion and adapt it to a more and more secularised milieu.

*Abraham Geiger*[151] (1810-1874) constantly endeavoured to show how tradition has changed and developed in every age, how it has always emerged anew. Tradition for him grows out of a static into a dynamic form. Even the

---

[151] On Geiger see collected essays: "Abraham Geiger, Leben und Lebenswerk" (Life and Life's Work), 1910, published by his son Ludwig Geiger, the literary historian. See also the diary of his youth and letters in Vol. V of the "Nachgelassene Schriften" (Posthum. Writings). On criticism of Geiger's concept of development and tradition cf. Leo Baeck's essay "Theologie und Geschichte" in "Aus drei Jahrtausenden" (Out of three millenia), Tuebingen 1958, transl. by M. A. Meyer in 'Judaism', summer 1964, pp. 214-285.

present age may not only create new traditions, but is obliged to do so in order to retain the vitality of religion. Geiger's work is always concerned with the problems of tradition in transition.[152]

Geiger's principal work "Urschrift und Uebersetzungen der Bibel in ihrer Abhaengigkeit von der inneren Entwicklung des Judentums" (Original Text and Translations of the Bible in their Dependence on the Inner Development of Judaism), appeared in 1857. In this work he sets out, by means of the ancient Greek and Aramaic Bible translations, the various shades of meaning of Bible passages, illustrating from these the earlier and later layers of Halakhah—the accepted religious interpretation of the Law. He showed how these various interpretations related to the party struggle between Sadducees and Pharisees. This struggle was seen by him as a conflict between the aristocratic conservative priestly nobility and the popular democratic Pharisees. The Pharisees were the creators of the oral Law, which they placed on a par with the written Word, the Bible. Geiger depicted the Pharisees as bearers of the living development in Judaism and as models for creating tradition in the present.

The concept of evolutionary development for Geiger is linked with a particular view of the history of Judaism. According to this view the pure, universal concept of God becomes more and more detached, in the course of Jewish history, from the bond with land and people. The Jews of the diaspora have remained Jews only through their religion. In the present age, following the elimination of civil and legal disabilities, the religious law that set them apart from the earlier hostile world and gave them a semi-national autonomy has become unnecessary. The Jews of today have now only one task, namely, to confess the one and only God. This task has retained its significance even with respect to Christianity and Islam.

These aspects are constantly reiterated by Geiger, notably in his lectures, "Das Judentum und seine Geschichte" (Judaism and its History), delivered between 1864 and 1871. In a rather different way than that of Zunz, Geiger saw in the attainment of civil equality the coming of the promised age, when all the barriers that still divide men, even on the part of Jews, could fall. Of Judaism there remained only a vague general abstraction, really equivalent —as with Mendelssohn's followers—to the religion of reason. For Mendelssohn the religion of reason still stood alongside and on a level with revealed tradition. But as a result of Kant, Mendelssohn's followers found the religion of reason and tradition to be in opposition to one another. For Geiger, on the other hand, the development of tradition viewed historically leads to the universal religion of reason.

Over and above the main works already mentioned, Geiger's scholarly

---

[152] The prize thesis, won by Geiger as student at Bonn university on the subject 'Was hat Mohammed aus dem Judentum entnommmem?' (What did Mohammed borrow from Judaism?)—for which he later received a Doctorate in Marburg—already relates to this theme.

activity is displayed in numerous minor writings. He was editor and almost sole author of two periodicals, the "Wissenschaftliche Zeitschrift fuer
juedische Theologie" (Scientific Periodical for Jewish Theology) in six
volumes, and following this the "Juedische Zeitschrift fuer Wissenschaft
und Leben" (Jewish Periodical for Life and Learning). Besides this he also
wrote for Hebrew magazines of his day. For him life and learning should
always go hand in hand. Theology is necessarily "practical theology".[153]
But for real theological, as for philosophical questions, Geiger had little
inclination. His concept of development was pragmatic. He sought examples,
historical cases of precedent. He was interested in events and people in
whom he saw outsiders and forerunners of his own aspirations, such as
Leon de Modena and Joseph Delmedigo of whom he had written. But in
Geiger's linking of the past with the present there lay a danger: "For practical
purposes, for the needs of the decade, one made a selection from tradition
and then called it development. This became a label—on whatever one had
actually selected or wanted to achieve through this selection.—One sought
its historical justification . . . by skipping over past centuries, thereby assert-
ing a direct link with a real or conjectured earlier epoch. A tradition had to
be artificially created".[154]   Yet with his new pragmatic interpretation and
application of the concept of development, Geiger gave to the Reform
movement an intellectual basis, creating thereby something very like a
theory of reform.

From an altogether different approach to that of Geiger a group of
scholars calling themselves the *positive-historical* school, applied the principle
of development to their Judaic work. Their most distinguished spokesmen
were Zacharias Frankel and his younger co-workers Heinrich Graetz and
Manuel Joel.
What with Geiger was development towards confessionalization and
denationalization, was with them a process carefully nurtured within a
popular religion and rooted in custom and ideas, behind which a living
people stood.
*Frankel* and his friends were likewise rooted in the ideas of the Enlightenment. As in the entire Wissenschaft of Judaism of the nineteenth century
they had no sympathy whatever for important phenomena that impressed
themselves upon Judaism for centuries, like mysticism or Ḥasidism, laughed
at or branded by them as un-Jewish aberrations. But stronger than the influence of rational tendencies of the Enlightenment upon this group was
the influence of the Romantic concept of a national spirit (*Volksgeist*).
For them development was the process within a Judaism continuously

---

[153] Cf. Baeck's Essay, op. cit. p. 280 ff.
[154] Thus Baeck criticised the Geigerian concept of development, op. cit. "Judaism", Summer 1964,
p. 278.

fashioned by history. As with Geiger there lay in this process a dynamic element, the vitality of Jewry and its will to live. However, Frankel and his followers did not take a revolutionary path. They did not select historical models or opinions in order to create a new Judaism that would seem strange to the traditional form of Judaism and its adherents. Their method was conservative-evolutionary, keeping their eye on Jewry in its entirety.

Perhaps to stress their connection with Jewish scholarship as a whole, *Zacharias Frankel* (1801-1875) wrote his two main works in Hebrew— an introduction to the Mishna, *Hodegetica ad Mischnam*, 1859, and an introduction to the Jerusalem Talmud, 1870. With these works, which represented his principle sphere of interest, Frankel became the founder of historico-critical studies in Talmud, a discipline lying outside the interest of the other scholars we have previously considered. But for all that, Frankel aroused the suspicion of the orthodox by his new critical method, which did not stop at the revelationary character of the oral Law accepted by tradition.

Frankel's scientific work on the Talmud, by its refuting of misconcepts held by non-Jews, had sometimes real emancipatory-political significance. In Saxony and Prussia it contributed towards the removal of the special Jewish oath and lingering discrimination against Jewish witnesses in public courts.[155]

A further sphere of Frankel's research was Hellenistic-Jewish literature, where he traced the influence of Palestinian Bible exegesis on the Septuagint and on the hermeneutic literature of the Alexandrian Jews. Here too the direction of his research is indicative. He does not investigate the effect of outside influences on Judaism, but the inner Jewish relation of a, so to speak, autochthonous interpretation upon a strongly Hellenised one.

The lasting importance of Frankel in the history of thought, however, is not so much due to his pioneering scientific work as to two foundations linked with his name and where his spirit still lived on till just before the Second World War and the destruction of German Jewry.

In 1851 Frankel founded the *Monatsschrift fuer die Geschichte und Wissenschaft des Judentums* (*MGWJ*) and three years later this former rabbi of Dresden became the first director of the Rabbinical Seminary in Breslau.

The *Monatsschrift*, as it is known to the present day, was not Frankel's first periodical. It was preceded by his more religious-politically than scholarly inclined 'Zeitschrift fuer die religioesen Interessen des Judentums' (Magazine for the religious interests of Judaism), 1844 to 1846, organ of the moderate party in the dispute with Reform and Orthodoxy. The 'Monatsschrift' however had nothing to do with that passing phase, becoming in its eighty-

---

[155] 'Die Eidesleistung bei den Juden in theologischer und historischer Beziehung' (The Jewish oath in theological and historical perspective), Dresden 1840, and 'Der gerichtliche Beweis nach mosaisch-talmudischem Criminal—und Civilrecht nebst einer Untersuchung ueber die preussische Gesetzgebung hinisichtlich des Zeugnisses der Juden' (Judicial Evidence according to Mosaic-Talmudic Law; a Contribution towards the Knowledge of Mosaic-Talmudic Criminal and Civil Law, including an Investigation on Prussian Legislation regarding the Testimony of Jews), Berlin 1846.

three years of publication the great international organ of the Wissenschaft of Judaism and a meeting point of everyone working in this field[156] until the Gestapo terminated it in 1939.

The other institution was made possible through an endowment in 1846 of the deceased Breslau community chairman and councillor of commerce, Jonas Fraenkel, who had been a friend of Geiger. Jonas Fraenkel had bequeathed his entire large fortune to charitable purposes. His will included real estate and a legacy for the founding of a Jewish theological college —probably on the advice of Geiger, who hoped thereby to realise his plans for the establishment of a Jewish academic faculty.

Several years elapsed before the Fraenkelian estate could be disposed of. The executors feared the general recognition of the college would be harmed and its rabbinical diploma impaired if a controversial party man like Geiger were at its head. They therefore appointed Zacharias Frankel director of the college, which was called *Juedisch-Theologisches Seminar Fraenkelscher Stiftung* (Jewish Theological Seminary of Fraenkelian Foundation) and opened in 1854.

The Breslau Seminary was the first academic rabbinical college in Germany.[157] Members of its first faculty were, beside Frankel: the historian Heinrich Graetz; the famous classical philologist Jacob Bernays, who later went to Bonn as librarian and professor extraordinary; the mathematician B. Zuckermann, who built up the seminary's library, and Manuel Joel, who at first taught the classical courses originally affiliated with the seminary, later to become lecturer in homiletics and the philosophy of religion and ultimately Geiger's successor as rabbi in Breslau.

This eminent body of scholars, teaching in the same institute and harmonious in their views, very soon made a perceptible influence on the communities in Germany and in neighbouring countries. Nearly all the rabbis serving in these communities gained their education in, and much of their intellectual stance from, the Breslau Seminary, the first to require of its students a simultaneous university course. In this way the seminary approximated to the ideal of a Jewish theological faculty, even if outside the official framework of the university. The Breslau Seminary became the model for a number of similar institutes in Germany and in other countries.

---

[156] Frankel handed over the editorship in 1869 to Graetz, who edited the 'Monatsschrift' till 1887, and from 1881-1886 together with P. F. Frankl, rabbi in Berlin and lecturer there at the "Hochschule fuer die Wissenschaft des Judentums". After an interval of five years, two disciples of Graetz, M. Brann and David Kaufmann renewed its publication. With Kaufmann's death in 1899, Brann was sole editor till 1920. From 1904 it became the organ of the 'Gesellschaft zur Foerderung der Wissenschaft des Judentums' (Society for promoting the Wissenschaft of Judaism). From 1921, on Brann's death, Isaac Heinemann was editor till 1938. The last volume, seized by the Gestapo, appeared in reprint in 1963. This eighty-third volume (1939) was edited by Leo Baeck.

[157] Already in 1829 in Padua, in the then Austrian Lombardy, a *Collegio Rabbinico* was founded, at which S. D. Luzzatto taught. The institute was later transferred to Rome, Florence and finally back to Rome. At the same time (1829) the old Talmud school in Metz was converted into an *École Rabbinique de France* and later transferred to Paris.

If the wide-ranging impact of Frankel was due less to his scientific literary achievements than to the institutions bearing his stamp—the Breslau Seminary and the Monatschrift, with its wide academic readership—then the influence of *Heinrich Graetz (1817-1891)* upon his own present and future Jewish generations was more direct. For them Graetz is the great *historian* of Judaism.[158]

Graetz's concept of history was shaped by various influences. For him the essence of Judaism is revealed in its history, in the course of which the ideal of Judaism unfolds. This basic idea, reminiscent of Humboldt and his contemporary Ranke, is linked in Graetz with a Hegelian trichotomy of Jewish history. Here the antithetical epochs—the largely political epoch of the pre-exilic period, the theocratic religious epoch of the Second Temple, and the reflective epoch extending from the destruction of the Temple by the Romans via the growth of rabbinic Judaism up till the present—are themselves dialectically divided into three in Graetz's schema. Thus prophecy, for example, is set within the political era of the First Temple, as a climax reflecting the contrast between theocracy and monarchy.

The third factor in Graetz's construction of history is the distinction which Mendelssohn made influenced by the Enlightenment, between the politico-legal element in Judaism and its share in the religion of reason. The lasting insight he gained from Jewish history is the inseparable bond between the religious-universal and the national elements in Judaism. Torah, land and people are, as he once put it, in "magical rapport". With this combination of religion and nation Graetz stands in strong contrast to Geiger and the various efforts of his day to divest Judaism of its particular qualities —Law, Hebrew language and hope for the future.

Graetz developed the above outlined concept of history in his essay, "Die Konstruktion der juedischen Geschichte' (The Construction of Jewish History) which he published in 1846 in Frankel's 'Zeitschrift fuer die religioesen Interessen des Judentums'.[159]

---

[158] Graetz's wide influence is especially due to the popular abridged version of his historical work, the three-volumed "Volkstuemliche Geschichte der Juden" (Popular History of the Jews), 1888, issued and re-issued, and even in the 1920's missing from few Jewish bookshelves in Germany. It was a favourite Bar-Mitzwah (Confirmation) gift, which enthused generations of young Jews for their people's past. Of Graetz's eleven-volume "Geschichte der Juden" the fourth appeared first in 1853 dealing with the period of Mishnah and Talmud, followed by the third and subsequent volumes. The last to be published were vols. I and II in 1872. In order to write them—they depict the Biblical period—Graetz made a journey to Palestine.

About Graetz himself there is literature in plenty. His biographies were written by M. Brann, his disciple and successor at the Breslau Seminary, and later by J. Meisels. S. W. Baron, inter alia, deals with his historiography; Hermann Cohen, Max Wiener, A. Lewkowitz, N. Rotenstreich and Hans Liebeschuetz deal with the intellectual-historical and historical-philosophical aspects of his historiography.

[159] The essay was republished by Ludwig Feuchtwanger as a Schocken book in 1935. This edition unfortunately does not include Frankel's important comments, which criticize the view of Graetz that monotheism is not a constitutive factor in Judaism. This reproof is then taken up in Hermann Cohen's essay "Graetz's Philosophie der juedischen Geschichte" in vol. III of Cohen's Juedische

In his magnum opus, the "History of the Jews", there is little to perceive of this "construction" with its Hegelian schema. Here Jewish history, from the early Christian era on, appears as a history of martyrdom of the Jews and of their spiritual endurance depicted in the life and work of Jewish scholars. What for Ranke, Droysen and the general historiography of the time is political history, becomes in Graetz the history of persecutions where the policy of secular—and still more of ecclesiastical—rulers is reflected in regard to the Jews. And in place of the concept of a "national spirit" which Graetz rejects because of its Romantic background and anti-Jewish inclination, he depicts the intellectual development of Judaism with a strong enlightenment-rationalist touch. Graetz is a historian, who takes sides and affirms or denies emotionally. The last volume, in particular, dealing with the first half of the nineteenth century and the beginning of the Reform movement, is full of trenchant and often unjust, one-sided judgments. Yet in the earlier volumes he criticizes just as vigorously mysticism, the Kabbalah, Talmudism and, always, the enemies—especially ecclesiastic opponents—of the Jews.

Graetz had to gather and prepare his source material largely himself. He did not find it, like the Ranke school, in the archives but in chronicles, books and literary works. His adaptation of this material occurs at the end of each volume in comprehensive notes, which themselves often assume the character of independent monographs. For present day users of Graetz's history these notes, with their numerous source data and analyses, still retain their importance. Here we can follow the pioneer historian at work with his intuitive "feel" for connections and his sometimes daring guesses and conjectures. The English translation of his "History of the Jews" that appeared in six volumes in the U.S.A. between 1891 and 1892 unfortunately does not include the notes, which make the work complete.

Graetz was also engaged in other spheres. He lectured on Bible in the Breslau Seminary and wrote, inter alia, a commentary on the Psalms. In his very first work "Gnostizismus und Judentum" (Gnosticism and Judaism) 1846, he is concerned with important religious historical themes. For many years he was editor of the "Monatschrift" and engaged in the controversy with Treitschke. But all these spheres of activity recede into the background in relation to his monumental historical work. As historian he is the Jewish counterpart to the eminent German historians of the nineteenth century.

The youngest member of the circle round Frankel at the Breslau Seminary was *Manuel Joel* (1826-1890). Joel[160] brought a new element into the Wis-

---

Schriften, 1924. Graetz reached his assertion out of an over-sophistication of the idealistic concept of an immanent idea. Frankel and Cohen maintain that Graetz withdrew this assertion. But much later Graetz wrote to his friend, Moses Hess, that he (Hess) was a complete—and he himself three-quarter—Spinozist. (Letter of 9.28.1868. Cf. Liebeschuetz p. 150 ff.).

[160] On Joel see MGWJ (1926, 70th year, p. 305 ff.). dedicated to his 100's birthday, with contributions by two former pupils, Caesar Seligmann and A. Eckstein, and by Max Freudenthal, Beermann, J. Heinemann and Karl Joel, the Basle philosopher and nephew of Joel.

senschaft of Judaism. He was probably the first—at least the first significant —scholar of the "Science" of Judaism who in training, interest and orientation was a *philosopher*. The pioneers of Jewish studies previously came from classical philology or from Oriental studies. As far as philosophy was concerned they stood for the most part on the fringe. Only Graetz—through his teacher Braniss at Breslau, quite an independent Hegelian—was, at least in his theory of history and early writings on Gnosticism and Judaism, more occupied with philosophical themes, though without deeper systematic interests. Even Munk and Steinschneider with their rich knowledge of Arabic philosophy were essentially orientalists. It was Joel who upset this balance. He too was a classical philologist. For a good knowledge of the classics was still a normal basic requirement in the first half of the nineteenth century for every academic study, doctoral theses being written in Latin. Joel in fact took the classical teachers' examination in Latin and Greek, and taught these, at the start of his career, in the Seminary's preparatory course for candidates with insufficient educational background for the Breslau Seminary and the university. In the main, however, he was and continued to be a philosopher. His teacher in Berlin was A. Trendelenburg, opponent of Hegelian philosophy and logician of the Aristotelian school. Joel quickly developed into a Kantian. But whereas Kant's influence on his contemporaries usually stemmed from his ethics with its rigorous moral law—which, as we saw, was felt to be congenial to the moral precepts of Judaism—it was the systematic impulses of Kantian philosophy that influenced Joel from the start. Joel's Kantianism was thus quite untypical for his day. He was a precursor of the Kantian Renaissance, which almost two decades later gave rise to neo Kantianism. In his treatment of the philosophy of religion from the systematic basis of Kantian philosophy, Joel has probably only one Jewish predecessor, the physician *Solomon Ludwig Steinheim* of Altona. In his detailed review of the second volume of Steinheim's "Offenbarungslehre" (Doctrine of Revelation) Joel's approach comes to its first and most concise expression.[161] Here he writes that, through Kant's critique of the proofs of God, "religion is freed of its only—at least its only dangerous— enemy.... Metaphysics and religion are sworn enemies"[162] Joel too sees religion founded on revelation. But for him the content of revelation are the postulates of practical reason. In this way revelation creates "objective morality, a moral life". It is the driving force behind reason. Revelation first enabled reason to demonstrate the correspondence between revealed truths and their postulates.[163]

[161] MGWJ Vol. VI, 1857, p. 38 ff and p. 73 ff.

[162] loc. cit., p. 38.

[163] op. cit. p. 40. This characteristically dependent relationship of reason upon revelation—also found in different form in the criticized Steinheim—is to be found again in Cohen's phrase, "Revelation is the creation of reason". Cf. Cohen, "Religion der Vernunft" (Religion of Reason), 2nd ed., 1929, p. 84. See also the essay of the present author "Steinheim und Kant" in Yearbook V of the Leo Baeck Institute, London 1960, p. 168 ff.

Joel's Kantianism came to the fore once again much later. In his "Relig-ioes-philosophische Zeitfragen" (Topical Religious-philosophical Problems) that appeared in 1876, he reiterates: "To me, and many others besides, it is always as though that which stands the test in our daily views, are only the spolia opima (copious spoils) of the 'long-since surpassed' Kant";[164] and, "One returns again and again to Kant".[165] Joel never abandoned this Kant-ianism of his.[166]

Joel's significance for the Wissenschaft of Judaism lies in the fact that he, the philosopher, became the historian of medieval Jewish philosophy. In a number of writings[167] he outlines the religious philosophies of Maimonides, Levi ben Gerson and Ḥasdai Crescas. He was the first to follow the lines of thought extending from these philosophers to the philosophy of Christian scholasticism and beyond to modern philosophy. He investigated, for ex-ample, the influence of Maimonides on Albertus Magnus, and that of Crescas on Spinoza. He devoted a special study to Spinoza's Jewish sources.

Joel did pioneering work not only for the inclusion of the Jewish medieval philosophy of religion in the general history of philosophy. In a double volume, "Blicke in die Religionsgeschichte des ersten und zweiten nach-christlichen Jahrhunderts"[168] (Glimpses into the History of Religion of the First and Second Centuries of the Christian Era), he explores the connections between paganism, Judaism and early Christianity. Here too he traced hitherto unnoticed culturo-historical associations.

Of the later generation of lecturers at the Breslau Seminary only a few became as well known as that first circle round Frankel. *Jacob Guttmann* (1845-1919) extended Joel's studies on the connections between the Jewish philosophy of religion and scholasticism. *Isaac Heinemann* (1876-1954) who edited the "Monatschrift" for many years, created in his "Philons griechische und juedische Bildung" (Philo's Greek and Jewish Education), 1932, a standard work of Philo studies, in which he shook and rectified outdated conceptions about Philo.

Following the Breslau model, similar institutions of learning very soon arose in London, Vienna, Budapest and New York.[169] American Reform Judaism founded the "Hebrew Union College" in Cincinnati in 1875; and

---

[164] Religioes-philosophische Zeitfragen in zusammenhaengenden Aufsaetzen besprochen von Dr. M. Joel (Topical religious-philosophical problems in related essays discussed by M. Joel), Breslau 1876, preface p. 5. This book deals with the positions of Kant and Schopenhauer vis-à-vis the historical religions, with Kant's philosophy of religion and with David Friedrich Strauss.

[165] op. cit., p. 37.

[166] Testimony of his nephew Karl Joel in MGWJ, Vol. LXX, 1926 p. 318.

[167] Most of them appeared in the annual Seminary Reports and were collected by him in his two-volumed "Beitraege zur Geschichte der Philosophie (Contributions to the History of Philosophy), Breslau, 1876.

[168] The two vols. appeared in 1880 and 1883, respectively.

[169] Jews' College, London (1856); Juedisch-theologische Lehranstalt, Vienna (1893); Landesrab-binerschule, Budapest (1877); Jewish Theological Seminary, New York (1886).

German neo-Orthodoxy established the "Rabbiner-Seminar für das ortho-
doxe Judentum" in Berlin, 1873. Similarly in Berlin, following Geiger's
call there as rabbi, the "Hochschule für die Wissenschaft des Judentums"
was founded in 1872. The latter had been planned as a purely scientific
establishment, independent in outlook, where scholars of the most varied
theological tendencies have always taught. However, in practice, the college
became a rabbinical training centre from which predominantly liberal rabbis
emerged.[170] For it was only in exceptional cases that Jewish scholars could
devote their time to scholarship without serving as rabbi.[171]

The Wissenschaft of Judaism had also created a new type of rabbi. Formerly the rabbi was a scholar distinguished by his thorough knowledge of
Talmud and of religious-legal literature. He was president of the local rabbinical court, and usually of a Talmudic academy as well, where he taught
Talmudic literature. But he was not a priest administering sacraments or
carrying out sacramental functions. This traditional type of rabbi must have
appeared obsolete to the new generation aspiring to adaptation and equality.
In the estimation of this generation, Talmudic scholarship had become
valueless, superfluous and meaningless, having no longer any direct bearing
on their life, and seeming rather to symbolize the old separation and exclusion from the life of their fellow-citizens. Since the Enlightenment,
rabbinic influence in Germany and Western Europe had been receding more

---

[170] When the "Hochschule" obtained corporation rights from the Prussian government, its name was
changed to "Lehranstalt fur die Wissenschaft des Judentums" in 1883, as one did not want to give a
Jewish scientific institute the status of a college. Only in 1923 could it be renamed "Hochschule",
until the National Socialists changed the name again to "Lehranstalt". With its enforced closing on
July 19, 1942 the last activity of a Jewish scientific institute in Germany ceased. The other two
establishments in Breslau and Berlin had already been closed at the end of the 'thirties.—It may be
worth noting that as early as in the beginning of the 'thirties a woman student, Miss Regina Jonas,
graduated as rabbi from the Berlin 'Hochschule'. After serving in Berlin for some years she perished
in the Holocaust.
[171] Of the eminent representatives of the Wissenschaft of Judaism we mention the following: *Seligmann
Baer* (1825-1897), Masoretic studies and editor of a scholarly edition of the Prayer book; *Abraham
Berliner* (1883-1915), work on Jewish medieval folklore, on the Jews in Rome and publication of a
scholarly edition of Rashi's commentary; *David Kaufmann* (1852-1899), author of 'Geschichte der
Attributenlehre' (History of the Doctrine of Attributes) and of genealogical-historical works; *Wilhelm
Bacher* (1850-1913), Iranist and historian of early Talmudic scholars; *Solomon Schechter* (1847-
1915) discoverer of the Cairo 'Genizah' and of the Hebrew original of the "Wisdom of Ben-Sira",
author of books on rabbinical theology, later President of the Jewish Thelogical Seminary in New
York, theorist of American Conservative Judaism; *Julius Guttmann* (1880-1950), son of Jacob Guttmann,
historian of Jewish religious philosophy; *Moritz Stern* (1864-1939), history of Jewish communities;
*Julius Aronius* (1861-1893), documents on early medieval history; *David Hoffmann* (1843-1921),
Talmud, Midrash and Bible scholar, opponent of Wellhausen; *Ismar Elbogen* (1874-1943), Liturgical
history and history of German Jewry; *Simon Dubnow* (1860-1941) murdered in Riga Ghetto, por-
trayer of world history of the Jewish people; historian of Russian and Polish Jewry and of Ḥasidism;
*Leo Baeck* (1873-1956) Midrash, history of religion, early Christianity as part of Jewish history. Of
those living today: *Gershom Scholem*, mysticism and Kabbalah; *Fritz Isaac Baer*, Spanish Jewry,
era of Second Temple; *Salo W. Baron*, Jewish social and religious history.

and more. One report of a community committee in Berlin on the function of a rabbi, defines him simply as a "Kauscher-Waechter', namely, one who supervises ritual slaughter! This illustrates the entire disregard of that generation for its scholars—once appreciated as the leaders and spiritual aristocracy of the Jewish people. And it was precisely then, at the turn of the eighteenth to the nineteenth century, that there were at the head of rabbinates in Germany several distinguished personalities, like Ezekiel Landau (1713-1793) in Prague, Raphael Cohen (1722-1803) in Altona and Akiba Eger (1761-1837) in Poznan.

The new age believed it needed other spiritual leaders, men whose tasks were modelled on that of Protestant clergy. Their education was to be attested by a university degree. Men were sought who were good speakers and who could outwardly represent aspiring Jewish citizenry. Less importance was attached to their traditional Jewish knowledge. Thus, from the beginning of the nineteenth century onwards we find in many places so-called preachers, or as they were frequently termed "teachers of the people", who, with a more or less basic Jewish knowledge, seemed to satisfy at least the other modern demands made on them. The very title of "rabbi" had fallen into discredit. In fact, a real rabbi in the traditional sense, like Isaac Bernays, preferred to be employed as a "spiritual official" and not to be titled rabbi but Ḥakham (wise one), the title of Sephardic rabbis—something that in Germany sounded at any rate exotic and therefore more fashionable.

The men of the Wissenschaft of Judaism very soon recognised the untenability of a situation, that threatened to hand over their religious and cultural heritage to the doubtful hands of ignorant speechifiers. The new historical approach to Judaism had in a certain way heightened Jewish self-awareness again. If Talmudic learning was no longer to be of overriding importance, the teachers of Judaism should nevertheless possess a sound historical knowledge of their religion. In this way there emerged the new type of German—and later of west-European and American—rabbi who obtained his education at the aforementioned new academic rabbinical colleges. However, that the Wissenschaft of Judaism served primarily for the training of rabbis, and that its representatives—with the exception of a few seminary lecturers—were also almost exclusively rabbis, presented a great danger for the new academic discipline.[172] Zunz and Steinschneider had already feared and resisted this threatening "theologization". Both men were in their lifetime fierce opponents of the Breslau Seminary and its teachers, and also opposed the Berlin Hochschule despite its purely scholarly

---

[172] Gershom Scholem, himself one of the most distinguished Judaic scholars and creator of a new branch of learning, Kabbalah-studies, has criticized the theologization of the Wissenschaft of Judaism severest of all in his essay, "Hirhurim al Ḥokhmat Israel" in Luaḥ Ha'areẓ, 1944/45, and later in Bulletin no. 9 of the Leo Baeck Institute, Tel Aviv, 1960: "The Science of Judaism then and now", p. 10 ff.

programme. Both constantly refused a call to and every co-operation with these institutes.

This theologization was, it is true, only from a sociological aspect. Systematic theological questions were far removed from nineteenth century Judaic scholarship.[173] In the few cases where they were touched upon, it was in historical perspective, as for example, in David Kaufmann's "History of the Doctrine of Attributes". But a "science" which lay chiefly in the hands of a profession whose tasks, objectives and mentality were, per se, remote from scholarship, could not remain untouched by these sociological realities. Its choice of themes was limited. One inclined towards an uncritical idealization of events and personages of the past. A sometimes obtrusive, apologetic and homiletic strain entered their scientific presentation. The newly enlightened well-to-do Jewish middle classes, who aspired towards social and legal integration, were intellectually quite unassuming. However, it was from them that the community committees—employers of the rabbis—were recruited. And their attitude to learning affected the scholarly aspirations of their rabbis in turn. One preferred, as Scholem puts it, to live in the drawing-room. Into that "enlightened" milieu, mysticism of every kind —Kabbalah, Ḥasidism—did not seem to fit. Concern with such things seemed to detract from the good modern impression one wanted to make. One also avoided the serious social problem presented by the beggar Jews in the seventeenth and eighteenth centuries. Only a generation that stopped asking what others would say, has been able to free itself also in the Wissenschaft of Judaism from such limitations.

[173] The numerous authors of religious school-books and catechisms, which appeared throughout the century, have nothing to do with Wissenschaft of Judaism.

# CHAPTER 15

# *Reform and Neo-Orthodoxy*

Efforts towards reform in Judaism came more and more into evidence from the end of the eighteenth century onwards. In the nineteenth century these efforts crystallized into various religious parties: the Reform movement proper, neo-Orthodoxy and a positive-historical middle grouping. In these parties and trends and their kaleidoscope of personal and local nuances was the vague feeling that the traditional forms of religious expression were no longer adequate.

One could now expect that this attitude would soon direct itself in particular against the constraint of the religious legal precepts that up till now minutely regulated Jewish life. It was precisely in this direction that some beginnings were already theoretically taking place. Thus Mordecai Gumpel Shnaber-Levison had distinguished between God as eternal truth and the divine works and commands apprehended in time—an interpretation only a step away from the relativization of the religious law. Saul Ascher had given the doctrinal content of Judaism priority over its sociological mode of expression, the "constituted" law, thereby explicitly opposing Mendelssohn. The younger Mendelssohnians had dropped Mendelssohn's synthesis of the religion of reason and revealed law, thereby not only de-grading the law but seeing in it a drawback for Judaism as the religion of reason.

Then there was—for Friedlaender, Bendavid, Saul Ascher and with them for ever-widening circles of arrived Jewish citizenry—the emancipatory political factor. The religious precepts lifted the Jew out of his environment, severing him from it or at least rendering natural social intercourse with non-Jews more difficult. This religious particularism was seen on the Christian side and by the Jews of the Enlightenment as an obstacle to the legal and social integration of Jews. Religious particularism also existed in Christianity with its various contending denominations and sects. Jewish particularism, however, was not only caused by dogmatic differences, as in Christian denominations, but by its distinct way of life moulded by the religious law.

Meanwhile the concept of nation had also changed. Previously it denoted only a special, recognisable but not necessarily ethnically homogeneous social group. However, since the Romantic era and the Wars of Liberation against Napoleon, the concept "nation" in German took on that emotional context that we still associate with the word today. So that now when the national particularism of the Jews was spoken of, an anti-Jewish, anti-emancipatory tone resounded in this reproach, which alarmed Jews as they strove for legal and civil equality.

Those well-to-do circles, influenced to a greater or lesser extent by education and culture, or in any case by the outward glitter of their surroundings, and craving for social prestige, began to feel ashamed of their Judaism. They sought to free themselves from it whether through baptism or through trying to conceal or laughingly make light of it. Probably, from the time of this generation that had become uncertain of itself, do we first find the phenomenon of Jewish self-hatred.—In some places like Prague, Prossnitz, Hamburg inter alia, where descendants of the clandestine Sabbatai Zevi followers or Frankists lived, the antinomianism of these circles had to some extent taken root. These groups, strengthened by Enlightenment tendencies, may have formed a potential reservoir for the Reform movement.[174]

Thus, when Friedlaender and Bendavid spoke of the "shameful ceremonial law"; when the young Zunz still wrote, "Until the Talmud is overthrown nothing can be done",[175] the urgent question had to be posed sooner or later: in what form Judaism, reduced to a religion of reason, was to be presented. For men like Friedlaender, Bendavid and Zunz wanted to safeguard religion, at least its Jewish character, freed from its traditional fetters. That was already implicit in the identification of the religion of reason with Judaism.

One would therefore have thought that the Reform movement would have concerned itself with the *question of religious law*. But from the start its central preoccupation was, surprisingly, an outward concern, namely reforming the synagogal service. Reform continued to be essentially *reform of the synagogue service*.

Various and sometimes mutually incompatible reasons had combined which, for the Reform movement, pushed the question of the law into the background. For an initially small but rapidly increasing number of Jews, practical observance of the religious precepts had lost its meaning. This departure from the traditional way of life was gradual and varied from one person to another. Yet modern education and the progressive secularization in which Jews and their environment were caught up, carried matters so far that religion lost its position as a guiding force in the life of both Jews and non-Jews. The question of the validity, re-interpretation or modification of the law was no longer of any consequence for these circles. When one dared

---

[174] Cf. references by Scholem. p. cit. p. 333.
[175] Zunz to Ehrenberg on Oct. 13, 1818, in Glatzer, *Leopold and Adelheid Zunz* p. 13.

at all to broach the subject it was mainly for other reasons, namely, emanci-patory political ones.

Nevertheless until the second half of the nineteenth century the great majority of German Jews, especially those in Poznan and southern Germany, had remained conservative in their attitude towards the religious law. Only with the migration from the rural and small urban communities into the cities did this outlook decline, very soon leaving the "Torah-true" groups nearly everywhere in the minority. Yet the extent to which religious practice was still observed even by the "liberal" majority, varied from family to family, from community to community.

Despite the frequent anti-talmudic slogans that were expressed, especially at the beginning, *there was in principle hardly any disavowal*—as by the Karaïtes—*of the talmudic tradition.* (A clear disowning of the Talmud and of dogmatic or practical adherence to the law deduced from it is probably only to be found in the pamphlet of the Frankfurt *Verein der Reform-freunde* (Society of the Friends of Reform) 1843. However, the tendencies expressed in it were rejected as attestations of unbelief even by radical leaders of Reform like David Einhorn.[176]) On the contrary, efforts were made to find a religious legal basis for the changes in life and worship that were suggested or adopted. One looked for cases of precedent in the Talmud or in the Responsa literature, and endeavoured as far as possible to attach oneself to a real or supposed tradition. *Michael Creizenach* (1789-1842) in Frankfurt published a reformed 'Shulḥan Arukh'.[177] *Aaron Chorin*, the pugnacious Hungarian Reform rabbi, gave even halakhic proofs for praying with uncovered head.[178] Holdheim argued against rabbinic law from the principles of the talmudic intellectual position. And Geiger's dynamic con-cept of tradition linked this to that of the ancient Pharisees and Tannaïtes.

In all the discussions concerning reform there was no question of *antino-mian* tendencies. The religious command, the divine call, has always been characteristic of Jewish religiosity, even when the accent of this call was placed on the ethical command as the kernel of which the ceremonial forms and customs were merely the shell.

The more Jewish culture and education declined and the influence of the city increased, the more there retreated into the *ethics* of Judaism whatever remained of Jewish consciousness. Of religious practice—and even that

---

[176] The Prayer Book of the West-London Synagogue of British Jews—the first British Reformed Congregation—advocated in its preface (1841) a biblical, non-talmudic Judaism, but without realising it in practice.

[177] Schulchan Aruch oder Encyklopaedische Darstellung des Mosaischen Gesetzes (Shulḥan Arukh or Encyclopaedic Presentation of the Mosaic Law), 4 vols., 1833, 1837, 1839, 1840.

[178] Aaron Chorin, Igeret Elasaf, Prague 1826, describes the journey of an African rabbi, Ibn Ḥorin—behind whom the author conceals himself—to Germany and Hungary, giving his observations on the customs of the German Jews.

which only approximated to it in the traditional sense—there were left mostly only residua.

The central interest of German Jewry until well beyond the middle of the nineteenth century—alongside the interest in emancipation—continued to be the synagogue service. Efforts at reform were focused on this and expressed a basic conservative tendency. Responsible Jews thought they could check apostasy from Judaism and the risk of baptism if the outward form of Judaism, the synagogue service, were made more respectable for Jews themselves and for the outside world.

By discarding the traditional Jewish costume—the long coat and beard— and by speaking German, the individual Jew had outwardly adapted to his environment. Jewish education had already been pushed aside to a large extent by secular education. Now the synagogue service was to be accommodated to the world's taste.

In the old synagogue or prayer room a relaxed homely and rather informal atmosphere prevailed, although old congregational regulations were concerned with preserving a certain decorum. One was not making a formal visit when one attended synagogue. The service was frequently a disorderly medley of praying voices, drowning that of the reader. It was an expression of the individual communicating with God. And, before and after the service, the local synagogues and learning-rooms were places where different groups sat together and "learnt" the Talmud or quite factually discussed the day's events.

With the decline of Jewish education, prayers in Hebrew and more so in Aramaic had become unintelligible for an increasing number of Jews. This was especially true with regard to the *Piyyutim*, poetic additions to the Prayers for the festivals. These contained many allusions to talmudic passages and ideas, for whose appreciation the linguistic and educational prerequisites were now lacking. The same applied to the sermon. In the Ashkenazi rite there was seldom any preaching—generally only twice a year apart from special occasions. These addresses of the rabbis were intended to elucidate religious precepts and entailed quoting and interpreting passages from the Talmud. Meanwhile fewer and fewer Jews were able to follow the preacher's arguments, whose language moreover was Yiddish interspersed with Hebrew quotations.

Now the individual and informal service of the *Judenschule*[179] —this word was often heard, and is heard even today, as ridicule or invective from non-Jews—was to be transposed into an orderly, aesthetically appealing "cult". It was to be made "worthier", as one put it. To this end synagogal orders of service were introduced during the first decades of the nineteenth century, often with official approval, setting out precise conduct and order

---

[179] "Shul" (school), the popular Yiddish name for the place where one prays and learns, indicates that learning in Jewish view is part of Worship.

for worship. The Protestant service provided a model, as the reforming efforts had originated in the Protestant surroundings of North Germany. German chorals were introduced, in many places a choir and an organ and, above all, the Sermon in German. The aim of these sermons was no longer to give instruction, but to follow the Christian ideal of edification.[180] The synagogue service came to be an *aesthetically* appealing performance offered to the congregation but scarcely based on its members active participation.

The first innovations in the synagogue service are associated with the name of *Israel Jacobson* (1768-1828). Jacobson, a Brunswick Court agent with strong educational interests, had founded a boarding school at Seesen in 1801, whose purpose—following the principle of the philanthropinists—was to foster understanding between religions in the spirit of the Enlightenment, and which from its inception accepted Christian alongside Jewish pupils. Jacobson became president of the Jewish consistory in the Napoleonic kingdom of Westphalia, and in this official capacity was now able to carry through his educational and liturgical reforms. In 1810 he had introduced the choral singing of German hymns and an *organ* into his school synagogue in Seesen. With the organ—at first within the private setting of a school service—a new element entered the synagogue service which was very soon to rouse heated discussion. The introduction or non-introduction of the organ became and remained the point on which parties divided. This is indicative of the entire superficiality of the situation. For even the synagogues which strictly adhered to the old custom had promptly taken over many elements of reform: orders of service, choir, sermon in German and even, to some extent, German hymns. But it was the organ, out of all proportion to its importance, that became the dividing line between traditional and neologist congregations, even if the latter changed nothing in content, text or scope of the prayers.[181]

After the dissolution of the kingdom of Westphalia, Jacobson moved to Berlin in 1815, where he started a synagogue service in his home on the pattern of that in Seesen. He soon had to move into the more spacious house of the banker Jacob Herz Beer, father of Meyerbeer the composer. A number of younger preachers such as Kley, Auerbach and especially

---

[180] Cf. Alexander Altmann, The New Style of Preaching in the 19th Century German Jewry, In Studies, pp. 65-116. Also by the same author: Leopold Zunz als Prediger, in Yearbook VI of LBI, London, 1961, pp. 3-59.

[181] In the Temple of Jerusalem Levite choirs sang to instrumental accompaniment, as many Psalm titles indicate. After the destruction of the Temple instrumental music altogether ceased as a sign of mourning, though it was retained for weddings and festivities. Instrumental music by Jews on the Sabbath seemed objectionable simply because instruments had on occasion to be tuned-up. More important than halakhic reasons against the organ was the psychological one, since the organ was well known as a specific component of the Christian service, although there were organs in synagogues in Italy, in the Orient and even in Prague.

Zunz[182] preached in this so-called "German synagogue". In April 1823 it was closed by royal command. Complaints had reached the Government from the Orthodox side about the new service, which was denounced as "deistic". The king forbade every deviation from the traditional Jewish service, particularly the sermon in German. In this way a stop was put to all innovations and reforms in Prussia for a long time.

One of the preachers of the Jacobsonian synagogue, Dr. Eduard *Kley*, was appointed director of the Jewish Free School in Hamburg in 1817. Here Kley organised a committee to implement a service on the lines of Jacobson's. This *Tempelvereinigung* (Temple Association) soon comprised many of the well-to-do Jews of Hamburg and was able to open a Temple in 1818. (The new name was intended to emphasize its diversion from the traditional synagogue.)

The purpose of the Temple Association was to make the synagogue service attractive again to a generation, that no longer found any religious or aesthetic satisfaction in the old form of worship and who had virtually ceased to understand the liturgy. Thus, Hebrew prayers were shortened and partly recited in German paraphrase, choral singing was introduced with organ accompaniment and a regular sermon delivered in German. To support Dr. Kley, Dr. Gotthold *Salomon* was called from Dessau, who soon acquired the reputation of an eloquent pulpit speaker.

On the initiative and with the financial help of Jacobson, the Alsatian rabbi Eliezer Liebermann published in 1818 four responsa by Italian and Hungarian rabbis in favour of a reformed service.[183] When in 1819 the Temple Association printed a revised Prayer Book reflecting their viewpoint, the Orthodox party in Hamburg published contra responsa by the most famous rabbis of the day. However, the arguments of these contrary opinions, according to which a change in the texts of the prayers was not permissible so as not to destroy the kabbalistic meaning behind their words and letters, made no impression upon the enlightened Jews. The religious legal objections moreover were not always valid, for prayer in the language of the country, for example, had never been forbidden. Also, as far as organ and instrumental music was concerned, there were expert opinions pro et contra. —The aesthetic innovations and modest textual changes in the Temple Prayer Book were not based on a well-reasoned principle. Such a principle was only stated fifteen years later by Abraham Geiger in his concept of historical development.

At the Leipzig Fair a filial service of the Temple Association was arranged

---

[182] Zunz relinquished his position in 1822, after a sharp sermon in which he had chastised the smug, self-satisfied and spiritless Jewish emancipated citizenry. At that time his anti-Talmudism had already changed to a conservative attitude. But throughout his life he remained true to his dislike of clerical-like behaving rabbis.

[183] Eliezer Liebermann published them under the name *Nogah Hazedek* and *Or Hanogah*, Dessau, 1818. The contrary responsa appeared under the title *Eleh Divre Habrit*, Hamburg, 1819.

through which this novel form of service became known to Jews from all over the world. The Hamburg Temple service came to be a conspicuous symbol and starting point of a movement, which drew widening circles of Jewry in Germany, England and the USA.

Meanwhile, however, the initiative had passed over to the traditional party in Hamburg which had the majority of the community and of its committee behind it. In view of the success of the Temple Association the committee saw the necessity of electing a rabbinical leader, possessing both rabbinic and academic training. Such a leader was found in the young Isaac Bernays.

*Bernays*[184] (1792-1849) had studied at the Wuerzburg Talmud School and in the philosophical faculty of Wuerzburg University. He was one of the first rabbis to have a completed academic training, as was soon in demand by many congregations. He had intelligence, education and initiative, all one would have looked for at that time in the Reform camp rather than in Orthodoxy. Bernays was and felt himself to be pioneer of a new kind of Torah-true Judaism, the later Neo-Orthodoxy, which in the wider sense was part of the Reform movement. He himself stressed the difference from the old rabbinate in that he was not appointed as "rabbi" but as "spiritual officer", calling himself not "rabbi", but according to sephardic custom Ḥakham (the wise one). This new designation of "spiritual officer" expressed in a dangerous way the tendency of the time of making the rabbi into a cleric of the Christian pattern and a mere divine service functionary. His successors, both in the Torah-true and the Reform parties, soon returned to the title of rabbi. Yet Bernays' attitude shows how much the word rabbi at that time had fallen into disrepute. The "Rav" of the old school was primarily the man of learning who mastered Talmud and religious law, and from knowledge of these was capable of reaching decision on religious and ritual matters. If over and above this he was philosopher, kabbalist, ethical teacher or a religious personality, who could be leader and example to his congregation, then these were desirable extras that enhanced his authority. The rabbi in central and western Europe and in the USA now came more and more to be "spiritual leader" (Geistlicher), teacher of the ethics and ideals of Judaism, pastor and social worker or Jewish scholar. Only a few still combined with this the necessary talmudic knowledge that gave them the ability to make religious legal decisions; and still fewer were recognized as rabbinical authorities also in east European Jewry. Bernays had started this development with the concept of "spiritual officer".

From the reformers in Berlin and Hamburg, Bernays took over for the traditional service of his congregation the German sermon and an order of service with an eye to aesthetic decorum. Through these innovations and

---

[184] Cf. Ed. Duckesz in the Yearbook of the *Juedisch-Literarische Gesellschaft*, vol. V, 1907, p. 297 ff.

his great gift of speaking he succeeded in making his synagogue attractive again for the educated. He gave public lectures in German—that too an innovation—on Jewish religious philosophy, and introduced secular subjects to the curriculum of the Jewish School in Hamburg.[185]

Bernays had been influenced in Wuerzburg by the philosophy of Schelling. It moulded—in conjunction with the mystical Judaism of his teacher, the Wuerzburg rabbi Abraham Bing[186] —his religious views. More than any of his Jewish contemporaries, Bernays was a romantic. He never distinguished himself as a scholar or writer. However, early on a remarkable magazine, *Der Bibelsche Orient*, that appeared anonymously in 1821, was attributed to him.[187] Here, proceeding from Herder's 'Vom Geiste der Ebraeischen Poesie' (Spirit of Hebrew Poetry), the emergence of Judaism from ancient pagan polytheism is described by means of strange etymology and symbolism. Whether this work stems from Bernays, or from a Jew at all, seems to me still uncertain. It expresses at any rate the notions of a Munich circle of Schelling enthusiasts to which Bernays could have belonged. Etymology and symbolism played a major role in Bernays' sermons and later also with Bernays disciple S. R. Hirsch.

This disciple, *Samson Raphael Hirsch* (1808-1888), was the organiser and theorist of Neo-Orthodoxy. Hirsch studied together with Geiger in Bonn, was rabbi in Oldenburg, Emden and later in Nikolsburg in Moravia. After the Frankfurt rabbinate had been occupied by Leopold Stein, a supporter of Reform, extremely Torah-true Frankfurt Jews united, left the local community and called Hirsch to be their rabbi in 1851. From Frankfurt Hirsch advocated the setting up of separate Orthodox congregations also

---

[185] In the course of time this school developed into the Talmud-Torah High School, which existed into the Nazi era—cf. I. Goldschmidt 'Geschichte der Talmud-Thora-Realschule in Hamburg, Festschrift zur Hundertjahrfeier der Anstalt' (History of the Talmud-Torah High School in Hamburg, Commemorative Volume on the Centenary Celebration of the Institute), 1805-1905, printed by S. Nissensohn, Hamburg 1905.

[186] Bing was pupil of the Frankfurt kabbalist, Nathan Adler, who had founded his own kind of Hasidism, contemporaneous with, but probably independent of, Polish Hasidism.

[187] On the question of authorship see Hans Bach, 'Der Bibelsche Orient und sein Verfasser' (The Biblical Orient and its Author) in ZGJD, VII, 1937, pp. 14-45. Bach tries to prove Bernays' authorship without fully convincing me. When in the "Biblical Orient" (Part II, p. 67), the "man" is spoken of who "had to rise" from his Biblical people and "prepare the way for the world reign of the same (i.e. of the original Biblical idea)", this sounds odd in the mouth of a Jewish author, for here a Messiah is spoken of who has already appeared. The author could hardly even be a Jewish Sabbatian or Frankist, since the tendency of the work throughout is not antinomian. One would be inclined rather to think of a Christian kabbalist like Franz Joseph Molitor, teacher at the Jewish Philanthropin in Frankfurt, or of some unknown person from the Munich circle round Franz von Baader, possibly with Judaic assistance from Bernays. See also the remarks (quoted by H. Bach) of Prof. Wagner, Bernays' teacher in Wuerzburg, who first had Bernays in mind, but had been notified from Munich that the author was previously a Catholic theologian. That von Kalb, a Wuerzburg university lecturer who had recommended Bernays to Hamburg, is not the author, as suggested by some, has been proved, in my opinion, by Bach.

SAMSON RAPHAEL HIRSCH

LEOPOLD ZUNZ

HEINRICH GRAETZ

HERMANN COHEN

LEO BAECK

ABRAHAM GEIGER

MOSES MENDELSSOHN
(in his late thirties)

GABRIEL RIESSER

THEODOR HERZL

DAVID FRIEDLAENDER

EMDEN'S TOMBSTONE (in Altona)

SOLOMON LUDWIG STEINHEIM

in other places, if necessary through secession from local communities where their leaders were followers of Reform. Indeed, he succeeded in 1876 in putting through the Prussian Parliament the so-called Law of Secession (Austrittsgesetz). This enabled Jews—at first purely on religious grounds —to leave the local Jewish community and form separatist communities with full legal status.[188]

Separatist communities in the Hirschian sense came into existence only in a few places.[189] Hirsch's propaganda found in the most esteemed orthodox rabbi of the day in Germany, the "Wuerzburg Rav" *Seligmann Bamberger* (1807-1878), Bing's successor, an energetic antagonist, who opposed the rift in the communities. There were now within Torah-true Judaism two groups: the larger group of *Gemeinde-Orthodoxie* (orthodox members within the local communities) and the numerical weaker but extremist *Trennungs-Orthodoxie* (secessionist orthodoxy) of the separatist (Hirschian) communities, who refused any cooperation with *non-orthodox* Jews.

The local communities very soon showed consideration to their Torah-true members,[190] who in the cities usually comprised the minority. For them special services—in synagogues without organs—were arranged and Torah-true rabbis frequently engaged. This solution, first initiated in Breslau after an embittered quarrel lasting some years, was adopted in many large congregations. Smaller communities chose rabbis, who were acceptable to all groups. In this way the traditional principle of the united community was safeguarded. The moderate character which the German Reform movement had generally adopted in its religious practice was thus determined. It abandoned the name 'Reform' and called itself 'Liberal Judaism'. The great

---

[188] In contrast to the Anglo-Saxon countries, Jewry in Germany and central Europe is organized in local communities, which comprise all the Jews dwelling in this place.—In 1920, following the 1918 German Revolution, the clause in the law that secession might only ensure on religious grounds was dropped. In this new form the law of secession took on an unexpectedly negative aspect. For now anyone could, without the odium of leaving Judaism, withdraw from the community in order to save tax. Indifference was thereby strengthened and smaller communities in particular were frequently hard hit financially, or else fell into degrading dependence on a few large tax-payers, who could terrorize the community administrators by threatening to leave themselves.

[189] Such communities existed in Frankfurt, Berlin, Cologne, Wiesbaden, and a few also in other German states and in Switzerland. The separatist congregation in Koenigsberg eventually rejoined the local community.

[190] The expression *Orthodoxy* is taken from Christian terminology and is only applicable in a limited sense to the much less dogmatically defined Judaism. In Germany therefore the term *gesetzestreu* or 'Torah-true' Judaism—had come into use for those circles who strictly adhered to the religious law. Another designation was *konservativ* in contrast to *liberal*, as the advocates of Reform referred to themselves from the end of the nineteenth century on. These latter expressions, stemming from politics, are not very helpful, especially in other countries, where they are linked with other associations and easily give rise to misunderstanding. In the U.S.A., for example, 'conservatives' are what the "liberals" were in Germany. In England the 'Reform' synagogue denotes precisely the middle trend, even though more reformed than in Germany in general—whereas "liberal" in England means the radical Reform orientation.

influence of the Breslau Rabbinical Seminary and its mediating tendency contributed to this development.

The importance of Samson Raphael Hirsch lies in the theoretical foundation of modern *Neo-Orthodoxy*, whose influence extended far beyond the narrow circle of separatists and even beyond Torah-true Judaism.

In 1836 Hirsch published, under the pseudonym of Ben Uzziel, the *Neunzehn Briefe über das Judentum*,[191] which were to become famous. There followed a year later: *Horeb, Versuche ueber Jissroels Pflichten in der Zerstreuung*,[192] then a translation of the Pentateuch with commentary and a similar edition of the Psalms and Prayer Book. Hirsch also edited a magazine *Jeschurun*[193] and wrote a number of polemical and religious philosophical pamphlets in connection with his fight against the reformers and in support of the secession movement. He also founded a high school in Frankfurt. His interest in education is certainly one of the most important aspects of his entire activity, and much of his impact is due to his personal educational influence.

Judaism, according to Hirsch's conception, is an historical phenomenon, but its source and life-centre is the Torah, understood by him as the unity of Biblical and oral Law. Torah is direct revelation of God, even in its latest rabbinical developments, and as such stands outside history, unchangeable and demanding obedience. Israel's historic mission is to realise the Torah within a mankind striving for pleasure and intoxication of the senses. Lessing's concept of the education of the human race is seen by Hirsch as the mission of Israel. True, Jewish life in the present is in need of reform but its goal must be "education, elevation of the age to "Thauroh""[194] —not levelling Torah to the age, not lowering the peak to the shallowness of our life".[195] Only in this perspective does Hirsch welcome emancipation. Through the removal of legal and political oppression, greater possibilities and freedom are given to fulfill the commandments. Emancipation itself is a sign of the concept of justice now being realised among the nations, this concept having its basis in the divine demands of the Torah. In this belief Hirsch was the continuer of the ideology of the Enlightenment, as were his Jewish adversaries on the liberal wing. But emancipation as it applies to Jews must

[191] "Igrot Zafon, Nineteen Letters on Judaism. Preliminary enquiry regarding publication of essays by the said author about Israel and its obligations", ed. by Ben Uzziel, 1836, 4th ed., Frankfurt 1911 and 1919, New York, 1966.

[192] "Horeb, Essays on Israel's Responsibilities in the Diaspora. Primarily for Israel's thinking young Men and Women", by S. R. Hirsch, Grand-ducal chief Rabbi of Oldenburg, Altona 1837.

[193] Appeared 1854-1870 and again 1883-1886. — A number of other magazines also appeared under the name *Jeschurun*. The most important of these are two scientific periodicals, *Jeschurun* by Josef Kobak between 1856-1878 and the *Jeschurun* by J. Wohlgemuth, organ of the orthodox Rabbinical Seminary in Berlin, appearing between 1914-1930.

[194] Hirsch always used the ashkenazic pronounciation of Hebrew customary in Germany, e.g. Thauroh = Torah, Yisroel = Israel.

[195] "Nineteen Letters", Letter 17.

not on this account cause an opposing and thereby anti-historical effect, i.e. freedom to break away from the divine commands now manifestly prevailing in the world.

The re-interpretation of the commandments—dealt with principally in his second book "Horeb"—and likewise the symbolism and etymology of his commentary works, clearly show that for Hirsch the ethical content lies behind the religious commandments, challenges and customs. For him too, religion is only a part of morality as with his Reform opponents.

The mission of Israel for Hirsch consists in the realisation of the divine Law and the living out of this Law in daily life among the nations. This was already Israel's task when it was bound to its statehood and to the soil of the Holy Land. Yet land and state were merely a passing means, not the goal of Israel, which it can henceforth fulfill in the Diaspora and even better in its civil freedom now begun. Hirsch in fact will not allow the title "nation" to be applied to Israel since in German usage this word is always linked up with state and country. In order to signify the singularity of the Israelite people, the Hebrew name *Am Yissroel* should be retained. The future hope of return to the Holy Land is reserved for God's decision, which man may not forestall by his own action.[196]

Thus for Hirsch Judaism comes to be a confessionalised and strongly denationalised religion of *Yissroel-People*, who are the bearers of the divine Law in the world.

Hirsch's influence upon his followers was fascinating. They felt themselves to be a chosen élite, who joyfully assumed their mission and the life of sacrifice of the uncompromising orthodox Jew. A certain high-spiritedness and solemnity in manner and bearing were characteristic of Hirsch and the men he influenced.

The neo-Orthodoxy inaugurated by Bernays and S. R. Hirsch had important intellectual-historical consequences. It differed from traditional Rabbinic Judaism by affirming secular culture and adopting its values as far as these did not conflict with Jewish ones. Thus there emerged the new modern type of orthodox Jew, who combined strict observance of the Torah with a broad secular, often academic, education. This *modern orthodoxy*, however, later abandoned for the most part its 'secessionary' character and much of Hirsch's romantic philosophy.

Hirsch's rival was his Bonn student friend *Abraham Geiger* (1810-1874). We have already considered the importance of Geiger for the Wissenschaft

---

[196] See letters 8 and 9 and, on the concept of people, "Horeb" para. 607 and 608. From these reflections the World Organisation of Orthodox Judaism—later developed under the influence of Hirschean orthodoxy—the *Agudat Israel*, had for a long time a decidedly anti-zionist character. Long before the establishment of the state, however, agudist circles had already actively begun to participate in the building up of the land of Israel and, in fact, founded their own kibbutz movement and participated in several government coalitions.

of Judaism in the previous chapter. Since for Geiger the same ideas and principles applied to academic research, teaching and life, I would refer the reader to what has been said there.

This combination of scholar, theorist and practical rabbi made Geiger a central figure of the Reform movement. His colleagues and the Jewish public recognized him as such, and he himself was well aware of the significance of this.[197]

Geiger's fundamental contribution to the Reform movement was his new concept of tradition, which itself according to him, is a link in the living evolutionary development of Judaism. This *dynamic concept of tradition*, however, was considerably limited by Geiger both through his "periodizing" of Jewish history and through a supplementary selective schema.

Geiger divides Jewish history into four periods. 1. The period of revelation, comprising the Biblical span of time. 2. The period of tradition, from the close of the Bible era till the end of the Babylonian Talmud. 3. The period of rigid legalism, i.e. the entire Middle Ages reaching into the eighteenth century. 4. The period of criticism, the modern era of release from the bonds of the preceding period.[198]

This very periodization of history brings a certain unhistorical element into Geiger's interpretation of tradition. For the living evolutionary development is applied only to three of the four periods: the biblical, the talmudic and the present. Twelve hundred years of Jewish history—the whole of the Middle Ages—have been insignificant according to Geiger. This epoch is passed over. The present, following Geiger, can only receive impulses from the first two epochs—the biblical and the talmudic—which can help it to create its own new traditions. The entire complex of tradition is thereby artificially reduced, its continuity interrupted.

Parallel to this limitation of the principle of evolutionary development to certain epochs, is a second scheme of selection, the aim of which is to distinguish the spirit of Judaism from its external manifestations. As a "manifestation of pure religious consciousness" Judaism has a significance exceeding time and nationality. For the sake of this significance, and in order really to be a world religion, the national elements in the manifestations of Judaism must be eliminated, especially national political aspects of the Messianic idea.[199]

---

[197] Cf. *Nachgelassene Schriften* (Posthumous Works), vol. V, p. 150.

[198] *Allgemeine Einleitung in die Wissenschaft des Judentums* (General introduction to the Wissenschaft of Judaism), Posthum. Wks. Vol. II, p. 63 ff.

[199] See letter of Aug. 25, 1843 in Posthum. Wks. vol. V p. 168: "Judaism is the original expression of pure religious consciousness. We adhere to it as those called to represent this awareness in different ages and to spread it beyond those professing it . . . The spirit of Judaism must be separated from its manifestations, as it has been especially encrusted during the long Middle Ages. Judaism, as called to become a world religion, yet emerging within a people whom it fully permeated, will have to be separated from all national elements necessarily picked up into its expressions." This will involve in particular "giving up belief in a future political unity of the Jews".

This universalist aspect once again narrows the concept of tradition since now also much from the first two periods of—in Geiger's eyes—legitimate tradition, viz. Bible and Talmud, would have to be eliminated.

The limitation of the historical principle of evolutionary development brought about by Geiger was certainly connected with the pressing practical tasks facing the Reform movement in the first half of the nineteenth century. It wanted to check apostasy from and the dangerous indifference to Judaism, and to show that even within the surrounding culture, which was—despite enlightenment and secularization—a Christian milieu, the Jew could safeguard the right to his own "refined" religious standpoint.

Moreover, the devaluation of Judaism to a statutory legalism—as Spinoza, the Enlightenment and Kant had depicted it—was the opinion prevailing in public as well as among many Jews. We saw this in the case of Lazarus Bendavid and Friedlaender. And neither Geiger nor his friends could escape the influence of this widespread judgement on Judaism. Geiger had admittedly included the law within the historical process of development, thus undermining the basis of the prejudice of the Enlightenment. Judaism for Geiger changed from a "statutory" phenomenon—as the Enlightenment had seen it—into an historical one. Yet, as though in an unconscious concession to general opinion, that epoch of Judaism was omitted which lay nearest to the present and which appeared to have moulded the prejudice of the surrounding world.

This moving away from authoritative and separatist rabbinism, the depreciating of the national in favour of the universal elements in Judaism, had also *emancipatory-political* significance. These points of view were taken over notably by the upper middle-class community dignitaries. They found in Reform theology an ideology that calmed their Jewish consciousness and legitimized the activity of those in the community committees, who, in thought, social habitus and lifestyle, were assimilated to the environment and aspired to full social and political integration. Conversely, it almost seemed that the Reform rabbis, perhaps without being aware of it, had become the mouthpiece of these circles of rank, their employers, in order to justify their religious-political ambitions. In this way there came about an interaction between these circles and Reform Judaism.

In practice all that was left of tradition was what seemed to promote the tasks of the day. Through this *pragmatic* character, which tradition had now taken on, Geiger's originally fruitful idea of historical evolutionary development of tradition was really neutralised.[200]

Geiger himself was much more reserved in his practical activity than in his

---

[200] Elements of genuine new formation in the Middle Ages also fell victim to the scheme of selection directed against medieval rabbinism as e.g. the Jewish philosophy of religion, mysticism and even Hebrew poetry, all of which belonged to that ostensibly "encrusted" period. Geiger himself only occasionally dealt with these themes, as e.g. with Maimonides and the poet Ibn Gabirol.

theoretical enunciations. Not only his regard for the communities—which in his day were still strongly bound to tradition—made him so inclined, but also his sense of history.

Of long lasting influence was the Prayer Book introduced by Geiger in Breslau in 1854. It became the basis for most subsequent liberal Prayer Books used in Germany.[201] In composition and text it resembled—apart from some abbreviations—the traditional Prayer Book. But all references to Zion, to sacrifice and to belief in a personal Messiah were deleted or rewritten. And instead of the usual literal translation into German, Geiger made a paraphrase of the Hebrew text into German.

Of other representatives of the Reform movement in intellectual history, perhaps only Samuel Holdheim, Ludwig Philippson and David Einhorn are significant. The religious philosopher Samuel Hirsch is considered in Chapter 18.

In contrast to Geiger's complicated idea of tradition, *Samuel Holdheim* (1806-1860) tried to establish a simpler and clear cut antithesis. He distinguished between the religious and national components in Judaism. The religious components have extra-temporal significance. They concern the knowledge of God and the divine commandments which lie behind the ethical conduct of man. Alongside these commandments are the laws existing from the time of the Israelites' own state which regulated the life of Jews as a nationally and politically organised commonwealth. These laws, according to Holdheim, appeared as divine commandments in religious garb. But the loss of national autonomy made them obsolete. This loss is an act of divine will, of similar clarity to that will through which the legal precepts were once given. The continued existence of these national laws—after the fall of the state—throughout the ages, has only been possible because the nations believed that marriage, inheritance and divorce are for the Jews bound up with their religion. The nations at the time should really have regulated these matters, for the right of the state is absolute over its citizens. In support of this Holdheim quotes Biblical and talmudic-rabbinic passages, such as the Talmudic rule *Dina di malkhuta dina* (the right of the state is a binding right). In his radicalism Holdheim overlooks the fact that the Christian Church also regards personal status, in particular marriage and divorce, to be religious matters and not a concern of the state. The latter

---

[201] Joseph Aub (1805-1880) modelled his Prayer Book on Geiger's for the "New Synagogue" in Berlin, opened in 1866. It was later used with slight alterations in all the liberal synagogues in Berlin. Manuel Joel, Geiger's successor in Breslau, retained Geiger's text but printed the traditional text alongside it. In this form, giving a choice of texts to follow, the Geiger/Joel Prayer Book found wide circulation. A change, somewhat in the conservative sense, was first brought about by the Liberal Union Prayer Book, which Ismar Elbogen and Caesar Seligmann had published in 1928 by commission of the Prussian Federation of Jewish Communities.

up till the present day has in part left these considerations to religion. Holdheim's argument[202] is quite unhistorical and absurdly casuistic and contradictory. He polemizes, for example, against Zacharias Frankel, who allowed Jewish pupils to attend general schools on the Sabbath if they refrained from writing. Holdheim held that such school attendance even when there was no writing, violated the spirit of the Sabbath and should be forbidden. On the other hand he is actually prepared to give up things for the sake of the state which according to his own definition belong to religion and not to state legislation. Jews as a minority must renounce themselves whenever the state, which has to protect Jewish religious interests, is burdened with unreasonable demands. When, for example, only one weekly rest day is practicable in the state, then Jewish officials or soldiers should be on duty on the Sabbath, and the gainfully employed should observe their day of rest on Sunday. Accordingly, he introduced a Sunday service in the Berlin Reform congregation in 1849 where he was rabbi, though a Friday evening service reminded one that this was only an expedient.

Holdheim was the most pugnacious representative of the most radical trend in Reform Judaism. Historical imponderables were unimportant to this protagonist of state absolutism. In comparison to the religious wrestling and seeking of Geiger, there is no indication of living religion in Holdheim's rationalist secular thinking.

*Ludwig Philippson* (1811-1889) was associated with efforts for renewal in Judaism since boyhood. His father Moses was one of the teachers at the Franz School in Dessau, founded on the pattern of the Jewish Free School in Berlin.

When he was just twenty years old Ludwig Philippson became preacher in Magdeburg where in 1831 he founded the *Allgemeine Zeitung des Judentums* which existed until 1920.[203] It reported on Jewish life and events all over the world. As its publisher Philippson had created a platform for himself through this widely circulated paper from which he initiated many stimulating suggestions which he often brought to fruition. His importance lay in his public activity as inspirer and organizer. It was he who called for the Assemblies of Rabbis that took place in Brunswick (1844), Frankfurt (1845) and Breslau (1846). His paper organized. fund-raising collections for various Jewish purposes including the setting up of a Jewish faculty. He founded the *Institut zur Foerderung der Israelitischen Literatur* (Institute for the Promotion of Israelite Literature), which published several scholarly works—among them some volumes of Graetz's history—and belletristic books of Jewish content. Philippson was himself a journalist and writer of

---

[202] See Samuel Holdheim, 'Ueber die Autonomie der Rabbiner und das Prinzip der juedischen Ehe'. (On the Autonomy of Rabbis and the Principle of Jewish Marriage), Schwerin, 1843.

[203] Its successor was the weekly newspaper of the Central Association of German Citizens of Jewish Faith—known as C.V.—which in its sub-title retained the old name.

great talent and wide knowledge. He translated the Bible, composed poems and dramas, wrote a voluminous *Israelitische Religionslehre* (Israelite Doctrine of Religion), sermons, text-books and philosophical and classico-philological works. For the nineteenth century he fulfilled the important function of an information centre on Jewish matters. He was aptly called the "janitor of the Wissenschaft des Judentums".[204] In the Reform movement he played—in virtue of his organising ability—an important mediating role between the various factions.

*David Einhorn* (1809-1879) differed from both the aforementioned by his lively and—in his own way—uncompromising religious conviction. More than once he had to show character and courage. As rabbi of Schwerin in Mecklenburg (1847-1851) in succession to Holdheim, he entered in the birth-register the name of a child, whose father did not want him to be circumcised. This led to a storm of protest not confined to the Jews of Mecklenburg. Even the theological faculty of Rostock—where Franz Delitzsch taught at the time—and the government accused him of heresy. Einhorn had to leave and became rabbi of a Jewish Reform association in Budapest. After a short period of activity he was expelled as a liberal revolutionary and his synagogue was closed in 1852 by the reactionary Austrian government, which had just put down the Hungarian uprising. As he could find no position—given the political situation in Germany in those days—he went to Baltimore, Maryland, USA, in 1855. On the outbreak of the Civil War he published in 1861 a pamphlet against slavery.[205] Bordering as it did the southern states Baltimore at that time held strong pro-southern sentiments. Following stormy protests outside his house he managed to flee and reached Philadelphia. Later he was rabbi of two synagogues in New York.

This outline of his turbulent career shows that Einhorn was no conformist. There is really no appropriate label, it seems to me, that unambiguously characterizes or classified him. He is generally taken to be one of the most radical reformers, and is reckoned to be among the rabbis who brought the ideas of the German Reform movement to America.[206] However, this characterization seems to me an over-simplification.

---

[204] Information from my teacher Ismar Elbogen.

[205] The pamphlet was a reply to the booklet by a New York rabbi, M. J. Raphall (1798-1868), who sought to justify slavery biblically, yet stressing that the Bible considered the slave as a person and not as a thing, as did the Americans in the southern states.

[206] Here we just mention a few of them: Isaac Mayer Wise (1819-1900), organizer of American Reform Judaism and founder of Hebrew Union College, Cincinnati; Max Lilienthal (1815-1882), who tried in vain to reform Jewish education in Russia and who subsequently went to the U.S.A.; Samuel Hirsch, religious philosopher (1815-1889) whom we have still to consider.—The American congregations consisted mainly of German immigrants. A large section of Jewish youth had gone to the U.S.A., notably from Bavaria after the Registration Law of 1813, limiting Jewish marriages. The American principle of "congregations"—valid for every religion—setting the individual synagogue in the place of the local community, facilitated reform. There was no need to consider deviating religious groups, who founded their own congregations.

Einhorn is one of the very few Jews of his time who had a genuine interest in basic religious questions. Among the rabbis he was—beside his opposite Samson Raphael Hirsch—probably the only *theologian*, who was as far removed from the historical pragmatism of Geiger as from the rationalist dialectic of Holdheim.

His sharp rejection of pantheism and of idealism, which he sees as two basic notions of heathenism, and his characterization of God as free Creator[207] is strikingly reminiscent of Solomon Ludwig Steinheim's "Doctrine of Revelation". The Mosaic theo-cosmology "pictures God as the highest reality and personality, a unique and eternal Being (not an abstraction disappearing as it were through one's fingers), who of his own free will has created heaven and earth with all that lives and moves therein and recognised it as good." But Einhorn formulates his stated 'Principle of Mosaism' quite vaguely and not very intelligibly.[208] He blames rabbinic Judaism for not having recognized this principle or for having misunderstood it. And he tries to exemplify this with the complex of sin, atonement and sacrifice, showing at the same time a thorough religio-historical awareness of tradition, including the forms of religious practice. The task of reform, according to Einhorn, is to see that Judaism "does not remain a mere verbal formula but that it breaks out again into flesh and blood". And "true reform is not content with an enlightened stomach but requires a deep religious sense . . . Jews who break with outdated doctrines do not do so out of frivolity but because they see in them a hindrance to living piety . . . No, we do not want a self-made cultus, not a Judaism cut to good taste".[209]

Einhorn, who at the Assembly of Rabbis advocated holding the synagogue service mainly in German, and indicated Messianism as Israel's task among mankind, sharply opposed substituting Sunday for the Sabbath.[210] It seems remarkable that the German language had for him taken on the halo of sanctity since, after all, the works of Mendelssohn, of the Wissenschaft of Judaism and of reform had been written in it. Einhorn objected to the introduction of English into the synagogue service, called for by the American communities on the grounds that the second generation of immigrants had already been born and brought up there. He warned, "Close your religious institutions to German and you will rob your children's understanding of the

---

[207] David Einhorn, 'Das Prinzip des Mosaismus und dessen Verhaeltnis zum Heidentum und rabbinischen Judentum' (Principle of Mosaism and its Relation to Heathenism and Rabbinic Judaism), 1854. p. 14 ff.

[208] Principle of Mosaism, p. 11 and 16.

[209] 'Ausgewaehlte Predigten und Reden' (Selected Sermons and Addresses) ed. by K. Kohler, 1880, pp. 39, 56 and 58.

[210] op. cit., p. 306: "'Transfer the Sabbath to Sunday' many cry—then 'tis remedied! Only the pity is that with this radical cure the patient would altogether die! I once heard in the Assembly of Rabbis in Breslau the ingenious remark: 'One could bury the Sabbath of course on Friday evening, but would wait in vain for its resurrection on Sunday'. And so it is."

precious writings on Jews and Judaism and you will expose Judaism to stagnation or even betrayal".—In all his onesidedness and uncompromising-ness Einhorn was a distinguished religious personality of the kind that was rare in those days. His sermons are perhaps the only ones of the entire nine-teenth century that are still readable today and often strike one as quite modern. His Prayer Book, *Olat Tamid*, 1856 had considerable influence on the first edition of the Union Prayer Book of American Reform Judaism.

The Reform movement was from its inception not an affair of some rebel-lious rabbis. It had risen, as we saw, largely out of a clearly sociologically-defined circle of the educated upper-class and "arrived" Jewish citizenry. Friedlaender, Bendavid, Jacobson and their many contemporaries and successors in the community-committees were ill-disposed to the rabbis, who for them represented the rigid authority of rabbinic Judaism. Even the new generation of rabbis already educated at the university who were gradually taking over from the older rabbinate, did not meet with their assimilatory requirements. For these Reform rabbis—apart from the central ideas of the Enlightenment—were stamped by the new historical thinking of their time. Their relation to the Jewish past—the religio-theological and religio-practical heritage of Judaism—had become a historical, at any rate a reflecting one, on the basis of which they wanted to safeguard the continuity of Judaism and shape it anew.

The leading men in the communities were largely out of touch with these ideas. For although never intending to deny their Judaism, their thinking was transfixed by the identity of Judaism with the religion of reason which they only wished to purge from historical forms and residues. Among these upper-class circles a "Lay-Reform-movement"—in contrast to that of the rabbis—began to get under way.

One cannot really speak of a "laiety" in Judaism, for since the destruction of the Temple there has been no priesthood. Traditional Judaism knew only more or less learned, or else unlearned ignorant, Jews. Even after the rabbinate became a salaried office in the late Middle Ages there existed everywhere learned family men, whose rabbinical training and qualification equalled that of official rabbis, indeed often excelling it, and whose authority found general recognition.[211] Only in the nineteenth century, with the rapid decline and devaluation of Jewish knowledge in Germany, could one for the first time really speak of a laiety. That was the time when Jewish knowledge was only acquired by the few experts, the rabbis, and no longer or only rudimentarily found among laymen.

It was this laiety, immersed in the world of thought of the Enlightenment, which the post-Enlightenment had influenced, though really only as a passing

---

[211] The most famous example is "the Vilna Gaon", Elijah ben Solomon, who never held office. Also Yair Ḥayim Bacharach and Jacob Emden were only official rabbis for a time.

fashion in its romantic aesthetic expression. Acquaintance with Goethe and Heine, Jean Paul and Hegel was for them a sign of modern education. As far as Jewish ties in these well-to-do educated or half-educated city circles were concerned, often only a certain sentiment of piety and a certain amount of general Jewish responsibility and belonging remained, which expressed itself in the struggle towards emancipation and in good works. Religious precepts and customs receded completely into the background.

After the first ardour with the embellishment of the synagogue service and the slight reforms of the Hamburg Temple, a great dissatisfaction began to show itself in these lay circles. Attempts by the Reform rabbis to justify the changes historically and even from the Talmud seemed to them a mere continuation of the rabbinic tradition they took for antiquated. The discrepancy between them and the forms and expressions of the Christian world, which was their model, continued to be too great. One of the leaders of this Reform Judaism of the laiety, Dr. Sigismund Stern in Berlin, raised the call for a "German Jewish church".

The dissatisfaction of the laiety was stimulated by two occurrences, which seemed to illustrate the delaying attitude and lack of clearness of the Reform rabbis.

Abraham Geiger had been chosen as second rabbi in Breslau in 1838, but due to the resistance of traditional circles supported at first by the government, could only take office after a two years conflict.

The other occurrence was the second dispute about the Hamburg Temple in 1841 following the revision of its Prayer Book. Expert opinion on the controversy surrounding this Prayer Book revealed a great lack of unanimity among the various trends of Reform rabbis. To one, this Prayer Book reform seemed to go too far; to another, not far enough and inconsistent.

Since no clear directive was to be expected from the rabbis, a "Society of the Friends of Reform" was founded in 1842 in Frankfurt-on-Main. They brought before the public a three-point programme: 1. "We recognize in the Mosaic religion the possibility of unlimited development. 2. The collection of controversies, discourses and precepts usually subsumed under the name of Talmud has no authority for us either in dogmatic or practical respect. 3. A Messiah, who will lead the Israelites back to the land of Palestine, is neither expected nor desired by us. We recognise no homeland other than that to which we belong by birth or civil connection".[212]

---

[212] Quoted from Caesar Seligmann's 'Geschichte der juedischen Reformbewegung' (History of the Jewish Reform movement), Frankfurt 1922, p. 105 f. The Programme originally contained two further points against the Biblical ritual and dietary laws and against circumcision. However, these points were omitted from the final proclamation. Writing to his friend M. A. Stern, a mathematician at Goettingen, who was associated with the founding of the above-mentioned Frankfurt society, the Jewish Emancipation fighter Riesser said, "One decided to leave out everything that concerns the Bible! Why? Out of reverence for the Bible, out of love to it and to Judaism? Motives which I for my part would respect? God forbid! Simply in order not to collide with the state authorities . . .

The Frankfurt renunciation of the entire historic Judaism roused the opposition of every group, including that of Holdheim. Einhorn called it "a document of disbelief".[213] Zunz wrote, "Suicide is not reform".[214] After the call of the moderate liberal Leopold Stein as rabbi to Frankfurt in 1844, this society dissolved. Its founder, Theodore Creizenach, converted to Christianity.

In 1844, the same year in which a German Catholic movement arose, as did in Protestantism the first Free Churches, a *Genossenschaft fuer Reform im Judentum* (An Association for Reform in Judaism) was formed in Berlin. Its inaugurator was the already mentioned Dr. Sigismund Stern, who delivered well attended lectures on "The tasks of Judaism and its Confessors". The association was more positive than the Frankfurt society. Their proclamation reads "We desire positive religion; we want Judaism. We hold firm to the spirit of Holy Scripture, which we acknowledge as a testimony to divine revelation. . . . But we want to understand Holy Scripture according to its divine spirit, not according to the letter. As the last of a great heritage in antiquated form, we wish to be the first to lay the foundation of a new edifice for ourselves and for the generations who will come after us. We do not desire, however, to break away from Judaism; we will bring no split into our unity.[215]

This association, which soon set about organizing its own synagogue service, continued to exist into the last years of German Jewry as the *Juedische Reformgemeinde in Berlin*. Holdheim became its rabbi in 1847. It was the only radical-reformed synagogue in Germany. Its services took place on Friday evening, Sabbath morning and Sunday. Already from 1849 onward the Saturday service was cancelled through lack of participation. Prayers were said without head covering and—apart from a few formulae—in German. Indeed, Holdheim himself found the service "half Jewish and unhistorical".[216]

By way of reply to the state of ferment among the laiety, Ludwig Philippson gave public notice in his paper of a convocation of an assembly of rabbis in order to reach a settlement of conflicting positions. At the three *Assemblies of Rabbis*, held each year from 1844 to 1846 in Brunswick, Frankfurt and Breslau, respectively, no one turned up from the traditional or Neo-Orthodox camps, and only a few conservatives attended. Frankel,

---

the Bible is taken care of as politely as possible, due to the fashionable affinity with Christianity and the high protection of the police." (Seligmann loc. cit. p. 106)—The correspondence between Riesser and Stern is published by Moritz Stern and Ludwig Geiger in the 2nd vol. of the ZGJD, old edition 1888, p. 47-75. The above quotation is also given by Isler in his biography of Riesser, p. 358.

[213] J. E. vol. X, p. 357.

[214] Zunz, 'Gutachten ueber die Beschneidung' (Responsum on Circumcision). Collected Works, vol. II p. 199.

[215] Seligmann op. cit., p. 121.

[216] Seligmann op. cit., p. 126.

who had been attending only the Frankfurt Assembly, left in protest when by a narrow majority the decision was adopted which made Hebrew only optional and not indispensable for the synagogue service. In order to secure a certain uniformity of outcome, Philippson and Geiger tried to limit the conference to selected practical matters and—in opposition to Frankel and Holdheim—to prevent a debate on the principles of reform. But even the decisions finally formulated on these single matters remained without practical result as they were not viable in the communities.

The laiety of the Reform Association in Berlin were particularly disappointed by the outcome of the Assemblies of Rabbis and henceforth went their own way. But the most consequential result of the Assemblies of Rabbis was Frankel's proclamation of a *positive historical* Judaism and with this he left the Frankfurt Assembly. His modification of the concept of evolutionary development which he applied to the whole of tradition and not to a selected part of it[217] gained acceptance in Germany. The Breslau Seminary—as whose principal Frankel was chosen in 1854—in conjunction with the rabbis and scholars educated there, helped to consolidate the victory of the positive historical tendency of the Reform movement in the communities. The renewed attempted revival of an Assembly of Rabbis (Kassel 1868) and the Synods of Leipzig (1869) and Augsburg (1871), which united rabbis and laiety, had just as few results as the assemblies of the 'forties. Both the League of Liberal Rabbis founded in 1898 and the Union for Liberal Judaism established in 1912 were a fusion of the Geigerian and Frankelian wings. The Liberal Prayer Book edited by Ismar Elbogen and Caesar Seligmann—both pupils of the Breslau Seminary—with its decidely positive historical spirit, was the last expression of this development of the Reform movement in Germany—in contradistinction to the more radical development in the USA and England.

In considering the Reform movement it should not be overlooked that only a minority of German Jews was at first affected by these new tendencies. This was at the start a small section of the Jewish upper and educated class—educated here in the sense of the surrounding culture. This group, grown out of the disciples of Mendelssohn, gradually attracted to itself wider circles of well-to-do and socially ambitious businessmen and intellectuals. These circles set the tone in the communities and in public discussion and journalism. Thus, in retrospective presentations, attention has not always been drawn to the fact that until the middle of the nineteenth century, the majority of Jews in Germany had no contact with the new tendencies. This majority of traditionally pious Jews, however, who were hardly

---

[217] Frankel and the lecturers at the Breslau Seminary themselves introduced at least one qualification, namely the devaluation of the mystic elements in tradition. Mysticism and Kabbalah were considered regrettable aberrations, which in fact temporarily obscured the unbroken rabbinic tradition without however destroying it.

even touched by Neo-Orthodoxy, began around the middle of the century to decrease in progressive tempo. But whole regions such as Poznan, Upper Silesia, West Prussia, southern Germany, and of the cities, Hamburg at least still preserved more or less their traditionally pious character. The same came true for the Jews in the small towns and country as well as for considerable minorities of the Jews in the cities. Only with the general inland migrations from the country into the cities—beginning about 1860—which affected the Jews very considerably, did traditionally existing ties loosen and the religio-political structure of German Jewry change.[218]

One need hardly point out that these traditionally pious groups, who did not accept the confessionalization of Judaism by Neo-Orthodoxy, were nevertheless more strongly influenced by the surrounding culture than the Jews of eastern Europe of the same period or even than the German Jews of the eighteenth century.[219]

---

[218] See Jacob Toury's Essay, 'Deutsche Juden im Vormaerz' (German Jews before the 1848 Revolution), Bulletin of LBI No. 29 (Year 8) 1965, p. 65-82, especially the charts on p. 81. Toury estimates that in 1843 55% of German Jews were "still not yet fully absorbed into the process of assimilation".

[219] The organ of this trend, 'Der Treue Zionswaechter' (The True Watchman of Zion) ed. in Altona, by S. Enoch and the chief rabbi Jacob Etlinger appeared in German language and print between 1845 and 1855.

In Lissa, the largest community in the province of Poznan at the start of Prussian rule in 1797, only two of the seven community elders could write German. In 1833, however, when Jewry in the province was newly regulated by the provincial governor von Flottwell, all 602 community members entitled to vote could speak and write German (see Louis Lewin, 'Geschichte der Juden in Lissa', Pinne 1904, p. 119). Parallel figures exist for the community of Poznan.

# CHAPTER 16

# The Legal and Social Position of Jews and Their System of Education in the Age of Emancipation

We have been trying till now to follow up an intellectual historical line of development which, proceeding from the Enlightenment and partly in opposition to it, led to a new Jewish historical awareness. However, it is not easy to separate the single threads of this development from one another. Frequently it is the same names and the same tendencies which meet us again and again under the various aspects. The Wissenschaft of Judaism too, just like the new religious groupings and the new attitude to the state and to citizens' rights, are all different facets of one intellectual historical situation. Initially, in order to attain civil equality, one had been prepared to make reductions in the Jewish content which frequently led to self-undoing. Now Gabriel Riesser was demanding for Jews equality with other citizens, and equality of rights based not on the renouncement of Jewish identity but on the liberal principle of the same right for all inhabitants of the German states. Even the old fashioned Orthodox, who had a certain reserve regarding aspiration to equality of rights—because with the emancipation of the Jews they feared an emancipation from Judaism—followed the new approach with great attention.

In all the German states, after the Congress of Vienna, the civil amelioration and rights, which had been granted to Jews before the Wars of Liberation, were now gradually being reduced again. In Prussia this retrograde step proceeded still relatively moderately. The Edict of Emancipation was limited to within the borders of the Prussian state of 1812, having no validity in areas which only fell or returned to Prussia after the Wars of Liberation. Even within this old Prussian territory several provisions of the Edict were annulled or qualified by royal Cabinet-decrees.

Around 1830 rumours spread in Prussia of the government's intention to rescind the Law of Emancipation and replace it with a new regulation, after the various provincial diets some years previously had submitted unfavourable reports on the consequences of this edict. A high ministerial official, Streckfuss, had presented a bill designed to make the legal status of Jews dependent on the extent of their assimilation. Streckfuss set out his suggestions in a pamphlet, which only appeared when the government had already rejected his bill.

The main points of Streckfuss's draft-bill, however, had influenced the "Interim Regulation for the Jews in the Grand Duchy of Poznan" which the provincial governor of Poznan, *von Flottwell*, enacted on June 1st, 1833. This regulation in Poznan, however, indicated not a reactionary but an emancipatory step, which redounded to the advantage of the Prussian Germanization policy of its Polish territories. The province, which only with the divisioning of Poland had become Prussian, and had subsequently been lost to the Napoleonic Grand Duchy of Warsaw, reverted—reduced in size—to Prussia in 1815. The Edict of 1812 did not apply to it. Since the days of Polish rule, a sizeable Jewish population lived here together with a majority of Poles and a minority of Germans. The Prussian administration sought to strengthen the German element, and on this score the Jews were meant to be of help. A section of the Jews of Poznan had already gone the way of the Berlin Enlightenment. One strove to adopt the German language and culture, although from a religious standpoint Poznanian Jewry preserved its traditional character into our present century.

The Flottwell Regulation divided the Poznanian Jews into two groups: those who could show a German education and some—not very large— private property, were called naturalised Jews. The rest—the large majority— remained in the category of protected Jews. The naturalised Jews were granted citizens' rights, especially the right to vote in municipal councils.[220]

The Flottwellian Regulation also gave the remaining Jews a powerful incentive to acquire German culture—something that was really not very difficult. For there were some Jewish schools with German as language of instruction already in the pre-Napoleonic era. Since 1824 they had to be established in nearly every community. The desired consequences of the Prussian policy very soon made themselves felt. In many towns in Poznan the Polish majorities in local councils were gradually reduced with the help of the Jewish vote. Later too, after 1848, resulting from these national political factors, the position of Poznan Jews there was better than that in other parts of Prussia. Jews in Poznan could obtain municipal or governmental positions more easily and earlier than elsewhere in Prussia, where

[220] The "naturalised" Jews had not yet received full citizens' rights. The number of Jews e.g. who might be voted to city parliaments were unevenly settled in various localities and could at most command a third of the seats. Emigration to other provinces of Prussia, though dependent on official approval, was always allowed. Flottwell failed to get the central government to include the Jews of Poznan in military service. Voluntary military service already existed since 1797 as well as parental exemption from recruitment tax, that was generally levied on Jews. (See A. Heppner and J. Herzberg, 'Aus Vergangenheit und Gegenwart der Juden in den Posener Landen' (From Jewish Past and Present in the Poznanian Provinces, Koschmin, 1901-1929, Part I p. 233 ff.

executive posts still virtually remained closed to them. With the Poznan Jews a particularly conscious Prusso-German patriotism thus emerged. They felt themselves to be champions of Germanism in the province. Not least through their resistance did the Polish uprising in the 1848 year of revolution fail.

As a result of the greater freedom of movement following the Flottwell legislation, a strong exodus of Poznan Jews began from the 'thirties onward, whose goal was mainly Breslau and Berlin. This led to a basic change in the structure of these two very important Prussian communities. Later, after the First World War, when Poznan fell to the newly re-emerging Poland, the Poznanian Jews opted for Germany and had to leave their home province. They migrated again mostly to Breslau and Berlin. But other communities in Germany at that time also gained through the Poznanian Jews an important increase of committed Jewish members, who now represented a new positive element among the largely indifferent Jewish urban society.

The resignations of Wilhelm von Humboldt and Hardenberg from political power and the sudden early death of the philosopher Hegel, brought to an end an era of national policy. The liberal nature of enlightened absolutism and of the Napoleonic monarchies was replaced by a new state philosophy characteristic of the period of Restoration.

Hegel's Prussian state absolutism had nevertheless still its roots in the rationalist ideas of natural law and of the Enlightenment. Real political Romanticism, whose precursor was the "Holy Alliance" of 1815, gained the mastery in the third and fourth decades of the century through Franz von Baader's theory of state and the philosophy of Schelling. These theories were brought together by *Friedrich Julius Stahl*, a baptized Jew, in his doctrine of the Christian State which formed the basis of the conservative parties and government policy.[221] Church and state or—as the slogan soon had it—throne and altar, stood on a par and in necessary correlation as "realisations" of divine action. The state, according to Stahl, as an earthly image of the kingdom of God, has to fulfil Christian teaching, just as the Church, conversely, has to give religious sanction to the acts of state. Non-Christians, standing outside this correlation of Christianity and state, would therefore have no possibility of participating in the administration of state. From these principles limitations were clearly set to the equal rights of Jews. The Jewish policy of the Prusian kings, Friedrich Wilhelm III and Friedrich Wilhelm IV, reflected these doctrines. And the Jewish policy of other German states was similar.

---

[221] Stahl's political activity as member of the Prussian Upper Chamber only developed after 1848. But his constitutional-legal writings from his time as lecturer in Munich and Erlangen in the 'thirties already expressed his political principles. His book *Ueber den christlichen Staat* (On the Christian State), did not appear till 1847.

But after the French Revolution of 1830, which in France brought the liberal "bourgeois royalty" to the helm, liberal tendencies were everywhere awakened. From these tendencies the Jewish struggle for emancipation received new impetus.

The enthusiastic champion of and spokesman for the Jews in this struggle was *Gabriel Riesser* (1806-1863) of Hamburg. Riesser was a grandson of Raphael Cohen, the last eminent rabbi of the Three Communities of Altona-Hamburg-Wandsbek. On his father's side he descends from the Katzenellen-bogen family of rabbis, famous since the Middle Ages. Yet he himself had few Jewish religious ties, moving nearly always since his student days in Christian circles. However, he was not prepared to pay the price of baptism in order to reach the desired academic career in Heidelberg or the call to the Bar in Hamburg. In many respects he was—what a generation later was called—a 'defiant Jew' (*Trotzjude*). He saw in the withholding of equality from Jews an offence against justice. He demanded equality of rights for Jews not because they were Jews and therefore—like every group in the state—are entitled to equality. Rather he saw the German Jews as fully German, differentiated from other Germans by virtue of their confession alone.

Riesser created a platform for himself through the publication of a periodical, to which he gave the provocative title *Der Jude* (the Jew). "Jew" at that time was considered almost a term of abuse. For this reason many Jews took it as such, preferring to call themselves "Israelites" or "Mosaites" and their religion "Israelite" or "Mosaic".

"The Jew" began to be published in 1831. In its three years of circulation it dealt with the legal position of Jews and the deliberations concerning them in the Chambers of Baden, Bavaria, Hanover and Prussia. Many of Riesser's essays in "The Jew" were also printed in book form.

"The Jew" took a new approach to the problem of the legal position of Jews, which Riesser first formulated in his work; 'Ueber die Stellung der Bekenner des mosaischen Glaubens in Deutschland. An die Deutschen aller Confessionen' (On the Position of Confessors of the Mosaic Faith in Germany. To Germans of All Confessions). This work "abandoned the stand-point of defending oneself against reproaches, placing first and foremost in the demand for equal rights the undertaking of equal duties and responsibilities with other citizens as an imperative, the granting of which is not to be bargained or traded for. Riesser does not engage in refuting attacks upon the religion of the Jews because they are irrelevant in this context. He opposes with the greatest moral indignation the commonly made suggestion of converting to the prevailing religion as the price of citizens' rights".[222]

---

[222] M. Isler, 'Gabriel Riessers Leben' (Life of Gabriel Riesser) vol. I of Gabriel Riesser's collected writings, 1867, p. 74.

Riesser included the struggle for citizens' rights for Jews in the overall political struggle of liberals and democrats. He lashed the customary official policy regarding the Jews in a language, which in its sharpness was new and unusual. This first publication was followed by a controversy with the Heidelberg Enlightenment theologian Paulus—who suggested withholding citizens' rights from Jews because of their national separation—and with the Hamburg High School teacher Eduard Meyer. Meyer, considered a liberal, had attacked Boerne and Heine as Jews, reproaching them for un-German demeanour. In his reply Riesser wrote words that became famous: "Whoever challenges my claim to my German fatherland challenges my right to my thoughts, my feelings, the language I speak, the air I breathe. I must therefore defend myself against him as against a murderer."[223]

This attitude was at that time not only widely held among Riesser's Jewish contemporaries but considered the accepted thing—also by Jews in France and England. And the majority of Jews later felt likewise until and even during the Hitler period.

But this confessionalization of Judaism that followed its national identification with the Germans, the French, etc. is a falsification of its character. Graetz and Moses Hess already recognized this. Judaism becomes a confession when it is seen through the glasses of the Christian view of religion, where religion is the relation of the redemptive need of the individual, or of a collection of individuals, the Church, to God. It is a question of the salvation of the soul. Whereas Judaism is a religion of a different kind. Here the religion of the individual is always united with a whole, related by common origin, faith and fate. Instead of an abstract institutional church there is here a people's covenant with God. This national factor *constitutively* linked with the universal religion of Judaism is what Riesser wished to leave out—just as Geiger and indeed Samson Raphael Hirsch had done and following them many generations of German Jews.

Riesser attributed only historical importance to the national common-origin element in Judaism, considering the Jews as real *Germans of Jewish confession*. They deserved civil equality, not as Jews in the German state, but as Germans in it. Riesser had thereby really abandoned the liberal starting point of the natural legal parity of all men and groups within the state. Instead, he adopted the argument of the representatives of the pure national state, which limits the civil equality of minorities who do not unconditionally give up their identity. In this German-national formulation Riesser succeeded in making the idea of Jewish equality into an item of the liberalism preceeding the 1848 Revolution.

When the revolution carried through the liberal ideas, at least temporarily,

---

[223] 'Boerne und die Juden, ein Wort der Erwiderung auf die Flugschrift des Herrn Dr. Eduard Meyer gegen Boerne' (Boerne and the Jews. A Retort to Dr. Eduard Meyer's pamphlet against Boerne) by Dr. Gabriel Riesser, Altenburg, 1832. Hofbuchdruckerei, p. 21 f.

Riesser became not only a member of parliament, but also vice-president of the National Assembly and member of the delegation, which offered the imperial crown to the Prussian king.

The long postponed regulation of the organisation of Jewry in Prussia came about a year before the Revolution of 1848. After lengthy negotiations in the "United Provincial Diet" a law was promulgated in 1847 which—with the changes that became necessary through the later Prussian and German constitutions—remained valid until the liquidation of the Jewish communities in 1938. In those areas which did not become Prussian till 1866, the previous laws applying to Jews remained in force. Hence, there eventually existed in Prussia, until the Nazi legislation of 1938, thirteen different laws relating to Jews, which originated from very different juridical conceptions. The *Law of July 23rd, 1847*, applying to Old Prussia, was based on individual communities, which were completely independent in the regulation of their affairs (this isolation and fragmentation of the communities being in fact the intention of the law-givers). They were organized purely as lay communities without the office of rabbi even being mentioned. In Hessen-Kassel and Hanover on the other hand—which fell to Prussia in 1866—there were district rabbis with supervisory authority over other rabbis in the province and over religious matters in the communities. Different arrangements existed e.g. in Schleswig–Holstein, in Nassau, in Frankfurt.[224]

The Revolution of 1848 and the constitution drawn up by the National Assembly had only temporarily removed legal discrimination against the Jews. Riesser of Hamburg, Moritz Veit of Berlin, Johann Jacoby of Koenigsberg and the Austrian Jews Hartmann and Kuranda became delegates to the National Assembly. Riesser was in fact vice-president. However, the reaction that set in after the failure of the revolution had in some countries consequences which were very crude.

In Prussian this occurred largely through administrative channels—what the famous historian, Theodor Mommsen, characterized as "administrative trickery"! Difficulties were set in the way of Jews seeking admission to public service, colleges, law careers, officers' corps. Only in exceptional cases did a Jew become full-professor. As judge he seldom got beyond the first stage of his profession, nor could a Jew become a Reserves officer. In 1851 Mecklenburg completely annulled equality of rights. From Bavaria, where the Registration law still existed, many Jews emigrated to the USA.

[224] Negotiations for the standardization of the laws regarding Jews in Prussia began in the Weimar era, but dragged on for years without any results. Not until 1922 could a "Prussian National Association of Jewish Communities" be founded. See the various writings of Ismar Freund, esp. his 'Die Rechtstellung der Synagogengemeinden in Preussen nach der Reichsverfassung (The Legal Position of the Synagogal Communities in Prussia according to the Constitution of the Reich), Berlin 1926. Also, the legal doctoral thesis, 'Die Organisation der preussischen Synagogengemeinden' (The Organisation of the Prussian Synagogal Communities) by Lothar Lazarus, Goettingen, 1933.

This law, like the settlement—and trading-restrictions, was not abolished in Bavaria until 1861. Only the Hanseatic cities adhered on this occasion to the attainments of the '48 Revolution. Gabriel Riesser at that time became judge of the Supreme Court in Hamburg. And when in 1869 Bismarck founded the North German Confederation, Jewish civil equality was secured in the *Law of July 3rd, 1869* passed by the Diet of the North German Confederation. Here it is written that: "All existing restrictions of civil rights derived from the differences in religious confession are hereby lifted. In particular opportunity to participate in community and national representation and to hold public positions shall be irrespective of religious affiliation". This provision, terminating all other contrary laws—which e.g. still existed in Mecklenburg and Saxony—passed into the Constitution of the Empire in 1872.

In practice of course, and especially in Prussia, the restrictions mentioned continued to apply until the foundation of the Weimar Republic.

The history of the political emancipation of the Jews was, as we have seen, a history of progress with many setbacks. Their *economic* development in the same epoch was different. At the start of the era of industrialization Jews enjoyed certain advantage in that they had no inherited connections with any particular hand trades or occupations, or in the public service—as was the case with a large section of the educated public. Jews in consequence were freer and always more open to break new economic ground, which the industrial age offered. Indeed, in the era of mercantilism, as already mentioned, some rich Jews had turned to factory enterprises. However, these undertakings were not very significant and not very permanent, having been created by the current political needs of the state.

At the turn of the nineteenth century the economic picture began to change. New technical and political factors began to affect the economy. On the one hand there were inventions like the steam-engine and the mechanical loom. On the political scene there were the great territorial upheavals bringing about a new political order in Germany. The 'Principal Resolution of the Imperial Deputation' of 1803—embodied in the act of Mediatization—had greatly reduced the number of independent German territories and greatly increased the remaining ones, notably after the dissolution of the clerical principalities. The Napoleonic Wars in their end-effect had really only brought about slight territorial changes in Germany, though costing vast sums of money and burdening all the warring countries with heavy national debts, especially to England. In order to pay their war debts and carry out administrative reform, these states required a new form of national credit. Likewise the farmer, on whose land coal and ore were now being discovered, needed capital to acquire new machinery to exploit these resources. Master weavers were in a similar position, desiring through purchase of looms to expand their domestic businesses into mechanized weaving mills. New here was the necessity of finding credit to develop, which apparently had not been available in the guild and class-structured economy of the past.[225]

As in earlier centuries so here too, Gentile financiers were cautious about accepting major and unknown risks in these new ventures. In the first half of the nineteenth century this function fell to the newly rising private banking enterprises largely created by Jews. Credit to the state and turnover of national loans—now issued in greater quantity—were promoted by several large banking houses, the best known being that of Rothschild. Alongside this large financier there now emerged a whole series of smaller and medium-sized Jewish banking businesses, whose main task was to provide credit for trade and commerce in the now rapidly thriving cities. The many Jewish banking and grain businesses also played an important role in agrarian districts in the building up of large-scale agricultural plant.

From this original position of giving assistance, Jewish businessmen soon went over to their own activity as entrepreneurs, especially in the new economic and technical branches, where they frequently became pioneers. From trading in old clothes they developed the manufacture of ready-made ware; from the rubble trade to copper and brass foundries. Also railway organizations, the new gas lighting coming more and more into use in the cities, later the electro-industry, were mainly founded by Jews. With the wireless in the 'twenties numerous radio shops were opened. This provided a further branch in technology and trade which at the commencement was largely taken up by Jews.

It has been a common phenomenon observed throughout the centuries, that a new enterprise would be taken up first by Jews, having been excluded from the traditional ones—agriculture, handcraft, etc.—only to see after some time the non-Jewish majority following suit and compelling the Jews once again to search for new avenues of business. So it has remained right into modern times, from the opening of department stores for the satisfying of mass-consumption in the growing cities to the entertainment industry for these cities, including theatre, cinema, radio etc., the press, international newsagencies and the latest branches of science.

The dynamic form of the nineteenth century and the function Jews fulfilled in it helped to bring about, within the economic sphere, a substantial improvement for a broad section of Jews. But this applied mostly to Jews in the cities. For the vast majority of Jews in Germany—especially in the south and in Silesia and Poznan—the first half of the nineteenth century brought no change in their economic structure. The majority of Jews, who at that time lived in the country and in the small towns, still made their living in the retail and second-hand trade, still also from pawnbroking and

---

[225] Cf. in this connection Raphael Straus: 'Die Juden in Wirtschaft und Gesellschaft' (The Jews in Commerce and Society), Frankfurt 1964.

in the country from livestock and wine. Only around 1860 did a change set in when, with the general inland migrations, they arrived in the cities and had to find there new branches of occupation in modern urban economic life.

Added to this at the end of the nineteenth century—and again following the First World War—was a new class of economically insecure people. They were comprised of Jews emigrating from Russia and Poland to the USA, a section of whom always got stuck in the transit countries of Germany, Belgium, Holland, France and England. Even those among the East-European Jews, who had achieved a certain degree of prosperity were, after the war with every crisis the most susceptible, since their circle of employers was much more limited, especially as many of them were traditionally religious and did not work on the Sabbath. Unemployment affected these circles all the more. And precisely the thrifty Jewish lower middle classes and shopkeepers, both of German and east-European Jewish origin, were hit by the inflation.

The efforts towards legal equality absorbed most of the energy of the leaders of German Jewry in the nineteenth century. Along with this, and as we saw, closely linked with the exertions for emancipation, was the interest aroused for or against Reform. Beyond these principal twin themes everything else was neglected.

This one-track line of vision had the most disastrous effect on *Jewish education*. The Jewish communities were led by well-meaning but not very far-seeing business people, who were successors of the prominent classes of eighteenth century society, strata who—at any rate until the middle of the nineteenth century—were more strongly assimilated to the surrounding culture than most of the community people.[226] By virtue of their greater ability at representation and their standing with the authorities, of their financial independence and German education, they had reached these positions of leadership. They felt themselves as custodians and trustees, who desired to steer their communities over into the conditions and realities of the new age. When, in this connection, they gave up old autonomous rights of the communities, this seemed to them not as a relinquishment or liquidation of the nature of the community, but as a matter-of-fact contribution towards the incorporation of Jews into state and society.

In this respect it was not at all seen or appreciated by them that such

---

[226] This difference noticeably expressed itself in the discussion over efforts at reform. Here the official community committees frequently supported the Reform party, whose protagonists largely came from the same social and cultural strata as themselves. Most of the community members, however, were still traditionally minded at that time. This was the case e.g. in Hamburg during the controversy over the Temple-synagogue; in Breslau during the conflict regarding Geiger; in Frankfurt, Berlin and in many other places.

abandonment was desired by the state from the Jews alone, whereas the major Christian denominations preserved their privileged position in and alongside the state. Rabbinical jurisdiction, disciplinary rights of the Jewish communities and their right to ban disappeared. But in Protestant state churches and in Catholic dioceses comparable ecclesio-legal and disciplinary functions and state-supported executive power continued to exist.

In matters concerning outward prestige of the communities, when equality of rights and the demand for equality could be demonstrated, money was gladly forthcoming. Thus, in the nineteenth century, many magnificent synagogues were built, often in a Gothic-Moorish hybrid style, which was looked upon as oriental.[227] Considerable sums were also made available for welfare causes—for hospitals, old peoples' homes and other institutions. But otherwise the principle of managing inexpensively was followed. And this was applied especially in educational affairs. Jewish education had lost its value for Jews of the nineteenth and early twentieth centuries. Why should one hand out such expenditure for something so unmodern as Jewish learning and scholarship? The "Cinderella" position, to which Jewish education and its pioneers were relegated, was expressed in part in an unworthy remuneration of teachers and rabbis. The teaching profession in Jewish schools became an expedient for Jewish university graduates unable to find posts in public school or university teaching. Rabbis, including liberal ones, came mostly from abroad, from Bohemia, Hungary and Galicia. This slender social prestige affected the attendance at religious schools and the interest and discipline of pupils. The relatively large number of religious classes and their nominal size does not therefore give a true picutre of school reality.

The intention of the men of the Enlightenment from Mendelssohn's circle in founding the "Free Schools" was to ease the way towards emancipation by including general education within the Jewish school system.

The new schools were orientated towards the theoretical ideals of Enlightenment pedagogies and the practice of the "Philanthropinists".[228] Young people were to be educated in such a way that they would gradually

[227]These buildings were often hidden in a square behind administrative premises. Only a few synagogues were built with their front facing the street or in open places. What in the seventeenth and eighteenth centuries was understandable and indeed often officially laid down, in order not to cause annoyance in the Christian world round about, was still continued after the desired emancipation, as though one hesitated to display Judaism openly. In Berlin the synagogue opened in 1866 in the Oranienburgerstrasse is built in the street front; the later edifices in Lindenstrasse, Kaiserstrasse and Luetzowstrasse in courtyards. Administrative buildings were even built around the 18th century 'Old Synagogue' in the Heidereuter Lane which had earlier stood by itself in the street.

[228]Thus, the educational Reform movement of the Enlightenment was called after the name of the "Philanthropin" founded by Basedow in Dessau in 1774 which, in its turn, influenced the Jewish educational movement of the Free Schools. The Free School in Frankfurt actually bore the name "Philanthropin" until its end in 1942.

and systematically become acquainted with the most varied aspects of human knowledge and behaviour within a school fellowship, stemming from the most diverse social and religious strata. Such education was intended to produce a useful citizen and a tolerant, enlightened person.

The principles of the Philanthropinists were reflected in different features, which we find again in the new Jewish schools. One of these was the wide choice of subject extending beyond the confines of the elementary school. Special value was placed on linguistic tuition. Beside German, which for most children used to Judaeo-German, was (at least at first) a kind of foreign language, French and Hebrew, and in some schools Latin, were taught.[229] Geography, Arithmetic and History were also on the curriculum. And when efforts soon failed to find handcraft or agricultural occupations for graduates of these schools bookkeeping was introduced as a subject.

From the educational viewpoint of the Philantropinists it can be appreciated that institutions of the Free School type valued having non-Jewish pupils so long as this was not forbidden by the government. There were probably non-Jewish teachers in all these schools, especially for languages and for scientific and technical subjects. For non-Jewish parents the ample educational possibilities offered by the Jewish schools at low school fees may have been a certain attraction. Some of the schools lost their Jewish character in the course of time and developed into non-denominational schools.[230]

The large number of subjects and the desired inclusion of Gentile pupils within the school organization necessarily led to a reduction in Jewish subjects. The new schools had indeed arisen in opposition to the old Jewish school system, the so-called *Heder* or "Talmud-Torah" school, where instruction was based on Hebrew literature, Bible with Rashi commentary, Prayer Book, Mishnah and finally on Talmud.

The Free Schools, on the other hand, had in many cases completely eliminated Talmud instruction from their curriculum. This should, as the founder of the Free School in Berlin explained, be left to the private initiative of parents—something that stood in marked contradiction to the declared aim of the new schools of serving those with little means. Even where Talmud was first taught to a limited extent, it had already disappeared from school curricula around 1800. In the course of the nineteenth and twentieth centuries the Talmud—once the crown of Jewish education—was quite forgotten in German Jewry. In rabbinical seminaries in fact it was

---

[229] For details of the Jewish school system see the Hebrew book by Mordecai Eliav: Haḥinukh Hayehudi be–Germaniah bimej Hahaskalah we-Ha' emanẓipaẓiah (Jewish Education in Germany in the Period of Enlightenment and Emancipation), Jerusalem 1961.

[230] This transformation was consciously completed by Dr. Anton Rée, for many years head of the Hamburger Stiftungsschule von 1815 (Hamburg Endowed School of 1815), the former Jewish Free School, and pioneer of the concept of the non-denominational school. In other areas this change was brought about by a drop in the number of Jewish pupils, as in Wolfenbuettel and Seesen.

relegated to the background in favour of many other branches of the Wissenschaft of Judaism. Only a few German rabbis—even among graduates of the Orthodox Rabbinical Seminary in Berlin—were able to understand Talmud on the same level as students from East-European *Yeshivot*.

Not only the Talmud but Hebrew instruction altogether was more and more reduced. In place of the earlier gradual and natural growth in familiarity with the sources, religion and practice of Judaism, there appeared the new instruction in the teaching of religion and morals. *Religious instruction* became a special subject, often without any intrinsic connection with the other subjects. It was taught, as has already been mentioned, through the media of catechisms and textbooks of similar nature. Biblical history took the place of the Hebrew Bible, and the Bible itself was read in German translation. The Jewish content of these Jewish schools was retained only in quantitatively and qualitatively diluted form.

There were, it is true, a number of Jewish schools, which despite similar diversity in non-Jewish subjects, successfully preserved a traditional Jewish character. The reform of the Talmud-Torah-School in Hamburg by Isaac Bernays in 1822 was probably the beginning of this modern orthodox school system. In 1824 there followed the Jewish Elementary Schools in the province of Poznan, and subsequently Samson Raphael Hirsch's Secondary School at Frankfurt and similar institutions.

These Jewish schools, however, recruited a steadily declining percentage of Jewish pupils.[231] Schools of the Free School type had for a long time the stigma of being schools for the poor, even though differentiated school fees were paid to them according to parental income. The few attempts following this pattern to found private schools, for pupils of well-to-do parents, remained stunted undertakings or else they had to try finally to amalgamate with public Jewish schools.

Most of the children of wealthy parents in the cities no longer attended Jewish schools but general ones. In Hamburg in 1845 all the girls and five-sixths of boys from these families attended public schools.[232] These schools now took the place of private Gentile teachers, who since the seventeenth and eighteenth centuries had taught in rich families. Very soon, however, the children from all Jewish strata were attending general schools. And this tendency from the beginning went beyond elementary education. Jewish pupils attended general secondary and grammar schools (mostly, it is true, only up till intermediate stage, the so-called "one year examination", a certificate that reduced the period of military service in Prussia to one year). The number of Jewish pupils in these institutions was relatively large. Out of 10,000 Jewish inhabitants in 1901, 333 Jewish pupils attended intermediate and high schools; whereas out of 10,000

---

[231] In places like Hamburg and Frankfurt, where there were well-founded and attractive Jewish schools of both orthodox and liberal outlooks, the percentage of pupils at Jewish schools was relatively high. A somewhat similar situation existed in the province of Poznan and to some extent in Westphalia.

[232] Eliav, op. cit., p. 345 ff.

Catholics only 32, and out of 10,000 Protestants 55 pupils attended these schools. Of Jewish pupils at secondary school level only 9% attended Jewish schools. A century previously Jewish secondary schoolboys were an exception. And those, after having had private tuition, mostly entered only the higher classes in order to prepare for university.[233] Hence, sometimes these secondary schoolboys were substantially older than their Gentile schoolfellows. Solomon Maimon and S. L. Steinheim e.g. attended the "Christianeum" in Altona. Jost was the first secondary schoolboy in Brunswick, and Zunz in Wolfenbuettel.

Within a century, therefore, a complete upheaval had taken place in the education of Jewish youth. Indeed one can no longer speak of Jewish education, especially in the case of Berlin and of most of the larger communities. In most cases these Jewish young people brought with them from their homes only rudiments of Jewish substance, and eventually transmitted even less to their children. Indeed, at most secondary schools —parallel to the religious instruction of the Christian confessions—there was Jewish religious instruction. However, what was achieved in the two periods in the week, devoted to that instruction, was scarcely more than a farce. Further complicating was the fact that teachers—usually the local rabbi—came from outside and did not belong to the teaching staff to whom the children were accustomed, and were on this account less respected. A similar state of affairs existed in the special religious schools, founded by communities for pupils at whose general schools there was no Jewish religious instruction. In these religious schools instruction was given for a few hours in the afternoon after the general school hours, thus lowering their status in the eyes of the pupils. Here too pupils—when they attended at all— seldom learned to read more than scanty Hebrew, the translation of several prayers, Biblical history and some Jewish history and teachings of Judaism.

For Jewish educationalists there was hardly any sphere of work and for Jewish scholars little money. The rabbi had become a religious functionary. Indifference and lack of knowledge in Jewish matters was the rule in the broadest Jewish circles. And this lack of knowledge was not found as something negative. It represented no deficiency in social values. One preferred to look down one's nose at those unable to converse on music, theatre or the latest literature. An exception were the even rarer conservative or orthodox families, who usually combined a well-grounded Jewish education with modern culture and preserved tradition in life and family. Alongside them there were the few really religious liberal Jews. Viewed as a whole, the Reform movement which originally wanted to deepen, revitalize and renew Judaism, had a few generations later almost brought it to extinction.

The consequences of this development in the history of thought soon became manifest.

---

[233] From the reports of the missionary Callenberg we learn that in 1744 one Jewish schoolboy in Anhalt attended a Christian school. Cf. A. Shohet, op. cit., p. 285, note 109.

# CHAPTER 17

# Participation in General Cultural Life

The far-reaching changes that the nineteenth century brought in the legal and social position of Jews in Germany, and the epoch-making shift of values in Jewish education, formed the background and basis of the new relation of Jews to general culture.

It is really a surprising phenomenon how Jews suddenly began actively to participate—often out of all proportion to their numbers—in almost every sphere of modern culture. This fact has in recent generations repeatedly excited attention. Earlier this attention was anti-semitically motivated. After 1945, however, the realization of the great loss has dominated men's thinking, a loss that German intellectual life has itself suffered through the physical destruction of the Jews or by their emigration.

The question may arise as to whether the participation of Jews in general or German culture still belongs to the scope of a presentation of Jewish intellectual history, whether it has to do here with events of German or general intellectual history, whose subject was incidentally Jews or people of Jewish descent. This question is only one example of the general problem as to what belongs to the scope and definition of the Wissenschaft of Judaism. There is no unanimity on the matter.[234] But this Wissenschaft has in fact from the start—without elucidating this question—also been occupied with areas of thought lying outside the Jewish thematic in its stricter sense. One recalls, for example, Steinschneider's papers on Jews as translators, as mathematicians, etc.

In some of the older traditional spheres of science Jews were always actively involved, as was the case for example in jurisprudence, medicine

---

[234] Cf. J. Elbogen, Ein Jahrhundert Wissenschaft des Judentums, in: Festschrift zum 50 jährigen Bestehen der Hochschule für die Wissenschaft des Judentums (A Century of the Wissenschaft of Judaism in the Commemorative Publication on the Fiftieth Anniversary of the Hochschule fuer die Wissenschaft des Judentums), Berlin 1922. Elbogen defines the Wissenschaft des Judentums as "Wissenschaft of Judaism standing in the living stream of development as a sociological and historical unity."

and mathematics. The Talmud and rabbinic literature formed the basis of Jewish law. The wide-ranging tradition of centuries of "learning", of Talmud study, had engendered familiarity with and interest in legal questions and juridical argumentation. A large part of the authority of rabbis derived from their legal competence. With the edging out or complete nullification of rabbinical jurisdiction and of the Jewish legal system through progressive emancipatory legislation, this tradition was broken. It found its continuation no longer with the rabbis nor within Jewish law but with the numerous Jewish jurists in the various civil legal spheres. Only with the admission of Jews to the Bar—since the second half of the nineteenth century—could unbaptized Jewish jurists act as barristers and some as judges.[235] The study of jurisprudence was thus a great attraction for the Jew, although the practice of it for him was limited to that of advocate. An administrative career, usually the great reservoir for jurists, was closed to them until 1918 and subsequently only seldom aspired to by them. The number of Jewish judges was small and only in individual cases were Jews offered promotion to higher legal positions. The Jewish solicitor was frequently engaged in Jewish community bodies and organizations. He often distinguished himself as juridical scholar and author with important commentary works, which combined theory and practice in the most varied spheres. Pioneering legal theory, in particular regarding constitutional law, goes back to Jewish jurists, e.g. Georg Jellinek, Hans Kelsen and Hugo Preuss. Kelsen and Preuss were the fathers of the Austrian and German republican constitutions respectively (1919).

Medicine and mathematics, and with them the natural sciences, were fields of learning in which the cooperation of Jews had been accepted by the non-Jewish world from days of old.

*Medicine* was for a long time the only academic department of knowledge accessible to Jews. Besides many medical practitioners there were always eminent physicians since Maimonides in the twelfth century whose works were heeded in the Gentile world. In the nineteenth century the anatomist and surgeon, Benedict Stilling (1810-1879), and the internal specialist, Ludwig Traube (1816-1876), were perhaps the first of a series of eminent Jewish doctors, who in the most diverse specialist fields of medicine extend to the present day. One thinks of, inter alia, Ferdinand Cohn (1818-1898) pioneer in bacteriology; Sigmund Freud (1856-1939) founder of psychoanalysis; and the creator of chemotherapy Paul Ehrlich (1845-1915) who with August von Wassermann (1866-1925) pioneered modern antibiotic research.

Unlike medical science *mathematics* did not open up any independent field of work, but then mathematics was more closely anchored to rabbinic

---

[235] Before admission to the Bar the few Jewish jurists at that time had opportunity only to act as syndics of Jewish communities, like Dr. Rubo in Berlin, or else they became—like Gabriel Riesser—journalistic advocates of civil equality.

scholarship. The complicated question of fixing the calendar had led to many prominent rabbis being occupied with mathematics and astronomy, such as Abraham ben Ḥiyya (who introduced Arab/Indian numbers, trigonometry and measurement systems to European mathematics) and Levi ben Gershom (Gersonides) in the Middle Ages, Moses Isserles in the sixteenth century, his disciple David Gans, co-worker with Tycho Brahe and Keppler, and Mendelssohn's teacher Israel Zamosć. Of more recent mathematicians I just wish to mention Adolf Abraham Fraenkel (1891-1965), who taught at Kiel and Jerusalem and came to the philosophy of mathematics from his own set theory. The founder of set theory, Georg Cantor (1845-1918) was baptized. Hermann Minkowski (1864-1909) had mathematically presented the space-time model of relativity, helping to create one of the foundations of the Einsteinian general theory of relativity with its consequences for physics and philosophy.

In modern *physics* Albert Einstein (1879-1955) stands on his own in the forefront of modern physics. He changed both the way of thinking in physics and its concept of the universe.

Several Jews also contributed decisive impulses to the twin pillars of the new concept of physics—that of Quantum and Atom physics.—One of the fathers of modern Atom physics is the Dane Niels Bohr, son of a Jewish mother. Among the many Jewish physicists should be mentioned Max Born (1882-1970), Lise Meitner (1878-1968), Otto Stern (1888-1969) and many others.

Of important *analytical chemists* let it suffice to mention Fritz Haber (1868-1934) and Richard Willstaedter (1872-1942).—Out of Ludwig Monds' (1839-1909) soda-factory developed "Imperial Chemical Industries", (the British I.C.I. concern).

The relatively large proportion of Jews in the various branches of natural scientific research has a clearly recognisable sociological cause. Young mathematical-scientifically or technically interested Jews had with few exceptions hardly any prospect of finding positions as engineers or chemists in industry or public service.[236] Due to the slender prospect of employment the number of Jewish students at technical colleges was small in comparison to that at the universities, apart from the faculty of Architecture which belonged more to the liberal arts. Nevertheless there was naturally a number of competent Jewish technicians and inventors, some of whom were also able to work as employers, as e.g. Siegfried Marcus (petrol-driven auto-

---

[236] Even at the end of the eighteenth century S. Sachs had as land-surveyor and civil engineer become governmental works' inspector and was allowed, despite the restrictions that set in following the wars of liberation, to retain his position. His cousin and pupil Meno Burg (1787-1853) was the only active Prussian army officer of Jewish faith. He taught at the School of Artillery and wrote textbooks on geometry. As 'Jewish major' he was in Berlin in the years before the 1848 Revolution a well-known personality, sometime also committee member of the Jewish community.

mobile), David Schwartz (airship), Emil Rathenau (General Electric Co.).
The physicist Hermann Aron invented the electricity meter and Emil Berliner
the microphone and gramophone.

Regarding the participation of Jews in German culture one thinks less perhaps on scientists, physicians and technicians as on the many *writers, journalists* and *artists* who appeared in the nineteenth and twentieth centuries.

The sociological factor, to which we attributed the inclination towards
science and research, applies here too. Full participation in aesthetic culture
seemed possible to the first generation of the nineteenth century only
through baptism. This step was very seldom taken for religious reasons.[237]
Since Judaism was found by these baptized persons not as something valuable
but as a hindrance to their integration, formal conversion to the majority
religion was an easy sacrifice in exchange for a career and the possibilities of
promotion. Best known is the example of Heinrich Heine, who viewed his
own conversion very critically and suffered in conscience and self-esteem
from this step throughout his life. The outward aim that baptism was meant
to achieve for him—a legal or public career—was not even reached. And his
love to Germany, like that of other baptized and non-baptized Jews, was
not reciprocated.

In the second half of the nineteenth century, however, general culture
had lost much of its specific Christian character. Commitment to Judaism
for many Jews was no stronger than that of their Gentile contemporaries
to Christianity. But now it was no longer necessary formally to discard
the Jewish faith in order to be integrated into German culture.

A certain impeding effect was soon exerted by the growing antisemitism,
which recurringly reminded Jews of their Jewishness. It engendered among
many Jewish intellectuals a "defiant Judaism". Yet this did not generally
prevent one from feeling so closely bound up with German culture that
no obstacle seemed to stand in the way of unreservedly entering into it.

To these Jewish intellectuals who formally remained Jews—just as their
Gentile colleagues remained formal Christians—and for whom their Jewish
make-up had become insignificant, belonged probably most of the numerous
Jewish writers, journalists, artists, politicians and scholars. Here too the
high proportion of Jews in journalism and in political or literary criticism
was not unconnected with the discriminations and limitations confronting
Jewish university graduates. Since a public career, the teaching profession
and largely also a university career were closed to them, they were driven to
writing and naturally to very critical journalism, which stood in opposition
to the existing institutions of state and society discriminating against them.

---

[237] Exceptions like August Neander (formerly David Mendel) and Paul (earlier Selig) Cassel who
became Protestant theologians, or Friedrich Julius Stahl, constitutional jurist, does not alter this
general finding which applies to the large majority.

Others were impelled to *artistic* expression as poets, musicians, actors. Perhaps they unconsciously desired to prove to themselves in artistic self-realisation their newly gained freedom. It was no accident that the theatre powerfully attracted Jewish youth. Here the leap out of the intellectual and social ghetto was manifested clearest of all. The heyday of this theatre as the expression of a liberated sense of life was reached perhaps by Max Reinhardt's stage productions, which transformed drama and theatre into an exhilarating and resonant artistic totality. The antipode to Reinhardt in Berlin was Leopold Jessner. He gave pride of place to the word and content of poetry. With him, as with Lessing and Schiller, the theatre became again a "moral institution". Characteristically he was also more religiously committed to Judaism than most other Jewish theatrical producers. Jews also became prominent in the newly emerging artistic technique of cinema, although more in the USA, the center of the movie world, than in Germany.

Jews were prominent very early on as *writers and journalists*. Of the early writers of the age of emancipation, all of whom were non-professional journalists, I have already written in previous chapters (Mendelssohn, Maimon, Bendavid, Saul Ascher). There followed the era of Ludwig Boerne and Heinrich Heine, both of whom chose baptism from despair and became a kind of modern Marrano. For generations of writers and journalists they became models of the combination of criticism, satire, linguistic elegance and political appeal.

In the next generation Aron Bernstein (1812-1884) was active in many spheres of progress and popular education. He was one of the founders of the *Genossenschaft fuer Reform im Judentum* (Association for Reform in Judaism) whose manifesto of 1844, quoted in Chapter 15, he penned. He also wrote stories rising out of the Jewish popular milieu. His main activity however lay outside the Jewish thematic. After the Revolution of 1848 he edited the *Urwaehlerzeitung* (Voters' Paper), which was succeeded by the first popular democratic daily newspaper, the *Berliner Volkszeitung*. Bernstein edited the latter jointly with the non-Jewish liberal politician, F. Duncker, and also wrote popular natural-scientific works. On a popular and realistic level there was a certain likeness to Leopold Zunz' peculiarly religious-democratic messianism, an expression of that faith in progress which saw Jewish and liberal political realisation in unison.

Moses Hess (1812-1875), later the pioneer of Zionism, also belonged to the first influential Jewish journalists. He was co-founder and editor of the *Rheinische Zeitung*, the organ of radicals and socialists of the 'forties. Karl Marx became its most famous co-worker. *Karl Marx*, who was baptised as a child, developed a strong anti-Jewish attitude. However, his philosophy and work on behalf of the underprivileged working-class may unconsciously betray his Jewish background.

The great era of Jewish journalism, however, began after the establishment of the German Reich of 1871. The city press had come into being in

Berlin, Vienna and Frankfurt and also in Prague. The most important of these papers were the "Berliner Tageblatt", the Vienna "Neue Freie Presse", the "Frankfurter Zeitung" and the Berlin "Boersenkurier". These papers expressed not exactly a radical but a quite perceptive liberalism vis-à-vis political, religious, and social discrimination. They met the literary-aesthetic interests of the well-to-do progressive bourgeoisie, and were distinguished for their literary section and especially refined theatre critiques. In all matters of the mind and spirit they sought to be modern, reflecting the latest movements and tendencies. On questions of religion or confession they took pains to be neutral—commensurate with their expressed enlightened impartial attitude—and not to cause offence. These newspapers gave expression to the marked cultural niveau of their readers, among whom the well informed and many-sided interested Jewish world of business formed a high proportion. The "Vossische Zeitung", rich in tradition (founded 1704), held a somewhat special position. It was more widely circulated in liberal academic circles—Jewish and non-Jewish alike. After its adoption by the Ullstein Press in 1912 it still remained representative of the heritage of the Berlin Enlightenment. Its editor Georg Bernhard (1876-1944) was probably the only one among the many Jewish journalists who was also active as a conscious Jew in the various Jewish organizations.—Jewish journalists were also editors and co-workers of the general newspapers of the German capital —the "Berliner Zeitung am Mittag", "Morgenpost", "Acht-Uhr Abendblatt", the communist "Welt am Abend"—and of many literary and political weeklies.

The broad strata of the German population in the small and medium-sized towns, as well as in the cities of western Germany, were hardly touched by the Berlin press, which was slandered by the antisemites as *Judenpresse* (the Jewish press). The lower middle-class read the local popular press, which was politically conservative, mostly reactionary and often openly anti-semitic. In these papers Jewish journalists were seldom let speak. The social democratic papers offered more possibilities for Jewish journalists but were frequently badly produced, and for readers like journalists not very attractive.

The step from political journalism to active participation in—and not simply critical observation of—*politics* was greater than one would have supposed. Relatively few Jewish journalists took this step of becoming parliamentarians—among them Georg Bernhard—and even in the Weimar Republic only a few Jews became ministers. The 'Paulskirche'—the German National Assembly of 1848/9—included seven non-baptized Jews: Gabriel Riesser, Johann Jacoby (1805-1877) from Koenigsberg; Moritz Veit (1808-1864) from Berlin; Wilhelm Levysohn (1815-1871) from Gruenberg in Silesia; the Austrians Ignatz Kuranda (1812-1884) and Moritz Hartmann (1821-1872), and Ludwig Bamberger (1823-1899).

Bamberger—later together with Eduard Lasker (1829-1884)—was an influential leader of the National Liberals in the German Reichstag. Both finally disassociated themselves from their party's pro-Bismarckian policy.

Another member of the Reichstag was Max Hirsch (1832-1905), co-founder of the Hirsch/Duncker trade unions.

Rabbi Joseph Bloch (1850-1923) held for many years a seat in the Austrian Parliament. He became known as exposer of the antisemite Rohling and as author of apologetical writings.

The organiser of the Labour movement, Ferdinand Lassalle (1825-1864), was not a parliamentarian. Yet his name has a place in active politics as founder of the General German Workers' Union, one of two groups from which the Social Democratic Party later emerged. Lassalle was associated for a while with the Jewish Reform movement. Although he soon turned his attention away from Jewish matters, he remained a Jew.

Several Jews became prominent in the Social Democratic Party, being mainly connected with the so-called revisionist wing of the neo-Kantian socialists. It was led by Eduard Bernstein (1850-1932), who, at the time of Bismarck's anti-socialist law, edited from Switzerland the social-democratic underground press. He soon disagreed with the theories of Marx, Kautsky and Bebel, and turning to Kant became the theorist of Revisionism in Socialism. Next to Bernstein, Kurt Eisner (1867-1919) was the most important of the revisionists. A disciple of Hermann Cohen, Eisner adhered to an ethical, radical-pacifist socialism. He proclaimed the Republic in Bavaria on 7 November 1918 where he was Prime Minister until his assassination on February 21st of the following year. The organ of the revisionist faction was the 'Sozialistische Monatshefte' (Socialist Monthly), founded in 1897 by the dentist Joseph Bloch (1871-1936). Through its independence and openness regarding intellectual and social questions, it was one of the most respected political periodicals until the Hitler period. In Austria Max Adler (1873-1937) represented neo-Kantian socialism. An ethical community-socialism was taught by Gustav Landauer (1870-1919), whose books 'Aufruf zum Sozialismus' and 'Beginnen' and letters in the 'twenties exercised a great influence on the Jewish youth movement. Landauer directed the department of culture in the Bavarian Soviet Republic and was murdered after its breakdown. The lyricist and dramatist Ernst Toller (1893-1939)—pupil of the sociologist Max Weber and follower of Eisner—having been a front-line officer in the First World War, became commander of the Bavarian revolutionary troops. During and after confinement he wrote and published a number of poems and dramas of a pacifist and socio-critical slant. He committed suicide in New York in 1939. The anarchist writer Erich Muehsam was murdered in a concentration camp in 1934. He too was involved in the short lived Bavarian Soviet Republic.

To these humanist socialists I would add the liberal socialist theorist and economist Franz Oppenheimer (1864-1943). He initiated experiments in new cooperative agricultural settlements in Germany and in Jewish settlements in Palestine before the First World War.

Some Jews found their intellectual home in Marxist socialism. Paul

Singer (1844-1911) was publisher of the social democratic newspaper 'Vorwaerts'.—As theorist, and due to her moral and humane significance, Rosa Luxemburg certainly holds a leading position. She was assassinated along with the non-Jew Karl Liebknecht in 1919. Also murdered in the same year was her counterpart, the peoples' commissioner Hugo Haase, former chairman of the Social Democratic Party, who after his party's vote for granting war credit to the German government in 1914 left the majority and helped to found the Independent Social Democratic Party.—Indeed, that Jewish politicians were so often victims of assassination shows that hatred of Jews was an additional determining factor in politics.

Of Jewish politicians in the Weimar era we mention: Walther Rathenau,[238] industrialist, cultural-philosophical writer and for a short time, until his assassination in 1922, Foreign Minister; Hugo Preuss who, as mentioned, drafted the constitution of the Weimar Republic; Rudolf Hilferding, Minister of Finance; the lawyer Paul Levi, who found his way back from communism to social democracy, and finally Ludwig Haas, who already before the November Revolution was Minister of the Interior in the Baden government, becoming later one of the leaders of the Democrat Party in the Reichstag and an outstanding figure in the Central Association of German Citizens of Jewish Faith (C.V.).—In the state of Baden, the home of Haas, there was already between 1868 and 1893 a Jewish Minister of Finance, Moritz Ellstaedter (1827-1905).

For most Jewish journalists, publicists and politicians, being a Jew was of marginal importance—if not altogether dismissed by them. But among Jewish *poets* and *writers* there were perhaps hardly any for whom it was not a central theme ·in their creative grappling. This goes back to Ephraim Kuh (1731-1790) in Breslau, and in fact really to the medieval minstrel Suesskind of Trimberg. Michael Beer (1800-1833), brother of the composer Meyerbeer, wrestles constantly with the problem of the outsider and stranger in his few dramas, which mirror in foreign non-Jewish disguise the role of the Jew in the age of emancipation.

Heinrich Heine (1797-1856), despite his formal conversion, never escaped the Jewish thematic. The new Jewish awareness of history, which was impressed on him as member of the 'Culturverein', was bound up for him with passionate and ever-disappointed love to Germany. The realisation that he did not succeed in synthesizing Judaism and Germanism, expresses itself in many of his incidental sarcastic comments.

---

[238] Insofar as Rathenau expressed opinion on Jewish matters he showed himself to be a marginal Jew. He wrote that he himself 'stood on the foundation of the Gospel' but declined baptism as he found a greater intellectual freedom in undogmatic Judaism. He said that Jews should discard everything that the surrounding world looked upon as foreign. See his 'Eine Streitschrift vom Glauben' (A Controversial Essay on Belief), Berlin 1917, p. 28, and 'Hoere Israel' (Hear, O Israel) in the periodical 'Die Zukunft' (The Future) of March 6th, 1897.

Without attempting any such synthesis, yet with unquestionable truth-fulness, Berthold Auerbach (1812-1882) sees Germanism and Judaism as co-existing side by side. He felt no tension between them. The antisemitism that set in towards the end of his life among the German educated class —and likewise the national-Jewish claims of his friend Moses Hess—seemed to him the collapse of his life-work. He faced the new tendencies with the same naive unbelief as most German Jews did in face of the later events that began in 1933.

Jacob Wassermann's autobiographic account (1873-1934) 'Mein Weg als Deutscher und Jude' (My Way as German and Jew), reflects the prominent novelist's wrestling with this synthesis, the belief in its possibility, but also the acknowledgement that it did not succeed.

As with Wassermann the Jewish thematic constantly recurs in Arthur Schnitzler, Arnold Zweig, Max Brod, Joseph Roth, Stefan Zweig and Lion Feuchtwanger. Feuchtwanger's Jews—the Josephus Flavius torn between Roman culture and Judaism or the court Jew, Jud Suess—illustrate the writer's own predicament when he says, "I am a cosmopolitan with my head, with my heart a Jew". Franz Werfel in later life was strongly influenced by Catholicism.

Another prominent novelist, the physician Alfred Doeblin, became a Catholic through his experience of being uprooted during the emigration. He describes the impact of social, technical and biological factors, which crush man with the same mythical power, as emigration later crushed the writer himself.

Franz Kafka (1883-1924) depicts the dispossessedness and helplessness of modern man in face of powers with which he has lost contact and for which he has lost understanding. Behind this outwardly general thematic is perhaps the hidden and intensive struggling of Kafka the Jew towards a new relation-ship with the Jewish religion, people and history, his longing for Jewish renewal.

In comparison with these strivings for a German-Jewish synthesis or for the inclusion of the Jewish problematic into general cultural situations, Richard Beer-Hofmann and in a different way Else Lasker-Schueler seem like Hebrew poets in the German language. Both of them consciously opted for the Jewish side—to the extent of expressing opposition to European culture. But they could only do so through the medium of German. For Else Lasker-Schueler the impossibility of integrating into living Hebrew after her emigration to Jerusalem, became a personal tragedy. A similar case was Karl Wolfskehl, exiled to New Zealand, who first clearly decided for Judaism under the impact of persecution. He too could only compose in German.

Much less in evidence than with the writers and poets was the Jewish element with the "music makers". The old synagogal music, confined to the singing of the cantor, had for centuries adopted the motifs of the Volks-

music of their environment and set it to Hebrew prayer texts. Jewish composers of the nineteenth and twentieth centuries continued this assimilatory
tendency. Tuition in music, which we already met with in seventeenth
century well-to-do Jewish homes, was probably always given by Christian
music teachers. With the ever increasing tendency at the close of the eighteenth century to accept general culture, Gentile musical culture also entered
into Jewish homes of the emancipatory era. The most illustrious Jewish
composers of the nineteenth century, Meyerbeer, Jacques Offenbach—who
later converted to Christianity—and Felix Mendelssohn-Bartholdy—baptized
as a child—were musicians who completely belong to the general history
of music and whose Jewishness or Jewish descent is a dispensible coincidence.
Meyerbeer nevertheless composed several pieces of music for the synagogue.
How little Judaism meant to most Jewish musicians is shown by Gustav
Mahler, who as a famous conductor and composer accepted baptism in
order to be appointed to the Vienna Court Opera. Not until twentieth
century composers like Schoenberg, Milhaud, Ernest Bloch do we find in
their newly awakened Jewish self-awareness a Jewish thematic and the rudiments of Jewish religious music. But with others in this period there is no
sign of Jewishness in their music—as in Kurt Weill, famous through his
music for the time-critical stage-works of Bert Brecht—or in the various
Jewish composers and conductors of operetta.

Modern descendants of the singers and musicians in the Temple service,
of fiddlers and music makers at weddings and festivals, are legion. With these
musicians a clear Jewish tone is barely perceptible. Only cantors changed
from synagogue to concert hall and opera singing, often returning to the
synagogue in later life..

Things were similar in the *fine arts*. In the antique synagogal mosaics we
find pictorial representations, even of people. From the Middle Ages we have
a great number of illuminated manuscripts. These found their continuation
in the later Jewish miniaturists and medallists and, in general, in rich Jewish
arts and crafts for embellishing utensils for services in home and synagogue.
In style, technique and mostly in choice of theme the paintings by Jews
—as well as their rarer works in sculpture—belonged to contemporary art
even when they used the Jewish thematic, as did e.g. Moritz Oppenheim,
Jozef Israels and Lesser Ury and occassionally Max Liebermann. Lesser Ury
also showed leanings towards Jewish religious painting, though not in the
variation of popular motifs as later contrived by Marc Chagall. It is not by
fortuitous choice of theme that Jewish destiny is depicted by Hermann
Struck, Ephraim Moses Lilien, Ludwig Meidner, Joseph Budko and Jakob
Steinhardt. Alongside them of course is a large number of artists who only
happened to be Jews.

A still further aspect of the participation of Jews in literary, musical and
artistic cultural life should be mentioned, namely the important role of Jews
as a receptive public. This seemingly mere passive function of echoing, and

in some cases of publishing and being patron, frequently contributed towards the success of new unusual tendencies in art and of their representatives. Some German Jews also gained international importance as antiquarian booksellers and art dealers.

In the *humanities* the position of Jewish scholars was particularly precarious. Schoolteaching, which in general was the great reservoir for graduates from the philosophical faculties, was virtually closed to them, especially as the number of Jewish schools was small, dwindling more and more in the course of time. Hence we find among historians and philologists of Jewish descent a very large number of baptized Jews, among whom are significant names like the Germanist Michael Bernays, the historians Philipp Jaffé and Emil Bernheim, the Semitic philologist Lidzbarski, the classical philologist Eduard Norden and others.

Those not wanting to give up their Judaism for the purpose of a career, but who at the same time did not wish or were unable to become rabbis, had to fend for themselves mostly with great difficulty and in unsuitable positions. We have already seen how Zunz and Steinschneider were temporarily in charge of Jewish schools. The Indo-European philologist Siegmund Feist was director of a Jewish orphanage in Berlin. Julius Fuerst was and remained a private lecturer in Leipzig, receiving the professor title only after twenty-five years. Moritz Lazarus had indeed already in 1860 been Professor of Philosophy in Berne, Switzerland. In 1867 he became professor at the Military Academy in Prussia.—However, at Berlin University in 1874 he was just honorary professor. Only the era of the liberal Prussian minister of culture, Falk, whom Bismarck during the *Kulturkampf* (struggle with the Catholic Church) placed at the head of the Prussian department of education (1872-1879), brought some temporary relief. Herman Cohen then became full professor of philosophy in Marburg, Ferdinand Cohn professor of medicine in Breslau.

Many scholars mentioned earlier as pioneers of the Wissenschaft of Judaism were in their subject *orientalists*, like Geiger, Fuerst, Steinschneider, Bacher. To these I would add the prominent expert on Islam, Ignatz Goldziher, who taught at Budapest University and Rabbinical College; the Hebraists Jacob Barth, David Heinrich Mueller and Harry Torczyner (Tur-Sinai); the lexicographer of talmudic literature Jacob Levy in Breslau and the Bible commentator Benno Jacob, rabbi in Dortmund—to mention the most important.

*Classical philology* in the nineteenth century produced two scholars who are still famous: the Latin lexicographer Wilhelm Freund (1806-1894) of Breslau whose monumental dictionary influenced the whole of—especially English/Latin—lexicography, and Jacob Bernays (1824-1881) who was amongst the first group of lecturers at the Breslau Jewish-Theological Seminary. Bernays' studies on Jewish influences upon Hellenistic literature and Greek philosophy belong to the greatest achievements in classical philology during the second half of the nineteenth century.

Of eminent *Germanists* we mention the German and English lexicographer Daniel Sanders (1819-1897) and Ludwig Geiger (1848-1919)—son of Abraham Geiger. The most popular biography of Goethe for a long time was penned by Albert Bielschowsky (1847-1902). It was subsequently overshadowed by that of Friedrich Gundolf (1880-1931), one of the Jewish members of the circle around the German poet Stefan George.

Among the *historians* should be mentioned: Harry Bresslau (1848-1926), disciple of Droysen and Ranke and a pioneer in the study of historical records. He was professor in Strasbourg and worked occassionally on the history of the Jews in the Middle Ages. His textbooks and studies in palaeography made him an authority on the interpretation and utilisation of medieval sources. Philipp Jaffé (1819-1870) was a tragic example of the frustration of the Jewish scholar. He was acknowledged as an outstanding medievalist. In spite of his Judaism he became a co-worker of the 'Monumenta Germaniae Historica' and ultimately professor extraordinary against the will of his superior Pertz, who had persecuted him over all the years with increasing hatred. Jaffé took his own life, having two years previously been baptized.

Eugen Taeubler (1879-1953) was in the next generation a historian of acknowledged repute and influence. He was co-founder and director for many years of the 'Gesamtarchiv der deutschen Juden' (Central Archives of the German Jews) and head of the 'Akademie fuer die Wissenschaft des Judentums' (Academy for the Wissenschaft of Judaism, see below, Chapter 19). In 1925 he became professor in Heidelberg. Although officially closely associated with Jewish historical studies his works chiefly deal with the history of the Roman Empire. He was the last assistant to Theodor Mommsen and in this way became deeply interested in social and legal history. Late Rome and Hellenism was his subjects which he compared and contrasted with the corresponding events in Jewish history, especially those of the early Middle Ages.

A decisive step forward in *psychology* is due to Sigmund Freud (1856-1939) through his psychoanalytic method. It has transformed our understanding of man and has had lasting consequences in almost every sphere of modern life and culture.

As a psychologist with strong philosophic strain, William Stern (1871-1938) investigated the formation of human personality. He is regarded as the founder of modern child psychology.

Max Wertheimer (1880-1943) in conjunction with the non-Jew Wolfgang Koehler developed the so-called *Gestalt theory of psychology*, which sees human actions inseparably interwoven in an overall complex and considers them from this overall pattern.

Kurt Lewin (1890-1947) applied the ideas of Gestalt theory to child psychology and to the solution of social conflicts. He was also concerned with the uncertain scientific status of psychology.

Freud's antagonist was Alfred Adler (1870-1937), founder of "Individual

Psychology" which became especially important in educational theory. Its emphasis on social attitudes, such as the inferiority complex and striving for recognition, largely replaced the Freudian principle of sexuality.

The Danzig born Hugo Muensterberg (1863-1916) taught in the USA. He is regarded as the founder of industrial psychology and psychotechnology. As a young lecturer he converted to Christianity.

The influence of Jews on *philosophy* began with Philo of Alexandria. Maimonides was probably the first Jewish philosopher of lasting consequence in Germany, notably through Albertus Magnus and Meister Eckhart. The influence of Kabbalah on the natural philosophy of the Renaissance and the resultant mysticism has already been touched upon.

Mendelssohn was the first actively involved German-Jewish philosopher. I have already dealt with Solomon Maimon and the Jewish Kantians in a chapter devoted to them. The neo-Kantianism of Hermann Cohen and Ernst Cassirer made an important contribution towards modern philosophy, a contribution which is perhaps of greater significance than is apparent today.

A considerable intellectual-historical influence also emanated from other Jewish philosophers. Heymann Steinthal (1823-1899) and Moritz Lazarus (1824-1903) founded the system of *Voelkerpsychologie* (Psychology of Nations), influenced by Herbart and Wilhelm von Humboldt. In this connection they were also concerned—especially Steinthal—with the philosophy of language. Steinthal's linguistic proficiency included the Chinese and Negro languages. Edmund Husserl (1859-1938) founded the phenomenological school which was very influential between the two world wars. Like some of his Jewish disciples—Edith Stein and the half-Jewish Max Scheler—he became a Catholic. It was out of phenomemology that modern existentialist philosophy arose.

An independent religious existential philosophy was taught by Franz Rosenzweig (1886-1929) and Martin Buber (1878-1965). Buber's philosophy of dialogue in particular has become very well known in Germany, England and the USA.

Close to their thinking is Hugo Bergmann, Jerusalem (1883-1975), who as an adherent of Brentano was later strongly influenced by Maimon and Cassirer. He was also concerned with the problems of modern physics and with various approaches towards a new logic.

Karl Joel (1864-1934) of Basle wrote influential intellectual-historical and educational-political works, not very far removed from Cohen's.

On scanning this brief survey of the participation of Jews in German culture we notice that they fall into two or three groups.

First, the large group of 'incidental' Jews whose only conscious link with Judaism is their origin, but who did not formally abandon it. The greater proportion of this group does not perhaps emerge as clearly in my survey as in reality—for it contains the large majority of Jewish intellectuals. Next to them is a smaller group, who occasionally participated in things Jewish, but for whom such matters did not occupy their central activity or interest.

But then there is the group, who wished their contribution to German intellectual life to be seen precisely as a *Jewish* contribution. Both sources of their being—the Jewish and the German—were for them a unity. They had no desire to deny either. As artists, scholars or scientists they knew that culture is the result of the meeting of various and in origin mutually different elements. They believed they were contributing creatively through their Jewish contribution to the kaleidoscope of German culture. The titles they sometimes gave their works are instructive. Franz Rosenzweig entitled a collection of his essays 'Zweistromland' (Twinstreamland). The educationalist and writer Jacob Loewenberg called his autobiographical novel 'Aus zwei Quellen' (Out of two Sources), Jacob Wassermann speaks of 'Mein Weg als Deutscher und Jude' (My Way as German and Jew). The most significant example in this group is Hermann Cohen. He approached Judaism through the medium of German philosophy. In his ethics, however, he gives this German philosophy a consciously Jewish basis.

Despite the apparently close involvement of Jews on every level with German culture, there remained in the world round about—often unconscious and often clearly and aggressively articulated—an embarrassed uneasiness, a reservedness in relation to Jewish cultural achievements. The readiness and sincere efforts of the German Jews towards a cultural symbiosis failed to find a response from the other side.[239]

---

[239] Cf. G. Scholem, "Wider den Mythos vom deutsch-juedischen Gespraech' (Against the Myth of the German-Jewish Dialogue), Darmstadt, 1964, reprinted in his collection of essays, Judaica II, Frankfurt, 1970.

CHAPTER **18**

# Portrayals of Jewish Self-Understanding I

Parallel to the intellectual-historical tendencies of the nineteenth century, as described in previous chapters, we find—probably for the first time in the history of Jewish thought—attempts at *portrayals of Jewish self-understanding*. The appearance of such self-portraits reveals, it seems to me, something quite new. When Judaism still held sway over the lifestyle and thought, society and home of the Jew, any such reflection on the meaning and nature of Jewishness and Judaism was unknown. There was no need for self-analysis or to justify one's own existence—especially to oneself—in the surrounding world.

Earlier there had been a Jewish *philosophy of religion* as well as polemical and apologetic writings. But the Jewish philosophers of the Middle Ages strove only to correlate the various philosophical schools of thought with Judaism. Yet Judaism itself for these authors remained the undoubtable basis, even when the attempted amalgamation of philosophical doctrines forced them to re-interpretations, which affected both the transmitted Judaism and philosophy. The authors of the old arguments and controversies with Christianity, Islam and Karaïtes, moreover, took the offensive insofar as they proceeded from their own undoubtable position. The "Kuzari" of Judah Halevi—a writing most nearly resembling a self-portrait of Judaism —confirms precisely this aggressive character, which seems out of keeping with a missionary work.[240]

Now that had changed. The appearance of and the need for self-portraits revealed a new situation. With its increasing estrangement, Judaism for many Jews was no longer found to be a naturally accepted basis. One thus looked

[240] This book by the poet and physician Judah Halevi (ca. 1085-ca. 1140), in the form of a dialogue between the king of the Khazars and a Jewish scholar, is also a discussion about philosophy and the other religions. This very popular book of the most distinguished of Hebrew poets in Spain, written in Arabic, was translated into Hebrew by Judah ben Saul Ibn Tibbon (1120-1190) and circulated in this form. David Cassel (1818-1893) translated it into German partly with the help of H. Jolowitz. The Arabic original was published by Hartwig Hirschfeld in 1886, from which German (1885) and English translations were made. Johannes Buxtorf (jun.) translated the "liber Cosri" into Latin in 1660.

for confirmation of one's Judaism through encounter with the intellectual and religious movements of the time. The apologetic tendency of the portraits of self-understanding is here directed not outwardly but inwardly.

This inward kind of apologetic was not confined to Judaism. In the prevailing religion, Christianity, we find that similar inclinations towards portraits of this self-understanding had become necessary. For religion in general had lost its leading role in intellectual consciousness. From Schleiermacher's *Reden ueber die Religion* (Addresses on Religion) to Harnack's *Wesen des Christentums* (The Essence of Christianity) one sought to win back—in Schleiermacher's words—"the cultured amongst its despisers" for an understanding of religion, for the truth or superiority of Christianity.

In addition to this general need, Judaism had still its own special problematic. Christian theologians equated religion with Christianity in a quite unconcerned matter-of-fact way. And the great philosophers, Kant, Schelling —and Hegel strongest of all—had, so to speak, scientifically confirmed the absolute claim of Christianity. Some cultured Jews who enjoyed keeping up with the latest mode in things philosophical and artistic, picked up these authoritatively proclaimed ideas. Shaking the primacy of Christianity, however, did not suffice to account for the religious independence of Judaism. One had to set Judaism—using where possible the methods and premises of one's opponent—in the place usurped by the majority religion. The inward apologetic was therefore linked with an *outward polemic that took the offensive*. Most self-portrayls followed this twin approach—with exception of the first and last which came from German Judaism, that of Mendelssohn and that of Franz Rosenzweig. All of them, however, addressed themselves to a Jewish public, for these portraits were an expression of their intellectual and acutely imperilled situation.

A further point is characteristic of these self-portrayals. Some of them were admittedly by rabbis. The most important attempts, however, were by men who were engaged with Jewish problems not because of their profession or office, but—if one may use a not very congenial expression as far as Jewish connections are concerned—by laymen: Mendelssohn, Steinheim, Lazarus, Cohen, Rosenzweig, Buber.

Most of the new self-portraits of Judaism have a philosophic or theological character. These include the great accounts of Jewish history, and they too interpret Judaism variously.

*Isaac Marcus Jost* (1793-1860), the first of modern Jewish historians who three times undertook to write a Jewish history,[241] belonged more than his successors to the thought-world of the Enlightenment.

---

[241] See footnote 150. On Jost cf. in particular N. Rotenstreich, p. 43 ff. and p. 143 ff.; Max Wiener, pp. 209-217; Salo W. Baron, History and Jewish Historians pp. 240-262, Philadelphia 1964; G. Herlitz Yearbook LBI IX, 1964 pp. 71-76 and the present author's article on Jost in the "Neue Deutsche Biographie', vol. X, 1974.

One could say that Jost, who throughout his life was an educationalist, also as a historian continued the popular educational undertakings of Mendelssohn and his circle. His endeavour to harmonize antitheses derives from the Enlightenment. Eighteenth-century reasonableness predominates in him, determining also his interpretation of religion. Yet he did not try to re-model Judaism into an ideology in conformity with the philosophies of the day. Here too Jost is a follower of Mendelssohn. But there is a significant difference between the two. Whereas for Mendelssohn the religion of reason together with the revealed Law binding on the Jewish stock, were the essentials of Judaism, for Jost it is—alongside the religion of reason—rather the history of this stock that takes the place of the law. However, he did not consider the Jewish stock as a nationality in the nineteenth century's sense.[242]

*Heinrich Graetz*, on the other hand, as we explained in Chapter 14, combined the history of ideas with the history of a people. The "magical rapport" of people, land and Torah determines his picture of Judaism. As a religion, a nation and in its history, Judaism for Graetz is a phenomenon sui generis—an idea developed within Jewish history. The outside world enters this history literally only from the outside, without being able to touch the inner world of Judaism. It can persecute, physically annihilate but not destroy. Jewry itself is for Graetz something passive. It is a victim of persecution, a community of martyrs, an object of history, but not an independent actively engaging factor. Out of this anonymous mass—patiently testifying to the living power and faith of Judaism—the personalities of prophets and teachers, heroes and martyrs, philosophers, poets and scholars step out, in whom the idea of Judaism unfolds in ever new vitality. They are the actors, who determine the development and history of Judaism. Graetz's history of martyrs and scholars has been depreciatively spoken of. Yet he perceived, with psychological insight, those in whom the Jewish people have seen the real heroes of their history, who have given them direction and stability on their way.

*Abraham Geiger's* account of Judaism has, in the course of time, undergone a noticeable change. In his main account, the lectures "Judaism and its History" and in the "Introduction to the Study of Jewish Theology", there emerges a rigid universalist, confessionalist interpretation of Judaism. In

---

[242] Recently it has been eagerly stressed that it is not the history of the ideas or religion of Judaism that Jost wrote, but "History of the Israelites", i.e. of a human group, and that only his latest work dealt with "Judaism and its Sects"—essentially a history of literature and of scholars. It is, however, entirely misleading for this reason to see in Jost a forerunner of a national Jewish or pre-Zionist interpretation of history, as does Herlitz but also Rotenstreich, Duenaburg and perhaps Baron. Jost is, in a way, a successor of the historiography of the Enlightenment. The pre-occupation of historians with human groups and societies seems to me just typical of the historiography of the eighteenth century from Hobbes via Vico to Rousseau, Schiller and Herder, with whom the transition to Romanticism began. Also, Jost's plea to retain Hebrew for prayer had—as Rotenstreich shows—nothing to do with national-Jewish motives. On the contrary, it is as a holy language that Jost assigns it a special religious function, as Hermann Cohen was later to do.

Geiger's view Judaism, from the great prophets onward, sheds more and more its particularist qualities. If in the Middle Ages, under the pressure of persecution, it was forced to cocoon itself again within the isolating shell of the Law, so now in the age of emancipation there exists the possibility and the duty to assume the real developmental line of prophetic Judaism once more. Not until the *Allgemeine Einleitung in die Wissenschaft des Judentums* (General Introduction to the Wissenschaft of Judaism), which he delivered at the 'Hochschule fuer die Wissenschaft des Judentums'[243], is a special value and weight attached to the connection of Judaism with the Jewish line. What is general in the universal religious idea is developed, according to Geiger, in the individual history of the Jewish people. Precisely in this attachment of the pure idea of God to a body of people who bear it, does Geiger see the advantage of Judaism in comparison with Christianity and Islam.

Geiger is now not so very far from the position of Graetz.[244] However, even in a more onesided way than in Graetz, Jewish history for him is a history of the Jewish religion and not so much that of its representatives.[245] What is surprising in Geiger and Graetz—despite this limitation—is their slight interest in theology. Both are essentially historians, Geiger being in addition philologically orientated. Where they touch on theological matters, these are interpreted historically or at best within the framework of a theologically pre-judged philosophy of history. With Geiger there is the added tendency towards the practical needs of the Reform movement.

A quite divergent view of Judaism from that of his predecessors was developed by *Simon Dubnow* (1860-1941).[246] His account was determined by the historical situation of East European Judaism. The national character of Jewry in Poland and Russia had there never been questioned by the Jews *themselves*. They were always in their Slavonic setting a closed national minority. Thus, for Dubnow, Jewish history is quite naturally the history of the Jewish people. Its theme is the affirmation of national autonomy in every age and under all conditions, even in the Diaspora in face of the various attempts of their usually hostile surroundings to break this autonomy, to limit and control it. Safeguarding their autonomy made the Jews into the subject of their history, not into its mere object.

The concept of national autonomism governed Dubnow's special interest for the organisational and social aspects of the communities. He was the first

---

[243] Both "Introductions" did not appear until the publication of the 2nd vol. of the posthumous works in 1876.

[244] The gradual approach of Reform to the positive-historical Judaism of the Breslau Seminary led in Germany to the rise of a dominant trend and to a religious party, which characteristically called itself no longer 'Reform' but "Liberal Judaism". (Cf. above, Chapter 15, p. 185.)

[245] Even where—as in the 'Urschrift'—he is concerned with the formation of politico-religious parties.

[246] Dubnow gave a theoretical account of his view of history in 'Die juedische Geschichte. Ein geschichtsphilosophischer Versuch' (Jewish History. A Historico-philosophical Essay). 2nd ed., Frankfurt, 1921, English translation by Henrietta Szold, 1903.

to use the sociological method in Jewish historiography, though he excluded the sociology of religion. Dubnow has little feel for the religious, trying to omit it as a positively determining factor from his view of history. "Judaismus", as he calls the Jewish religion, is for him not a root but an expression of national culture. With the free-thinking anti-clerical Enlightenment, as it developed in France since the eighteenth century. Dubnow shares "the antipathy to the recognition of metaphysical powers in the world and thereby he lacks understanding for the efficacy of religious powers in Judaism".[247] Dubnow's secular view of Judaism is not less onesided than the religious view of his predecessors. It is most vividly presented and found a strong response especially in East European Jewish thinking and in emerging Zionism.[248]

Portrayals of Jewish self-understanding in the stricter sense are attempts to present the particularity of Judaism through the medium of and in relation to contemporary *philosophical* trends of thought.

The first of these modern reflections on Judaism was Moses *Mendelssohn's* "Jerusalem". Here a Jew had portrayed his Judaism for the first time in the German language and gave grounds for its independence. He equated it with the natural religion of reason. To the astonishment of his contemporaries he showed Judaism as a religion free from dogma whose real Jewish content was confined to the revealed Divine Law.

In the Jewish camp Mendelssohn's thesis affected both the Reform movement and Neo-Orthodoxy. The outside world was surprised by Mendelssohn's expressed claim that Judaism was still entitled to enjoy the same rights in the modern civilized world—alongside the prevailing Christian confessions. He desired not the subordination of one religion to others, but acceptance and tolerance for Jews and Judaism. "Whoever does not disturb the public peace, whoever deals rightly in conformity to the civil laws, in relation to you and his fellow-citizens, let him speak as he thinks; let him call upon God in the way of his fathers and seek his eternal salvation where he believes it to be found. Let no man in your countries be a knower of the heart or judge of the thoughts; let no one assume a right which the Almightly has reserved to himself! If we render to Caesar what is Caesar's, then give ye yourselves to God what is God's! Love the truth! Love peace!".[249] Mendelssohn's plea for religious equality for Judaism is linked with his demand for their civil equality.

Mendelssohn, philosopher and Jew of the Enlightenment, could rightly

---

[247] J. Elbogen, 'Zu S. Dubnows Geschichtswerk' MGWJ, Vol. 70, 1926 p. 147.

[248] Dubnow was a national Jew but not a Zionist. He tried to consolidate and politically organize national autonomy of Jews as a national minority in their mass-settlements in Eastern Europe. He was one of the initiators of the Jewish autonomist parties, which came into being in Poland and other border countries of Russia after the First World War. One such party was already founded by him in Czarist Russia in 1906.

[249] The closing sentences of Mendelssohn's 'Jerusalem.'

content himself with this demand for the equality of religions. He needed only to criticize the tendencies of Christian Enlightenment theology which tried to depreciate Judaism. The Enlightenment in Germany had quite naively seen the universal religion of reason—common to all men—in Christianity. Judaism was viewed as a national political law imposed on the Jews by a divine despot. In virtue of this it seemed excluded from every share in the religion of reason, if one did not deny it the name of religion altogether —as Kant still did. That was the consensus from Spinoza to Kant, from which even Mendelssohn had not entirely escaped. For he too had separated the religion of reason from the divine revealed Law laid upon Jews, confirming in this way, as it seemed, the generally accepted thesis. But he had not only equated the religion of reason with the dogmatic content of the Jewish faith, thereby upsetting the monopoly claim of Christianity to it. He had also placed both elements in Judaism side by side, the religion of reason and religious action, whose religious efficacy resides in the revelation to Israel. Eternal and historical truth are united in the faith and life of the Jews.

A generation later a decisive change had taken place in the surrounding world. Romanticism had displaced the Enlightenment, consigning it almost to the scrap-heap.

The new philosophical development began with Fichte. *Fichte* developed Maimon's interpretation of the Kantian 'thing-in-itself', as an infinitesimal margin value, into a subjectivism. The "I" faces the 'non-I'. However, this 'non-I' is dependent on the "I", which postulates it. In this subsumption of the object into the subject the shift to speculative Idealism[250] took place, which as "German Idealism" began to hold sway during the first decades of the nineteenth century. Its great representatives were Fichte, *Schelling* and *Hegel*. With Fichte it took on an ethical dimension through linking the "I" with freedom and the will. Schelling's idealism brought in nature as reflection of the "I", whose medium of expression is art. The unconscious in nature's producing and acting is identical with the consciousness of the "I". This philosophy of identity in Schelling was finally transformed by Hegel into an eternally logical process of the dialectical self-movement of the Spirit.

Common to all these systems of Idealism is a mystical pantheism—strongest in Schelling—who early on arrived at a remarkable philosophy of myth. But also in Fichte the Divine will is one with the world. The blissful life is found in union with God as the One, Absolute. And with Hegel the "phenomenol-

---

[250] Friedrich Heinrich Jacobi had early on warned of this possible consequence of Kantian philosophy—in 1787 indeed, seven years before the appearance of Fichte's 'Doctrine of Wissenschaft' (Cf. F. H. Jacobi, Works, Vol. II, 1815, p. 36 ff and p. 310). Kant himself had protested against Fichte's Doctrine of Wissenschaft in a public declaration in the 'Jena Allgemeine Literaturzeitung' (No. 109, 1799, Cf. vol. VIII p. 306 in Vorlaender's ed. of Kant) and in a letter to Tieftrunk of April 5, 1798.

ogy of the Spirit", its expressions and self-movement in history, nature and religion, culminated in absolute knowledge.

It was a *pantheism of the spirit* which dominated the various ways of thinking in that epoch. The key concept introduced into the history of philosophy by Romanticism was 'spirit' (*Geist*)—one of the vaguest and most ambiguous of terms. Its very long ancestral line includes the Platonic Idea and the active intellect of Aristotelianism, concepts of the philosophy of nature of the Renaissance, the "substance" of Spinoza, animist and biblical-religious elements and, in particular, the specifically Christian interpretation of "Holy Spirit". All these elements cumulatively contributed to the concept of 'spirit' in German Idealism.[251] It appears as a dynamic concept, but in its main expressions it was really a static concept in the philosophy of the first half of the nineteenth century.[252]

A second feature of this time, closely associated with the philosophy of spirit, was the *dailectical method.* It appeared as thesis and antithesis, and then as a synthesis combining and integrating the two. This triad led or mis-led to the easily suggested analogy of the Christian Trinity. "The religious philosophy of Idealism was in its most significant and influential achievements a philosophic proof of Christianity. If the older rationalist school had seen the content of rational religion to be belief in God, freedom and immortality, the profound truths of religion were now located in these specifically Christian doctrines, which had previously been looked upon as super-rational and supplementary to the above-mentioned rational principles".[253] The irrational dogmas of the Trinity, of God becoming man, etc. were equated with the historical development of the spirit and its dialectical movements, especially in Hegel. In this way the absoluteness of the *Christian* religion came, as it were, to be philosophically established.

The German Jews who were just beginning to become integrated into the German language and culture and actively to participate in both, were suddenly faced with intellectual streams of thought, which in no way resembled their guiding examples as seen in Lessing and Mendelssohn. Instead of the same recognition for all who were striving along various ways to the common truths of the religion of reason, as Mendelssohn and his followers

---

[251] Geist (spirit), it seems to me, is a characteristic creation of the literature and philosophy of German Idealism. It has nothing analogous to it in general philosophical terminology. It corresponds neither to the French 'esprit,' nor the English "spirit" or "mind" which clearly have a religious and psychological colouring respectively. Also the expression, so common in Germany, of *Geisteswissenschaften* and *Geistesgeschichte* are apparently untranslatable. It is indicative that neither Kant nor F. H. Jacobi use the term *Geist*.

[252] See Schelling's "indifference" with its powers, Hegel's "world spirit," whose dialectical self-movement occurs within itself.

[253] Julius Guttmann, "Philosophies of Judaism," Routledge & Kegan Paul, London 1964, p. 306, translated from the revised and enlarged Hebrew edition of his German 'Die Philosophie des Judentums,' Munich 1933.

had expected, one was confronted anew by the absolute claim of the dominant religion. And this claim appeared in the heavy armour of the prevailing
philosophy of the day which declared it was the absolute philosophy.

Jewish reaction to the new and dangerous challenge to Judaism was relatively weak, as most of the educated remained true to the attitude of the
generation of the Enlightenment. Tenaciously they continued to see their
German view of culture embodied in Lessing, Mendelssohn, Schiller and
Kant, barely allowing themselves to waver in the modern streams of thought
passing over them. We saw how even with the pioneers of the Wissenschaft
of Judaism–Zunz, Geiger, Graetz, even Samson Rafael Hirsch–the heritage
of the Enlightenment outweighed the more superficial effects of Idealist
philosophy. For philosophical-theological discussions there was hardly any
interest. These generally took place outside the Jewish public with only a
few outsiders participating in them. They had from the beginning no prospect of entering into the non-Jewish world. For this reason only a few made
the attempt to meet the challenge of Idealist philosophy to Judaism.

These few attempts towards a self-portrait of Judaism amongst those who
consciously argued with the newly created philosophical situation, were
again varied. Varied also in the way they reacted to the attack. But they all
took pains to demarcate Jewish monotheism from the pantheistic tendencies
of those philosophers they followed, and to set an absoluteness of Judaism
in place of that of Christianity.

*Nachman Krochmal* (1785-1840) lived since early youth in Zolkiev,
Galicia. He was son of a wealthy businessman from Brody. His father,
through travelling to Berlin, came into contact with Mendelssohn and his
circle. The son broadened his traditional talmudic education by extensively
reading the medieval Jewish philosophers–Saadiah, Maimonides and the
philosophic Bible commentator Abraham Ibn Esra. This was something rare
in the Galicia of that day, when Ḥasidism was widespread. He also read the
modern philosophers of his day from Kant to Hegel.[254] Alongside the
classical he also acquired knowledge of the oriental languages. He did all this
as a self-taught man, who after the death of his well-to-do parents and
parents-in-law had to take up accountancy. Offers of positions as rabbi, like
those from Berlin, he refused. In his lifetime he submitted only a few contributions to the Hebrew periodical 'Kerem Ḥemed'. Krochmal's great work,
*Moreh Nevukhe Hazman* (Guide for the Perplexed of the Time) was–in
accordance with his testamentary wish–edited by Zunz eleven years after
his death in 1851.[255]

---

[254] Krochmal was one of two pre-subscribers in Galicia for Hegel's collected writings.

[255] Simon Rawidowiez edited a complete Hebrew edition of Krochmal's works (Kitve R. Nachman
Krochmal, Berlin 1924) with a full introduction. After Rawidowicz's death a second issue of this
edition appeared (London and Waltham, Mass., 1961). Other literature: Zunz's Introduction to his

Krochmal's main impact during his lifetime consisted in the personal influence he had on a number of friends and pupils—S. J. Rapoport, Rabbi Zevi Hirsch Hajes of Zolkiev and the Hebrew poet Meir (Max) Letteris. Renak[256]—with Zunz and Rapoport—is considered one of the pioneers of the Wissenschaft of Judaism. Yet in contradistinction to these two and to the predominant historical direction of this Wissenschaft, historical research for Renak stands within the firm framework of a philosophy of history, to a certain extent as exemplification of the latter.

More than his Jewish contemporaries in Germany, Krochmal resembled the Jewish scholars and philosophers of earlier centuries, in that he could still proceed quite naturally from the secure basis of his Judaism. He had no need to prove either to himself or to his Jewish readers the validity and soundness of the Jewish position. He did not need to smooth out two conflicting intellectual positions, to harmonize his Judaism with contemporary philosophy. Rather he found Judaism again in the philosophy of Idealism. In an, at first, naively charming way he equates philosophy with Judaism.[257] Judaism for him is the expression of the absolute Spirit.

Both Schelling and Hegel have had a special influence on Krochmal. The Hegelian influence is reflected notably in his terminology. He also took over from Hegel the historical-philosophical method, transforming the latter's logical-dialectical triad, however, into a *morphological-genetic* one. In this way Krochmal assumes a relatively independent stance.[258] Probably only because he wrote in Hebrew has this unusual position of his eluded the historians of German Idealism.

The spirits of peoples (Volksgeister), according to Krochmal, are governed by three stages, of birth, blossom and decline, after which they quit the process of world history to be superseded by another Volksgeist. But since the individual spirits of peoples also share in the absolute Spirit, as parts of its self-movement, their intellectual-spiritual achievements continue to exist

Krochmal edition; a biography by his disciple Meir (Max) Letteris, Vienna 1853 (all these, like Krochmal's own writings, are in Hebrew). Also, J. D. Landau, 'Nachman Krochmal, ein Hegelianer' (Nahman Krochmal, a Hegelian), Berlin 1904, and by the same author "Short Lectures on Modern Hebrew Literature," London 1938; Simon Rawidowicz (opposed to Landau) "War Nachman Krochmal ein Hegelianer?" in HUCA, vol. V 1928, pp. 535-582. Cf. also the comprehensive extracts by A. Lewkowitz and Rotenstreich. Julius Guttmann, who in the German edition of his 'Philosophie des Judentums,' Berlin 1933, only gives ten lines to Krochmal, adds an extensive chapter on him in the later Hebrew and English editions.

[256] Krochmal is thus called in Hebrew literature after the acronym of his name, *R*abbi *N*achman *K*rochmal.

[257] We shall find a similar approach, e.g. in Samuel Hirsch. However, for Hirsch absolute philosophy and absolute religion are identical, and only as a second step is this absolute religion equated with Judaism.

[258] One could call him "a Hegelianized Schellingian", as does Rawidowicz. With equal right one may call him a Hegelian strongly influenced by Schelling and Herder, as does Landau. But this dispute between Landau and Rawidowicz would perhaps be settled if one granted Krochmal a way of his own in the Idealist philosophy of history.

even after their physical decline—for instance, in art and literature, science and philosophy.

The people of Israel too, according to Krochmal, are subject to this three-fold genetic process of development. But the Jewish people are excluded by him from this schema, for, following every decline, with them a new beginning, a new historico-genetic cycle, takes place. This special position is biblically-theologically grounded and confirmed and justified in Krochmal's philosophical premises, which equate *Judaism* with *absolute Spirit*. If other peoples participate in the absolute Spirit only in part, Israel does so in its totality.[259]

With this close bond between absolute Spirit and Judaism which breaks the historiosophical schema, Krochmal has abandoned the teleological nature of the Jewish doctrine of history. In the universal absolute Spirit, divine and human spirit, religion and philosophy merge. Thus Krochmal adopts the Idealist pantheism of spirit. God becomes a *neutral* concept of spirit without the attributes of will, freedom and implicitly even of morality.

In this way an altogether paradoxical consequence ensued. Krochmal, who wrote in Hebrew and was more closely and organically bound to the rabbinic and philosophic tradition of Judaism than contemporaneous Jewish scholars in Germany—Zunz, Jost, Geiger—was in lifestyle and self-understanding an orthodox Jew. However, he shows himself in his doctrine of history remarkably un-Jewish. His impact on the Hebrew reading Jewish intelligentsia in Galicia and Eastern Europe was nevertheless great and decisive. Here his historical outlook, his presentation of historical developments and of single events, had a stimulating effect, paving the way for the scholarly treatment of Jewish history. Yet the increasingly reservedness of this East European intelligentsia to Jewish religious questions may, in large measure, go back to Krochmal's philosophy of spirit which in its outcome relativized religion.

If Krochmal made a comparatively independent contribution to the philosophy of speculative Idealism, Formstecher and Hirsch sought to affirm the individuality of Judaism each within a certain Idealist school of thought —the one within that of Fichte and Schelling, the other within that of Hegel.

*Solomon Formstecher* (1808-1889)[260] set himself the task "of considering Judaism as an absolutely necessary phenomenon within mankind". Judaism exists as a phenomenon, which is subject to historical development, and as

---

[259] Krochmal can quote many biblical passages for this. He also combines the idea with that of Shekhinah, the indwelling of God in the people of Israel.

[260] Formstecher was born in Offenbach. Apart from his four student years in Giessen he remained throughout his life in his birthplace, where he became preacher in 1831 and rabbi in 1842. He took part in the three Assemblies of Rabbis. The title of his main work is 'Die Religion des Geistes, eine wissenschaftliche Darstellung des Judentums nach seinem Charakter, Entwicklungsgang und Beruf in der Menschheit' (Religion of the Spirit. A Scientific Account of Judaism According to Its Character, its Course of Development and Task among Mankind), Frankfurt 1841. Besides this he published sermons, textbooks and several essays.

an idea. But in each of its developmental stages it is a part of mankind that "advances and recedes with mankind".[261]

In this self-assigned task Formstecher attributes absoluteness to Judaism according to its idea. His starting point is the *Schellingian world-soul*, which manifests itself in various powers. At the peak of these physical powers is man, who is above them in virtue of his self-consciousness and self-determination. However, if man possesses this, how much more must the world-soul, the bearer of all phenomena—to which indeed man himself belongs—possess self-determination and be a free independent spirit or God.[262] "God is a self-conscious free Being, self-reliant, independent of all phenomena." He is Creator of the world, not out of necessity but freely. "Without God no world, but not without world no God."[263] Nature which is determined by necessary laws, and the free spirit which is peculiar to man, stand opposite one another in the world.

The spirit of man is part of the *universal life* of Nature. It objectifies itself in the sciences of physics and aesthetics. However, in its *individual life* as human spirit it recognizes the true in logic, the good in ethics. The good does not reside in Nature. *Revelation* is the "message of that which is good placed by God in the human spirit".[264] The subjective recognition of revelation occurs through reason. *Reason cannot create the good; it can only judge what is good*, thus corresponding to revelation.

Collective knowledge and the endeavour to realise it is for Formstecher religion. But "if the content of Spirit is a twofold ideal, then there must be, can only be, not more than *two religions*, namely a religion for the ideal of universal life and one for that of individual life. The former we call *heathenism*, the latter *Judaism*".

The two parts of the world soul, Nature and Spirit, are also set opposite each other by Formstecher in the religions. Heathenism is the service of Nature, Judaism the service of Spirit. The God of Judaism creates—"as Spirit standing over Nature"—the whole world out of nothing by his simple word.[265] God is "a pure ethical Being. He has indeed created both Nature and Spirit . . . yet he is at the same time an extra-mundane God, who has no need—like a mere world-soul—of the world in order to be". The ideal of Judaism realises itself in its history. In Judaism "history is recognized as a manifestation of the free life of the Spirit in which, for this reason, only a psychological course of development can be pursued." During this course of development the relative truth of Judaism will become the absolute truth of the religion of the Spirit. In this connection Formstecher rejects

---

[261] 'Religion of the Spirit,' p. 12, 13.
[262] op. cit., p. 18.
[263] op. cit., p. 20 ff.
[264] op. cit., 32 ff.
[265] op. cit. p. 63-67.

all a priori constructions of history, whether they be analogies applied to
history from nature, such as childhood and youth, manhood and age, or
whether they be polarities. That would be a misjudgement of freedom and
an acknowledgement of a pagan fatalism.[266] —It is, therefore, a remarkable
rejection of both the method of Herder and that of—to Formstecher as yet
unknown—Krochmal, as well as of the Hegelian dialectic of history.

Parallel to the inner history of the Jews which Formstecher divides into
two great epochs: prophecy—beginning with the Patriarchs—and tradition
—from the return from Babylon to Moses Mendelssohn—is the relation of
Judaism to pagan mankind. This relation, which Formstecher calls "mission",
is a stirring of Judaism out of itself through paganism back to itself, according to the act of thinking which returns to itself as a movement of the
subject through the object. Thus, the mission of Judaism severs itself as
something independent of Judaism".[267] The severed bearers of this mission
are the daughter religions, Christianity and Islam. These are considered
representatives of a relative "transitory truth", spreading Jewish ideas
among the nations but thereby assimilating heathen conceptions. In contrast,
Judaism "throughout the storms of world history always preserves the
absolute true picture of mankind"[268] till the end of time, when the transitory bearers of mission shall have completed their task and Judaism proved
itself the absolute religion of the spirit.

With the aid of Schellingian terminology, Formstecher, by imparting to it
a strong ethical strain, gives an apotheosis to Judaism. He tries in vain to
break through the basically indifferent pantheistic principle of Schelling's
world-soul. Spirit and the religion of the spirit have for him pre-eminence
over nature. His priorities among the activities of the spirit are those aimed
at the good—more at knowledge of the good than the good deed itself.
Formstecher seeks to make the concept of God "extra-mundane" and
thereby to ensure for it a monotheistic character. He wants to protect His
power of creation and freedom, seeing in freedom—in the wake of Fichte
—the essential quality both of the divine and human spirit. In general, he
endeavours to retain all the basic theological concepts of Judaism: from
revelation—which he completely intellectualizes—to the election of Israel,
expressed in the leaving of the missionary task to the "transitory" daughter
religions, in order not to impair the purity and absoluteness of the religion of
the spirit. And finally to the teleology of the last days.

Yet Formstecher is not capable of convincingly going beyond the scope
of Schelling's system—not even of his terminology. What remains of this
Judaism—despite the constant and clever use of biblical and rabbinic material
—is a pure *abstraction*. It is only religion of the spirit. That Jews also exist—

---

[266] op. cit., p. 198.
[267] op. cit., p. 365.
[268] op. cit., p. 451.

living people and not mere abstract processes of an absolute Spirit—is for-gotten by him.[269]

*Samuel Hirsch* was faced with a task similar to that of Formstecher;[270] but Hirsch's was perhaps the more difficult. For as a *Hegelian* he had to measure himself against Hegel, the philosopher, who more emphatically than Fichte or Schelling had maintained that the absoluteness of Chris-tianity and the devaluation of Judaism was the consequence of a compel-ling dialectical-historical process.

One important difference to Formstecher's attempt is already to be found in the title of Hirsch's work. Not the "Religion of the Spirit" but the "Religious Philosophy of the Jews"—not an abstract Judaism but the "Religious Views of the Jews" is what Hirsch wishes to present.[271] In this respect he appears to remain entirely within the framework of the Hegelian theory of history, which performs the movement of the world-spirit within the spirits of nations. Hirsch quotes a wealth of religio-historical and ethno-graphical material on the religious outlooks of many peoples and cultures, following the parallel presentation in Hegel's 'Philosophy of Religion' and in other contemporary sources. But it is precisely in this application of the history of religion that Hirsch emancipates himself from the dialectical system of Hegel, just as he always leaps beyond the speculative Hegelian system—the trinitarian dialectical triad—whenever fundamental Jewish religious positions are concerned. Whereas the genuine Hegelian process knows no real contradiction between the various religious conceptions —letting them all, as partial truths, have a lingering effect upon the absolute religion, Christianity—Hirsch, like Formstecher distinguishes sharply between paganism and Judaism. With Formstecher this was the contrast between the religion of the universal life of nature and that of the individual life of the spirit. It is the tension between two—in principle equally possible—positive

[269] On Formstecher see especially Schoeps' account in 'Geschichte der juedischen Religionsphilo-sophie in der Neuzeit' (History of Modern Jewish Philosophy of Religion) Berlin 1935, pp. 65-92.

[270] Samuel Hirsch, born 1815 in Thalfang near Trier, was rabbi in Dessau and Luxemburg. He took an active part at the Assemblies of Rabbis in Brunswick and Frankfurt. In 1866 he went to Philadelphia as successor to Einhorn, where he held office till 1888. Already in Germany—and even more in the USA—he was one of the spokesmen of radical Reform, and one of the first to introduce Sunday services in the USA. His main work, 'Die Religionsphilosophie der Juden oder das Prinzip der juedischen Religionsanschauung and sein Verhaeltnis zum Heidentum, Christentum und zur absoluten Philosophie' (The Religious Philosophy of the Jews. The Principle of the Jewish View of Religion and its Relation to Paganism, Christianity and Absolute Philosophy)—written while still in Dessau—appeared in Leipzig in 1842. It was the only one published of a multi-volumed planned work: 'Das System der religioesen Anschauung der Juden und sein Verhaeltnis zum Heidentum, Christentum und zur allgemeinen Philos-ophie fuer Theologen aller Konfessionen sowie fuer gebildete Nichttheologen' (The System of the Religious Outlook of the Jews and its Relation to Paganism, Christianity and General Philosophy for Theologians of All Confessions and Educated Non-Theologians). He died in 1889 in Chicago in the house of his son Emil Gotthold Hirsch, who like him was a significant Reform rabbi and inter alia author of the most important theological articles in the Jewish Encyclopaedia.

[271] On Hirsch see Schoeps op. cit., pp. 93-132 and Emil J. Fackenheim's Essay "Samuel Hirsch and Hegel" in "Studies" ed. by Altmann pp. 171-201.

factors whereby the religion of the spirit is simply given pre-eminence over the religion of nature. According to Hirsch, on the other hand, it is not two positive factors standing side by side, but one positive factor and its negation. Paganism is the *negation* of truth and freedom. It is the *absolute false religion*, which is confronted by the *absolute true religion, Judaism*.[272] For Hegel the non-Christian religions are parts of a dialectical process culminating in Christianity. For Hirsch the dialectic of paganism culminates not in the true religion but in self-refutation of the false one. Paganism as a deification of nature "is not a partial truth but a total falsehood. And from this falsehood the dialectical process can only lead to further falsehoods, at most to the recognition of the futility of all falsehoods", to scepticism with which Hirsch concludes his presentation of pagan philosophy.[273] Hegelian philosophy, as a derivative and culmination of pagan philosophy, is actually described by him on one occasion as "sublimated paganism".[274]

However, in our discussion of Hirsch's religious philosophy, we have somewhat anticipated. How did Hirsch arrive at his sharp distinction between paganism and Judaism? In the first place absolute philosophy for him is identical with absolute religion[275] —this again a deviation from the Hegelian position. But it is only an apparent deviation, since the primacy of knowledge —whether religious or philosophical—takes us back again to man and his thought, and therefore back to philosophy.

Hirsch's religious philosophy has its starting point in man.[276] Man comes into being when "the child no longer refers to itself in the third person but as 'I'—i.e. not until it has elevated itself from awareness of the world to self-awareness. Only when man has first learned to say 'I' does he become a real human being, does he tear himself away from the natural, from all earlier stages of existence and become an individual person . . . What is

---

[272] The above is a good example of Hirsch's dependence on and emancipation from Hegelian ideas. The dialectics of the historical process are abandoned but the conceptual dialectics retained and stressed. Hirsch remains a Hegelian, but often a Hegelian against his will and with a sharp critique of Hegel at some points. The phrase in the title of his book—"absolute philosophy"—is Hegel's. And on p. 412 he draws a graphic schema of the history of philosophy which is bracketed to face the words: "Hegel the sum total of all philosophy!". At the same time, he criticises the Hegelian schematic: "One may consider the Hegelian philosophy of religion—e.g. its treatment of the religion of the Indians and that of the Jews—as though it were nothing more than a pure childish joy, that the preconditioned schema could be found again . . . First Hegel indicates the conceptual stage of a given religion, followed by a concrete presentation, as though it were proof of what he had stated beforehand." His helpless dilemma vis-a-vis Hegel is expressed in the sentence: "One is no longer a Hegelian— the pity is that one is nothing besides!" p. 289. This sentence—levelled at D. F. Strauss—is applicable to Hirsch himself.

[273] op. cit., p. 437 ff.

[274] op. cit., p. 98.

[275] Philosophy, according to Hirsch (cf. p. *XVII*), cannot give to religion any other knowledge than that already present in religion.

[276] One can hardly compare this focus on man with the "anthropological tendency" of the Hegelian 'Left', as e.g. in Feuerbach, or give Hirsch priority over Feuerbach, as indeed Schoeps proposes. Cf. Schoeps p. 105.

implied then in this very meaningful saying of 'I'? Nothing other than freedom itself . . . Freedom is that something which first makes man a man". But this is only an empty abstract freedom. Nature has taught him to say 'I', yet this does not mean that he is free from nature. For "nothing can be free from nature. Where freedom is, there naturalness ends. Freedom wants to be won". To become free, i.e. to become his own master and not nature's slave, is man's task. The abstract innate predisposition towards freedom should be actualized into real freedom. "But this is also the essential and only true concept of religion. The religious life is nothing other than this eternally real freedom perpetually realizing itself".[277]

Hirsch sees "the basic error of the religiosity of our time" in the fact "that it is incapable of conceiving religion as anything other than a relation-ship of man to God . . . One cannot speak of a relation to God. Only things relate to each other".[278] But if religion only "expresses man's relation to himself, then the basis, the root, of this relation to himself must be God".[279] "Freedom in principle and the ability to acquire it (is) a gift of God" that makes it possible for man to become free.[280] This *freedom* founded on man created in God's likeness holds good with regard to the problem of *sin*. "Man is not sinful by nature. Everything natural is neither vice nor virtue as such . . . but man can in no way remain in this pure natural state. He is torn between his naturalness and the freedom transcending it. It is man's essential disposition to free himself, which implies the *possibility* of making oneself unfree. Pure naturalness is given to man—it is already there—but it is he who makes himself free or unfree". The *capacity for sin* then exists for him as well as the capacity for virtue. "But this possibility for sin should remain a pure possibility and should never become a reality".[281] From this mere possibility of sin it follows that sin is not necessary, not our fate, not *original sin*. The principle of paganism however—according to Hirsch—lays down that "man must sin, and that being so, naturalism, sen-sualism is absolute master".[282]

Abraham is the first man to free himself from this principle of paganism, who resists all temptations and becomes the beacon showing all mankind that it is possible to realise freedom, and thereby triumph over the pos-sibility of sin. His absolute true religion has been handed down to his descen-dants as a legacy and task. The mission of Judaism to humanity is manifested in the history of the Jews and in their special way of life. Judaism is an *intensive* religion which should be effectual through its example.

In its initial stages with Jesus and the Gospels, *Christianity* still remained

[277] op. cit., p. 12 ff.
[278] op. cit., p. 25 ff.
[279] op. cit., p. 29.
[280] op. cit., p. 48.
[281] op. cit., p. 41 ff.
[282] op. cit., p. 110 ff.

within the framework of Judaism. It was Paul in his mission to the Gentiles who first made it into an *extensive* religion, and by adopting the heathen doctrine of original sin and redemption caused the schism between Judaism and Christianity. But Hirsch hopes that the church will one day discard the false Pauline doctrines.[283] Then, at the end of days, "God will be recognised as One and men as free images of Him". Then too, "Israel will still foster and cultivate its own particular cult, but a cult which will be honoured and loved by all men, in which all men will have a mediate, but Israel an immediate, share". This cult symbolises the Jewish national vocation—an attitude one would hardly expect from a radical Reform rabbi—in which "the philosophy of religion or the ideal of freedom has been fulfilled, proving how freedom has established itself despite the possibility of sin in the world".[284]

Hirsch illustrates his doctrine of religion with countless quotations from Bible, Talmud, Midrash—even from the Zohar—in order to find in the rabbinic pronouncements support for his own speculative ideas and their conclusions. In all his efforts to present his philosophy within the strict context of Jewish tradition one could easily forget that Hirsch was one of the most radical of Reform rabbis.[285] His attempt nevertheless remains confined to a presentation of religion based on intellect and on the concepts of Idealist philosophy. Yet despite his efforts he finds no exit from the immanence of the intellect. His *concept of God* is a pure intellectual abstraction, which is not even made intelligible but is presupposed. It seems on occasion like a *deus ex machina*, from which it is difficult to see how it fits in with his speculations on freedom and sin.

For all that Hirsch is a noteworthy, powerful systematic thinker. His unsuccessful confrontation with Hegel can thus readily be described—in Fackenheim's words—as a heroic failure.[286]

Alongside Krochmal's interpretation of Judaism as an eternal rebirth within the historical process and alongside Formstecher's religion of the spirit, Hirsch portrays Judaism as a religion of the freedom of man. These three instances of applying philosophic Idealism to the Jewish view of religion all come to grief in that they dovetail religion into immanental processes of the spirit, regarding the spirit as an embracing world principle, to which Creator and creature and the otherness and togetherness of the God/man relationship are foreign. These interpretations could not do justice to Judaism as the thoroughgoing representative of a theistic religiosity, even though constant and serious attempts were made to hold firm to the Jewish

[283] op. cit., p. 765.

[284] op. cit., p. 882.

[285] Cf. e.g. p. IX where he claims to understand the Jewish customs and ceremonies in their absolute necessity, flatly refusing every form of biblical criticism and showing the necessity—not just the possibility—for miracles (See pp. 537-620) and the like.

[286] Cf. Fackenheim, op. cit., p. 201.

theistic positions in relation to those pantheistic processes of the spirit and to harmonize them with the latter.

In direct contrast to the portraits of Judaism presented by the spirit of Idealism, with which we have so far been concerned, is *Solomon Levi (or Ludwig) Steinheim's* "Doctrine of Revelation"—the first volume of which appeared in 1835, i.e. prior to the works of Formstecher, Hirsch and Krochmal.[287] If the latter approached the Jewish religion as philosophers, even though often consciously breaking through the systematic hold of Idealist philosophy, the physician and scientist Steinheim approached it as *theologian*. His theology was indeed influenced by philosophical considerations. However in philosophy—"philosophism" (Philosophema) as he styles the philosophic approach—he sees the continuation and sublimation of paganism as the *opposite* of the revealed doctrine of true religion. By means of his extreme supernatural concept of revelation he wants to keep religion free from all apparent or latent admixture with any man-made religious or philosophical world-view. This is why he polemizes—often viciously —against a metaphysics that competes with theology and metaphysics' "dogmatics of construing reason".[288] His opponents are Plato, Spinoza, Leibniz; among the Idealist philosophers Fichte, Schelling, Hegel; and among the theologians Schleiermacher. He sees his allies in Aristotle and Bayle, Lessing, Friedrich Heinrich Jacobi and Jaesche.[289] He constantly refers to *Kant*, though frequently seeing him through the eyes of Jacobi and Jaesche.

---

[287] Steinheim was born in Bruchhausen in 1789, studied in Kiel and Berlin and lived from 1813-1845 as physician in Altona, later mostly in Italy. He died in 1866 in Zurich. See the memorial volume 'Salomon Ludwig Steinheim zum Gedenken' (In Memory of Salomon Ludwig Steinheim), on the centenary of his death, ed. by H. J. Schoeps in collaboration with the present author and Gerd Hesse Goeman (Leyden 1966). On Steinheim's doctrine cf. present author's essays, 'Die philosophischen Motive der Theologie S. L. Steinheims' (The Philosophical Motifs in the Theology of S. L. Steinheim) in the memorial volume and 'Steinheim und Kant' in Yearbook LBI, vol. V, London 1960. See further Joshua O. Habermann: "S. L. Steinheim's Doctrine of Revelation," in "Judaism" 1968.

The 1st vol. of Steinheim's work 'Die Offenbarung nach dem Lehrbegriff der Synagoge' (Revelation according to the Teaching of the Synagogue) with the sub-title 'Ein Schiboleth,' was published in Frankfurt in 1835; the 2nd vol. not until 1856 in Leipzig with the sub-title 'Glaubenslehre der Synagoge als exakte Wissenschaft' (Doctrinal Belief of the Synagogue as an Exact Science). Vol. III: 'Die Polemik, der Kampf der Offenbarung mit dem Heidenthume, ihre Synthese und Analyse' (The Polemic, the Struggle of Revelation with Paganism, Its Synthesis and Analysis) (exemplified by Christianity), Leipzig 1863. The 4th Vol. contains 'Five Monomachies' (Altona 1865), the most important of which is the argument with Luther. In the literary remains were preliminary studies for a 5th vol., including a comparison of Schopenhauer with Kant from the standpoint of the doctrine of revelation. Steinheim gives a shorter account of his doctrine of revelation in 'Moses Mendelssohn und seine Schule in ihrer Beziehung zur Aufgabe des neuen Jahrhunderts der alten Zeitrechnung' (Moses Mendelssohn and his School in Relation to the Task of the New Century) Hamburg 1840. In this work he first introduces his Kantianism.

[288] Vol. II, p. 6.

[289] On Jaesche cf. the present author's note in the memorial vol. p. 75 ff.

Steinheim's aim—as the title of his second volume implies—is to raise the *doctrine of Judaism to an exact science*. Just as astrology gave rise to astronomy, alchemy to chemistry, magic to physics, so theology should be elevated from theosophy and the theology of feeling à la Schleiermacher to a science.[290]

Steinheim's turning to religion and his re-turning to Judaism was the result of his serious personal struggle with Christianity. Several of his closest friends had accepted baptism, and he himself was frequently tempted to convert. It was out of his entirely personal struggle with Christianity that the knowledge of Judaism unexpectedly dawned on him.

What distinguished Judaism from all other religions for Steinheim was that it is a revealed religion, founded on divine revelation. The *criterion of revelation* lies in its content. This content is not to be found in deductive thought. It actually contradicts the latter. "For" as Lessing once said—and Steinheim quotes him here—"what is revelation that does not reveal?" God would surely be playing a capricious game with us if he revealed something, which human intelligence could discover itself. "Thus I concluded that everything subsumed under the name of revelation, whose facts and content correspond to what we know, for that very reason cannot be called revelation".[291]

Steinheim himself was surprised by the paradox of his discovery, according to which the general view—which sees the truth of revelation precisely in its agreement with religious consciousness—should be completely reversed. Yet he follows up his new insight with onesided consistency. The first volume of his work in particular aims to show the difference between revelation and non-revelation, i.e. the false application of the concept of revelation. Steinheim finds non-revelation in paganism, in the myths and natural religions of the various nations. With the Greeks it is myth that gives rise to philosophism, philosophic metaphysics, in which pagan thought exists to our own day. What is common to paganism and philosophism is that in these man creates his own god.[292] This is not the God of revelation, the free Creator of nature, but a god *bound* to nature and its system of law or identical with it. The genuine *content of revelation—God, Freedom, Creation* are foreign to both natural consciousness and philosophism. They are something new which cannot be discovered or constructed from the presuppositions of natural thought or philosophism. This genuine revelation only exists in the revelation to Israel. Nevertheless it is not always identical with the revelation at Sinai, or in the Pentateuch or Hebrew Bible. Even here Steinheim only recognizes as revelation that which corresponds to his selective concept of it. Christianity on the other hand, according to Steinheim, has inter-

[290] Vol. II, p. 38.
[291] Vol. I, p. 10.
[292] Vol. II, p. 28.

mingled the original Jewish elements of revelation with foreign pagan ones. Through these Christianity became already in the Synoptics—with exception of Mark—but also in John, Paul and finally in the Athanasian symbol, a hybrid religion.

Yet Steinheim, the natural scientist, is not an irrationalist. He accuses Schleiermacher of having "dislodged impartial reason from its judgement seat and set infectious feeling in its place".[293] Steinheim places the criterion in the *concept of reason* itself. He distinguishes dogmatic from critical reason. Dogmatic reason is that of philosophism, metaphysics. It wants to make deductive statements a priori about the perceptible and imperceptible world. Whereas critical reason proceeds inductively and a posteriori both in the perceptible material sphere—as in the sciences—and in theology. It leads not to knowledge of facts and things—as dogmatic reason does—but to understanding.

Dogmatic reason cannot stand in face of revelation. It is "taken prisoner" by revelation, as Steinheim says, using again a quoted expression of Lessing from the deistic philosopher H. S. Reimarus. The reason-part of revelation, however, is founded upon critical reason i.e. it can be found not by a priori construction, but by a posteriori induction alone.[294] "The faith of the Jew is . . . founded on research, induction; he believes only that to which these force him, like the thinker his unprovable hypotheses, the chemist his atomic weight".[295]

All *constructions* of nature, whether they appear as Idealism, materialism or as Romantic natural philosophy, break down on the *problem of reality*, the problem of the real object. Steinheim elucidates this by a series of examples, from which he concludes: "In all natural objects there resides something of a wonder. This is the incommensurable, indissoluble in the process of thought".[296]

The subsequent step from the object of natural science to the content of the doctrine of belief was taken by Steinheim in close reliance on *Kant's Critique of Pure Reason*. Having confirmed the wonder character of the real object by extending the Kantian concept of the antinomies from metaphysics to natural science, he now established this with the aid of Kant's "analogies of experience". The object of experience cannot be construed. Philosophy can only give a rule as to how to look for it in experience. Even for Kant the real object is a wonder. Steinheim can now give us an analogy, a line of direction, by which to understand the content of revelation—but not to construct it. "Natural history has become the propaedeutics of theology".[297]

---

[293] Vol. II, p. 38.
[294] Vol. I, p. 71 and passim.
[295] Vol. II, p. 19.
[296] Vol. II, p. 54.
[297] Vol. II, pp. 70-74 and Kant's Critique of Pure Reason, 2nd ed. pp. 222, 228, 229.

After Steinheim has created a basis for the doctrine of revelation through his interpretation of Kant he comments on the content of this doctrine: "God is the wonder of an incomprehensible personality".[298]

Person for Steinheim signifies ethical-spiritual individuality, self-conscious reflecting freedom in action. Freedom is "the highest attribute of God and the highest glory of man, the common focal point in which both world problems—physics and ethics—converge". Divine freedom is expressed in creation. Free creation ex nihilo is the best example in Steinheim's concept of revelation. In speculative metaphysics one never gets beyond the contradiction between: "Out of nothing comes nothing"—assuming the eternity of matter—and the law of causality: "No effect without cause". We avoid this contradiction by making creation the first act of God, and His will the first free cause of this act, and by stating the dogma: 'Out of nothing, something, everything'. This too is inconceivable, but it is not subject to contradiction and therefore not impossible". The difference between the divine and the free human will is that the former creates matter itself for his work, whereas man can only work with material already given.[299]

Steinheim also recognizes his doctrine of creation in Kant.[300] His treatment of the problem of immortality and of history relies heavily on him. He takes over Kant's philosophy of history en bloc, quoting him page after page.[301]

History—closely connected with creation and freedom—begins with man made in God's likeness. Then follow the covenants made with Noah, Abraham and Israel. These covenants presuppose a certain equality of both partners and are the foundation of society and state. This ideal theocratic state existed in Israel only before the monarchy, which Steinheim rejects as a relapse into the pagan "state of privilege" based on inequality.[302] However, history will finally reach its goal in the Messianic kingdom of God proclaimed by the prophets.[303] "The higher idea of history according to revelation consists in this worthy participation in the completion of the great plan of creation" through man, "who helps to complete the work of the great Father and Creator".[304] This is the old central Jewish concept of the

---

[298] Vol. I, p. 82.

[299] Vol. II, p. 166 and p. 147 ff.

[300] He quotes examples from the Critiques of Pure and of Practical Reason and from Jaesche, who refers to Kant. See vol. II pp. 146 and 362 and the note of the present author on Jaesche in the memorial vol. on Steinheim, p. 75 ff.

[301] From Kant's 'Mutmasslicher Anfang der Menschengeschichte' (Conjectural Beginning of the History of Mankind) and 'Ideen zu einer allgemeinen Geschichte in weltbuergerlicher Absicht' (Idea for a Universal History with Cosmopolitan Intent). Cf. e.g. Vol. II p. 186 and 211 ff., 355 ff. and passim. Cf. also Steinheim's booklet on "Mendelssohn and his School," p. 37 and pp. 101-137.

[302] Vol. II, p. 237.

[303] Vol. II, p. 240 ff.

[304] Vol. II, 243 ff.

challenge to man to co-operate in the realisation of the kingdom of God. Steinheim again finds parallels for this idea in the Kantian teleology of history.

I have already referred to the autobiographical motif in Steinheim. His work is a self-portrayal in the strictest sense of the word, namely the portrait of *a Jew finding his way back* to his religion. This religion which he demarcates as alone pure from all non-religion, mixed religions and philosophic constructions of the world, this "doctrine of revelation" is for Steinheim Judaism. He sets Jews the task as a special community to preserve and spread this religion in its purity and rigour. In the profusion and wide range of his polemics, however, it is often forgotten that Steinheim's "Revelation according to the Teaching of the Synagogue" is really intended to be a self-portrait of Judaism.

But the only response which this portrayal of Judaism evoked—standing, as it does, in marked contrast to the accepted ways of thought—was an estranging astonishment. Thus Steinheim, one of the great theologians of Judaism and the only one of his century, remained an outsider. In earlier Jewish intellectual history he had a fore-runner in Juda Halevi, likewise an anti-philosopher, theologian and physician. Geiger, however, to whose first periodical Steinheim at first contributed, behaved outspokenly hostile to him, as did also Formstecher who refused "to learn theology from a physician". Samuel Hirsch wrote: "To my knowledge Steinheim is the first who, well-intentioned enough, tried to identify Judaism with nonsense!"[305] Orthodoxy blamed Steinheim for his selective concept of revelation and non-Torah-true lifestyle. Graetz and Frankel certainly viewed him as an eccentric to be tolerated. It is only in our century that attention is again turning to him.

---

[305] Samuel Hirsch, *Religionsphilosophie* (Philosophy of Religion) p. 554, footnote.

# CHAPTER 19

*Portrayals of Jewish Self-Understanding II*

The writings of Steinheim, Formstecher and Hirsch were published in the years 1835-1842.[306] In the course of the next half century there was certainly no lack of portrayals of the Jewish religion. More than a hundred and sixty such books appeared between 1785 and 1894,[307] but most of these were textbooks for Jewish religious instruction or else outlines of a popular or apologetic nature. This literature was produced by Jewish teachers and rabbis of the most varied outlook, among them Formstecher and Samuel Hirsch; Kley, founder of the Hamburg Temple and director of the Free School there; Solomon Plessner, one of the first Orthodox preachers in the German language; the moderate Reform rabbis Joseph Aub and S. Herxheimer;[308] the Conservative Moravian rabbi, H. B. Fassel, who wrote a Jewish doctrine of morals based on the post-Kantian philosophy of Wilhelm Traugott Krug;[309] and many others.

During the next half century between 1840 and 1890 the formal civil equality of Jews had gradually established itself in the German states. Their cultural and conscious integration into German life towards the end of this epoch had probably reached its peak. This generation of a success-conscious ascending citizenry, which felt politically secure, was not very pretentious in Jewish spiritual matters. One had at most a sentimental nostalgic interest

[306] Since Steinheim's "Mendelssohn and His School" already anticipated his close relation to Kant, later developed in vol. II of his "Doctrine of Revelation", it may perhaps be said that around 1840 the system of Steinheim was also largely completed.

[307] See Jacob J. Petuchowsky's "Manuals and Catechisms of the Jewish Religion in the Early Period of Emancipation", in "Studies in 19th Century Jewish Intellectual History" ed. by A. Altmann, Cambridge, Mass. 1964, pp. 47-64.

[308] His "Yesode Hatorah", published in 1830, was probably the most widely read of these textbooks. The present author's copy is the 34th edition from the year 1897. Herxheimer was rabbi in Eschwege and Bernburg. He died in 1884.

[309] 'Zedek und Mischpat—Tugend und Rechtslehre', bearbeitet nach den Prinzipien des Talmuds und der Form der Philosophie des seligen W. T. Krug ("Zedek and Mishpat—Virtue and the Doctrine of Right" According to the Principles of the Talmud and the Philosophy of the Deceased W. T. Krug), Vienna 1848.

in the now happily surmounted past. This era produced novels like "Dichter und Kaufmann" (Poet and Merchant) by Berthold Auerbach, who then applied the same approach to non-Jewish themes in his "Schwarzwälder Dorfgeschichten" (Village Stories of the Black Forest), Aron Bernstein's "Voegele der Maggid" (The Popular Preacher) and Leopold Kompert's and Karl Emil Franzos' widely read stories of the Bohemian and Galician ghettos. They were the popular and sentimental side-effects of the same historical interest that was academically reflected in the works of the Wissenschaft of Judaism.

Many non-academic portrayals of the Jewish religion which appeared at that time also testify to the simple taste of the readers for whom they were written. Their purpose was to make Judaism amenable to "enlightened" and in many cases, semi-educated German Jews, with a corresponding justification of its value. Titles like "Das rationale Judentum" (Rational Judaism) by the Breslau/Koenigsberg preacher and educationalist Isaac Asher Francolm (1840) give an indication of this trend. A Conservative rabbi in Gleiwitz, Dr. H. S. Hirschfeld (1812-1884), had written an unclear quaint book "Ueber das Wesen und den Ursprung der Religion" (On the Nature and Origin of Religion), in which a medley of opinions intermingle.

The most voluminous and widely read of these books and the most momentous in its claims was the "Israelitische Religionslehre"[310] (The Israelite Doctrine of Religion) by Rabbi Ludwig Philippson (1811-1889) of Magdeburg, the versatile initiator, organiser and publisher. He was a man of wide learning, whose academic qualities were pushed into the background by the journalist and religious politician in him. Neither does his work alas bear the stamp of the theologian and philosopher, but of the journalist and spiritual adviser. It is catechetically designed, each section beginning with a question, which is answered with lengthy explanations. Philippson defines religion as the relationship—expressed in the Hebrew idea of covenant (Brith)—of man to God. "The awareness and concept of a divine Being come to us from three sources: Firstly, from the feeling of dependence on a higher Power. Secondly, in the desire of the human spirit towards something higher . . . its longing heavenward. Thirdly, the consciousness of man consists essentially in the combination of cause and effect . . . Every cause is the effect of a first and highest cause, the divine Being".[311] Schleiermacher's theology of feeling, a metaphysical longing and the Aristotelian primus motor of the medieval Jewish and scholastic philosophy, are here further united with a Steinheimian concept of revelation: "Revealing means conveying something hitherto unknown which man by himself could not know or experience."[312] This religio-philosophic conglomeration, with commen-

[310] Leipzig 1863, 3 volumes.
[311] See "Israelit. Religionslehre", 1861, pp. 1-7.
[312] op. cit., p. 39.

surately long explanations, is hardly enjoyable today in its moralising triviality.

Well above these works in stature is "Die Biblisch-talmudische Glaub-enslehre nebst einer dazugehörigen Beilage ueber Staat und Kirche, histor-isch dargestellt" (The Biblical-Talmudic Doctrine of Belief, including an Ap-pendix on Church and State Historically Presented) by Dr. Moritz Duschak (1815-1890), rabbi of Gaya in Moravia and later in Cracow. It lies some-where between an historical Wissenschaft of Judaism and an implicit trans-ference of Talmudic theology to the present. Here the "collective-truth" of Judaism is arranged into various aspects, all of which—though some are more important than others—are treated alike. Duschak was perhaps philo-sophically influenced by the speculative theism of the younger (J. H.) Fichte, whom he quotes (p. 178).

Only at the end of the nineteenth century does a turning-point, a renewal, of a genuine Jewish philosophy of religion begin, and through it a renewal of Jewish self-expression and self-portrayal.

In 1898 the first volume of *Moritz Lazarus'* "Ethik des Judentums" (Ethics of Judaism) appeared.[313] Lazarus (1824-1903), who took his starting-point from the post-Kantian philosopher Herbart, applied Herbart's psychol-ogy to the study of peoples. In conjunction with his brother-in-law, Heymann Steinthal[314] (1823-1899), he developed his own discipline of "Voelker-psychologie" (Psychology of Nations). Lazarus became professor in Berne, Switzerland in 1860, professor at the Berlin Military Academy in 1866 and honorary professor at the University of Berlin in 1874. In politics and in Jewish affairs he was active from an early age. Already in 1850 he advocated Prussia's hegemony in a booklet, "Die sittliche Berechtigung Preussens in Deutschland" (The Ethical Justification of Prussia in Germany). He became president of the "synod", which in Leipzig (1869) and Augsburg (1871) re-sumed the efforts at reform by the Rabbinical Assemblies of the 'forties on a broader basis, but again without success. Lazarus was one of the initiators in founding the "Hochschule fuer die Wissenschaft des Judentums" in Berlin, and published many essays and lectures on Jewish questions. He was in-volved in the controversy with Heinrich von Treitschke, his lecture, "Was heisst national?" (What does "national" mean?) delivered in 1880 in this connection, becoming especially well known. Here his psychology of nations tries to give subjective substantiation to the concept of "national", since

---

[313] The second volume was published posthumously in 1911.

[314] Steinthal, a linguistic genius, applied the discipline especially to philology and the philosophy of language, including the negroid languages and the Chinese. He became private lecturer at Berlin University in 1850 and Professor Extraordinary in 1863. From 1872 he was also lecturer for Jewish religious philosophy at the newly established "Hochschule fuer die Wissenschaft des Judentums". His writings on Judaism appeared in a collected volume, "Ueber Juden und Judentum", after his death in 1907. Steinthal also edited, inter alia, a new edition of Wilhelm von Humboldt's writings on the philosophy of language.

objective criteria–like race, origin and political borders–failed to constitute the concept of nation. Only language and the will to belong to a community with a common language and culture, thus remain.[315]

Lazarus' "Ethics of Judaism" is closely connected with his academic achievement. The "psychology of nations" was a modification of the national spirit of Romanticism, though Lazarus is far removed from the idea of "Volksgeist" in Romanticism. "Volksgeist" in his psychology of peoples is no longer interpreted historically, as a temporal representation of the world-spirit, but socio-psychologically, as that which unites individuals within a nationally and culturally homogeneous group. This "collective spirit"–as Lazarus variously calls it–also possesses continuity.

This *socio-psychological interpretation* of the ethical outlooks of the Jews made Lazarus' portrayal in his "Ethics of Judaism" very vivid and really popular. Lazarus drew on copious material from Bible, Talmud and Midrash, from rabbinic literature, from ancient and living custom. At the same time he not only disregards the ethical philosophical literature produced by Judaism, but distinctly rejects it in places. He is methodically correct here in that he does not see in the reflected philosophical ethics–which preserves the con-nection with general philosophy–the unaffected expression of the Jewish *Volksgeist* which can be interpreted psychologically. He therefore attacks –among others–Maimonides, but also Baḥya, the eleventh century author of "Duties of the Heart", saying: ". . . the point is not to create free philo-sophical ethics, but to present the real existing ethics of a school of thought, of an era, of a people and of a religion".[316] "The examples of the Alex-andrians, later of Maimonides (had) frightening consequences . . . Philosophic thought did not deepen the ethical but deflected and submerged it in foreign depths. Thus with Baḥya ethics is merged into mysticism, leading of neces-sity to an all too aristocratic ethics".[317]

But this demarcation from philosophic ethics, especially from that of the Medieval Jewish philosophers, is not consistently carried through by Lazarus. His book claims to present an *ethics* and should therefore be more than a description of popular customs and views, for ethics is a part of systematic philosophy.

Thus Lazarus himself has to enter "foreign" depths". He takes as his example the *Kantian ethics* with its principle of autonomy, trying to apply Kant's concept of autonomy to the ethics of Judaism.

Religion for Kant is the "recognition of every duty as a divine com-mand". According to him the ethical law leads towards religion "by means

---

[315] Lazarus published his occasional writings on Judaism in "Treu und Frei" (Faithful and Free) in 1883. His second wife, whom he married in 1895, was the authoress Nahida Remy, who had con-verted to Judaism and written several books of Jewish content–"Das juedische Weib" (The Jewish Wife) in 1892 and others.

[316] Lazarus, "Ethik des Judentums", vol. II, p. XVII.

[317] op. cit., p. XVIII.

of the concept of the highest good as the object and goal of pure practical reason".[318] The teleological function of the highest good, which corresponds to the postulate nature of the Kantian concept of God, links (in Kant) religion and ethics—the autonomy of the free human will with the will of God—as pledge of the realisability of the moral law.

Lazarus now tries to apply this connection to Judaism: "The Jewish ethics is originally a theological one . . . That which is ethically good and pleasing to God—ethical law and divine regulation—are for Judaism completely inseparable concepts". Already in the oldest biblical sources the thought appears: "It is not through a divine act of will or by divine command that the ethical law originates, but from the very nature of God himself . . . Therefore the sum of all morality is condensed in the commandment, "Ye shall be holy"—not "for I desire it", or "for I command it", but rather "Ye shall be holy, for I am holy". It is not on any dogmatic concept of God but on the idea of God's morality, i.e. on the nature of morality itself, that the ethical law is founded. Not as commander, but as prototype of morality is God simultaneously the original source of all human morality".[319] In this foundation of morality, as it is found in biblical and rabbinic Judaism, Lazarus sees the *autonomy* of Jewish ethics expressed, despite its religious and—in Kantian terminology—real heteronomous foundation.

Lazarus rejects especially sharply the application to Jewish ethics of the utility principle, a eudaemonic doctrine of good. Also the question of the highest good which Kant had allowed here for the combination of religion and ethics, is according to Lazarus far removed from Judaism. "In rabbinic learning the question of the goal of morality is not: 'What is the highest good man may attain?', but 'What is the right way?' 'What is the good way one should take?' The thinker's view is directed here not to results but to the intentions of ethical action".[320] Reward and punishment are indeed frequently spoken of in scripture. But these terms, according to Lazarus, are used for purely educational or psychological reasons. Hence, though not acting for altruistic reasons at first, one learns in the end to act unselfishly. Apart from this popular educational outlook "numerous sayings were not merely generally known but also acknowledged, which expressly reject reward as the basis of the law and as an inducement for its fulfilment."[321]

Lazarus portrays Judaism as an ethical doctrine reflected in the life and opinions, forms and institutions of the Jews. This doctrine of ethics is religious. But religion for Lazarus is confined to ethics. The doctrine of God

[318] Kant, Critique of Practical Reason 2nd ed., p. 129.

[319] Lazarus, vol. I pp. 85-90.

[320] op. cit., vol. I p. 125. See also "Mishnah Avot" (Sayings of the Fathers), Ch. 2.1 and Ch. 2.13.

[321] op. cit., vol. I pp. 130-134 & 405 ff. (Appendix, note no. 26). Among other passages in Talmud and Midrash, Lazarus refers in particular to the well-known saying of Antigonus of Sokho: "Be not like servants who serve their master in the hope of receiving reward; be rather like those servants who serve their master with no expectation of reward, and let only the fear of heaven be upon you".

in Judaism is entirely taken up for him in the holiness of God, from which he derives the demand of the ethical and the sanctifying of human action. Other aspects of Jewish teaching about God, such as the oneness of God, the Creator of the world, are not dealt with by Lazarus. His rather inconsistent attempt—in contrast to his declared opposition to philosophical ethics—to give Jewish ethics a philosophical basis, to place it within the framework of the Kantian doctrine of autonomy, lacks clear and systematic precision. Nevertheless Lazarus possesses a keen intuitive eye for connections and for the ethical content of religious phenomena. He is a typical representative of the attitude of mind and outlook on life of the German Jews in the second half of the nineteenth century—at least of those within Liberal Jewry, to whom an interest and active participation in Jewish questions and affairs were an inner need. These contemporaries regarded Moritz Lazarus as the most distinguished and illustrious representative of Judaism.

In his critique of the "Ethics of Judaism" *Hermann Cohen* accuses Lazarus of cheap popularity, of methodic-philosophical inadequacy and neglect of medieval Jewish philosophy. Cohen ends his critique with the hope "that a scientific portrait of our religion may again ultimately emerge—based on historical research, including that of our dogmatics, and in living homogeneous relation to scientific philosophy".[322] These lines of Cohen—written in 1899—are probably the first mention of a task he had set for himself and which he was only able to fulfil towards the end of his life. Indeed the title of his main religious-philosophical work, "Religion der Vernunft aus den Quellen des Judentums" (Religion of Reason from the Sources of Judaism), seems to be referred to in this first intimation.

Cohen was born in 1842 in Coswig, Anhalt. He left the Breslau Jewish

---

[322] On Cohen, see the present author's doctoral dissertation "Die Stellung der Religion im systematischen Denken der Marburger Schule" (The Place of Religion in the Systematic Thought of the Marburg School), Berlin 1930, p. 14 ff. and p. 54 ff; Guttman op. cit., p. 345 ff; Rotenstreich op. cit., vol. II p. 53 ff; Jakob Klatzkin, 'Hermann Cohen', Berlin 1922; Siegfried Ucko's doctoral dissertation "Der Gottesbegriff in der Philosophie Hermann Cohens" (The concept of God in the Philosophy of Hermann Cohen), Berlin 1929; H. Liebeschuetz, "Hermann Cohen and his Historical Background", in YLBI XIII, 1968, and in his book "Von Georg Simmel zu Franz Rosenzweig", ch. 1, Tuebingen 1970. See also the preface by S. Ucko and the postscript by J. Ben-Haim to the Hebrew translation of Cohen's "Religion of Reason", Jerusalem 1971. Cohen's "Religion of Reason" is available in English translation by S. Kaplan, N.Y. 1972, and a selection of his writings on Judaism in English translation by Eva Jospe, New York, 1971.

A special place is taken by Franz Rosenzweig's introduction to the essays of Hermann Cohen on Judaism (Juedische Schriften), which Bruno Strauss published in 3 vols. in 1924. Rosenzweig, who stood close to Cohen in his (Cohen's) last years, gives an unusually vivid picture of his personality, but interprets Cohen's religious philosophy from his own standpoint. He construes a breach between the Cohen of the philosophic system and the Cohen of the Berlin years. This existential-philosophical interpretation of Cohen—very widespread forty years ago and then probably for the first time critically treated by the present author—has been generally abandoned today. But see S. H. Bergmann, Faith and Reason, New York 1961, and Walter Goldstein "Hermann Cohen und die Zukunft Israels" (Hermann Cohen and the Future of Israel), Jerusalem 1963, for a different view.

Theological Seminary early to switch over to philosophy. From the Steinthal/
Lazarus' psychology of peoples he turned to Kant. The first edition of his
revolutionizing interpretation of Kant–"Kant's Theorie der Erfahrung"
(Kant's Theory of Experience)–appeared in 1871. Friedrich Albert Lange,
author of the "Geschichte des Materialismus" (History of Materialism),
brought him to Marburg in 1873 as private lecturer. On Lange's death there
three years later, he became his successor, remaining in Marburg until 1912,
when he resigned in protest against an increasing German policy of filling
university chairs of philosophy with psychologists–as later on with sociol-
ogists. He was the only Jewish holder of a chair of philosophy in Germany
before 1919, and one of the very few Jewish full professors at all. How
precarious Cohen's position was is seen from the fact that he never became
Rector in Marburg (a position rotating among the full professors) and never
received a call to another university.

After his further Kantian studies: "Kants Begruendung der Ethik" (Kant's
Foundation of Ethics) 1877 and "Kants Begruendung der Aesthetik" (Kant's
Foundation of Aesthetics) 1899, Cohen proceeded to build up his own
system.[323] His religious writings complement these systematic works.[324]

From 1912 until his death six years later Cohen taught Jewish religious
philosophy at the "Hochschule fuer die Wissenschaft des Judentums" in
Berlin.

Around Cohen and his non-Jewish disciple and colleague Paul Natorp
there gathered the "Marburg School", whose influence ranged over wide
branches of philosophy, science and politics.

Cohen belonged to those philosophers whose biography is important for
an understanding of their philosophy. His exposed position as a Jewish
full professor of philosophy at a German university was for him a source
of intellectual and emotional tension. He felt responsible for both poles of
this magnetic field: as philosopher for his subject and its cultivation at the
university, and as Jew for his Judaism–and all this, both in relation to Jews
and to the academic world in an era of rising antisemitism among scholars
and students in all faculties, especially in the humanities and theology. He
approached his Judaism as a philosopher, whose philosophy for its part
embodied basic Jewish ideas.

In character Cohen was very emotional. This trait, through which he
exercised great personal influence on friends, pupils and public alike, also

---

[323] "Das Prinzip der Infinitesimalmethode und seine Geschichte" (The Principle of the Infinitesimal
Method and Its History) 1883; "Einleitung mit kritischem Nachtrag zur 7. Auflage von F. A. Langes
"Geschichte des Materialismus" (Introduction with Critical Supplement to the 7th edition of F. A.
Lange's History of Materialism) 1896 and to the 9th edit. 1914. "Logik der reinen Erkenntnis" (Logic
of Pure Knowledge) 1902; "Ethik des reinen Willens" (Ethics of Pure Will) 1904; "Aesthetik des
reinen Gefuehls" (Aesthetics of Pure Feeling) 1911.
[324] "Der Begriff der Religion im System der Philosophie" (The Concept of Religion in the System
of Philosophy) 1915; "Religion of Reason from the Sources of Judaism", 1919. 2nd edition 1929.

appears in his writings, often interrupting the rigour of his argument. One also senses how he struggled against his emotion, forcibly suppressing the thoughts and implications that seem to him impermissible from his methodical premises. He himself once referred to this inner situation in a letter: "My fate is of a kind all its own. If there are people who make the 'sacrificio del'intelletto', then I make the 'del sentimento'. You know how much I ... am involved in the inner life of our religion, but here, too, abstraction is my destiny".[325] This letter was written the same year in which Cohen's first major religious-philosophic work—"Religion und Sittlichkeit" (Religion and Morality)—appeared.[326] It was precisely in this book that Cohen gave "abstraction"—i.e. the absorption of religion into ethics—its most radical expression.

This tension runs throughout Cohen's entire work. In fact his *terminology* in its decisive expressions illustrates a content, which seems to go beyond a formal methological function. He calls his method of philosophy "Logic of Origin" (Ursprung) which "creates" its object—words reminiscent of the semi-mythological terminology of the pre-Socratics, Plato and Democritus. Other termini are taken directly from the religious vocabulary of Judaism. He speaks of God; of the idea of one humanity first proclaimed by the prophets; of messianism.

Cohen's philosophizing had always been determined by latent or manifest *theological themes*. There was just one period of his life in which he was rather indifferent to religion, when mere feelings of piety linked him to Judaism. That was the years between his leaving the Breslau Seminary and the commencement of his work on the philosophy of Immanuel Kant.

The détour via Kant brought Cohen back into a new relation with religion and to an awareness of his Judaism. Yet this détour also set the perspectives of his portrayal of Judaism, fixing its methodical boundaries. These boundaries remained decisive for Cohen to the end of his life.

These methodical boundaries were of course trammels, which Cohen had laid upon himself. He retained a certain freedom in relation to them which, in the face of new knowledge, enabled him to fasten them differently or more loosely.

In this Cohen was freer than his Jewish predecessors, who grew up under neo-Platonism, in medieval Aristotelianism or in the clearly defined systems and schemata of Schelling's and Hegel's thought. Their possibilities of fitting Judaism into these *pre-given* thought-schemata were limited. Whereas Cohen himself had created his own system and its method, within whose framework he could move.

Cohen's philosophy goes back to his *interpretation of Kant*. Here Kant is

---

[325] Hermann Cohen's "Briefe", edited by Berta & Bruno Strauss, Berlin 1939, p. 77 (Letter of February 27, 1907).
[326] In "Juedische Schriften", vol. III pp. 99-168.

scrutinized with philological exactitude and placed in the continuity of the history and philosophy.[327] Kant's problematic and method is compared with that of Plato and Leibniz, and found to be rooted in the method of Galileo and natural science. The ominous "thing-in-itself", which was a stumbling-block for an interpretation that did not advance beyond the threshold of Kant's "Critique of Pure Reason", is shown by Cohen in its function as an idea, which indicates the direction knowledge should take and makes objective experience possible.

In his own philosophy Cohen goes beyond the basic Kantian position. He abandons the notion of "pure intuition"—which in Kant complements the rational understanding—in order to avoid misinterpreting the thing-in-itself as a thing. The object is not given a priori, but becomes the object of knowledge—becomes definable—only through the infinitesimal process of cognition itself, analogous to the procedure of mathematical science. For Cohen no problem can in principle lie outside the process of cognition. Rather it is through this process that the objects of knowledge become possible. Thus, following Cohen, logic constructs the world with the method of science. Ethics linked to the method of jurisprudence appears as the task of realising morality and justice among mankind. Aesthetics relates to the method expressed in the work of the artist. Every tendency of cultural awareness is raised to cognition through the one method, whose foundation the *logic of Origin* (Ursprung) has laid. Natorp had called this overlapping method *panmethodism*.

The philosophy of German Idealism transformed Kant's doctrine of experience into a work of "I", into a subjective Idealism. With Hegel this "I" became the universal world-spirit, in whose eternal dialectical movement life is represented.

Cohen's Idealism is distinct from this speculative Idealism in that it avoids its subjectivism. Instead of a pantheism of spirit which puts "I", spirit, world-spirit, nature and God into one, with Cohen the concrete *task* of knowledge is to determine its object, to produce and actualize it. By means of its relation to the method of natural science, "critical Idealism" is immune to the dangers of speculation. In virtue of this relation, which is lacking in Fichte, Hegel and even in the scientifically educated and interested Schelling, Cohen remained close to Kant and thus founded the *Neo-Kantianism* of the Marburg School.[328]

---

[327] The joint-effect of the philological—which has "always to be in order"—and the historical is a particular hallmark of the working method of Cohen. We also find it in Natorp and especially in Ernst Cassirer.

[328] Solomon Maimon had already understood the Kantian "thing in itself" as an infinitesimal border-concept. He too switched from the negative criticism of Kant in his doctrine of "definability" to the construction of the objective world. Yet it seems to me that Maimon's use of the differential to determine the integral is not really very different from the function of form in relation to matter in Aristotle. Cohen's "origin", on the other hand, is directed by the Platonic "idea as hypothesis", whose Aristotel-

In the methodic basic tendencies of Cohen's "Logic of Origin" there already shimmer through, it seems to me, religious and in particular *Jewish-religious motifs*, which soon take on clearer contours with respect to knowledge and creation. There is, to begin with, the concept of God, which unexpectedly entered Cohen's horizon during his work on "Kants Begruendung der Ethik" (Kant's Foundation of Ethics) in 1872. He wrote to a friend "It will seem strange to you that I avail myself of the Kantian God, and stranger still that I am convinced that every attempt in ethics made without such a God lacks thought and principle. You see, He has actually fanaticized me, as it befits a God. But you will find that you yourself will believe in this God".[329] After years of religious indifference Cohen has here discovered God and faith. And his concept of God already appears here in that same form in which he later expresses his ethics and philosophy of religion. Here God is really no longer the "Kantian God", a postulate of ethics, "found to fill a gap"[330] but becomes the *principle* on which ethics is founded.

This new concept of God is for Cohen bound up with *truth*. Logic, too, employs the terms true and false. But this, according to Cohen, is imprecise terminology. The distinction in logic should rather be between correct and false.[331] The expression "true" has another meaning. Its opposite would be "untrue" or a "lie". True applies to morals, since it has an ethical value. In Cohen, therefore, "truth signifies the accord and harmony between the theoretical and the ethical".[332] The God of truth, however, is not a linking medium between logic and ethics, between the knowledge of nature and ethical effort—this is man's task. Cohen rejects any such union of nature, God and man. Such a unification—often sought in the history of philosophy and found among the Greeks, in Spinoza and in the Idealist philosophy of identity—leads to pantheism. Cohen replaces this false unity with the *oneness of God*, marking off his distinctiveness from all other beings.[333] Yet transcendence, which the concept of God acquires through His uniqueness is not, according to Cohen, a metaphysical but a functional transcendence. In order to make possible the realisation of ethics, a world must be there. It is this connection—between the world and ethics—which the idea of God safeguards and guarantees. He is the origin of nature and morality—or in the religious language of Cohen's "Ethics": "God is the Creator of nature and the principle of morality". In this way he arrives at the Jewish concept of God as the principle of ethics.

---

ian reinterpretation into form Cohen most sharply opposed. (Hypothesis is used here in the original sense of 'laying the basis').

[329] "Briefe", p. 42.

[330] "Ethik", p. 444 (p. 440 of 2nd edition).

[331] op. cit., p. 88 (p. 86 in 2nd edition).

[332] op. cit. p. 91 (p. 89 in 2nd edition).

[333] Cohen first does this in his essay "Der Stil der Propheten" (The Style of the Prophets) in 1901, when he was working out his own philosophic system. Cf. his "Juedische Schriften", vol. 1 p. 265.

Cohen bases his ethics not only on the Jewish concept of God. Ethics as a part of culture, whose content is human relations, is constantly illustrated by him with material from Bible and Talmud. The concept of one humanity—foreign to Greek thought—has been discovered by the prophets. This concept is associated with the Jewish ideal of the Messianic age, which for Cohen is the goal of ethics, the task individuals, peoples and nations strive to fulfil, in order to bring about the "unity" of mankind. In this goal of history the concept "world-history" is discovered by the prophets.

With the transference of basic Jewish-religious concepts to ethics, it may seem that religion itself has been made superfluous. Indeed, Cohen took this view in his "Ethics" and in his already mentioned essay "Religion and Morality". This viewpoint represents the climax of his "sacrificio del sentimento".

Nevertheless, Cohen acknowledges Judaism's right to exist and continue. It should and must retain within itself what Mendelssohn called "the association of genuine theists"—that group of people, who, throughout the course of history, has to preserve and hand on the pure idea of God and ethical demands and ideals.

*Religionized ethics*—if the term be permitted—could not be Cohen's last word on the question of religion. In the "Ethics" emotional impulses were already subliminally at work, due to his rootedness in Judaism. Cohen's deeper knowledge of a life-fulfilling and life-directing religion, could not be replaced by artificial formal-methodic constructions. Religion is, for Cohen's inner sense, more than a "natural condition" which can be disposed of by transferring its philosophically relevant elements to the "cultural condition" of ethics. Precisely those elements taken up in the "Ethics"—the idea of God, monotheism, mankind—challenged anew the question of the concept of religion and its place in Cohen's system of philosophy. It is clear that these concepts give religion itself a share within the totality of reason, and not just through its inclusion in ethics. What place must religion—and religion for Cohen is always the strict monotheism of Judaism—occupy in the system of philosophy? This question is dealt with in his two books on religion: "Der Begriff der Religion im System der Philosophie" (The Concept of Religion in the System of Philosophy), 1915, significantly dedicated to the Marburg School and thereby stressing its connection with Cohen's earlier approach; and "Religion der Vernunft aus den Quellen des Judentums" (Religion of Reason from the Sources of Judaism), published posthumously in 1919.

The element of reason in religion seemed to make an additional systematic branch necessary. Religion seemed able to claim recognition as an independent branch of culture. Yet, on the other hand, the problems of religion reach into other spheres of thought. The concept of the one and only God—through his relation to being and becoming, and to truth, as we saw earlier—links religion with Cohen's logic. At the same time it is this concept, with its demands on man, which is the principle of ethics. Religion has also a part in aesthetics through the literary value of the biblical writings, notably the prophets and psalms. However, now that its various aspects were dealt with in ethics, logic and aesthetics, no place was left for religion itself in the system of philosophy.

Especially problematic was the relation of religion to ethics, since the central question of religion was the relation of God and man. But the problem of man was dealt with in the Ethics, which itself is aware of the God/man relationship. Two branches of thought, in other words, were concerned with the same subject. This is why Cohen had in the first place incorporated religion into ethics.

This coordination of ethics and religion is not altered in Cohen's writings on religion. His doubt, however, as to its adequacy also remains. He grants religion—within the retained framework—not quite independence, but an individuality which complements ethics. This complement—the new aspect that religion adds to ethics—concerns the relation of God and man. The God of the "Ethics" now seems to Cohen to be a remote God, and the mankind of the "Ethics" too far removed from the needs of the individual.

In the "Ethics" it was precisely the task of man to free himself from the trammels of his individuality, his natural condition, in order to become a *social* being. This liberating process was the origin of justice, of the legal form of the state, leading to the idea of the "unity" of mankind.

The religious concept of man in Cohen has its starting point in the *individual*. The individual suffers and sees his fellow-man suffering. In the Ethics "fellow-man" was simply the first rung in the ladder culminating in mankind. But now fellow-man becomes the neighbour, who calls for our responsibility, our help and sympathy. In compassion for one's neighbour, the poor and the suffering, Cohen sees—like Samuel David Luzzato before him—the origin of religion. He measures the individual in terms of his "suffering-with" his neighbour which frees him from the fetters of his own egoism. Empathy leads to self-knowledge, to the recognition of one's weakness and sin.

Ethics had handed over sin as human failure to the law. In aesthetics, the individual artist, the genius, is really an "overman" (Uebermensch), who is already no longer an individual.

The sinful suffering person, on the other hand, is the single man who henceforth faces the single God, so that "the one unique and single God gives new meaning to his own uniqueness: He is uniquely there for man, insofar as man is to be thought of as a single and unique individual".[334] This relationship leads to the new basic concept in Cohen's religious philosophy, namely, *co-relation*.

To be freed from sin (which became original sin only in myth, but in religion is always the sin of the individual) is brought about through the

---

[334] "Der Begriff der Religion im System der Philosophie", 1915, p. 61.

"return" (in Hebrew "Teshuvah") of man. God who accepts return becomes the Redeemer. Yet this co-relation "avoids identification (of man and God)".[335] Even in the act of returning man and God remain distinct. The most that man can attain is the *nearness of God* (Psalm 73.28).

Cohen's modifications in his concept of *God* remain more within the framework of his systematic writings, and they are terminological rather than substantial. His religious language, now used with lesser restraint, has scarcely changed anything in the methodic logical functions. As in the earlier writings, the unique Being of God is separated from the existence of nature, thus making God the origin of Becoming in nature and of its conservation as well as the origin of ethics. *Creation* is referred to as the "original attribute of God". "If the unique God were not Creator, then Being and Becoming would be the same, and nature itself would be God. But that would mean that God is not. For nature is the Becoming, of which Being must be the origin".[336]

It is when applied to man, who is part of the creation of nature, that "the special problem of human reason arises". This kind of creation—the relation of the one God to man's reason—Cohen calls *revelation*. "That is the most general meaning of revelation, namely that God comes into relation with man . . . For the view that God also reveals himself in the world is an imprecise idea . . . drifting into pantheism. God never reveals himself in something, but only to—in relation to—something. And it is only man who can be the corresponding link in this relationship"[337] between God and human reason. From this Cohen draws the terse conclusion: "*Revelation has created reason*".[338]

Here too, co-relation comes in. The reason of man as creation of God implies a reason-relationship of man to God. Reason makes him "at least subjectively, as it were, the discoverer of God".[339] One may notice the careful reverential accumulation of qualifying phrases: "at least", "subjectively", "as it were". The religious content of Cohen's Judaism is perhaps nowhere more directly expressed than in the words just quoted. Rabbinic literature has in this connection an appropriate expression: *Ke'we'jakhol* ("as one might be allowed to say"), when it wants to express religious content that almost seems blasphemous.

Nevertheless, even in the writings on religion, *God* remains an *idea* with the full methodological content of an idea in Cohen's system. "God becomes a person only in myth"—so one reads in the "Ethics" with reference to Maimonides.[340] But the co-relation had created a personal relation to this

---

[335] op. cit. p. 105.
[336] Religion of Reason, 2nd edit. p. 77.
[337] op. cit., p. 82.
[338] op. cit., p. 84.
[339] op. cit., p. 103.
[340] "Die Ethik", p. 457 (p. 453 in 2nd edit.).

idea in the nearness of God, in the love of God and love to God. God is at the same time therefore not thought of as an abstract single unique Being, but quite concretely as "the single unique One".[341]

The freedom reserved by Cohen for man corresponds to God's "attributes of action", which he took over from Jewish medieval philosophy. They are —like creation—logically necessary origins of divine action.

Despite its religious terminology Cohen's philosophy of religion is simply the application of logical, methodical relations. Yet it probably contains the most universal and profound understanding of religion attainable for a "religion of reason", for a philosophical doctrine of religion. And this applies not just to the *Jewish* philosophy of religion.

Judaism for Cohen is not necessarily the only religion of reason, but it is the only historical example from whose sources one can illustrate such a religion. These sources of Judaism, which for Cohen were living and with which he was fully acquainted, supplement and complete his systematic structure.

During the first quarter of this century Cohen was the recognized representative of German Jewry and Judaism. As a religious thinker in modern Judaism he is one of the few very great.

*Franz Rosenzweig* (1886-1929) came from a strongly assimilated Jewish family. Several of his relations—some a generation earlier—had become Christians. His relative and close friend of his youth, Rudolf Ehrenberg, was born a Christian. Rudolf's cousin, Hans Ehrenberg, baptized as a young man, switched from teaching philosophy to theology and became a clergyman. Hans' brothers, Paul and Victor, however, remained Jews. All of them —like Franz Rosenzweig—were great-grandsons of Zunz' teacher, Samuel Meyer Ehrenberg, head of the Samson School in Wolfenbuettel. Rosenzweig himself was near to embracing Christianity but finally decided for Judaism.[342]

Rosenzweig is often considered a disciple—indeed the last disciple—of Hermann Cohen, but this is true only in a limited sense. Rosenzweig's relationship to Cohen was completely different, for example, from that existing between Fichte and Kant. This could be spoken of as a pupil-teacher relationship, since Fichte considered himself a Kantian and continuer of Kant's philosophy. The same cannot be said with regard to Rosenzweig. His relation to Cohen was more a personal one. When he almost by chance visited Cohen's lectures at the Berlin "Lehranstalt fuer die Wissenschaft des Judentums", he fell under the spell of the old man's personality—the first real philosopher he met who was more than a mere professor of philosophy. This meeting was of great importance for the consolidation and elucidation of Rosenzweig's attitude to Judaism. Cohen for his part found the veneration of the very

---

[341] Religion of Reason, p. 49.
[342] See his Letters (Briefe, p. 71 ff.).

much younger man as the good fortune of his old age. And Rosenzweig in his introduction to Cohen's Jewish Writings and in many references had drawn the picture of Cohen's personality in understanding and love. Franz Rosenzweig never belonged to the Marburg School. It was only much later that he came to know Cohen's philosophical writings, when in the First World War he had some of Cohen's books sent to him at the front. As late as 9 March 1918, a few weeks before Cohen's death, he asked him with which of his books he should begin in order to redress his lack of knowledge on Cohen. However by that time the basic concepts of his own work were already formulated.

When Rosenzweig came to Cohen in November 1913 he was no longer a beginner in philosophy. A year later he had discovered a philosophic-historical manuscript, which he considered a transcript in Hegel's handwriting of a work by Schelling from the year 1796, and called it "the oldest systematic programme of German Idealism". His dissertation "Hegel und der Staat", published only after the war in book form in 1924, was probably also then already completed. The decisive influences on him were not from Kant but from Hegel and Schelling. The "balance wheel moving my thinking is the epoch around 1800", so he wrote at the time he conceived the idea for his "Stern der Erloesung" (Star of Redemption). "I have to see everything from this intellectual focal point of mine—what to me should be quite apparent. From any other approach my reasoning quickly runs aground".[343]

His own philosophizing stood under the influence of the great systematic attempts of Romantic Idealism. He saw in them the zenith and last word of the history of philosophy—exactly as Hegel had seen himself. But from this Idealist philosophy, which deduced God, world and man from one principle, making abstract generalisations out of them, Rosenzweig wanted to dissociate himself. It was from particular man, the individual "with fore- and surname", from nature in her particular development, from the living God of whom we know nothing—may know nothing—in philosophy, from these three premises that Rosenzweig sought to proceed; from their reality, their givenness, that preceeds and lies outside the Being, which philosophy ascribes them. Thus Rosenzweig became one of the earliest *existential philosophers*. When about a decade after the composition of the "Star of Redemption"—written in 1918 on the Macedonian front—Heidegger's "Sein und Zeit" (Being and Time) appeared, Rosenzweig welcomed it as an expression of the "new thinking".[344]

Rosenzweig, however, acquired his initial existentialist ideas by borrowing from *Hermann Cohen*, i.e. from Cohen's function of "origin" and with express reference to him.[345] Of God, the world and man we know nothing.

---

[343] Shorter Writings (Kleine Schriften, p. 358).
[344] op. cit., p. 355 ff. R. refers here to the discussion between Heidegger and Cassirer.
[345] Star of Redemption, London & New York pp. 20-21.

But this not-knowing is the beginning of our knowledge of them.[346] Still, these border concepts apparently reached methodically in Rosenzweig are hypostatized by him and take on again—against his express intention—an *ontological* character. Despite his efforts to protect their individual features directly expressed and stamped by the situation, they become in reality *generalisations*, bases for a schematic construction. God, world and man correspond then to creation, revelation and redemption, and again to knowledge, experience and petition (prayer) as the means by which these can be experienced and brought into relation with each other. These relations themselves exist in juxtaposition, linked together by an "and". This "and" is compared by him to the Cohenian co-relation and later Buberian "I-Thou" relationship.

This general framework of the "new thinking" is now applied to the history—or more precisely religious history—of Judaism and of Christianity. Hence, Judaism and Christianity are portrayed as two related, but in tendency distinct, expressions of revelation. This portrayal is given as a description of two different forms of religious life.

Nevertheless, it does not deal with the actual life of real Jews or Christians in any sociological, statistical or, let us say, religio-psychological sense. Rosenzweig's Jews and Christians are rather *theological abstract types*. His Jews in particular are not those of the present but of the pre-emancipation era. They appear as a people withdrawn from the present and cut off from their ties to land, state and language. Their outlook is not aimed to the Messianic future; instead they look back upon history, so to speak, from this vantage-point. For this reason he calls them "the eternal people". Christianity, on the other hand, is the bearer of revelation in the here and now, with its political associations and dangers. It is constantly only 'on the way' to the divine goal, which has been pre-given to the Jews and is their eternal possession. Rosenzweig's declared non-Zionism—not anti-Zionism—was founded on this. The Jews as an eternal people must avoid temporal political involvement. The land of Israel may only be a holy land, Hebrew only a sacred language.

The "Star of Redemption" owed some of its popularity in Jewish circles to its historico-theological portrait of traditional Jewish life, customs and festivals. This made it—against the author's intention and wish for it to be understood as a system of philosophy—into a "Jewish book", which suited the sentimental romantic mood of the post World War years and the beginning of the Hitler period.

Rosenzweig has a firm place in the history of philosophy—especially Jewish philosophy—as one of the founders of religious existentialism. But

---

[346] op. cit., pp. 23, 45, 62.

his influence on the late history of German Judaism was chiefly as a popular educator and through his personal example.

In an appeal to Hermann Cohen entitled "T'is Time" ("Zeit ist's"),[347] Rosenzweig suggested from the battle-front a new way of raising the level of Jewish religious instruction. The suggestion was to promote teaching and research by founding an "Academy for the Wissenschaft of Judaism". By creating posts for academically qualified teachers of religion at secondary schools and at adult Jewish educational centres, this would give young scholars the opportunity to engage in scientific work without studying for the rabbinic profession. Cohen took up the plan, but it fell through with his death. All that remained of this comprehensive plan was an "Academy for the Wissenschaft of Judaism" as a pure research institute, which did in fact give a number of young scholars a start, but never followed up the suggestions of applying this to youth and adult education.

Rosenzweig wanted to make his own trek back to Judaism into a general one for his own generation. In 1920 he became director of studies for Jewish adult education in Frankfurt. He tried to renew in modern form the old Jewish ideal of "learning" in the proper sense of *learning together*. Not as lectures offered to an anonymous public audience, but as teachers and pupils working together in areas of Jewish knowledge—the leader preferably not a specialist himself but a fellow-learner. This "Freies Juedisches Lehrhaus" was soon imitated in other places. After 1933, in the time of enforced Jewish self-rediscovery, the new Lehrhaus method became the basis of Jewish adult education in the final years of German Jewry.

During the last seven years of his life Rosenzweig suffered from a progressive paralysis of the limbs and powers of speech. Despite this he continued to work, writing essays, translating and publishing Judah Halevy's poems, in which he realised a new ideal of translation that was to become well-known through his joint Bible translation with Martin Buber. These translations sought to resemble the original as closely as possible in language, choice of word, rhyme and rhythm and to preserve its peculiar linguistic character.

Rosenzweig's tentative way back to the *religious law*[348] became exemplary for a small group of young Jews, notably from the youth movements. This personal example of Rosenzweig, the liberal Jew, who affirmed the commandments and their pervasion of life, became hallowed for his friends through his heroic struggle against his personal destiny.

*Martin Buber* (1878-1966) met Rosenzweig for the first time in 1914. But it was not until 1921, after Buber's move to Heppenheim and his active participation at the Lehrhaus in Frankfurt, that their acquaintance grew into

---

[347] Shorter Writings (Kleinere Schriften, p. 56 ff.).
[348] see 'The Builders' (Die Bauleute, Kleinere Schriften, p. 106 ff.).

friendship and close co-operation, whose memorial was to be their combined translation of the Bible. After Rosenzweig's early death Buber continued and completed the translation alone.

It was not only through the Bible translation in the 'twenties and 'thirties that the name of Buber and Rosenzweig are associated. Their aims—and in part their methods—in adult education also ran parallel. At the commencement of the Hitler period Buber as head of the 'Coordinating Centre for Jewish Adult Education' had made the idea of the Frankfurt Lehrhaus the basis of the last important attempt to give new backbone to a German Jewry suddenly awakened from the dreams of assimilation. Buber differed in this respect from Rosenzweig and his conception of communal learning, being in disposition and aptitude more a teacher, lecturer and *orator*. He wanted to constrain his audience to think along with him and understand without being brought in as co-learners. Indeed, he wrote once, towards the end of his life: "I have no doctrine; I am leading a dialogue".[349] But this was largely a one-sided dialogue. Many of Buber's writings were originally speeches and were referred to as such by him. Even the Ḥasidic stories are mostly sayings, parts of conversations, which are really monologues. They proceed from a posed question. But while keeping the questioner—the dialogue partner—in view, they effectively exclude him.

Buber's style of speaking and writing contributed to the great influence on his audience. It was the style of the generation of Rilke and Stefan George, poetically elevated and somewhat exalted, which often concealed the intended meaning rather than explaining it. Only in the last thirty years of his life did this often estranging unintelligibility give way to a greater precision and simplicity, which one would no longer have expected from the Buber of the "Tales of the Ḥasidim" or even of "I and Thou". Perhaps during these latter years in Jerusalem the enforced confrontation with the spoken Hebrew may have influenced the linguistic clarity of his late writings.

Buber and Rosenzweig felt themselves akin in their religious philosophy. But this affinity should not be over-emphasised. Their personal development began from different presuppositions. Rosenzweig—as we saw—took as his starting point the great systematic attempts of speculative Idealism. He himself wanted his "Star of Redemption" to be regarded as a system of philosophy. Buber's approach, on the other hand, was from the positive facts of the *history of religion*, from the interpretation of Ḥasidism but also from the Chinese teaching of Tao. In these phenomena of the history of religion he discovered human and religious primordial relations, which he developed into an *anthropology*, not in the sense of physical or psychological anthropology, but of a meta-physical anthropology, in the literal sense of the word.

The basic concept of this anthropology, according to Buber, is the *I-Thou*

---

[349] Works (Werke, Vol. I, p. 1114. In Schilpp/Friedmann German edit. p. 593).

relationship. This is developed as an inner-human relationship of an "I" to another "I", namely, a "Thou". Or as a human-divine relationship of the human "I" to a divine "Thou", and of the divine "I" to a human "Thou". Buber calls this, "the dialogical principle". It is not meant to be a mere intellectual relationship but to embrace man and fellow-man in their psycho-physical totality. It is to see God not as an idea but in his complexity as Creator, Lord, loving and loved Father. It seems to me noteworthy, that for Buber the partners in dialogue are not polarized but are members of a relationship who themselves remain, as it were, in suspense. Through this pure *functional*—and not ontological—nature of the principle of dialogue, Buber differs from the real existential philosophy. For this reason I should only hesitatingly call him an existentialist philosopher. Buber seeks this functional significance of "I" and "Thou", without presenting any systematic viewpoint, in the various aspects of culture, i.e. in history or psychology, in social behaviour or politics, in philosophy or religion. That this functional significance is, nevertheless, far removed from the functional concepts of the Marburg philosophers, like Cassirer, or from Natorp's "pan-methodism", is clearly shown by his entire bypassing mathematics and science, especially those sciences from which the functional concept derives. They are disregarded as spheres of "It", which are outside the I-Thou-relationship.[350] A philosophy, however, which does not include mathematics or the mathematical sciences in its methodology remains, it seems to me, incomplete.

Born in Vienna, in 1878, Buber was brought up and educated in the house of his grandfather, *Solomon Buber*, in Lemberg, in Galicia. Solomon Buber (1817-1906) was a leading businessman and for a while president of the Lemberg Chamber of Commerce. He was also an important representative of the Wissenschaft of Judaism which was indebted to him for his standard Midrash editions with their comprehensive introductions and commentaries.

Before his twentieth birthday Martin Buber took part in the First Zionist Congress in Basle, though not as a delegate. His Jewish involvement and activity were concentrated at the beginning on the political, then soon on the cultural, aspects of Zionism. Together with Weizmann he founded the Democratic Party within the Zionist Congress which clashed with the diplomatic approach represented by Herzl and supported the intensification of the colonization of Palestine and the cultural preparation of the people for Zionism. It was from this more or less secularised cultural Zionism[351]

---

[350] When Carl Friedrich von Weizsaecker, in his important contribution to the Schilpp/Friedmann collected volume *"Ich und Du und Ich und Es in der heutigen Naturwissenschaft"* ('I and Thou' and 'I and It' in Modern Science), also resolves the "It" into a "Thou"—from the twofoldness of the "I" of the scientist as theorist and experimenter—this is, in all probability, not an application of the principle Buber had in mind.

[351] Buber founded and managed for several years the Jewish Verlag in Berlin, publishing from 1916-1924 the periodical "Der Jude", the representative organ of the younger generation influenced by Zionism. Hermann Cohen tried to create a non-Zionist balance to this in the "Neue Juedische Monatschefte" (1916-1919).

and at first, probably, from a folklore-literary interest that Buber's explora-
tory work on the meaning of Ḥasidism began, which from about 1905
became "the mainspring of his own thinking".[352] It was through Ḥasidism
that he drew gradually closer to the Jewish religion.

The re-telling of and commenting on the Ḥasidic legends and sayings
became the generally best known aspect of Buber's lifework. Later, through
his association with Rosenzweig at the Frankfurt Lehrhaus and in the
Bible translation, there was his involvement with Biblical and also with New
Testament theology. In between were the "Reden ueber das Judentum"
(Addresses on Judaism)—first collectively published in 1923 and delivered
between 1909 and 1919—which made a deep impression on Jewish youth
in Germany. It used to be said jokingly in those days that everyone has to
pass through "buberty" sometime in life!

Buber once described Judaism as "a phenomenon of religious reality . . .
proclaimed in and through Judaism and for the sake of which (reality)
. . . Judaism exists".[353] This reality, according to Buber, allows no abstract
subdivisions or limitations, which would regard Judaism only as a religion,
or as a culture or mere historical connection. Judaism came into being
when the tribes of Israel were addressed by the divine Word and accepted
this divine call. This dialogical "Covenant" relationship has determined
Jewish consciousness throughout history. This consciousness expresses the
Jewish kind of faith as *Emunah*, as "trust" of the collective people demanding
confirmation, which in its turn makes this communal trust possible. It is
upon this Jewish concept of faith anchored in peoplehood that Buber's
religious and cultural Zionism is founded.

Buber contrasts the "Emunah" type of faith with "Pistis", the faith of
the individual not bound up with a people which characterizes post-Jesus
Christianity.[354] Jesus himself is claimed for Judaism—as by Buber's predecessors in the nineteenth century and earlier—to be really one of the
purest expressions of the Jewish type of faith. Buber even wrote: "But a
Judaism striving for the renewal of its faith through the rebirth of the individual, and a Christianity striving for the renewal of its faith through the
rebirth of the nations, would have something of unspeakable value to say to
each other, and which would render mutual help to an extent scarcely imaginable today".[355]

Buber's contrast of "Emunah" as collective faith with "Pistis" as individual
faith is neither etymologically nor theologically tenable. For the Greek
word "Pistis" and its verb "pisteuein"—as also the Latin *fides*—likewise
express faith and trust. "Emunah", or rather the verbal form "he'emin",

---

[352] Schilpp/Friedman, p. 29.
[353] "Der Jude und sein Judentum", p. 3.
[354] Werke, vol. I, p. 653 ff.
[355] op. cit., p. 782.

is first applied to Abraham as an individual in the first and basic passage
in Genesis 15.6. Here Abraham's faith is quite obviously individual faith.
Buber himself stresses in a passage of the Ḥasidic Tales: "We say: (at the
beginning of the main prayer, the Tefillah) God of Abraham, God of Isaac
and God of Jacob; we do not say: God of Abraham, Isaac and Jacob, thereby implying that Isaac and Jacob did not rely upon Abraham's tradition
alone, but sought the Divine for themselves.[356] —In Christianity the place of
the people's covenant with God is taken by the Church founded through
the sacraments. Here too, faith is, as opposed to Bubers thesis, collective
faith—it is the faith of the Church.

In the dialogical relationship Martin Buber has worked out with great
refinement and clarity the basic religious relationship peculiar to monotheistic religion, especially with regard to Judaism. In Judaism dialogue
takes place without a mediator between man and God. Dialogue is not
projected onto a man become God or God become man, as happened in the
Greek mysteries and in Christian theology under their influence. The Jew
responds to the call of God and sanctifies his life by accepting the commandment. And God responds to the prayer of man, hearing it and reconciling
the returning sinner. Buber rightly emphasises that the divine call requires
a decision from man. If man does not respond, then the call is vain. Only a
response makes dialogue possible.

Man can respond through his way of life. But here a certain breach in
Buber's Jewish position becomes manifest. He confines the religious pene-
tration—the "sanctification"—of life to the interhuman sphere, to ethics.
Buber strove throughout his life for the realisation of social justice and love.
As a religious socialist, and within the Zionist policy in relation to the Arab
neighbours, he was thoroughgoing, often opposing the public and official
view. Yet in principle he is closer to the position of Mendelssohn's followers,
who limited Judaism to a *religious ethical doctrine*, although Buber empha-
zises the national aspect (the collective covenant) in this context.

In an open letter to Buber, "The Builders", Franz Rosenzweig draws
attention to his evasive attitude to the law. The question here is not a matter
of a more or less thoroughgoing acceptance of the forms of traditional
Judaism. It concerns the Jewish principle of including even the smaller
transactions of daily life in the religious context, also beyond the interhuman sphere. What is seen both by Orthodox and Reform Judaism as a
characteristic of Judaism falls short with Buber, precisely with the philosopher of the dialogical principle and the narrator of the Ḥasidim, who
were completely rooted in fulfilling the law. Buber can therefore scarcely
be regarded as the reprsentative of modern Jewish thought—as he is looked

---

[356] op. cit., vol. III, p. 51 ff.

upon particularly by the non-Jewish public—although his influence was and is important.

*Leo Baeck* might well be called the last *representative* of German Judaism. The personal authority emanating from him may have obscured his importance as a religious thinker, scholar and even as a diplomatic-political representative of German Jewry in face of the Nazi authorities.

*Leo Baeck* (1874-1956), son of Samuel Baeck,[357] rabbi in Lissa, was rabbi in Oppeln, Duesseldorf and since 1912 in Berlin, where he lectured at the Hochschule for the Wissenschaft of Judaism. During the First World War Baeck was a German army chaplain. In 1933 he became chairman of the Reich's Representation of German Jews. Under the most trying circumstances—following the assassination of his closest co-workers, Otto Hirsch, Heinrich Stahl, Arthur Lilienthal inter alia—he remained leader of his community, which he refused to leave.[358] He was deported to the concentration camp of Theresienstadt in 1943, surviving there by pure accident. His last years in London were interrupted through travelling to Israel and Germany and lecturing for several months each year at Hebrew Union College, Cincinnati.

Leo Baeck's "Das Wesen des Judentums" (The Essence of Judaism) first appeared in 1905. His revision of it after World War I went through many editions. The title of the book is reminiscent of "Das Wesen des Christentums" (The Essence of Christianity)—a series of lectures by the eminent Protestant Church and dogma historian, A. von Harnack, delivered to students of all faculties in 1899 in Berlin and later published in book form. By means of an extensive de-theologization Harnack tried to make Christianity amenable to the religiously estranged youth of his day, giving in the second half a comparative outline of Church history. The figure of Jesus of Nazareth is divested of all Christological references and portrayed—against a dark backcloth of the Judaism of his time—as a unique religious ethical personality. Harnack's book was probably the best-known and most widely read portrait among the interpretations of liberal Protestantism, and was at the same time intended as an apologia of Christianity.

Baeck's intention in his similarly titled work was not to pursue—vis-a-vis Harnack's contentions—an apologia of Judaism. (This task was accomplished by him in a review of Harnack's book in MGWJ in 1901 and by Joseph Eschelbacher in his "Das Judentum und das Wesen des Christentums".) Like Harnack Baeck had a wide public in view—Jews and non-Jews. Yet his

[357] Samuel Baeck became known through his "Geschichte des juedischen Volkes und seiner Literatur" (History of the Jewish People and Its Literature), 1874. He taught Jewish Religious Instruction at the Gymnasium in Lissa and succeeded in introducing it as a special subject in the High Schools in Prussia. He wrote important sections in the collected volume "Juedische Literatur", which Rabbi J. Winter and the non-Jewish Hebraist, August Wuensche, published between 1892 and 1895.
[358] See Fuchs in the YLBI, XII 1967, p. 28.

"Essence of Judaism" is in no way an apologetic book. It is rather a portrait of Judaism, a presentation of its characteristic and permanent "essence" over and above temporal phenomena and developments. Baeck gives neither a philosophy of religion nor a theology, not a religious history of the Jews and not a phenomenology. Yet all these aspects and tendencies are present in his method. Baeck, the disciple of *Wilhelm Dilthey*, founder of the descriptive psychology of "understanding", set himself "the historico-psychological task of letting the Jewish spirit speak for itself.[359]

The method of this self-portrayal of the Jewish spirit is a peculiar dialectic. Baeck encompasses the depth and breadth of religion by endeavouring to present it in *paradoxical* antitheses. What perhaps is true of all religion is characteristic in a specially meaningful way in Judaism. For here the religious paradox goes far beyond general theological statements to the *historical paradox* of the existence and survival of the Jewish people. Examples of such paradoxes are: the nearness and remoteness of God; mystery and commandment; love and severity; universalism and election. These pairs of paradoxes are always related to each other, mutually conditioning and qualifying one another. They are never resolved into a third, a synthesis, a medium or mediator. The tension between the poles is maintained even in their correlation.

This method of presentation avoids the danger of a one-sided rationalization and ethicalization of religion, leaving the picture open for the mysterious and the mystical, for the individual's claim to recognition.

Especially illuminating in Baeck's method is his treatment of the paradox of the universalism and election of Israel. He refers to Judaism as the *classical* form of religion: "It is only in Israel that an ethical monotheism has existed, and wherever else it is later found, it has been derived directly or indirectly from Israel. The existence of this form of religion was conditioned by the existence of the people of Israel, and so it became one of the nations, which have a vocation to fulfil. This is what is meant by the *election* of Israel". This concept of election is apparently not based on a priority in time—which would be a very dubious argument for proving a theological concept. Baeck bases Israel's election, although it is seen as a historical fact, on the uniqueness of that fact. (His argumentation somewhat resembles that of, e.g. Steinheim or Formstecher, who stressed the uniqueness of revelation vis-á-vis the mixed religions, and the religion of the spirit vis-á-vis the transitory religions, respectively.) The pecularity residing in such a historical fact, according to Baeck, gives the life of the people its meaning by being understood "as a mutual relationship, a covenant between them and God". It is in the awareness of this covenant that Israel gained "the strength to be unlike others, the will to be different and to remain unconcerned about numbers and success".

---

[359] "Wesen des Judentums", preface to 2nd edition.

"The religion of Israel has always emphasized its *pecularity*. Prophetic teaching demanded segregation from the way of life of neighbouring peoples, and the oral tradition had to erect 'a fence around the Torah' ". Yet this national particularism linked itself, through its relatedness to the demanding God, to the awareness of an ethical task, of a *world historic mission*. "The idea of election thus implies its necessary correlation, the idea of mankind—a humanity destined to true religion . . . The hope of mankind is the hope of Israel. The word of God to mankind is none other than the word of God to his people . . . the more strongly universalism was emphasized, the more the special task and position of Israel could and had to be accentuated . . . The prophets speak of the world and its salvation, but they speak *to* Israel". Baeck lays special emphasis on the connection between the universal and the particular in Judaism. The survival of Judaism—like the future of mankind—depends upon the old historical experience that here is "a people who live alone and apart from the nations", as the blessing of Balaam expressed it. "They grasped the idea that existence itself could be a kind of proclamation, a sermon to the world". This is how Baeck sees Judaism and its historic task. It is "something unancient in the ancient world, something unmodern in the modern world. Thus the Jew was to live as a Jew: the great *nonconformist*, the great dissenter of history".[360] Baeck continued this thematic in his book "Dieses Volk" (This People), which he commenced in the concentration camp of Theresienstadt and completed in London. Its leitmotif is "Jewish existence".

The portrayal of the pecularity of Judaism, especially in contrast with the religious and cultural phenomena of the Ancient world, is the real theme of Leo Baeck's scholarly work. The direction of his thought is already shown in his inaugural lecture to the Berlin Lehranstalt on 'Griechische und juedische Predigt' (Greek and Jewish Preaching).[361] The argument with gnosticism and early Christianity is treated in his Midrashic studies,[362] in which he himself saw his real contribution.[363] It is within this thematic complex that Baeck's argument with Christianity is also to be found. This began in "The Essence of Judaism", and received its real polemical offensive character in the study "Romantische Religion"[364] of 1922 where he contrasts Christianity as "romantic religion" with "classical" Judaism. This contrast is also seen in his essay "The Faith of

---

[360] "The Essence of Judaism" (New York, 1961), pp. 61, 62, 68, 69, 73, 260, 261.

[361] Reprinted in "Aus drei Jahrtausenden", p. 142 ff.

[362] Especially the important essay "Zwei Beispiele midraschischer Predigt" (Two Examples of Midrashic Preaching) in MGWJ, vol. 69, 1925, p. 258 ff and in "Aus drei Jahrtausenden", p. 157 ff.

[363] Baeck's oral expression in a discussion with the present author (ca. 1931).

[364] "Aus drei Jahrtausenden", p. 42 ff.

Paul" written thirty years later.[365] "Das Evangelium als Urkunde der juedischen Glaubensgeschichte" (The Gospel as a Document of the History of the Jewish Faith),[366] 1937, places the Gospels within the framework of the Midrashic and early talmudic literature, stressing the Jewish kernel in relation to its Greek modifications. Precisely these writings on Christianity reveal how little Baeck was an apologist and how much he was an agressive polemicist of his cause. For he does not defend Judaism or give it equal status alongside the predominating religion but argues from the standpoint of the superiority of Judaism.[367]

To his involvement with the trends of late Antique religious philosophy belong Baeck's studies on Jewish mysticism, especially on "Sefer Yeẓirah", the first complete mystical work of the late or post Talmudic period, in which he discovered terminological echoes of Proclus, or at any rate of neo-Platonic philosophy.[368]

Baeck also participated in the theological discussion on the basic principles of Judaism. In his important essay "Theologie und Geschichte", 1932, he demarcates the theology of Judaism from historicism and from the pragmatic non-historical concept of evolutionary development in Geiger. Baeck sought to base the theology of Judaism upon a critical historical concept of tradition, which attempts to grasp "the universal idea and special tradition of Judaism, its world-historical individuality".[369] The question "Does traditional Judaism contain dogma?" is answered in the negative by Baeck[370]—though he could only do so through a very narrow interpretation of the concept of dogma taken from Christian dogmatics.

[365] Judaism and Christianity p. 139.

[366] Published by Schocken (No. 87) Berlin 1938.

[367] See foreword by Walter Kaufmann to "Judaism and Christianity".

[368] MGWJ vol LXX (1926) and vol. LXXVIII (1934). Cf. Kurt Wilhelm, Leo Baeck and Jewish Mysticism, Judaism vol. II, 1962, p. 125 ff.

[369] "Aus drei Jahrtausenden", p. 41.

[370] Op. cit., p. 12 ff. The discussion was enlarged upon following an essay by the Iranist and orthodox rabbi Prof. J. Scheftelowitz in Monatsschrift vol. LXX (1926), who criticized Baeck's thesis of "dogma-less" Judaism. Baeck replied with the above essay. The discussion in MGWJ is continued in the same and subsequent issues (vol. LXXI, 1927). After a reply by Scheftelowitz, the liberal rabbi Felix Goldmann of Leipzig entered the debate, affirming what Baeck had denied. Julius Guttmann, philosopher, historian and colleague of Baeck at the Hochschule, concluded the discussion in his essay "Die Normierung des Glaubensinhaltes des Judentums" (Determining the Faith-content of Judaism) in MGWJ, LXXI, 1927, p. 241 ff. Cf. also Joseph Schechter, 'Mimadda l'emunah' (From Science to Faith), Tel-Aviv 1953, p. 50 ff.

In the present author's opinion there are principles in Judaism that could be called dogmas. However, these are not articles of faith, essential for the ultimate salvation of the believer. Rather, they are principles that indicate the limits of what would be considered Jewish and what not. Mendelssohn, we remember, stressed rightly that there are no commandments in Judaism to be believed but only to be done. The ancient sages in the time of the Bar-Kokhba uprising stated three things obliging the Jew to undergo martyrdom if forced to transgress them: idolatry, unchastity and murder. This shows that Jewish dogmas are religio-ethical demands. Some rabbinical scholars tried to phrase them in

Baeck's great commanding influence, however, goes beyond the writer and scholar, beyond the preacher and organiser. He wrote and spoke not about Judaism but out of Judaism,[371] out of the fulness of inherited and self-acquired Jewish wisdom. It is this Judaism which determined his life and action. His name became the symbol of the past values and history of German Jewry.

With Leo Baeck we conclude these portrayals of Jewish self-understanding. In the years following World War I there did appear several books which sought to bring Judaism before a wider public, especially the Jewish public. But none of these have become representative for modern Judaism.[372]

various ways, e.g. Maimonides in thirteen articles, others, in three as did Joseph Albo and later in a different way Steinheim. Shnaber-Levinson left only one principle: God, from Whom all else is deduced as time-dependent. Jewish dogmas are therefore quite different from the way Christianity understands its own dogmatics. Measured by these, Baeck is right, but it is impossible to deny that there are essential principles in Judaism, though less fixed and rigid.

[371] Cf. Liebeschuetz in YLBI vol. XI 1966, p. 26.

[372] I mention: *Max Dienemann*, "Judentum und Christentum", 1914; *Max Brod*, "Heidentum, Christentum, Judentum" (Paganism, Christianity, Judaism) 1921; *Judah Bergmann*, "Das Judentum", 1933; *Emil Bernhard Cohn*, Judentum, Ein Aufruf an die Zeit" (Judaism, An Appeal to the Time) 1923; *Hans Joachim Schoeps*, "Juedischer Glaube in dieser Zeit" (Jewish Faith at this Time) 1932.

# Modern East-European Jewry

The Jewish Enlightenment in Germany was the result of more than a century long process. Its kernel had so to speak grown naturally, until from Mendelssohn's time on it gained foothold in every stratum of the Jewish population. In German and west-European Jewry there was hardly any serious resistance to the new trends, for rabbis themselves had been influenced by them. And where rabbis did try to resist them—out of real concern about nihilist consequences, about the threatening decline in Jewish education and for fear of destruction of traditional authority and of apostasy —it was a half-hearted rearguard action without inner credibility.

In *Eastern Europe* it was different. When the ideas of Mendelssohn and the Hebrew writings of Wessely and the 'Me'asfim' reached Galicia and beyond to Poland, they encountered hostility of a more robust nature. Here the Enlightenment found no ready prepared soil. It collided with the still traditionally cohesive lifestyle of the Jewish masses, who found it foreign and rejected it as an outside element. In this way the Enlightenment in Eastern Europe acquired a different character and function.

The east-European Enlightenment is better known by its Hebrew name, *Haskalah*. Its adherents were called the *Maskilim*. This different name already suggests that a peculiar development was here in process.

In an earlier chapter we traced the development in Eastern Europe up until Ḥasidism. I indicated that the Ḥasidic movement, in its loosening and at first anti-authoritarian dynamics, represented a certain parallel to the Enlightenment within German Judaism. This comparison holds true for the culturo-historical function of both movements.

Nevertheless the motifs of Ḥasidism and of the Enlightenment were opposed to one another. Ḥasidism arose as an emotional revolt of the socially depressed non-educated classes against intellectual Talmudic learning, which held sway over the communities and life of the Jew. It was an irrational protest of inner religiosity.

The Enlightenment, on the other hand, in the name of universal reason, called for the inclusion of values and viewpoints of the surrounding culture within the Jewish mental horizon, giving in fact priority to them. Reason and the religion of reason stood in contrast to emotional piety.

The face of Ḥasidism, however, had also changed. It lost its rebellious character when its leaders—the 'Zadikim'—no longer based their authority on their charismatic inheritance alone, but on their rabbinic scholarship. Therefore it was in fact the old rabbinic scholarship, represented by the Mitnagdim—opponents of Ḥasidism—that retained the upper hand, whereas Ḥasidism did so in numbers and expanse. Yet it was the irrational elements in Ḥasidism which continued to attract the masses.

At the end of the eighteenth century the Enlightenment coming from Germany clashed with the already firmly-established and still expanding Ḥasidism. This clash between Haskalah and Ḥasidism in Eastern Europe was more serious in its consequences than the parallel clash of Haskalah with the as yet unshaken rabbinism, which was actually able to absorb Ḥasidism. This was because the non-Ḥasidic rabbis and the Maskilim came from the same talmudically educated upper-layer of society. They spoke, as it were, the same language and employed a similar rational argumentation, so that their differences were less apparent. The real mutual opponents were the *Ḥasidim* and *Maskilim*. It was from the great controversy between them, which dragged on for a century, that modern east-European Judaism arose.

Already before the rise of the Haskalah movement there were individual Jews in Galicia, Poland and Lithuania who were acquainted with secular learning and modern culture. These were mostly scholars who, having lived for some time in Germany, had returned to their homeland; also businessmen who, through visiting Berlin or the Fairs, had come into contact with these movements in Germany. But scholars like Israel Zamość, Solomon Dubno or Naḥman Krochmal's father in their native milieu were quite isolated cases. They retained the knowledge acquired abroad for themselves without intention or opportunity of spreading it.[373]

Only after an influential and outward-reaching centre of the Enlightenment had been formed around Mendelssohn and his circle, following Mendelssohn's Bible translation and the publication of the "Me'assef", did the formation of similar circles begin in other countries. These first groups stood in close personal or literary contact with the Mendelssohn circle. Similar manifestations of the sense of belonging together occurred again within the small Jewish framework which we observed when dealing with the élite of the non-Jewish Enlightenment.

---

[373] Solomon Maimon tells in his autobiography of a Lithuanian rabbi, who between 1770-1775 lent him books on physics and medicine. This rabbi had returned from Germany 31 years previously. In all those years not a single Jew from Lithuania had requested any such German secular books for himself.

The first centre of the Haskalah was in Austrian Galicia. A smaller circle was formed at about the same time in Lithuania, but it was not till later that it achieved greater importance. Both these countries had traditionally close links with the German Jewish centres and now also with those of the Enlightenment in Berlin, Koenigsberg and Breslau.

In Galicia a culturo-political factor contributed to the cohesion of adherents of the Enlightenment, namely the advocacy of the Josephian Reforms for Jewish school education. But as the Ḥasidic population largely rejected these schools, their adherents fell into the dubious position of being regarded not just as heretics but even as collaborateurs of the hated governmental policy.

The programme of the Haskalah was a continuation of the popular educational methods of Mendelssohn and even more so of Wessely. One wanted to impart new knowledge to the Jewish population, especially the youth, and extend their horizon beyond mere preoccupation with the Talmud. By attending to Hebrew grammar which was neglected in the old school, the 'Ḥeder', a pure Bible-orientated Hebrew was cultivated in order to break away from talmudic style and themes. The Maskilim were hostile to the dialectic practised in the Talmud schools, the so-called 'pilpul', which pursued mere sagacity at the expense of promoting real knowledge—even of the Talmud itself. And in the manner of the Enlightenment they fought against every form of superstition, which they saw especially prevalent among the Ḥasidim. An additional aim was to prepare young people for practical occupations by furthering their secular knowledge and linguistic ability.

The Haskalah was a *Hebrew* movement, using the Hebrew language. The value of learning foreign languages, especially German, was naturally emphasized, but the Judaic-German folk language was considered a horrible jargon and rejected. Neither the rabbis nor the Maskilim wrote in Yiddish. Like Mendelssohn, one preferred to use either Hebrew or literary German as the written language. Therefore, the medium of popular education was to be Hebrew, the literary language of all more or less educated Jews.

This either/or approach of the Maskilim led to a certain contradiction within their own broad educational programme. For by dropping the popular Yiddish, the circle of those reached by the Haskalah was reduced again to an upper social stratum of the educated. The Yiddish Enlightenment, on the other hand, which only began in the middle of the nineteenth century and which created modern literary Yiddish, was popular in its choice of theme and thus became the political medium of the broad Jewish strata, including the Jewish working class.

A large amount of Haskalah literature comprised translations from other languages, thus making the works of the most important writers of world literature available to the Hebrew reading public. Especially patronized were literary works dealing with Biblical personages. Geographical and scientific knowledge was also widely circulated by means of translation or through original Hebrew writings. Fables, collections of proverbs and other writings of an ethical nature were eagerly translated into Hebrew. Original Hebrew writings were often modelled on foreign works.[374] The satirical literature of the Haskalah had a real originality of its own and was therefore of poetic and culturo-historical importance. It levelled its critique in the main against Ḥasidism. The satirists drew a bead on the Ḥasidim's belief in miracles, their currying favour with the Ẓadikim, as well as on the tyranny of wealthy community heads and intolerant rabbis who could not see beyond the Talmud or the Shulḥan Arukh.

Some patrons of the arts who were themselves literarily active, supported other Maskilim financially and through their influence. Thus *Joseph Perl* (1774-1839) in Tarnopol, for example, gave personal and economic backing to the satirist and physician Isaac Erter and to the scholars Naḥman Krochmal and S. J. Rapoport and protected them against persecutions on the part of the Ḥasidim. *Joshua Zeitlin* (1742-1822), one time agent of Prince Potemkin, gave asylum to an entire group of writers and scholars on his estate.

The Hebrew of the Haskalah, despite its biblical style, was a *secularized language*. This change was not expressed in a new choice of theme, for centuries earlier there already existed among the Ashkenazi Jews writings of scientific, mathematical and historical content. This secularization was based rather on the new *value-hierarchy of the Enlightenment*, with which Mendelssohn and Wessely had begun, namely on the priority of the surrounding over traditional Jewish values. In the Haskalah this new scale of values had already become the accepted standard. Nevertheless the older Maskilim remained Torah-true not only in practice or for tactical reasons, but for their own self-understanding. That the well-meaning representatives of the traditional rabbinate themselves took offence at this reversion of values we have already observed in the case of Wessely. To other rabbis, notably Ḥasidic circles, the strong Haskalah accent on Bible study, grammar and biblically styled language—which differed from rabbinic Hebrew—were signs of heresy. The older Maskilim, who sometimes levelled a religio-legal and philologically based critique at Ḥasidic customs, were already suspected as enemies of tradition.[375] Real anti-talmudic tendencies only occured in later Haskalah.

Reform of the synagogue service, which occupied the main interest in

---

[374] Regarding the poetic quality of this literature see Silberschlag, Parapoetic Attitudes and Values in Early 19th Century Hebrew Poetry, in Altmann, Studies etc., p. 117 ff.

[375] The most extreme was the Enlightenment rabbi, Manassah Ilyer (1767-1831) who belonged to the circle of scholars around Joshua Zeitlin. He ventured to challenge the decisions of the Shulḥan Arukh and to interpret the Mishnah differently from the Gemara.

Germany, did not extend to Eastern Europe.[376] The introduction of the organ was probably not even discussed. Abbreviations or re-formulation of prayer passages with a national content would have been repugnant to the national sentiments of the Jewish population in their Slavonic surroundings, which sentiments the Maskilim affirmed. Prayers in the language of the country would have been meaningless as they would not have made them or their religious content more understandable. The vernacular—German in Galicia, or Russian or Polish in areas speaking these languages—was foreign to most of those who attended synagogue, whereas even the uneducated were familiar with the Hebrew prayer-book.

*Efforts at Reform* by the Haskalah applied at first only to Kabbalistic and Ḥasidic customs and to rabbinic regulations, which in the changed social and political circumstances were seen as unnecessary encumbrances. One sought a balance between life and doctrine. The argumentation here was less historical and theoretical—as in the West—than educational-practical and juridical.[377] And this was in keeping with the Talmudic training of the Maskilim themselves and with that of their environment.[378] It was only later generations of the Haskalah who went further and applied their critique to the validity of the religious Law. After the Enlightenment philosophy of Mendelssohn had been overtaken by the positivist and materialist philosophies of the nineteenth century, a radical critique of religion became increasingly noticeable. Instead of a balance between doctrine and life, as in the earlier Haskalah, doctrine was repressed and actually opposed vis-a-vis the requisites of life. And this tendency consolidated itself, when the ideas of socialism penetrated to the Jewish intellectuals of Eastern Europe. But when finally the raising of the educational and living standards of the Jewish population was the only task, then the question regarding the right not only of a Hebrew Haskalah but indeed of a special Jewish community to exist, remained an open one.

This question of existence found its answer in the idea of *national Judaism*. The literary development of one of the leading Maskilim in the second half of the nineteenth century, *Moses Leib Lilienblum* (1843-1910), exemplified all the stages of this escalation from the Yeshivah, via the critique of religion and socialism, up to protagonist of the early Zionist movement. The way of many Jews in Russia, Poland and Galicia until recent times was

---

[376] Unless one ranks the 'Choir Synagogues' among the synagogal reforms, the first of which was founded by Joseph Perl in Tarnopol in 1815, and which spread to several synagogues in Uman, Wilna, Odessa etc, where larger Maskilim groups existed.

[377] Cf. Rotenstreich, vol. I, p. 148.

[378] That it is not lacking in historical interest is shown by names like Krochmal and Rapoport among the older Maskilim, Simḥah Pinsker—discoverer of the Babylonian system of Hebrew vocalisation, which was displaced by the vocalisation used today—and the historian and educationalist, Samuel Joseph Fuenn, around the middle of the century.

similar to his, and typical of thousands of young Jews, particularly in the period between the two World Wars.

Before discussing the re-orientation of Haskalah towards the new Hebrew cultural movement, I should like to consider other consequences of this Enlightenment movement.

Reform of *Jewish education* had been a principal concern of the Enlightenment in Germany. Instead of the 'Ḥeder'—the classroom in the home of the often poorly trained teacher—better equipped schools were to be set up with qualified teachers and a fixed curriculum.

In Austrian Galicia the introduction of Jewish state schools provided the possibility of carrying through such a school reform. These modern schools even spread to Russia—at first as private schools—as early as the 'twenties of the nineteenth century. Like their models in Galicia, they were based on a combination of Hebrew and German with religious and secular subjects. Teachers were appointed from Germany and Austria. In 1840 the Russian minister of education, Uwarov, commissioned the Munich-born *Dr. Max Lilienthal* (1815-1882), head of the Jewish School in Riga, to carry out a reform of Jewish schools in Russia.

Lilienthal pursued his task with enthusiasm. However he not only encountered resistance—already experienced in Galicia—to the innovations which aimed at breaking through the traditional and time-hallowed school system, but found opposition among the Maskilim as well. For them he was not radical enough. To win support from the leading rabbis he included the Ḥeder within the new school system. Ḥeder teachers were to be put under school supervision, but this did not materialise in practice. The newly founded government schools for Jews and the two rabbinical schools, which were part of the whole complex, were attended by a mere handful of students, since people preferred the old Ḥeder and Yeshivah.

Lilienthal soon fell under understandable political suspicion. The Jewish policy of the Czar *Nikolaus I* more than that of his predecessors, had as its aim the de-judaization—with force no less—of his subjects. In inner Russia, especially in Petersburg and in Moscow, only the very wealthy "merchants of the first class" had right of residence. All other Jews were confined to the western and Polish provinces of the empire. The borders of this 'pale of settlement' were frequently redrawn, in consequence of which forceful expulsions of Jewish communities repeatedly took place, with those suddenly made homeless forfeiting their property. In the pale itself they were subject to severe disabilities, which led to a hitherto unknown increasing pauperization. The most dreadful kind of pressure, however, was the inclusion of Jews in military service, which for them began at the age of twelve. Jewish communities had to declare how many children were available, so that in order to reach this quota, children—often only eight years old—were seized both by police and by community officials from the streets for the army. The government believed that through hunger and stress children could be the most easily forced to change their religion. Conscripted children were dispatched to remote provinces of the empire in order to deprive them of all Jewish influences. As long as these child soldiers did not perish from shock and privation, they had to do military service for twenty-five years. But of those who survived most remained true to Judaism.

Everything proscribed by this government concerning Jewish matters was looked upon by the Jews of Russia as a new element in the policy of de-judaization. Lilienthal himself, eventually realising he was being misused, fled to the USA in 1845.

In the Russian government schools for Jews, *German* and not Russian was used as the teaching medium. Russification of the Jewish upper classes only occurred under the reign of the more liberal *Alexander II*. He opened the Russian universities to Jewish students and also the high schools as a preparation for them. Soon Jewish periodicals were appearing in the Russian language to which many Maskilim contributed.

Parallel with this assimilation to the Russian was that to the Polish language in the provinces of Poland. This was especially the case among the youth, who had been actively involved in the various Polish uprisings and stood in solidarity with the Polish freedom movement. The great mass of the Jewish population, however, continued to speak and read Yiddish.

After several feeble beginnings dating back to the eighteenth century, Haskalah also commenced using *Yiddish*, which for a long time it had stubbornly rejected.

Whereas the older Judeo-German literature had found a continuation in the writings of Ḥasidism, in the many collections of Ḥasidic legends and sayings of the Ẓadikim, Yiddish emerged as a modern literary language only now when the men of Enlightenment were beginning to use it. In this new literary genre—using the spoken language[379] of the people—appeared popular educational translations, short stories, satires and novels. Notably conspicuous was the large number of theatrical plays, which brought the life of the people visibly and tangibly nearer to the public. In Yiddish literature the social dimension is strongly represented, yet linked to a romantic senti-mental idealisation of the Jewish small town (Shtetl). Jewish poets and writers became known in world literature through translation of the works of men like J. L. Perez, Shalom Alechem, Mendele Mocher Sefarim, Shalom Asch. Many magazines and later daily papers appeared in Yiddish. The Jew-ish socialist 'Arbeiterbund', the 'Bund' (Union) as it was known, became an influential political party consciously using the Yiddish language. And among the Yiddish-speaking immigrants in the USA, Jewish socialists founded a strong trade union movement. Finally a Yiddish scholarly literature emerged,

---

[379] A distinction is made today between east-European and west-European Yiddish—or Judeo-German—which lacks Slavonic elements. West-European Yiddish has virtually disappeared today.

and in Vilna in 1925 the Institute for Jewish Research (YIVO) was founded, which still exists in New York and Warsaw. Today, of course, especially after the decimation of Polish and Russian Jewry in the Second World War, the Yiddish language and literature are dying out. In the USA English has taken the place of Yiddish among the children and grandchildren of immigrants, as has Hebrew in Israel. Nevertheless, Yiddish is still spoken or understood to some extent by many Askenazi Jews.

The intellectual Jewish youth in Eastern Europe, who grew up around 1870, were faced with three *alternatives*. These young people, coming mostly from a Ḥasidic milieu, had passed through Ḥeder and Yeshivah. Through their first contact with the surrounding culture, the forbidden fruit, which Haskalah literature conveyed to them, they fell into radical doubt, and from the discarding of the religious precepts they passed over to open unbelief, often becoming hostile to religion. They identified Jewish religion with the social misery of their environment and with Ḥasidism's hostility to secular education. They reacted to the new liberating influences in different ways.

One section assimilated completely into their Russian or Polish surroundings. The children of oppressed Jews sided particularly with the politico-revolutionary streams of the Russian intelligentsia. They became revolutionaries, socialists and later communists who rejected a separate Jewish existence as reactionary.

A second group identified themselves with the poverty-stricken Jewish masses, fighting for the right of the national Jewish minority, for their political emancipation and social rehabilitation. To this section belonged the protagonists of Yiddish, the language of the people. It also included a liberal middle-class element, the *autonomists*, centred round the historian Simon Dubnow. They demanded national autonomy and minority rights for Jews in Russia and in the later succession states (created by the dissolution of the Russian and Austro-Hungarian Empire in 1919). Beside this, a socialist wing was formed, the 'Bund', already referred to, with a similar political tendency.

The third choice was the national Jewish one, which was inspired by Hebrew Haskalah literature and whose adherents formed branches of *Hovevei Zion* (Friends- or Lovers- of Zion). They soon merged with Zionism.

The latter, whose concerns and aspirations were at first utopian, and who for several decades were probably the smallest of the Jewish groupings, became the most important. It was they who were to revolutionize the life and history of Jewry. For here was a desire to change life completely in a way no longer possible in Poland or Russia, but only by a decisive withdrawal from the diaspora countries and settlement in the old homeland, in the Land of Israel.

The roots of "Love for Zion" lay in the religious attachment of the

Jews to the Holy Land, and in the longing for redemption linked with it. These two factors had not yet been historically relativized in Eastern Europe or reinterpreted into a pure belief in progress. Even in their secularized form, adopted by the religious-critical Maskilim, they had been retained as national hopes. For it must be remembered that the Jews of Eastern Europe lived in an undoubtedly nationally minded milieu side by side with Russians and Poles speaking their own national languages. Here too, they were minorities, but not disappearing minorities dispersed among people with a single common language as in Germany. The constant pull and psychological constraint towards assimilation did not exist in Eastern Europe.

This latent religious national love of Zion through the centuries had largely remained no more than an emotional longing. Seldom did it stir larger Jewish groups, only once the whole of Jewry—in the period of Sabbatai Zevi. But these early movements had a much stronger religious character than a consciously national one. And in the Lurianic Kabbalah messianism was widened into a cosmic redemption, which included national redemption within it.

Thus *national Judaism* in a very real sense first became a phenomenon in the nineteenth century. It was connected to some extent with the national movements in Europe and could be called an assimilation to them. At any rate national Judaism was a consequence of the devaluation of the religious dimension within the religious-national structure of Judaism. This devaluation thus placed the national aspect of that structure in the foreground and even regarded it as the sole valid factor.

The national Jewish current was already expressing itself round the mid-nineteenth century in romanticized literary form. The biblical era of the monarchy was rediscovered in novels and poems as the national golden age. Happiness and prosperity of a free country folk on their own soil was poetically idealized, while the gloom of the present was a frequent subject of satire.

Change in their structure of occupation, especially the possibility of working the soil, had been an old dream of the Jewish Enlightenment. Experiments in Germany in this direction were time and again frustrated,[380] but in Russia they had notable success. There a large number of agricultural settlements were founded—at first indeed through a benevolent disposition of government. Although development of these colonies was considerably constricted due to the increasing anti-Jewish policy of the authorities, a hundred thousand Jews[381] lived in them towards the end of the nineteenth

---

[380] Of these experiments in Germany, only a few agricultural schools and teaching farms continued to exist after the First World War. Best known of these was the "Gartenbauschule" in Ahlem near Hanover.

[381] See relevant statistics in JE, vol. I, col. 256. The 'Lexikon des Judentums' (1967) gives the same figure for 1914.

century—a sign that they fulfilled a desire of the Jewish population to till the soil. The idealization of the peasantry in Hebrew literature possibly emanated from these longings and attempts to realize them. But the shift of emphasis—from Russia to their own national life in the Land of Israel —is clearly discernible. After all, governmental restrictions and mass anti-semitism made it hardly feasible for Jews to live on the land, or indeed, to lead a normal life in Russia or in Poland. The Land of Israel, where once Jews had lived a normal life, seemed to be the only alternative.

It was no longer a question of the old demands of the Enlightenment and of Haskalah. From these the new generation, which had gone through the school of the older Haskalah, consciously turned away. Mendelssohn, previously the revered model of the Maskilim, was branded by *Perez Smolenskin* (1842-1885) as the great corrupter, who had initiated the denationalization of west-European Jews. Smolenskin, moreover, disfavoured the romantic association with the Jewish past and tradition. He sought to divest Jewish messianism of its religious content and to interpret the future hope of the Jewish people from a national political perspective. His national and areligious interpretation of Judaism is still a force to be reckoned with.

Contemporaneous with Smolenskin—and again, of consequence today —was the emergence of a *national-religious* understanding of the Jewish task and future. Its first representative was the Lithuanian rabbinic scholar, *Yeḥiel Michael Pines* (1843-1913), who since 1878 lived in Jerusalem as representative of the English Jewish philanthropist, Sir Moses Montefiore. Through his symbolic interpretation and defence of Torah-true Judaism after the manner of S. R. Hirsch and S. D. Luzzatto, Pines exercised an influence on youth studying at the Jerusalem Yeshivot. He also had close relations with Russian Jewish students of the *Bilu* movement,[382] for whom he was model and patron.

In Israel there also took place the epochmaking culturo-historical transformation of Hebrew from a literary into a living *spoken language*. Indeed, in the eyes of the first prominent Hebrew lyricist, J. L. Gordon (1830-1892), Hebrew was a mere standby for the little understood Russian.[383] This change of language which first gave the basis to a new national culture, is linked with the name of *Eliezer Ben-Yehudah* (1858-1922). When he came to Jerusalem, in 1881, he began unremittingly to speak only Hebrew. Soon a small band of friends was following him, among them Pines. The old-new language—not completely foreign to any Jew—was soon permeating the schools in the newly founded settlements and from there entered the every-

---

[382] The Bilu movement (an acronym formed from the words of Isaiah 2.5: Bet Yaakov Iekhu w'nelkhah—O House of Jacob, come let us go . . .) arose among students of Kharkow University following the pogroms in 1881. The hitherto social-revolutionary students then decided to actualize their social and life-reforming ideas in Erez Israel.

[383] See Boehm "Die Zionistische Bewegung" (The Zionist Movement), Berlin 1920, p. 61.

day life of the "Yishuv" (Jewish population in the Land of Israel). From Israel it slowly reinfluenced parts of east-European Jewry. During the years between the World Wars there developed in the new states, established in the former outer provinces of Russia, a widespread complex from Kindergarten to Grammar School using Hebrew as the medium of instruction.

Ben-Yehudah, who was also one of the most distinguished Hebrew philologists, began with the publication of a "Thesaurus totius Hebraitatis", the seventeen volumes of which were only completed thirty-five years after his death.


In Russia early in 1881 Czar Alexander II was assassinated. His ultra-reactionary successor, Alexander III, began his reign with an extreme intensification of the policy towards Jews. They lost the franchise and the right of representation in the cities obtained under Alexander II. Right of residence outside towns and outside Jewish agricultural settlements was withdrawn and existing rights here restricted. The borders of the Pale of settlement were again repeatedly redrawn. In the towns outside the pale police raids were carried out on Jews and thousands of artisans ejected.

This curtailment of rights, creating great misery among the Jewish population, was accompanied by brutal outbursts of antisemitism. A wave of *pogroms*, which was supported—indeed often organized—by the authorities raged from April 1881 for several years in Russia and Poland. Murder, rape, arson and plunder of Jewish residential areas and businesses were justified on patriotic and pious grounds. This led to a vast exodus of Jews from the Czarist kingdom. Their place of refuge was chiefly the USA, where hundreds of thousands of destitute refugees landed after long privation.

This eruptive *migratory movement* out of Russia changed the *demographic structure* of world Jewry, as only the banishment of Jews from Spain centuries earlier had done. If at that time the communities in the Mediterranean countries, especially the Balkans, became Sephardic, so now the Jewish communities in the United States and England—hitherto mostly influenced by German Jewry—took on a predominantly east-European Jewish character. The same was true in Belgium, South Africa, South America and notably Argentina.

Germany and Austria were in respect of this migration merely transit countries.[384] The refugees who got stuck here were for the most part quickly integrated into German Jewry. Only after World War I, when following the pogroms in the Ukraine and the upheavals in Eastern Europe, a second stream of Jewish refugees came to Germany—who because of the new

---

[384] Due to the limited admission of Jewish students to Russian universities (numerus clausus) that was introduced by Alexander III, many of them came to universities in Germany, Switzerland and France, where they became an important factor in early Zionism.

American immigration laws could not sail further—did an "east-European Jewish problem" arise in the German communities.

In Canada, and in large measure in Argentina, agricultural colonies were established on estates acquired by the Jewish Baron Hirsch. There several tens of thousands of Jews were settled. However, in the course of time, most of them or their children moved again into the cities. It was clear that in order to bring about a fundamental change in the structure of occupation and settlement of Jews, an emotional commitment to their new occupation and to the soil was necessary.

Such a commitment was only offered by settlement in Erez Israel (the Land of Israel) which at first was a very modest Jewish attempt at settlement. The great west-European relief organisations had never taken this country into consideration, since it manifestly appeared to them to offer no solution to the refugee problem on a large scale.

In the year of the first pogrom, 1881, the Odessa physician Dr. *Leon Pinsker* (1821-1891), wrote a pamphlet 'Auto-Emancipation'.[385] Pinsker was probably not thinking here of a national regeneration, as did Smolenskin in his somewhat similar line of thought, but had a legal-political solution of the Jewish problem in mind. Under the influence of this booklet, the 'Hovevei Zion' societies were founded in order to assist emigration to Erez Israel and to promote settlement there. In the 'eighties and 'nineties Hovevei Zion founded a number of settlements in Erez Israel, which, due to the financial and organizational help of Edmond de Rothschild, were finally able to be consolidated.[386] These settlements were the starting point for the later development of the Jewish national home and the State of Israel.

The rise and development of Zionism do not belong to this chapter, where we have only briefly delineated the impulses proceeding from east-European Judaism. The life-reforming tendencies lying at the basis of the Jewish national movement from its inception, were decisively expressed in the second stream of emigration to Palestine after the Revolution of 1905. Like the 'Biluim' twenty years earlier, students and intelligentsia with Russian and Hebrew education went to Israel at that time.

For this generation Hebrew was the natural basis of life. Their aim, which they sought to realise under the most trying circumstances, was the erection of a new and just Jewish society relying on its own toil. And labour was to be Jewish labour, whereas the settlers of the Rothschild settlements had now already gone over—like small plantation owners—to employ cheap Arab labour. For this reason the new socialist immigrants formed collective

---

[385] 'Auto-Emancipation—a warning call to his clansmen from a Russian Jew', 1882. Pinsker was son of the above-mentioned first Judaic scholar in Russia, Simhah Pinsker. The booklet was published in German.

[386] Similar societies were also formed in Germany, England and other countries. The centre in Odessa became known as the 'Odessa Committee'.

groups without outside wage-labour and exploitation. Indeed, an equalitarian society emerged, where everyone shared equally in work and reward, where everyone contributed according to his ability and received according to his needs. Types of the smaller kevutzah and the larger kibbutz came into being in the years before World War I, and many were established since then.

In the movement of this so-called 'second' Aliyah (lit. 'ascent', i.e. immigration into the Land of Israel), there were two groups. The one was strongly orientated towards Marxist socialism. The other, which strongly influenced the first, cultivated an ethical-humanitarian socialism, the kind of which Gustav Landauer was calling for at the same time in Germany, *Aaron David Gordon* (1856-1922) was the theorist and personal example of this latter kind of socialism. He was over fifty years of age when he came to Israel. This reformer, teacher and writer embodied for youth the possibility of a radical renewal of life for the individual and for society. He advocated for Jewry "Deliverance through work" which could be realised in Erez Israel if everything, including the meanest tasks, were performed by Jews. For Gordon the relation to work was accompanied by a new reverential relation to nature. In the same way his writings express a religious ethical relationship to all creatures. He saw in all this a renewal of Judaism. A. D. Gordon was the spiritual father of the first kevuzot and thereby of the *Kibbutz movement,* which after World War I determined the social ethos of the Yishuv until the 'thirties.

We observed how since the mid-nineteenth century east-European Haskalah had become more and more critical of, indeed hostile to, religion—under influences from abroad and as a reaction to the prevailing obscurantism. The latter, with which aspiring youth constantly crossed swords, falsified their view of religion. In ever widening circles in Eastern Europe there spread a lax and often hostile attitude to the Jewish religious law and even to religion in general. Even for circles who, like Aḥad Ha'am, emphasized Jewish cultural values, this national culture was a secularized one. Religion represented within it an important historically significant worth, but it had lost its central position in the hierarchy of values. Many were of the opinion that religion probably preserved Israel in the diaspora, but that now with the rebirth of the nation its role had ended. Others argued very similarly in favour of a cosmopolitanism, which now, in the hour of its realisation, had removed the differences between religions and nations. Both views were arguments for assimilation whether it appeared in national or international garb.

It was precisely the most active sections of the Jewish generations who up until World War II and thereafter from the concentration camps streamed into Erez Israel—who had grown up in this frame of mind. They also determined thereby the cultural situation in present-day Israel, for the national-religious elements among this youth were only a minority. A liberal religious

Judaism, as existed in Germany, had remained unknown and incomprehensible to it. In Reform Judaism one only saw, since Smolenskin, the trend towards denationalization, which had long dominated it. Appreciation of the positive aspect of the Reform movements and of the feasibility of a modern religious Judaism, was lacking in Eastern Europe.

Remarkably, that which has just been said, appears not to apply to the large Jewish masses, who emigrated from Poland and Russia to the USA. Here these hundreds of thousands of east European immigrants made contact with the moderate liberal congregations—known in the United States as Conservative synagogues—thus helping this hitherto weak branch of the then largely radical-reform Jewry of the USA to become the most prominent sector in present-day American Jewry. Others joined the Reform synagogue, while again others remained Orthodox—even partly in the sense of the east-European 'Shtetl'. This linking up with religious congregations was not entirely a matter of religious motives, but included sociological factors in American life.

Be that as it may, modern Judaism as it exists today in Israel, the Americas and Europe has been fashioned by very heterogeneous trends. Common to them all, however, is a living Jewish community consciousness, whether this be areligious-nationally, religious-nationally or purely religiously motivated. The descendants of east-European Jewry are today's determining factor in world Jewry.

# CHAPTER 21

## *The New Jewish Self-Awareness*

We have already in other connections touched upon events, which determined the last fifty years of German Jewry. That epoch had begun with the cultural preponderance of Jewry in central Europe. But very soon, at the turn of the century, this preponderance was lessening.

In the United States of America and later in Erez Israel new centres of a modern scholarly, cultural and socially active Jewry had been formed. Modern east-European Judaism, which came into being by rejecting the central European concept of emancipation, had begun to develop new national forms of life in Erez Israel, which was to become more and more significant for world Jewry. A new centre of the Wissenschaft of Judaism arose in the USA, which in greater freedom and with much greater means quickly grew to universal importance. Only the German-Jewish achievements in Jewish philosophy and modern understanding of religion still await further development, of which promising beginnings are already evident.

Characteristic of this development is the history of the *Jewish Encyclopedia*, still indispensable today, published in twelve volumes in New York between 1901 and 1906,[387] after its editor Isidore Singer had for years tried in vain to interest Jewish circles for such a work in Europe. In this encyclopedia whole areas found their first scholarly presentation. Although very many of its some four hundred contributors were European Jews, it appeared as a first representative work of America's younger Jewry that

---

[387]It appeared in reprint in more compact volumes in 1965. The German 'Encyclopaedia Judacia' initiated by Jacob Klatzkin and Nahum Goldmann only reached letter 'L' (10 vols. 1918-1934). An English edition in 16 vols. was published in Jerusalem in 1972 virtually rewritten. The five-volumed 'Jüdisches Lexikon' (1927-1930) has a popular scholarly character. During World War II the ten volumed 'Universal Jewish Encyclopedia' was brought out in New York, The Spanish 'Encyclopedia Judaica Castellana' in ten volumes appeared in Mexico between 1948-1951. The Russian 'Jewreskaja Enziklopaedia' was printed in 16 vols. between 1906-1913, and the Hebrew 'Ozar Yisrael' edited by J. D. Eisenstein in New York (1907-1913) runs into 10 volumes. The large, still incomplete 'Encyclopedia Hebraica' (begun 1949) is a general Hebrew encyclopedia with important Judaic contributions.

could not be ignored. Despite the great demographic changes they simultaneously had to overcome, the Jews of the USA were able to organize
and complete such a scholarly undertaking, which the old world could
not emulate.

At a time when no one could have foreseeon the holocaust it was of
providential significance that modern Judaism had begun to break away
from its geographical concentration in Europe. It was this decentralization
which after World War II made possible the continuation of Jewish history.

During the last fifty to sixty years the intellectual history of modern
Jewry has undergone a momentous structural change. In Germany, around
the mid-nineteenth century, the whole of educated Jewry had participated
in the arguments about legal, social and cultural emancipation and Reform.
These were still themes which at that time concerned everyone. But after
civil equality had been formally attained with the establishment of the
German Reich—and about the same time in Austria-Hungary—the necessity
of being involved in Jewish questions seemed to have disappeared. Even the
Reform movement was usually considered less from a religious than from an
emancipatory-political aspect. The sluice gates were now opened for the
Jewish intellectuals. This led to an increasingly ramifying participation in
general culture, whereas Jewish culture and Jewish matters seemed of
concern only to the few who were involved by reason of their profession,
like rabbis, teachers, heads of the Jewish communities and organizations.
Judaism was becoming a poorly paid and unpromising administrative affair
divorced from the literary, aesthetic, scholarly and political questions, which
preoccupied the middle and upper classes of German Jewry. In these matters
of general culture people readily inclined towards avantgarde trends which
frequently had their origin in the genuine pathos of the struggle for emancipation with its background of natural right. But now this pathos was continuing without any such impetus. Jewish writers and journalists did not
notice how much the cultural and political outlook of the educated German
public—whose representatives they thought they were—had meanwhile
changed.

And here we should notice a further aspect. Graetz concluded his history
—which ends with the year 1848—with the statement that Jews had indeed
more or less achieved equality of rights as individuals, but that the *emancipation of Judaism*, the recognition of *its* equality, was still not within sight.[388]
The emancipation of individual Jews was in fact still subjected to many
restrictions. The civil service, the officers' corps and 'society' remained
closed to them. In those spheres of life, of course, where most Jews were
closely involved—in business, the professions, literature and art—develop-

---

[388] See Graetz's concluding words of vol. XI (written in 1869).

mental scope was fully given them and gladly utilized. Yet Judaism was probably intentionally excluded from the new legislation pertaining to equality of rights. The Jewish faith did not stand on the same legal or social footing as the major Christian confessions. It continued in the German Empire to be the tolerated private religion of a small minority and in relation to Christianity was considered inferior. The tendency—since Joseph II, Clermont-Tonnerre, Humboldt and Hardenberg—still remained the same. It was, by means of emancipation and assimilation of Jewish individuals, to cause Judaism to disappear as a special entity. The revival of national-romantic ideas of the 'Christian state' in the 'seventies strengthened this tendency, which now united both liberal and conservative Germans. No Jewish demand found such unanimous rejection among antisemites, liberals and socialists as that calling for the equality of Judaism; whereas for Jews this was merely the logical consequence of civil equality.[389]

The above-mentioned facts: the diminution of the central importance of German Jewry, the confinement of interest in Jewish matters to a minoritity and the lack of equality of Judaism in state and society, still have consequences to the present day.

But around 1890 a new era of Jewish *self-consciousness* began, affecting circles—far beyond the minority just mentioned—who until then had little interest in Jewish questions. There now arose in these wider circles a latent feeling of solidarity, often as an expression of hurt pride or defiance.

This reaction was provoked by the new secularized form of antisemitism and by the Russian pogroms of the 'eighties which confronted the Jews in Germany with refugees from Eastern-Europe and east-European Judaism.

*Modern antisemitism* is a combination of several factors. Its background is socio-psychological: the attitude of a majority to a minority. The minority is mostly met with distrust, disapproval, jealousy and disdain, because it often diverges from the lifestyle, values, religion or nationality of the majority. From dislike to bedevilment is often only a step. This fate of the minority has always struck the Jews to a terrible degree. In this context, the social, occupational and legal restrictions imposed on the Jews, distorted their image considerably because of the resultant unnatural occupational structure. Their Gentile neighbours, however, got used to that structure and resisted any change to it.

Added to this was the theologically motivated anti-Jewish hostility of the churches. The continuance of Judaism, and the adherence of Jews to it, stood in the way of their claim to be the new and the true Israel replacing the Old Covenant.

---

[389] The devaluation of Judaism was also reflected in liberal Portestant theology and its Old Testament scholarship. The more it abandoned dogmatic-Christological positions, the more strongly it had to assume an ethical-religious distance from Judaism.

A further factor was the resumption of the old "Germanomania" of the early nineteenth century with its Christian Germanic ideal of peoplehood. This tendency was given political significance by the 'Christian state' as a doctrine determining the policy of the conservative parties towards Jews. But it also found access to the right wing of the German liberals, e.g. with Eduard Meyer (senior)—against whom Riesser polemized—and with the theologian Paulus. It found its most powerful historical expression in the historian Heinrich von Treitschke in 1879.

Linked to these socio-psychological, theological and romantic-nationalist elements in the rise of modern antisemitism, were factors from a very different quarter: the anti-Jewish hostility of many influential circles of the Enlightenment. These drew their arguments from the anti-Jewish litera-ture of antiquity and also from eighteenth-century deistic criticism of the Bible which asserted an innate moral inferiority of the Jews provable and unaltered since biblical times. These Enlighteners—like Voltaire in France and H. S. Reimarus in Hamburg—were precursors of that historically fateful phenomenon, *racial antisemitism*.

The other source of this antisemitism—mingled with some of the above ideas—which finally gained the upper hand, was the *theory of race*. The doctrine of the inequality of the human races was first developed by the French diplomat and writer, Count Gobineau, in 1853. In its antisemitic form this theory depicted the Jewish race as inferior and detrimental vis-á-vis the Germanic race, which felt itself called to rule.

Antisemitism in Germany became politically significant at the end of the 'seventies. To achieve the unification of the Reich and afterwards during the *Kulturkampf* against political Catholicism, Bismarck had relied upon the National-Liberals. He now sought to make friends again with Conservative groups, as he wanted to introduce a military budget for several years in ad-vance and pass the anti-Socialist Laws. He also tolerated the exploitation of anti-Jewish public feeling, which put the blame on Jewish speculators for the long economic crisis following the overheated boom of the period of pro-moterism. In the Reichstag's General Election of 1878 the Jewish question played a role for the first time. The court chaplain, Stoecker, founded at that time a Christian Social party in order to alienate the working and lower middle-classes from the Social Democrats. In his propaganda he resorted to crass anti-Jewish slogans, while the Berlin historian, *Heinrich von Treitschke*, made antisemitism respectable among the German educated class. Treitschke, regarded as a liberal, and who was also a National-Liberal parliamentarian and editor of the influential 'Prussian Yearbooks', wrote in 1879 " 'The Jews are our misfortune'—that is the concurring judgement of the best educated circles!" He called for complete assimilation of the Jews and the relinquish-ing of every 'peculiarity' preventing this before they could be regarded as Germans. Without demanding direct conversion to Christianity Treitschke stressed that religious unity also belongs to the national character. His first essay led to a vehement controversy.[390] Involved in this—alongside several antisemites, who brought in the aspect of race that Treitschke steered clear of—was the famous historian Theodor Mommsen in opposition to Treitschke and antisemitism. On the Jewish side, Graetz, whom Treitschke had apostrophized as prototype of an un-German disposition, Lazarus, Joel, Hermann Cohen and the historian Harry Bresslau engaged in the controversy. Moritz Lazarus organized a quite ineffective committee of Jewish notables. Nothing more happened at first in the Jewish camp. Seventy-five men in public life —among them Professors Droysen, von Gneist, Mommsen and Virchow— published a protest against introducing antisemitism into the universities. But the strongly increasing antisemitic trend among German students and in the academic world originated in large measure in the lectures of Treitschke, who helped prepare the way for the later rapid victory of National Socialism.

In the following years the wave of antisemitism grew. Antisemitic parties obtained seats in the Reichstag (parliament).

Jews, particularly in remote districts, were often physically assaulted and economically boycotted. In Xanten in 1891 and between 1900 and 1903 in Konitz it came to accusations of ritual murder and court trials. In 1892 the influential ruling Conservative party in Prussia included an anti-Jewish clause in its official programme—the 'Tivoli Programme'.

In 1890 a number of prominent non-Jews had formed a 'Society for Protection against Antisemitism', to whose founders the constitutional jurist von Gneist, the philosopher Rickert, the literary historian Erich Schmidt as well as the novelist Gustav Freytag and Theodor Mommsen belonged. The society published literature of an informative nature, including a periodical, but it could not really counteract the antisemitic propaganda. This society existed until 1933.

In leading Jewish circles in Berlin the idea was contemplated of making direct petition to the Kaiser.

Then at the beginning of 1893 there appeared a pamphlet 'Schutzjuden oder Staatsbuerger?' (Protected Jews or Citizens?). Its author was *Dr. Raphael Loewenfeld*, a writer who had translated Ibsen and founded the Schiller Theatre in Berlin and one who seemed remote from Jewish questions. Loewenfeld explained that a petition of free citizens to the Kaiser would be unworthy and would represent the mentality of bygone protected Jews. The German Jews should not leave their defence in the hands of a well-meaning society of non-Jews, but defend themselves.

In response to this call the *Centralverein deutscher Staatsbuerger juedischen Glaubens* (Central Association of German Citizens of Jewish Faith),

---

[390] Cf. Walter Boelich, 'Der Berliner Antisemitismusstreit' (The Berlin Antisemitism Controversy), Frankfurt 1965. This contains the most important essays and pamphlets. H. Liebeschuetz gives a detailed analysis of the controversy in 'Das Judentum im deutschen Geschichtsbild' (Judaism in the German Idea of History), Tuebingen 1967, Chaps. 5 and 6.

generally known as *C.V.*, was set up, very soon to become the largest organization in German Jewry.[391]  The object of the 'C.V.' was "to bring together German citizens of Jewish faith, irrespective of religious or political persuasion, in order to confirm them in the active safeguarding of their civil and social equality as well as in the unwavering cultivation of the German way of thinking".[392]

The C.V. was active in giving legal advice and protection in cases of attacks of antisemitism, kept an eye on the antisemitic press for defamation, offences and punishable dealings against Jews, many instances of which it brought to court. It also distributed articles, leaflets and books on Judaism of an enlightening and didactic nature. Its essentially rational and scholarly argumentation was helpless in the face of the irrational elements of Jew-hatred. Nevertheless its achievements cannot be too highly estimated. But the main service it rendered was that it was the first to give expression to the new Jewish self-consciousness and pride. This is why it found such a response in German Jewry. Jews in remote places in particular no longer felt forsaken. Now they had an address where they could expect moral and legal support.

The ideology of the C.V. was in keeping with the tradition of the era of emancipation—as Gabriel Riesser, Lazarus and especially Hermann Cohen had left their imprint on it—namely that synthesis of Germanism and Judaism, according to which the German Jew could be fully German and at the same time fully Jew. In Jewish reality, however, as we saw, a *preponderance of Germanism* had emerged which elbowed the Jewish element in Jewish consciousness to the side. Whereas the C.V. included Zionists even in its central committee during the pre-World War I years, the society developed into an outspoken anti-Zionist organization in inner Jewish policy and polemics. Only in the 'twenties did it alter its position, at any rate an influential minority within it, which supported the building up of Palestine. Yet the C.V. remained non-Zionist, being considered in Zionist propaganda as the inner-Jewish opponent. Not until a few years before the national socialist upheaval was a certain co-operation between both groups reached.[393]  But the C.V. did not come to grips with the inner problems of German Jewry, because it wanted to remain neutral regarding political and religious differences of opinion. The result of this was that it gave nothing positive to the broad strata of urban Jews that could have raised them out of their Jewish

[391] In 1927 the C.V. had over 70,000 members in 3,260 centres throughout Germany. See 'Lexikon des Judentums', column 141.

[392] Paragraph 1 of the Statutes. The last part of this sentence led after some years to the withdrawal of the Zionist members, making the C.V. for a long time an anti-Zionist organization.

[393] See A. Paucker 'Der Juedische Abwehrkampf' (The Jewish Resistance Struggle), Hamburg 1968.

indifference. The struggle against antisemitism, important as it was, could not be the sole content of Jewish life or take its place.

The reawakening Jewish self-consciousness found its historical—and not just its intellectual historical—expression in *Zionism*. Zionism finally revolutionized Jewish life throughout the world, giving it, especially after the establishment of the state of Israel, a new goal and focus.

In the previous chapter I tried to depict the natural growth of a Hebrew, Palestine centred, national Judaism out of the Jewish national minority in Eastern Europe. Here the Ḥovevei Zion movement arose as a life-reforming protest against both the unnatural structure of Jewish economic and occupational life and the traditional form of schooling and education. This movement was an offshoot of Haskalah, but had absorbed from the surrounding culture, in addition to secular elements, romantic-national traits which it linked with social Idealism—both of which were of biblical origin.

Zionism in Western Europe lacked the basis of a Jewish peoplehood and with it, to a large extent, the Jewish outlook and culture rooted in the education and milieu of east-European Jewry. It also lacked the stimulus of acute outward pressure. For in western Europe antisemitism and the various kinds of social and occupational discrimination were only considered to be marginal phenomena, which blurred and slowed down the pull towards integration into the surrounding culture without basically stopping it.

It was therefore only a *minority* within the minority still interested in Jewish matters which until 1933 was affected by national—Jewish and Zionist ideas. It was, for all that, a very active group, which not only influenced Jews but made an important contribution to German journalism and literature in general. Yet this influence came essentially from the second generation of Zionists, namely that immediately preceding and following World War I.[394]

Characteristic of the earlier German and west-European Zionism was its political and at the same time philanthropic drive. In contradistinction to the pure philanthropic attempts at agricultural settlements, as for instance by Baron Moritz von Hirsch in Argentina, was the concept of a *political* solution of the Jewish question in Moses Hess, Pinsker, Herzl. Yet one had always in mind the east-European Jews in particular, for whom such a political territorial solution was intended.[395] Western Zionism—like American Zionism today—was basically a Zionism for others, if not in theory then in practice.

---

[394] One recalls, inter alia, the writers Richard Beer-Hofmann, Else Lasker-Schueler, Max Brod, Arnold Zweig; the philosophers Hugo Bergmann, Martin Buber, Felix Weltsch, the publicist Robert Weltsch.

[395] This does not apply to Herzl, who at first had only Western and Central European Jews in mind and never properly realised the significance of east-European Zionism, which urged immediate practical colonization.

Nevertheless, this western Zionism was likewise centred in an idea—an idea that struck one as being revolutionary in the century of emancipation which questioned and denied all previous striving by proclaiming that the Jews were a people. Non-Jews—and not just antisemites—had constantly affirmed the peoplehood of the Jews. The Jews of the nineteenth century, however, used many arguments to dispute that Judaism had a national character. After the modern national state had replaced the 'natural right' concept of state, it felt obliged to call for the national unity of its citizens.[396] Only on this basis did it seem possible to demand and obtain the emancipation of the Jews.[397]  It was on these grounds that Gabriel Riesser demanded equality for Jews, not because they were Jews or that the principles of equality and toleration entitled them to it as human beings, but because they were Germans. The vast majority of German Jews considered themselves as such, differing from other Germans only in virtue of their religion—and areligious Jews perhaps in virtue of their origin. Analogous examples were the Huguenots or the French settlement in Berlin. They had become Germans and their Germanness was not doubted, even though they preserved their distinctiveness in churches, schools and institutions, and to some extent even in language.

A second major argument against national Judaism had been highlighted particularly by the Reform theologians. The universalism of Judaism seemed to contradict a Jewish nationality. The dispersion appeared as a divinely willed annulment of the Jewish state and nationality in favour of a new task, namely to give an example of pure monotheism throughout the world to all mankind. For Geiger Jerusalem is only an honoured historical memory to be respected as such, but without any significance for the Jewish present.

Heinrich Graetz could not have caused greater offence towards this view —which the great majority of German Jews shared—than by depicting Jewish history as a religiously motivated history of a *people*. Geiger's lectures 'Judaism in History' are nothing more than a counter-portrait of Jewish history from the universalist standpoint. The Jewish participants in the debate with Treitschke hastened to disassociate themselves from Graetz, the 'Palestinian', as Cohen described him on that occasion.

The first modern Zionist was *Moses Hess* (1812-1875). In his youth Hess[398] received a traditional education from his rabbinically trained grand-

---

[396] This also holds true for Austria, where at least in the 19th century a strict policy of Germanization was pursued in respect of Slavonic nationalists, and in Hungary a Magyarization policy.

[397] However when Zionism demanded from the state equal citizenship for Jews, it referred back to the natural right concept of state, pointing out that minorities are entitled to civil equality as human beings without making this explicitly or implicitly conditional upon their integration into the majority.

[398] Re biography see Edmund Silberner 'Moses Hess, Geschichte seines Lebens' (The Life of Moses Hess), Leiden 1966; also the earlier biography by Theodor Ziocisti, Berlin 1921 and 'The Life and Opinions of Moses Hess' by Isaiah Berlin, Cambridge 1959.

father in Bonn. After he had acquired a self-taught philosophical education he severed his Jewish ties as a young man, becoming a writer and journalist. He became the pioneer of an ethical-philosophical socialism. Taking his starting-point from Spinoza, Rousseau and Fichte, he saw in history—in contradiction to the Hegelian school, especially to Marx—not an objectively determined process, but a human task. Corresponding to the human dynamics, which characterized history, was the dynamics of the development of nature. Hess's views on the value and future of Judaism corresponded for a long time to those of Spinoza in the Theologico-Political Treatise, for he considered himself a "disciple of Spinoza".[399] After the Revolution of 1848 Hess lived mostly in exile—in Paris, Belgium and Switzerland. Like many German émigrés he still saw in the France of Napoleon III the torchbearer of democratic and social ideals and of the liberation of nations.

During the Damaskus Blood-libel affair in 1840 Hess' Jewish passion flared up for a while, only to be suppressed for two decades due to his political activity on behalf of the suffering proletariat.

The account of Hess's return and the re-shaping of his philosophical, religious and social ideas are expounded in his *Rom und Jerusalem, die letzte Nationalitaetenfrage* (Rome and Jerusalem, the Last National Question) published in 1862, a year after he had returned to Cologne under political amnesty granted by the King of Prussia.

Before writing this book, Hess had been very preoccupied with anthropology and the doctrine of race then in vogue in France. These themes and Hess' experiences of antisemitism even among his socialist friends are reflected in his work. He maintained that the European nations, although having granted the Jews formal equality, still regarded them as foreign, even though they had striven to the point of self-effacement to assimilate. As race or nation,[400] the Jews are indestructible. They were in history and are today—and as Hess hoped, would be in the future—a fundamental factor in world civilization.

For Hess race is not simply a pregiven destiny but carries with it the historic dimension of a task, which he sets the Jewish people. This task is to further the unity of nature and mankind, as called for by Spinoza and seen by Jewish messianism as the religious goal of history. This oneness will follow the realisation of a society free from exploitation and class domination. The Jews are to set a living example of this society in their own national Jewish state. They cannot do this in the dispersion, but only as a conscious national and political entity. Therefore the Jews should proceed to re-settle Palestine.

---

[399] Hess' first work is entitled 'Die heilige Geschichte der Menschheit. Von einem Juenger Spinozas' (The Sacred History of Mankind, by a disciple of Spinoza), Stuttgart 1837.

[400] Hess seems, as Silberner remarks, to use both expressions indiscriminately without any clear distinction.

The realisation of this task, according to Hess, is not at all utopian. Many hitherto oppressed nations are now on the way towards national renewal and political liberation. Italy, writes Hess, is at this moment finding national unity, with France on her side. The national emancipation of the Jews is part of these national movements already hinted at in the renewal of Hebrew literature. As for Rome, so liberation must also come for Jerusalem. And just as the Italians were supported by the French, so the political interst of France in the Middle East (construction of the Suez Canal; military expedition into Syria in 1860) may be used for the establishment of an autonomous Jewish settlement in Palestine.

Of course, continues Hess, the emancipated Jews of the West will not easily be won over for emigration to Palestine. The "cultured Jews of Germany" had—through the fault of the reformers—confessionalized Judaism and lost their sense of national identity. But the Jews of Poland and the Balkans still retain their national consciousness, and will still be willing to play their part in this original Jewish messianic task.

Hess' book caused some excitement, but was largely rejected by Jews and non-Jews alike. The spokesmen of Reform Judaism, Philippson and Geiger, were the most critical. Philippson accused Hess of hypocrisy for glorifying traditional Judaism, while at the same time not observing the religious laws in his own life. In an essay[401] Geiger described him as an "almost complete outsider who, bankrupt in socialism and other swindle, now concerned himself with nationalism". Graetz alone agreed with him,[402] whereas the Neo-orthodox, gratified with his attack on the Reform movement, kept benevolently reserved. Hess' old friendship with the writer Berthold Auerbach, who had described himself in a letter to Hess as "a Germanic Jew, a German as good as they come"[403], came to an end because of 'Rome and Jerusalem'.

Hess' attempt to interest the *Alliance Israélite Universelle*—and through it French government circles—in the Palestine project remained unsuccessful. Hess was forgotten. Not till nearly forty years later, at the First Zionist Congress, was Hess again referred to as a forerunner of Zionism. Herzl did not yet know him at the time of his writing 'The Jewish State'.

Seldom is the full extent of the loss of substance that befell German and west-European Jewry in the nineteenth century so clearly, directly and visibly in evidence as when Hess and Herzl are compared. Both were

---

[401] See 'Alte Romantik und neue Reaktion', in Juedische Zeitschrift fuer Wissenschaft und Leben, vol. I, 1862.

[402] Graetz had by pure chance read the manuscript of the book and secured a publisher for Hess. The title was Graetz's suggestion. Hess for his part translated the 3rd vol. of Graetz's History into French.

[403] Correspondence of Hess, edit. by Silberner, p. 376.

journalists. Both sought a political solution to the Jewish question. Both had
something prophetic, pointing to the future, which seemed utopian and which
they endeavoured to realize. Both belonged to the well-to-do Jewish educated
classes. Both had a marked sense of social responsibility. Yet the almost five
decades separating them reveal the full extent of the change that had taken
place during that period.

Hess, the Jew of the era of emancipation, had immersed himself in the
philosophic, political and social questions of his day and had forgotten the
relevant Jewish problems. Yet the foundation of his education was Jewish.
In the hour of his return, that which was long buried came alive again. His
'Rome and Jerusalem' shows not only a knowledge of Jewish history,
acquaintance with new developments in Hebrew literature and with the
social problems of the east-European Jewish masses. It shows that he can
also cite at length Hebrew quotations from the Midrash. His earlier knowledge is immediately at hand again.

*Theodor Herzl* (1860-1904), born forty-eight years after Hess, possessed
nothing of this background of religious and Jewish cultural experience and
education. One could call him, after he had completed his law studies,
taken up literature and become a journalist and author of successful plays
and short stories, a typical assimilated Jewish intellectual. He seemed to have
adapted without reservation to German and European culture. He once
thought of solving the Jewish question not through private individual baptism
but through baptism en masse, to be performed in full festive procession.

Herzl was thus an outsider in a quite different degree from Hess. It is
not that he had been estranged from Judaism and its problems, but was
rather a stranger to them. Then as correspondent of the Vienna 'Neue Freie
Presse'[404] in Paris he experienced the *Dreyfus Trial*.

Confronted by the flood of antisemitic attacks on Dreyfus and on Jews
in general and in face of the frenzied hate of the people, Herzl saw in a flash
the questionableness and pointlessness of assimilation and the necessity of
a radical re-think. The result of this re-thinking was the recognition that the
Jews were a people; that their predicament, existing everywhere in the most
varied forms and expressions, demanded a political solution in a Jewish state.

Early in 1896 Herzl's slim volume *Der Judenstaat* (The Jewish State)[405]
—destined to become famous—appeared. It begins: "The idea which I have

[404] From 1896 till his death in 1904 he was literary editor of this paper, in which Zionism was not
allowed to be mentioned. Even Herzl's obituary in it passes over his Zionist achievement in silence.
The paper's Jewish editors saw in Zionism a danger threatening the civil position of Jews. Out of concern for his family Herzl thought he should not relinquish the editorship despite the constant humiliation connected with it, as he had exhausted his own means and that of his parents for the Zionist
cause.
[405] 'The Jewish State' went through many editions and translations. On the history of Herzl's development see his 'Tagebuecher' (Diaries), Berlin 1922. Re biography see Alex Bein 'Theodor Herzl' and
Amos Elon's biography 'The Pride and the Pity', 1974.

developed in this pamphlet is an ancient one: It is the restoration of the
Jewish State.

The world resounds with clamor against the Jews, and this has revived
the dormant idea.

I claim no new discoveries; let this be noted at once and throughout my
discussion. I have discovered neither the Jewish situation as it has crystallized in history, nor the means to remedy it. The materials for the structure
I here sketch exist in reality, they are quite tangible; this anyone can establish to his own satisfaction". The "propelling force" behind this plan is
"the plight of the Jews. Who would dare to deny that this exists? Now
everyone knows how steam is generated by boiling water in a kettle, but
such steam only rattles the lid . . . But I say that this force, if properly
harnessed, is powerful enough to propel a large engine and to move pas-
sengers and goods". The introduction ends: "It depends on the Jews themselves whether this political document remains for the present a political
romance. If this generation is too dull to understand it rightly, a future,
finer, more advanced generation will arise to comprehend it. The Jews who
will try it shall achieve their State, and they will deserve it."[406]

After this description of the task, there follows its historico-sociological
justification: "The Jewish question still exists. It would be foolish to deny it.
It is a misplaced piece of medievalism which civilized nations do not even
yet seem able to shake off, try as they will. They proved they had this
high-minded desire when they emancipated us. The Jewish question persists
wherever Jews live in appreciable numbers. Wherever it does not exist, it
is brought in together with Jewish immigrants. We are naturally drawn into
those places where we are not persecuted, and our appearance there gives
rise to persecution. This is the case, and will inevitably be so, everywhere,
even in highly civilized countries—see, for instance, France—so long as the
Jewish question is not solved on the political level. The unfortunate Jews
are now carrying the seeds of antisemitism into England; they have already
introduced it into America.

Antisemitism is a highly complex movement, which I think I understand.
I approach this movement as a Jew, yet without fear or hatred. I believe that
I can see in it the elements of cruel sport, of common commercial rivalry,
of inherited prejudice, or religious intolerance—but also of a supposed need
for self-defense. I consider the Jewish question neither a social or a religious
one, even though it sometimes takes these and other forms. It is a national
question, and to solve it we must first of all establish it as an international
political problem to be discussed and settled by the civilized nations of the
world in council.

We are a people — *one* people.

---

[406] 'The Jewish State', translated by Sylvie d'Avigdor, quoted from 'The Zionist Idea', edited by
Arthur Herzberg, New York 1976, pp. 204-207.

We have sincerely tried everywhere to merge with the national communities in which we live, seeking only to preserve the faith of our fathers.
It is not permitted us. In vain are we loyal patriots, sometimes superloyal; in
vain do we make the same sacrifices of life and property as our fellow-
citizens; in vain do we strive to enhance the fame of our native lands in the
arts and sciences, or the wealth by trade and commerce. In our native lands
where we have lived for centuries we are still decried as aliens. The majority
decide who the 'alien' is; this, and all else in the relations between peoples,
is a matter of power. It is without avail, therefore, for us to be loyal patriots,
as were the Huguenots, who were forced to emigrate. If we were left in
peace. . . .

But I think we shall not be left in peace.

Oppression and persecution cannot exterminate us. No nation on earth
has endured such struggles and sufferings as we have. Jew-baiting has merely
winnowed out our weaklings; the strong among us defiantly return to their
own whenever persecution breaks out."[407]

The Jewish state would not only solve the plight of the Jews. It would
also free the nations from the Jewish question and eradicate the root cause
of antisemitism. The relatively few Jews who would remain in the Diaspora
would no longer constitute a problem for other countries and peoples, so
that they could assimilate normally.

Herzl then sets out the details for establishing the state. A representative
Jewish group of morally upright and respected men—Herzl was thinking here
of English Jews—was to form a 'Society of Jews'. Their task was to create a
political basis and look into statistical and economic data. As the negotiorum
gestor of Jewry they were to obtain a nationally legally recognized charter,
which would make possible for Jews the formation of an autonomous commonwealth under the protection of neutrality. Herzl had thought of Argentina or Palestine. But then realising the emotional bond of Jews to their
ancient homeland stretching over millenia, he decided for the latter. Therefore the movement was called *Zionism*, the return to Zion. The Jewish state
in Palestine was to remain under formal Turkish sovereignty. The Jews
would as a quid  pro quo liberate Turkey from the 'Dette Ottomane', the
oppressing international finance-surveillance. The executive organ of the
Society of Jews would be a 'Jewish Company', which would "be the liqui-
dating agent for the business interests of departing Jews and organize trade
and commerce in the new country".[408] Emigration would be orderly and
planned over the years. With the help of modern technical planning the
land would be prepared for houses and employment etc.

The response to Herzl's booklet was profound. In the western world and
in Central Europe it was only very small groups of Jewish intellectuals who

[407] op. cit., pp. 208-209.
[408] op. cit., p. 220.

first found in Herzl's national Judaism the possibility and justification for remaining Jews without having to be religious Jews. The great majority of western Jews sharply rejected Zionism. It contradicted too strikingly emancipated Jewry's habit of thought. They saw in it a danger to their newly acquired civil position. It seemed to render their patriotism suspect and to aid and abet antisemitism, because a main argument of antisemites, that of the foreignness of Jews, would be confirmed on the Jewish side through Zionism.

In Eastern Europe, whose Jewry with its plight and inner resources were previously little known to Herzl, hearts went out to him. Even *Hovevei Zion*, which at first reacted reservedly, yielded to his suggestive authority.

From 23-31 August 1897 the *First Zionist Congress* met in Basle. It founded the 'World Zionist Organization' and made Herzl its President. The first paragraph of the Basle programme reads: "Zionism aspires to the creation, under public law, of a homeland for the Jewish people in Palestine". Herzl once described the new organization as "the Jewish state underway". He exhausted himself in an incredible number of many-sided political, diplomatic and organizational initiatives, dying in 1904 at the age of only forty-four. Something of the prophet and the seer emanated from him. Wherever he appeared, he spellbound Jews and non-Jews alike by his dignity, integrity and enthusiasm.—The above extracts convey perhaps something of this.—Having returned to his people, Herzl became the symbol and prototype of the best innate energies within Jewry. He became the founder of the State of Israel, which was proclaimed fifty years after the First Zionist Congress.

Even after his turning to Zionism, Herzl in many respects remained a *Jew on the periphery* of Judaism. He was much too sensitive not to feel the significance of the religious and cultural powers inside Judaism and Jewry. But they hardly determined his world view. At the First Zionist Congress he did declare that the return to Judaism would have to precede return to the Jewish homeland. However, this was possibly a mere diplomatic concession to the Torah-true members in congress. His unfamiliarity with Jewish lifestyle, not to speak of Jewish knowledge, and his ignorance of Hebrew is apparent in his 'Jewish State' and even more in the later novel 'Altneuland' (Old New Land). This novel reveals little of the new Jewish life and culture, which were to have been developed in the Jewish state. He stresses, on the contrary, in an outspokenly apologetic manner that was otherwise foreign to Zionism, how tolerant and unprejudiced the Jews and the institutions of the new commonwealth were. The dominant factor in Herzl is the national political aspect. Yet he proclaimed his political goal with such breathtaking urgency that precisely in the firmly-rooted Jewish masses of Eastern Europe he awakened deep messianic feelings. They were not bothered by the lack of Jewish and Hebrew culture in this western Jew, whose person acquired and retained a legendary halo within his own life-time.—And indeed, it turned out that Herzl's urgency was justified in the light of the holocaust forty-three years later.

The most important national-Jewish critic of Herzl was the Hebrew culture-philosophical essayist Asher Ginsberg (1856-1927), known under his pen name *Ahad Ha'am*. He criticized the neglect of national cultural elements—especially Hebrew education—in Herzl's programme and policy. The sceptic Ahad Ha'am did not envisage an early realisation of the Jewish state, and believed therefore that for the present one should come to grips with at least part of the Jewish plight, namely the 'inner struggle', the spiritual dependence and weakness of Jewry. In the new settlements of Erez Israel there were beginnings of a new Hebrew culture to be supported and extended. The new type of Jew growing up there would—from the spiritual centre of Palestine—react upon the diaspora, strengthening and encouraging Jewry throughout the world.

In the course of time Ahad Ha'am's cultural Zionism became the foundation of Zionist cultural activity both in Israel and in the diaspora. The one time very strong antithesis between political and cultural Zionism has long since disappeared and his once very strong criticism has been out-dated. Development has since proceeded in both directions—that of Herzl's and that of Ahad Ha'am's—hand in hand.

A precursor of Herzl and Ahad Ha'am was *Nathan Birnbaum* (1864-1937),[409] founder of the first national Jewish Students' Society in Vienna in 1882. He coined the term 'Zionism' for the new movement in 1890. After the First Zionist Congress he became the first general secretary of the Zionist organization in 1897. But he soon came into conflict with Herzl's policy of attaining Zionist aims through diplomatic proceedings. Birnbaum gave priority to the acute needs of the Yiddish-speaking masses. According to him national and cultural autonomy should first be secured for the Jewish people there—just as other minorities in the Hapsburg monarchy and in the Russian Empire strove for it. In order to work journalistically and politically for the idea of autonomy in the diaspora, he learnt Yiddish and moved for some years to Czernowitz. In the years preceding World War I Birnbaum converted from a free-thinking atheist position to that of an orthodox Jew. In many books and essays written in German and Yiddish he called for the renewal of Jewry through return to a living Torah-true Judaism. But even in the orthodox camp—he was for a while general secretary of the World Orthodox Organization *Agudat Israel*—he continued through his

---

[409] Cf. the essay of Solomon A. Birnbaum in 'Men of the Spirit', edit. by Leo Jung, New York, 1964, pp. 518-549.

deeply religious dynamism and search for truth to be an indeed respected but often embarrassing and suspected outsider. Yet precisely because of his diversified development he had a considerable influence on people of very different outlook.

# CHAPTER 22

# The Last Decades of German Jewry (ca. 1910-1942)

The new Jewish self-consciousness—in its twofold expression in the C.V. and in Zionism—had only captivated a small minority of German Jews at a deeper level. In most of the large communities, in Berlin, Vienna and other cities, the bulk of Jews and the Jewish intelligentsia were barely affected by the new movements and remained indifferent to the Jewish problematic. They felt more at home in the arts, theatre and literature of other peoples than in the history and literature, or social and religious matters of Jewry.

Baptism for social or occupational reasons; leaving Judaism or the communities out of political ideology or simply to save tax; mixed marriages, where the children were mostly lost to Judaism—all these factors played a drastically reducing role. Mixed marriages in fact became a serious danger.[410]

Most community members were "Three-day-Jews", attending synagogue only on the High Holidays without feeling really involved in the service. (Though, in comparison with church attendance, Jews probably did not do too badly.) The essential bond linking them with Judaism was their piety towards the parental home which sometimes extended to all Jews. The existence of antisemitism and the resistance to it was a further consolidating factor. Membership of the C.V. was thus often the only manifestation of Jewish solidarity.

In large communities with a rich tradition like Frankfurt and Hamburg, where Torah-true Judaism was more strongly represented, things looked better. Both had good Jewish High Schools, which served to strengthen the background in Jewish knowledge in these communities. In the medium and smaller sized communities Jewish life and Jewish interest was somewhat more intensive, and the personal influence of the local rabbi stronger. Here the close contact of the few, who largely belonged to the same economic and social stratum, was obviously necessary and easier to manage.

---

[410] See F. A. Theilhaber, "Der Untergang der deutschen Juden" (The Decline of the German Jews), Berlin 1911.

A conscious Judaism was, of course, preserved by the Torah-true minority and by most of the immigrants from eastern Europe. But a decline in the Jewish interest of the latter's children had already set in due to the assimilating influence of their new milieu and the diminution of Jewish instruction, leading at times to a radical politically conditioned withdrawal.

The return to a self-conscious Judaism came from *Jewish student* circles. These students stood in the forefront of antisemitic attacks and abuse from the time when the "Verein deutscher Studenten" (German Students' Union), under Treitschke's influence, began to dominate the universities in Germany and most student societies and associations had affiliated with it. The Jewish businessman in the city preferred quietly to pass over antisemitic incidents, wanting to close his eyes to them or ignore them. However, such evasiveness was not possible for the student, as he came into more direct contact with Gentile fellow-students and could not avoid awkward situations.

The first Jewish student alliance whose members were prepared to uphold Jewish honour, was formed in Breslau in 1886. Like other organizations they wore colours and fought hard duels. They wanted to be proud Jews, engaged in sports activities and kept up Jewish history in order to be physically and mentally equipped for their tasks. But they equally felt themselves good Germans and tried to show the equivalue of the Jewish alongside the non-Jewish within the German nation.

After similar associations had been set up at other universities, these formed themselves in 1896 into the *Kartell Convent deutscher Studenten juedischen Glaubens*—the "K.C." (Kartell-Convent of German Students of Jewish Faith).[411] The inner-Jewish stream within the K.C. was the C.V. ideology, to whose initiators many K.C. members belonged, remaining leading members in the authoritative bodies of the C.V.

The movement for the renewal of national Judaism spread relatively late to Germany. Yet even here it began in the pre-Herzlian era of Zionism.

First to emerge were associations of Russian-Jewish students, who brought the national Jewish aspirations of east-European Jewry with them. Through associating with these, a few German-Jewish students came to experience a living national Judaism, which for them was a hitherto unknown Jewish world.

In 1895 the first society was formed in Berlin, called *Verein juedischer Studenten*—the V.J.St.—(Jewish Students' Society). The name intentionally alluded to that of the antisemitic *Verein deutscher Studenten* (German Students' Society). The object of the V.J.St.-groups, which soon sprang up in other universities, was a living Judaism with a Zionist flavour. Just before

---

[411] See Asch and Philippson, Self-Defence at the Turn of the Century: The Emergence of the K. C., in YLBI, vol. III, 1958.

World War I these groups affiliated with other pronounced Zionist groups into the *Kartell juedischer Verbindungen*—the K.J.V.—(Federation of Jewish Societies).[412]

Whereas the K.C. had never any great influence among the large number of indifferent and assimilated Jewish students and academicians, the Zionist societies were able to exercise a strong influence on the much smaller circle of German Zionists. They contributed decisively to the formation of a specific Zionist ideology, which distinguished Zionism in Germany from that in Eastern Europe and in Anglo-Saxon countries. Zionism in Eastern Europe rested on the undisputed fact of a national peoplehood. This national character of east-European Jewry was so influential in America that even there Zionism had no need of any ideological justification. In fact, its main function there was—and still is largely—fund-raising. The situation was similar in England, where after the Balfour Declaration Zionism was in addition regarded as an English patriotic activity.[413]

In Germany, on the other hand, this Jewish national awareness could not be taken for granted. Here an *ideological foundation* was necessary for Zionist self-understanding and propaganda. Zionism was understood as 'post-assimilatory' Judaism—a form of Judaism which, having assimilated and absorbed European culture, had now found a new appreciation of Jewishness in its national character. After World War I Kurt Blumenfeld, ideologist of the Zionist student body and chairman of the "Zionist Organisation in Germany", became the educator of German Zionism and a prominent figure in German Jewry.[414]

The Wissenschaft of Judaism was likewise turning its attention to new problems, e.g. in the field of historiography (Dubnow, Baron) to demographic, statistical and sociological studies. It was also interesting itself in folklore and legend, in research into the Kabbalah (Scholem) and the relationship between religious-historical and cultural-historical themes (Baeck). The modern Jewish conception of religion had de-confessionalized Judaism, depicting it as a complexity, a phenomenon sui generis, not as a mere religious denomination. Rosenzweig, Buber and Baeck also tended in this direction.

Several Jewish poets introduced evidence of the Jewish regenerative process and its problems into German literature, while some creative artists did the same for the Jewish thematic in art.

Not all representatives of the new tendencies were Zionists or even 'national'

---

[412] See Walter Gross, The Zionist Students' Movement, in YLBI, vol. IV, 1959.

[413] It is a glorious chapter in English Zionism, that it stood solidly behind the political and military struggle of the "Yishuv" in Erez Israel even after the Mandatory Government's change in policy when Zionism was hardly considered an expression of British patriotism.

[414] Only in few community administrations did the "Jewish People's Party"—the community political group close to the Zionists—achieve any real influence, and even here only in coalition with the Conservatives and just for a limited time. Administration in most urban communities was in the hands of the Liberals for whom the Jewish Community was a purely religious body.

Jews.[415] The intellectual historical impact produced by the Zionist idea, very soon extended beyond the circle of Zionists, gradually reaching wider circles, especially the youth.

Before turning to this development, which really became fruitful only after World War I, let us briefly look at some manifestations of the two preceding decades. They were probably connected with the greater sensitivity of Jews in Germany following the upsurge of antisemitism. In relation to this new sensitivity, these manifestations had symptomatic importance. First there were the *Vereine fuer juedische Geschichte und Literatur* (Societies for Jewish history and literature), which in 1893 formed an alliance, organizing a popular Jewish lecturing body—especially for smaller communities, where prominent speakers otherwise seldom appeared—and, since 1898, publishing a Year Book.

In some of the larger communities, Jewish adult education centres were vegetating on the periphery of Jewish life. Rosenzweig's reform in the sphere of education at the Frankfurt "Lehrhaus" gave new life to this institution.

The lodges of the "B'nai B'rith Order", which sprang up in Germany from 1882 onwards,[416] arose out of the need for communal cohesion. Their programme combined social togetherness, welfare and Jewish cultural lectures. The selective principle of the organization limited membership to a small social upper stratum of businessmen and intellectuals. The lodges served as a kind of bond, which protected parts of this class from complete indifference to things Jewish. Like the literary societies, they formed a conservative, but not culturally forward looking, element.

World War I caused a caesura in the regenerative tendencies within German Judaism.

The wave of patriotism at the outbreak of war gripped the whole spectrum of German Jewry. At that time German propaganda tried to make use of the ties of world Jewry with the German language and culture by seeking to gain the sympathy both of the emigrated Jews in the USA and the Yiddish speaking masses in Eastern Europe and the USA for the German cause in the fight against Czarism.[417]

The English and French governments propagated among the Jews their intention of liberating Palestine from the Turks. The Central Powers (Ger-

---

[415] For instance, Baeck, Rosenzweig, Jacob Wassermann, Lion Feuchtwanger.

[416] The Order was founded in 1843 in the U.S.A. by German-Jewish immigrants in order to strengthen Jewish cultural and social ties.

[417] During the First World War Hermann Cohen tried to indicate the parallel destiny of Germans and Jews in three essays and to represent it as a duty of non-German Jews to see in Germany a second spiritual homeland. See Cohen, "Jued. Schriften", vol. II.

many and Austria) had less room for manoeuvre over the Palestine question, because of their alliance with Turkey. Since Herzl's death (1904), however, the headquarters of the Zionist World Organization was in Germany. This circumstance was exploited both by the Germans and the German-Zionists. A careful attempt was made to obtain concessions from Turkey for a Jewish autonomy for the post-war era. A "Pro-Palestine Committee" was set up by semi-official German and Zionist circles.[418]

Yet the other side was freer and quicker in its opportunity to act. The "Balfour-Declaration" was announced on November 2nd, 1917, according to which the British government advocated the establishment in Palestine of a national home for the Jewish people without prejudicing the civil and religious rights of non-Jews there or the rights and political status of Jews in other countries. The Balfour Declaration became part of the later mandate on Palestine entrusted to Great Britain by the League of Nations.

With this, the aim of Zionism was for the first time *internationally* recognized and the possibilities given for its further development.

Attempts by the German government to obtain a similar declaration through the Central Powers ultimately failed because of Turkish resistance. The end of the war would in any case have rendered such a declaration obsolete.[419]

In the post-war era the centre of political Zionist activity moved from Berlin to London, where *Chaim Weizmann* (1874-1952), the Russian-Jewish professor of chemistry in Manchester, now became the recognized leader of Zionism and later First President of the State of Israel.

This turning point for Erez Israel and the preceding competitive negotiations affected the Foreign Offices in London and Berlin as well as a small number of Zionist functionaries while by-passing the majority of Jews in Germany. Palestine still lay outside their interest and concern. Indeed, unless I am mistaken, the significance of the Balfour Declaration was only really appreciated by the German Zionists after the war had ended.

Already before 1914 a certain change in the demographic structure of the Jewish population had taken place in some parts of Germany. Ever since the Chmielnicki persecutions of 1648 there had always been a small *influx* of Jews from Eastern Europe into German communities. After the Russian Pogroms in the 1880's, some of the flow of refugees to the USA got stuck in Germany. At the turn of the twentieth century a larger number of Austrian Jews—mostly from Galicia—emigrated to Germany, as well as

[418] Between 1917-1918 the committee published several booklets on economic-political questions in Palestine, mainly by Jewish authors.
[419] See Egmont Zechlin, "Die deutsche Politik und die Juden im Ersten Weltkrieg" (German Politics and the Jews during World War I), Goettingen 1969, chapter 22.

Jews from Russia following the pogroms in the wake of the revolution of 1905. The largest immigration of foreign Jews into Germany occurred in the decade between 1900 and 1910,[420] when the number of immigrants rose to 37,000.[421]

Treitschke had already begun to exploit east-European immigration for antisemitic purposes. During, and especially after, World War I it was made into an issue of antisemitic propaganda. During the war Jewish workers were brought to Germany from the occupied Polish areas to work in industry. Jewish prisoners-of-war doubled this labour force. Neither of these groups, who in many cases had lost family and home through the war and post-war chaos, could be easily repatriated. After the war Jewish refugees reached Germany, fleeing from the pogroms which accompanied the Russian Civil War. At the same time the earlier usual emigration to the USA was made more difficult by the stiff new immigration laws, which particularly curtailed immigration from Eastern Europe. Antisemitic propaganda in Germany argued that the east-European Jews took work-places, food rations and housing accommodation from the demobilized soldiers, thus making them a conspicuous object of Jew hatred. This theme was later continued and intensified by national socialist propaganda. Nevertheless, economic problems were soon solved with the help of Jewish organizations.[422] The census of 1925 shows that during the fifteen years since 1910 the number of foreign Jews remaining in Germany had only risen by about 31,000,[423] i.e. considerably less than between 1900 and 1910.

More fundamental than the economic and political question of east-European Jewry was the inner Jewish problematic of the *integration of Jews from Eastern Europe* into the Jewry and Jewish communities in Germany.

Welcome, on the one hand, was the increase and the intellectual renewal acquired by German Jewry through this conscious Jewish element, which for the most part was still closely linked with tradition and religion—an element that filled the gaps caused by apostasy, mixed marriage and indifference.

These newcomers, on the other hand, were different from the resident

[420] Cf. S. Adler-Ruden. Ostjuden in Deutschland, 1880-1940 (East-European Jews in Germany, 1880-1940) Tuebingen 1959.

[421] These figures are given by Adler-Rudel on pp. 164-166. At the time of the census in 1900 out of 580,833 Jews, 41,133 were foreigners (7%). The proportion of foreign Jews in Saxony in 1900, however, comprised 45.5% (In Leipzig 60.1%); in 1910 59%, (in Leipzig 67.6%); 1925 65.2 (Leipzig 80.7%). The percentage of Jews in the entire German population dropped from over 1% in 1900 to 0.8% in 1930.

[422] With the help of the American "Joint Distribution Committee", (known simply as the "Joint") the Jewish organizations founded a workers' welfare department.

[423] As the number of Jews in Germany had declined the east-European share in the Jewish population rose to 19%. The above figure also indicates the higher birthrate of east-European Jewish families.

Jews in many respects. Resentment against Polish Jews is perhaps as old as the severance of the German branch of Ashkenazi Jewry from the Polish branch. Then in the era of emancipation, when the 'High German' language, European culture and dress had been adopted by German Jewry, one arrogantly looked down upon the "backward" Jews from Eastern Europe. (This resentment, however, was reciprocated by the Polish Jews who ridiculed the "uneducated" Western Jews, who had lost their Jewish culture and were all too ready to assimilate.)

This mutual prejudice and resentment complicated existing difficulties and tensions. The largely straitened economic circumstances of the newcomers, to whom the language, customs and business conventions of their new environment were unfamiliar, meant their having to accept social assistance from the communities. This led to a social cleavage between the economically secure German Jews and those from Eastern Europe, which easily took on a form of patronising haughtiness. But the east-European Jews not only cost the communities money; they also paid taxes to them, thus claiming a rightful say in community affairs. The communities for their part often feared being overruled by a majority of the newcomers and thus losing their character, especially those communities which were liberal in their synagogal service. In some parts of Germany, notably in Saxony, where already before World War I the majority of Jews were east-European, this was a real possibility. No legal basis existed, whereby the right to vote for community representation could be limited to German citizens. The introduction of a waiting period before attaining eligibility to vote was discussed and actually accepted in places. Such attempts, however, were generally rejected. It contradicted too strongly the Jewish sense of solidarity to make distinctions between Jew and Jew, particularly during the high-tide of antisemitism.

East-European circles usually opened their own synagogues and small prayer rooms, and often formed their own societies. They lived close to their synagogues, which they attended twice daily, and whose milieu often took on the nature of voluntary ghettos.

During the 1920's Berlin became for a while a centre of east-European Jewish intelligentsia, who opened Hebrew and Yiddish publishing houses and printed their own periodicals. The Hebrew poets Bialik, Tschernichowsky, Agnon and many other writers lived in Germany at that time. Hebrew and Yiddish theatre performances had great success. These cultural influences also affected German Jewry. This meeting with living Judaism, which many had come to know as soldiers in Poland or in east-European Jewish families and places of worship, became for many German Jews a reorientating impetus towards Judaism. In strongly assimilated circles of artists and intellectuals, Jewish folklore and folk art actually became modern. By their presence in the German communities, east-European Jews—despite many restraining barriers—contributed towards the heightening of Jewish awareness in German Jewry.

At the end of the nineteenth-century groups of "Wandervoegel" (Ramblers) had formed themselves from among high school pupils and students. This was the beginning of the *German Youth Movement*.

The "Wandervogel" developed out of school-aged hiking groups into a movement with its own distinct lifestyle. Walking was intended to bring city youth into contact with the countryside and with historical sites in town and country. The youth movement rejected the artificial social conventions of the cultured citizenry from which they came, and the patriotic and moral clichés of their parents in the heyday of Wilhelmian Germany. The youth also demonstrated their protest in their simple unconventional dress, and by abstaining from alcohol and tobacco. They sought unspoilt naturalness in folksong and folkdance. In the art of that time there developed the 'youth style', which strove for simplicity of line and ornament, and stood in contrast to the pompous hybrid style of the day. Through their experience in youth activity many went on to education and social work, in which spheres the influence of the youth movement in the 'twenties was great.

The activities of the youth movement, which comprised a mere fraction of middle-class youth, were copied after the First World War by other —mostly political or religious—youth organizations, few of which were attached to the youth movement.

When in October 1913 Germany officially celebrated the centenary of the Battle of Leipzig—the decisive victory over Napoleon—the youth movement assembled in protest on the Meissner Hill near Kassel. Aspiring towards an alliance of the various organizations, they united under a common formula. This 'Meissner Formula' announced the will of the 'Free German Youth': "to shape our life according to our own decision, in responsibility and inner truthfulness." This 'Meissner Formula' became the common basis of the entire youth movement, and also of the Jewish youth movement, which developed about the same time.

But alongside this *culturo-critical* trend, with its passion for ethical natural right, there existed in the youth movement from the beginning a *romantic* one. (Just as both trends characterized nineteenth-century liberalism.) Although the youth movement stood out against the nationalist paroles of Wilhelmian society, the detour via the romantic submergence into old German folk custom had led it to a basically racial position. The question of accepting Jews was widely discussed in magazines and organizations of the youth movement. Only a few had Jewish members, most of them refusing openly or de facto to accept them.

The influence of the German Youth Movement had also spread in part to Jewish youth. Only a few of the latter had found their way to the "Wandervogel". Particularly those young Jews who took the Meissner Formula seriously, had sufficient Jewish self-awareness not to enter into anti-Jewish alliances. The *Jewish Youth Movement* began to form alliances of its own.[424]

In 1912 the *"Blau-Weiss"* (Blue-White) *Jewish Wanderbund*, a youth organization with Zionist aims was founded.[425] It adopted the programme and lifestyle of the German Youth Movement—outings, informal house gatherings and discussions. However, it sought to emphasize Jewish national characteristics rather than German ones. This did not hinder the "Blue-Whites" from cultivating German folksongs and folkdances with the same enthusiasm as they did with their newly acquired Hebrew and Yiddish songs and dances. After World War I preparation for settling in Palestine became their main task. In 1922 the organization accepted a programme committing its members to live in Erez Israel. The realization of this commitment was to be their common aim. In this way the "Blue-Whites" broke through the narrow sphere of a 'youth culture' in which the general movement was largely stuck.

Many "Blue-Whites" attended training centres for agriculture and craftmanship. Students also chose subjects useful for developing the new country. The first Blue-Whites to go to Erez Israel founded an agricultural settlement there and "Blue-White workshops". But difficulties were very soon to arise. A serious economic crisis began in Palestine in 1925. This led to unemployment and a strong re-emigration back to Europe of middle-class Polish immigrants, who in the preceding years had largely built the new city of Tel-Aviv. This setback adversely affected those workshops assigned to urban contracts.

Added to this was the social isolation of the "Blue-Whites" in Israel. They had come with good technical know-how, but found it difficult to pick up Hebrew and to fit into the life of the Yishuv. Above all, they found little contact with the strong Jewish workers' trade union, the main pillar of economic and Hebrew-cultural development. Few serious efforts were made to overcome this isolation. The "Blue-Whites" of that time still had a parental home and a future in Germany, whither many of those disappointed returned.[426] Some of the Blue-Whites did stay on in Israel, but only as individuals. Their great effort towards realizing the Zionist dream seemed shattered.

This disappointment spread to the majority of the organization's members waiting in Germany. Its basic rule, which had called for such a complete

---

[424] See Essays in "Der Morgen", 9th Year 1933, YLBI vols. IV, VI; BLBI vol. IX; also H. Meier-Cronemeyer in: "Germania Judaica", 8th yr., 1969.

[425] Characteristic of the taboo on Zionist ideas at the time of the founding of the "Blue-White" is that the movement officially followed "no political or religious aims". The "Blue-White" was often accused of concealing its Zionist character.

[426] The fact of having a home to return to—even today—prevents many American and west-European immigrants from striking permanent roots in Israel. The subjective difficulties of acclimatizing in a new country are, however, over-rated and too many give up too soon.

change in their accustomed way of life seemed unattainable in its severity. In the autumn of 1926 the Blue-White organization was dissolved. Some of its younger members joined the Zionist Scout Movement, *Kadimah*.

In 1916 a second Jewish Youth Movement was founded, the *Deutsch-Juedische Wanderbund Kameraden*. It was, so to speak, the antithesis of the Blue-White League. If the latter was Zionist and had formulated its aims into a binding rule, the Kameraden were non-Zionist and not ideologically committed. In this respect they resembled the Free German Youth Movement. A formula was never found for the aims of the Kameraden. It was simply quite vaguely described as "The Youth Movement of people of German-Jewish kind".

Thus the organization contained very heterogeneous strands, organized more or less in factions. There was in it a "Jewish strand" which was strongly influenced by Franz Rosenzweig.[427] Belonging to it were the first leaders of the "Comrades", who during and after the First World War sought a new Jewish orientation. The German dimension in the phrase "German-Jewish" seemed to them to require no special cultivation. It was natural property, so to speak, through education, school, literature and milieu, whereas Judaism had become quite unknown to Jewish youth. All their energies would have to be dedicated towards the conscious restoration and revival of the Jewish dimension.

Alongside was a "radical socialist circle". And finally, a third group wanted to content itself with an insular youth life, which was very attractive for the younger members but offered no sense of commitment.

Despite the diverging strands and tensions, the Comrades lasted for sixteen years, dissolving only towards the end of 1932.

Of its successor organizations the *Werkleute* (workers)—coming from its Jewish trend—opted for Zionism. During the first Hitler years they founded the kibbutz *Hazorea* in Erez Israel. Strongly influenced by Buber, this kibbutz—whose founders included a number of theological students of the Berlin 'Hochschule'—merged with the Left-socialist kibbutz federation of the Hashomer-Hazair.

In connection with the "Comrades", the *Aelteren-Bund Kameraden* (Older Comrades)—organizationally independent of the Wander-League —also deserves mention. The "Ae.B." was a small order-like body,[428] which tried to approach the problems of the Jews in Germany from a Jewish and largely religiously-orientated standpoint. It rejected the confessionalization of Judaism which was widespread in non-Zionist circles. The rebuilding of

---

[427] In 1920 Rosenzweig had participated in the first assembly of the "Comrades".

[428] The "Older Comrades" had only 50-60 members, some of whom did not come from the Comrades. Among the "Ae.B" 's were many jurists, students at the Hochschule for the Wissenschaft of Judaism, medical doctors, engineers, political economists. Only a few were non-academic. During his student days the present author served as secretary of the Ae-B. for several years.

Palestine was affirmed, though they did not consider it as their own way. The Jewish communities and organizations in Germany were to be the sphere of activity of the "Ae.B.'s", who worked not as an organization but as individual members.

The "Ae.B.'s" found a certain response to their ideas among some leading lights of the C.V. But the young men, who happened to be just settling down to life in Germany, did not succeed in finding their place in Jewish community work. Already between 1930/31 the Aelteren-Bund Kameraden had fizzled out. Their ideology was overtaken by the events soon to occur in Germany.

In the 'nineties the B'nai-B'rith Lodges had set up youth clubs in many places—after the pattern of the English-American Y.M.C.A.—which were affiliated to the *Verband der juedischen Jugendvereine Deutschlands* (Federation of Jewish Youth Societies of Germany)—the "neutral association", as it was called. It was the numerically largest Jewish youth organization with a membership of some tens of thousands—though often only a nominally and strongly fluctuating membership.

After World War I the ideas of the youth movement also permeated this organization. A small wing influenced by the youth movement set up the *Jung-Juedischer Wanderbund* (Young Jewish Wander-League) in 1920. The J.J.W.B. soon opted for Zionism and somewhat later for Zionist socialism. It regarded itself as the recruiting movement in Germany for the Jewish labor movement in Erez Israel. Like the Blue-Whites its members prepared themselves by undertaking training in agriculture and in skilled labour for a life in collective settlements in Erez Israel. Of the three major organizations of the Jewish Youth Movement, it was the only one that found closer contact with east-European Jewish youth in Germany. In 1929 the first group of the J.J.W.B. in Palestine, in association with a group from Lithuania, established the Kibbutz "Givat Brenner".

The 'Young Jewish Wander League' was just more or less beginning when the Blue-Whites were coming to an end. It represented a later generation of the youth movement. Its settlement activity began at the end of the economic crisis in Palestine and during the first large wave of emigration out of Germany. Its social and emotional background was nearer to that of the Yishuv —due to its large membership of east-European origin. This enabled the J.J.W.B. to realize its basic ideas more than other youth organizations.

The net result of the Jewish Youth Movement was quite positive. If members and organizations often lived in a romantic illusory dream-world and frequently failed in time of testing, they nevertheless awakened a sense of responsibility for Judaism throughout an entire stratum of Jewry and the will to a Jewish future. Thus they set ethical and social standards which permanently influenced many in their attitude to life, and which enabled them to be somewhat better prepared ideologically, psychologically and even professionally for the coming storm than others in German Jewry.

We have gone into detail with the Jewish youth movement, since it was the last important manifestation of German Jewry's intellectual history. This most promising last generation of German Jewry could not come of age. The same holds true unfortunately for Jewish youth almost throughout continental Europe.

It should not be forgotten, moreover, that the above organizations[429] comprised only a small proportion of Jewish youth. The Blue-Whites probably had for a time 3,000 members; the Comrades and the J.J.W.B. between 1,500 and 1,600 each. The vast majority of youth, insofar as they were not Torah-true, remained indifferent to things Jewish. Apart from a small politically interested section which went over to left-wing socialism or communism, the large majority of Jewish youth were content with art and literary interests.

The German youth movement made a strong impact upon Jewish youth in *Eastern Europe*, where it met with the latter's efforts at national and social renewal. A. D. Gordon's ideas—redemption of the Jewish people through their own labour on the soil of Erez Israel—and the Zionist socialist ideals blended with a lifestyle of the Youth Movement. This blending gave rise to organizations like the "Hashomer-Hazair", "Gordonia" and others. Deeply influenced by the youth movement was the "Hehaluz" (Pioneer) organization, whose members, during their preparatory time in Europe (for immigration to Israel), lived in collective settlements or groups and remained together in kibbutzim after their *Aliyah* (the coming of the Jews to live in Erez Israel). But these kibbutzim were not egoistic dream realisations, like the few experiments at settlement undertaken by the German non-Jewish Youth Movement in the 'twenties. The kibbutz movement had to surmount the dangers and difficult conditions of the old-new country. The hard "must" of necessity compelled them never to give up. East-European Jewry—with the east-European youth movement at its head—had freed and channelled the moral and national energies into illusionless resistance—as was later demonstrated by them during the uprisings in the Warsaw and other ghettos and in Israel's struggle for independence.

In the wake of the lost 1914-1918 War, Germany experienced a high tide of *antisemitism* in unprecedented intensity. Jews were made the scapegoat for each difficulty and crisis in politics and economics: for the military collapse and the revolution against the Kaiser, for black-marketing and

---

[429] Alongside the three major organizations there was still a number of smaller groups. For example the German-Jewish Youth Fellowship, whose links with the C.V. were stronger than those of the Comrades; the already-mentioned 'Kadimah'; the Jewish Liberal Youth Association; the Orthodox 'Ezra'; the religious-Zionist 'Ze'ire Mizrahi' and others. Not every group had adopted the forms of the youth movement. The "Reichsausschuss juedischer Jugendverbaende" (Federal Committee of Jewish Youth Organizations) was the umbrella organization of the various Jewish youth associations.

inflation, for the economic crisis and mass unemployment. A number of Jews, who became prominent during the revolutionary disorders and in the early years of the Weimar Republic, were assasinated: Rosa Luxemburg, Kurt Eisner, Hugo Haase, Gustav Landauer, Walther Rathenau and others. As organizer of the war economy, Rathenau had enabled Germany to endure four years of war. As Foreign Minister he had freed the German Reich out of its political isolation, making it again into an active factor in world politics. However, his Jewishness made him a central target of hate.

The gradual yielding of the democratic parties of the center to the pressure from Left and Right, the shift of the political balance to the Right through the inclusion of the antisemitic German National People's Party in the coalition government, and above all, the rapid growth of National Socialism, were alarming occurrences. All this led to a setting aside of the ideological differences between the C.V. and the Zionists and to some cooperation. Yet no one envisaged any serious threat to the legal position of Jews, let alone their very existence.

Jews were quite accustomed to antisemitism. It had nearly always accompanied the life of the Jewish community in one form or another of Jew-hatred, always costing Jewish life and property. But it had never been able to destroy Judaism. Jew-hatred and modern racial antisemitism had never been able to prevent the close association of German Jews with German culture. Neither had it lessened indifference or apostasy.

The coming to power of the *National Socialists* struck the Jews in Germany like an unimaginable and unforeseen natural catastrophe. The first illusions that the Nazi regime would only be transitional, that the conservative coalition partners could keep it in check and within the rule of law, soon vanished before the facts. Yet many still cherished these illusions for a long time.

The immediate introduction of discriminatory provisions in 1933, which were developed into a complicated legislative system on the basis of the principle of race, not only aimed at eliminating Jews from the German state, its economy and culture. Their intention was also to label them as inferior beings, as despised and outlawed 'sub-humans' (Untermenschen) whose physical destruction was the ultimate outcome.

But at the beginning no one could have surmised such a development. One had hoped to be able to protect the core of German Jewry as a particular group—even though compulsorily separated. In the Autumn of 1933 the three major Jewish organizations—the Centralverein (C.V.), the Zionist Organization and the Territorial Federations of Communities—founded the *Reichsvertretung der deutschen Juden* (The Reich's Representation of the Jews in Germany) headed by *Leo Baeck*. Its director *Otto Hirsch*, earlier a high ranking ministerial official in Wuerttemberg was murdered in Mauthausen concentration camp in 1941.

This Reichsvertretung, set up after decades of abortive attempts and preparatory work, was the first full representative body of German Jews —the first, in fact, in their two thousand years' history.

The new organizational framework was also the outward expression of the profound emotional reaction of the German Jews. Now their homeland, the German state, its culture and society, indeed the right to live, were suddenly taken from them. Jews who had long since thrown their Jewish ties overboard, who no longer knew their religion, suddenly saw themselves confronted with their Jewishness. This being made aware of their Jewishness occurred under outward compulsion. However, it no longer permitted—as earlier—evasion through indifference or baptism. One was suddenly a Jew whether one liked it or not. This new realization gave rise to a new concern for the unknown, unnoticed or ignored fact of Judaism. Robert Weltsch, editor of the "Juedische Rundschau" in Berlin, coined at that time—on 1 April 1933, Boycott day on Jewish shops and professions—the phrase, "Wear it with pride, the yellow badge!"

In every circle of German Jewry, an interest began in Jewish religion, history and culture. This return to the roots of Jewish being gripped all sections, giving them moral stay, self-confidence and comfort in the face of the degradation in Nazi Germany.

Between 1933 and 1939 a kind of Jewish renaissance was reached in Germany to an extent never thought possible. Now these trends, which during past decades had led a small minority to a new positive Jewish stance, showed their providential importance. Out of this minority emerged the people who stood available as teachers for the new tasks.

The Reichsvertretung set up the "Co-ordinating Centre for Jewish Adult Education", led by Martin Buber and Ernst Simon. It was based on the pattern of the "Free Jewish Lehrhaus", founded by Franz Rosenzweig, and organized a whole network of courses, lectures and teaching conferences in many places.[430]

Concurrent with these provisions for adults, who wanted to find their way back to an understanding of Judaism, was the concern for youth. For Jewish pupils, who had been ousted and finally barred from the general schools, a network of schools had to be created. Teachers excluded from public school service had to be re-educated to teach in these Jewish schools, and new teachers had to be trained.

From the start of National Socialist rule, Jewish university teachers lost their posts. Soon Jewish students were not allowed to study. Some academics found new places of work at foreign universities, mostly under uncertain conditions similar to those of a post doctorate scholarship, often most inappropriate to their scholarly repute and rank. Such conditions were even offered to world renowned scholars up to Nobel Laureate standing.[431] Many

---

[430] See Ernst Simon, Aufbau im Untergang (Reconstruction in a time of Ruin), Tuebingen, 1959.
[431] See e.g. Toni Cassirer, Mein Leben mit Ernst Cassirer, New York, 1948, and Ronald W. Clark, Einstein, The Life and Times, New York and Cleveland, 1971.

students had to abandon their studies as they could not afford to continue them abroad.[432]

The "Juedischer Kulturbund" (Jewish Cultural Society)[433] functioned more on the fringe of Jewish educational and cultural activity. It met the musical and literary inclinations of German Jewry by means of theatrical productions and concerts, providing at the same time employment for many Jewish actors and musicians expelled from theatres and concert-halls. The cultural society presented works by Jewish authors or with a Jewish theme, being finally restricted to such works by the authorities.

The exclusion of Jews from the German state and nation became increasingly sharper in its effectiveness. It started by dismissing Jewish officials, college teachers, editors, leading to the compulsory Aryanisation (taking over by Aryans) of Jewish businesses and firms, to the Nuremburg Racial Laws, to confinement of Jewish physicians and lawyers to Jewish clients and to dispossessing them of their professional titles. It subsequently led to the wearing of the Star of David, to the compulsory resettlement of Jews in specified places and housing areas, finally to their deportations to occupied Poland and from there or directly from Germany to the extermination camps. During the 'Crystal Night'—night of "broken glass" as the Nazis euphemistically called it—in 1938, synagogues throughout the entire land were nearly all destroyed. In 1939 the Reichsvertretung and the Jewish communities were dissolved and replaced by the Organization of Jews in Germany (Reichsvereinigung der Juden in Deutschland), established by Nazi law and strictly controlled by the Gestapo (Nazi secret police). The deportations that began in 1941—in the annexed and occupied territories already towards the end of 1939—were carried through in large measure in 1942 and 1943, and the "final solution" almost completed within the next two years. Remnants of Jews in concentration camps were saved on the brink of extermination or starvation in 1945 by the allied armies. Apart from Jews in so-called "privileged mixed-marriages", only a handful of Jews survived in Germany. The very few who, in constant fear, succeeded in surviving underground, did so with the help of non-Jewish acquaintances, who took care of them at the risk of their own lives.[434]

The problem of emigration confronted probably every Jew in Germany from 1933 on. Even those so deeply rooted in their homeland and place of birth—largely people in advanced years—that they would not think of emigrating themselves despite their dreadful situation, tried to send their

---

[432] Only a very small number of lecturers and students were admitted to the Berlin Lehranstalt for the Wissenschaft of Judaism—as the "Hochschule" was again renamed—which had now incorporated a department for humanities. Leo Baeck still continued teaching here as the only remaining lecturer with a handful of students till 1942. The Breslau Seminary and the Berlin Orthodox Rabbinical Seminary had already been closed by the Nazis in 1938.

[433] Cf. Herbert Freeden 'Juedisches Theater in Nazi Deutschland', Tuebingen, 1964.

[434] See H. D. Leuner, When Compassion was a Crime (London, 1966).

children and younger family members abroad. Many, especially politically prominent Jews, already had to flee the threat of arrest from the start of the new regime. Following the wave of arrests after the 'Crystal Night', leading personalities—notably rabbis—were released from concentration camps on condition that they leave Germany immediately. But even for those still not living under such direct compulsion, it became psychologically more and more difficult to live under the pressure of increasing humiliation. Added to this was the growing impossibility of earning one's living and the rapid disappearance of savings, particularly after the expropriations and the compulsory contribution of one billion marks levied upon Jews following the Crystal Night.

Zionism, which had hitherto appealed only to a minority of German Jews, took on an especial attraction under these circumstances. The events in Germany had clearly justified it. From all that had happened, the deeply injured Jewish pride concluded that only their own solution in the old Jewish homeland remained desirable. If one had to leave the present home-land then one would not wish to go to just any country where Jews could perhaps experience a similar fate as in Germany and again be considered foreign. One wanted to bring Jewish wandering to an end, at least as it affected one's family. For this reason the majority aspired to Ereẓ Israel, where they could live as Jews among Jews. At any rate children and young people were to be rescued and sent there first. The "Youth Aliyah" set up at that time brought groups of children and young people to Ereẓ Israel, where they were reared and educated in Kibbutzim and youth villages, later to contribute significantly to the State of Israel in nearly every field.

Only some parents were able to follow them. Until 1935 Palestine was the main immigrant country of German Jews.[435] However, in the wake of the Ethiopian-Italian War an economic crisis set in, involving serious unemployment in Palestine. Subsequently there was the Arab unrest of 1936-1939 which was in part supported by Germans. The result was a drastic curb on immigration by the British Mandatory government which finally made legal Jewish immigration almost impossible and led to illegal immigration, even before World War II and to the resistance activities of Palestine Jewry against British policy.

Emigration to other countries became increasingly more difficult. The first hurried emigration was into the neighbouring countries of Germany. These often served as transit stations until permission to emigrate overseas was obtained. With the successive occupation of each country by the German armies, Jewish refugees and resident Jews alike fell into the grip of the German extermination machine. All countries impeded the immigration of

[435] Cf. Werner Rosenstock, Exodus 1933-1939, A survey of Jewish Emigration from Germany, YLBI, vol. I.

Jewish refugees by limiting intake and through bureaucratic formalism. The attempt by an international refugee conference in Evian in 1938 to solve the refugee problem on an international basis failed. In the end the international city of Shanghai was the only place to which Jews could still emigrate freely. Refugee ships sailed the seas without finding harbour only to be eventually returned to the hands of the Germans and death.

A serious obstruction to emigration was the draconian German regulations which gradually made any transfer of property impossible. No country, however, agreed to accept poor possessionless Jews. Nevertheless, of the 500,000 German Jews, more than half were able to leave Germany between 1933 and 1939. The United States took over 100,000 of them; Erez Israel somewhat less than this. Great Britain stood in third place, taking over 50,000. The remainder dispersed among many countries.

Of the brief upsurge in Jewish learning between 1933 and 1939 not much remained. Time was too short to communicate real knowledge, and the result was only a flare—a euphoria—before the end.

The awakened Jewish interest was very soon pushed aside by the occupational, linguistic and other difficulties of integrating into the new countries. The newcomers grouped up everywhere into immigrant associations, founding their own synagogues according to the accustomed liberal or orthodox order of service in Germany, and with a sermon in German. But how much of their Jewish heritage they conveyed to their children in the lands of their adoption, will probably have to remain inconclusive. This was easier in Erez Israel insofar as children there were educated in Israeli schools and thereby found deep Jewish intellectual and spiritual roots.

Since World War II some smaller Jewish communities have grown up in Germany. They comprise Jews, who survived in the underground or through having a non-Jewish marriage partner; of people who came out of concentration and death camps or from the camps for 'displaced persons' and who at first lingered on in Germany without intending to stay. Then there were those returning who could not accustom themselves to the language, climate or economy of the countries to which they had emigrated. There is also a certain number of newcomers. The statistics of these communities show a downward trend and a high proportion of old people. Great efforts are nonetheless being made to create out of these very diverging elements a new community life and consciousness. Whether a new German Jewry will arise from these beginnings must remain an open question. That depends not least on how the German environment will accept this new development.

In German non-Jewish circles of recent years an active and previously unknown interest in Jewish history, Jewish religion and in Israel has revealed itself. The loss to German culture brought about by the destruction of German Jewry is being constantly emphasized. At several universities chairs and lectureships in Judaic studies have been created and institutes estab-

lished. The Free and Hanseatic City of Hamburg has founded its own Institute for the History of the German Jews. Many state and national archives
have published works on or memorials of the history of Jews in their local
areas. All these—for the most part by non-Jewish Judaic scholars and historians—fulfil the important task of researching the history and seeking to
understand the history and customs of a people, who have lived with and
alongside them for more than a thousand years. Yet concern with the
German-Jewish past should not obscure the reality of a Jewish present or
the fact that Jewish history continues.

From the great tradition of German Judaism many problems and impulses
also affect the new centres of Jewish life. In previous chapters we have repeatedly drawn attention to this.

But to this inheritance two events are now added which have decisively
changed the self-understanding of modern Jewry: the eradication of one
third of world Jewry and the establishment of the State of Israel. The first
event—of which barely a family of Ashkenazi Jewry was left untouched—has
shaken blind faith in assimilation and in progress even for many Jewish
intellectuals, whose Jewish awareness had almost ceased. The rise of the
Jewish state signifies not only refuge and a new chance in life for a large
section of the Jewish people. It also means a source of new emotional and
spiritual strength for Jews in the diaspora.

During the past thirty-five years a new chapter of Jewish history has
begun, to which that depicted in this book is perhaps a prelude.

# Bibliography I

*Further literature is given in the notes.*

Abbreviations

MGWJ = Monatsschrift für Geschichte und Wissenschaft des Judentums Breslau, Frankfurt, 83 volumes 1851-1939

JQR   = Jewish Quarterly Review, London, 1889-1909, Philadelphia (since 1910)

ZGJD = Zeitschrift für Geschichte der Juden in Deutschland, old series, 5 volumes, Berlin, 1887-1892; new series, 6 volumes, Berlin, 1929-1937

JJLG  = Jahrbuch der Jüdisch-Literarischen Gesellschaft, 22 volumes, Frankfurt, 1903-1932

HUCA = Hebrew Union College Annual, Cincinnati (since 1924)

LBI   = Leo Baeck Institute, London, Jerusalem, New York

BLBI  = Bulletin, Leo Baeck Institute, Tel-Aviv, (since 1957)

YLBI  = Year Book, Leo Baeck Institute, London, (since 1956)

ZRGG = Zeitschrift für Religions- und Geistesgeschichte, Köln, (since 1949)

JJS   = Journal of Jewish Studies, London

JSS   = Jewish Social Studies, New York

JE    = Jewish Encyclopedia, 12 volumes, New York 1901-1906, reprint New York 1963

EJ    = Encyclopaedia Judaica, Berlin, 10 volumes (A-Lyra) 1928-1934 (in German)

EJ (e) = Encyclopaedia Judaica, Jerusalem 1972, 16 volumes (in English)

*Adler-Rudel, S.*, Ostjuden in Deutschland 1880-1940, Tübingen 1959.

*Agus, Irving A.*, Urban Civilisation in Pre-Crusade Europe. A Study of Organised Town-Life in North-Western Europe during the Tenth and Eleventh Centuries, based on the Responsa-Literature. 2 Volumes, New York, 1965.

*Altmann, Adolf*, Das früheste Vorkommen der Juden in Deutschland. Juden im römischen Trier. Trier 1932.

*Altmann, Alexander*, Moses Mendelssohn, A Bibliographical Study, Philadelphia 1973.

— (Editor) Studies in 19th Century Jewish Intellectual History, Cambridge, Mass., 1964.

— The New Style of Preaching in 19th Century German Jewry. In: Altmann Studies (see above).

— Zur Frühgeschichte der jüdischen Predigt in Deutschland. Leopold Zunz als Prediger. In: YLBI volume VI, 1961.

*Aronius, Julius*, Regesten zur Geschichte der Juden im fränkischen und deutschen Reiche bis 1273, Berlin 1902.

*Baron, Salo W.*, A Social and Religious History of the Jews,. (until now 16 Volumes). New York and London (1937), 1953-1973.

— Die Judenfrage auf dem Wiener Kongreß. Wien and Berlin 1920.

— History and Jewish Historians. Philadelphia 1964.

— The Jewish Community its History and Structure to the American Revolution, 3 volumes. Philadelphia 1942-1948.

*Bergmann, Hugo Sh.*, Faith and Reason, New York 1961.

— The Philosophy of Solomon Maimon, Jerusalem 1967.

*Berliner, Abraham*, Religionsgespräch gehalten am kurfürstlichen Hofe zu Hannover 1704. A Hebrew Manuscript, edited and translated in German, Berlin 1914.

— Aus dem Leben der deutschen Juden im Mittelalter, zugleich als Beitrag für deutsche Culturgeschichte. Nach gedruckten und ungedruckten Quellen, Berlin 1900.

*Böhm, Adolf*, Die Zionistische Bewegung. Berlin 1920.

*Boelich, Walter*, Der Berliner Antisemitismusstreit. Frankfurt 1965.

*Dubnow, Simon*, Die jüdische Geschichte, ein geschichtsphilosophischer Versuch. German translation by Jos. Friedländer, 2nd edition, Frankfurt 1921.

— Weltgeschichte des Jüdischen Volkes. German translation based on the 5th Russian edition by A. Steinberg, 10 volumes, Berlin 1925-1929.

— Geschichte des Chassidismus. German translation by A. Steinberg, 2 volumes, Berlin 1931.

*Duckesz, Eduard*, Zur Biographie des Chacham Isaak Bernays. In: JJLG volume 5, 1907.

*Elbogen, Ismar*, Geschichte der Juden in Deutschland, Berlin 1935.

— *Elbogen-Sterling, Eleonora*, Geschichte der Juden in Deutschland (second edition of the above mentioned work, brought up to date to 1945 and annotated by Eleonora Sterling, Frankfurt 1966).

— Ein Jahrhundert Wissenschaft des Judentums. In: Festschrift zum 50-Jährigen Bestehen der Hochschule für die Wissenschaft des Judentums, Berlin 1922.

— Zu S. Dubnows Geschichtswerk. In: MGWJ 70, 1926.

A Century of Jewish Life, translated by Moses Hadas, Philadelphia 1944.

— Der jüdische Gottesdienst in seiner geschichtlichen Entwicklung. 2nd edition. Frankfurt 1924.

*Eliav, Mordechai*, Haḥinukh Hayehudi be-Germaniah bime Hahaskalah we Ha'Emanẓipaẓiah (Jewish Education in Germany in the Age of Enlightenment and Emancipation). Jerusalem 1961.

*Eschelbacher, Josef*, Die Anfänge allgemeiner Bildung unter den deutschen Juden vor Mendelssohn. In: Beiträge zur Geschichte der deutschen Juden, Festschrift zum 70. Geburtstag Martin Philippsons. Leipzig 1916.

— Das Judentum und das Wesen des Christentums, Vergleichende Studien. 2nd edition Berlin 1928.

*Fackenheim, Emil L.*, Samuel Hirsch and Hegel. In: Altmann, Studies (see above).

*Fischer, Horst*, Judentum, Staat und Heer in Preußen im frühen 19. Jahrhundert. Tübingen 1968.

*Freund, Ismar*, Die Emanzipation der Juden in Preußen. 2 volumes, Berlin 1912.

— Die Rechtsstellung der Synagogengemeinde in Preußen und die Reichsverfassung. Berlin 1926.

*Friedlander, Albert A.*, Leo Baeck, Teacher of Theresienstadt, New York 1968.

*Gebhardt, Carl*, B. de Spinoza, Theologisch-politischer Traktat, German translation and introduction by Carl Gebhardt, 5th edition, Hamburg 1955.

*Germania Judaica*, After the death of M. Brann edited by I. Elbogen, A. Freimann and H. Tykocinski. Volume 1 from earliest times till 1238, Tübingen (1934) 1963; volume 2 (in two volumes) from 1238 to the mid 14th century, edited by Zvi Avneri, Tübingen 1968.

*Ginsburg, Sigmar*, Die zweite Generation der Juden nach M. Mendelssohn. In: BLBI, 1957/58.

*Glanz, Rudolf*, Geschichte des Niederen Jüdischen Volkes in Deutschland. Eine Studie über historisches Gaunertum, Bettelwesen und Vagantentum. New York 1968.

*Glatzer, Nahum N.*, Leopold Zunz, Jude, Deutscher, Europäer. Tübingen 1964.

— Leopold and Adelheid Zunz. An Account in Letters. London 1958.

— Untersuchungen zur Geschichtslehre der Tannaiten. Berlin 1933.

*Graetz, Heinrich*, Geschichte der Juden von der ältesten Zeit bis auf die Gegenwart. 11 volumes. Berlin, Breslau, Leipzig 1853-1875.

— Die Konstruktion der jüdischen Geschichte, edited by Ludwig Feuchtwanger, Berlin 1936.

*Graupe, Heinz M.*, Die Stellung der Religion im systematischen Denken der Marburger Schule (Doctoral thesis and book). Berlin 1930.

— Steinheim und Kant. In: YLBI, volume 5, 1960.
— Kant und das Judentum. In: ZRGG, volume 13, 1961.
— Die philosophischen Motive der Theologie S. L. Steinheims. In: Salomon Ludwig Steinheim zum Gedenken. Ein Sammelband edited by H. J. Schoeps, Leiden 1966.
— Mordechai Gumpel Levison. In: BLBI, volume 5, 1962.
— Jewish Testaments from Altona and Hamburg (18th Century). In: Michael II, Tel-Aviv 1973, (in Hebrew).
— Die Statuten der Drei Gemeinden Altona, Hamburg, Wandsbek, Quellen zur jüdischen Gemeindeorganisation im 17. und 18. Jahrhundert. edited, introduced and translated into German, 2 vols., Hamburg 1973.
— Juden und Judentum im Zeitalter des Reimarus. In: Hermann Samuel Reimarus. Ein "bekannter Unbekannter" in Hamburg, edited by "Jungius Gesellschaft der Wissenschaften", Hamburg, Göttingen 1973)

Guttman, Julius, Die Philosophie des Judentusm. München 1933.
— Philosophies of Judaism. London 1964 (enlarged translation of the above).
— Kant und das Judentum. Leipzig 1908.

Guttmann, Michael, Das Judentum und seine Umwelt. Berlin 1927.

Hamburger, Ernst, Juden im öffentlichen Leben Deutschlands. Tübingen 1968.

Heppner, A. u. Herzberg, I., Aus Vergangenheit und Gegenwart der Juden in den Posener Landen. 2 parts, Koschmin 1901-1929.

Hertzberg, Arthur, The French Enlightenment and the Jews. New York, Philadelphia 1968.

Jacobs, Noah J., Salomon Maimon's Relation to Judaism. In: YLBI volume 8, 1963.

Jost, Marcus, Geschichte des Judentums und seiner Sekten. Volume 3, Leipzig 1859.

Katz, Jakob, Die Entstehung der Judenassimiliation in Deutschland und deren Ideologie (Doctoral thesis). Frankfurt 1935, (reprinted in the following volume).
— Emancipation and Assimilation, Farnborough, Hants, England, 1972.
— Tradition and Crisis. Jewish Society at the End of the Middle Ages. New York 1961.
— Exclusiveness and Tolerance. Studies in Jewish-Gentile Relations in Medieval and Modern Times. Oxford 1961.
— Jews and Freemasons in Europe, 1723-1939. Cambridge, Mass. 1970.
— Die Anfänge der Judenemanzipation. In: BLBI XIII, 1974.

Kayserling, Meir, Moses Mendelssohn. Sein Leben und Wirken. 2nd edition, Leipzig 1888.

Kaznelson, Siegmund (Editor) Juden im deutschen Kulturbereich. Ein Sammelwerk, 3rd edition, Berlin 1962.

*Kellenbenz, Hermann*, Sephardim an der unteren Elbe, ihre wirtschaftliche Bedeutung vom Ende des 16. bis zum Beginn des 18. Jahrhunderts. [Vierteljahresschr. für Sozial- und Wirtschaftsgeschichte, volume 40], Wiesbaden 1958.

*Kisch, Guido*, Forschungen zur Rechts- und Sozialgeschichte der Juden in Deutschland. Zürich 1955.

— The Jews in Medieval Germany. A Study of their Legal and Social Status. Chicago 1948.

— Das Breslauer Seminar. Jüdisch-Theologisches Seminar (Fränkelscher Stiftung) 1854-1938, Tübingen 1963.

— *und Kurt Roepke*, Schriften zur Geschichte der Juden. Eine Bibliographie der in Deutschland und in der Schweiz 1922-1955 erschienenen Dissertationen. Tübingen 1959.

*Klatzkin, Jakob*, Hermann Cohen, 2nd edition, Berlin 1922.

*Klausner, Josef*, Geschichte der neuhebräischen Literatur. German edition by Hans Kohn, Berlin 1921.

*Klemperer, Gutmann*, Ḥaye Yehonatan, Rabbi Jonathan Eibenschütz. Eine biographische Skizze. Prag 1858.

*Kober, Ad.*, Grundbuch des Kölner Judenviertels. Bonn 1920.

*König, Balthasar*, Annalen der Juden in den preußischen Staaten (1790). Berlin 1912 (reprint).

*Landau, Juda L.*, Short Lectures on Modern Hebrew Literature. 2nd Edition, London 1938.

— Nachman Krochmal, Ein Hegelianer. Berlin 1904.

*Lazarus, Lothar*, Die Organisation der preußischen Synagogengemeinden. (Doctoral thesis) Göttingen 1933.

*Lewin, Louis*, Aus dem jüdischen Kulturkampf. In: JJLG XII, 1938

— Die jüdischen Studenten an der Universität Frankfurt a.d. Oder. In JJLG XIV, XV, XVI, 1921, 1923, 1924.

— Geschichte der Juden in Lissa. Pinne 1904

*Lewkowitz, Albert*, Das Judentum und die geistigen Strömungen des 19. Jahrhunderts. Breslau 1935.

*Liebeschütz, Hans*, Das Judentum im deutschen Geschichtsbild von Hegel bis Max Weber. Tübingen 1967.

— Von Georg Simmel zu Franz Rosenzweig. Tübingen 1970.

— Hermann Cohen and his Historical Background. In: YLBI XIII, 1968.

— Between Past and Future. Leo Baecks Historical Position. In: YLBI XI, 1966.

*Littmann, Ellen*, Studien zur Wiederaufnahme der Juden nach dem Schwarzen Tode. (Doctoral thesis) Köln 1928.

— Saul Ascher, First Theorist of Progressive Judaism. YLBI V, 1960.

— David Friedlaenders Sendschreiben an den Probst Teller und sein Echo. In ZGJD, VI, 1936.

*Meisl, Josef*, Haskalah, Geschichte der Aufklärungsbewegung unter den Juden in Rußland. Berlin 1919.

— Protokollbuch der Jüdischen Gemeinde Berlin (1723-1854). Jerusalem 1962 (Hebrew and German).

*Meyer, Michael A.*, The Origins of the Modern Jew. Jewish Identity and European Culture in Germany 1749-1824. Detroit 1967.

*Michael*, On the History of the Jews in the Diaspora, Collection of Essays, volume II. Edited by S. A. Simonsohn and Jacob Toury, Tel-Aviv 1973 (Hebrew and German).

*Monumenta Judaica*, 2000 Jahre Geschichte und Kultur der Juden am Rhein. Edited by K. Schilling, Köln 1963.

*Mosse, Werner E. und Paucker A.* (Editors) Deutsches Judentum in Krieg und Revolution, 1916-1923. Tübingen 1971.

— Entscheidungsjahr 1932. Zur Judenfrage in der Endphase der Weimarer Republik. 2nd Edition. Tübingen 1966.

*Neubauer, A. und Stern, M.*, Hebräische Berichte über die Judenverfolgungen während der Kreuzzüge. Berlin 1892. Reprint Jerusalem 1971.

*Pelli, Moshe*, Mordechai Gumpel Schnaber, The First Religious Reform Theoretician of the Hebrew Haskalah in Germany. In: JQR LXIV, 1974.

*Perelmuter, Moshe A.*, R. Yehonatan Eybeschütz we yaḥaso el Ha'Shabta'ut (Rabbi Jonathan Eybeschütz and his Attitude towards Sabbatianism). Tel-Aviv 1947.

*Petuchowski, Jakob J.*, The Theology of Haham David Nieto. New York 1954.

— Prayerbook Reform in Europe. The Liturgy of Liberal and Reform Judaism. New York 1968.

— Manuals and Catechismus of the Jewish Religion in the Early Period of Emancipation. In: Altmann, Studies.

*Priebatch, Felix*, Die Judenpolitik des fürstlichen Absolutismus im 17. und 18. Jahrhundert. In: Festschrift für Dietrich Schäfer zum 70. Geburtstag. Jena 1915.

*Rawidowicz, Simon*, Kitve R. Naḥman Krochmal (Writings of R. Naḥman Krochmal) 2nd edition; London-Waltham, Mass. 1961.

— War Nachman Krochmal Hegelianer? In: HUCA volume V, 1928.

*Reissner, Hans G.*, Rebellious Dilemma. The Case Histories of Eduard Gans and some of his Partisans. In: YLBI II, 1957.

*Richarz, Monika*, Der Eintritt der Juden in die akademischen Berufe. Jüdische Studenten und Akademiker in Deutschland 1678-1848. Tübingen 1974.

*Rosenzweig, Franz*, Einleitung zu Hermann Cohen. Jüdische Schriften. Edited by Bruno Strauß. Berlin 1924.

*Rotenstreich, Nathan*, Hamaḥashavah ha-Yehudit be-et haḥadashah (Jewish Thought in Modern Times). 2 Volumes Tel-Aviv 1945, 1950.

— Jewish Philosophy in Modern Times. New York 1968.

— The Recurring Pattern. London 1963.

*Roth, Cecil*, History of the Marranos (1934). Cleveland, Meridian Books 1960.
— History of the Jews in England. 3rd Edition, Oxford 1964.
— A Short History of the Jewish People. London 1959, New York 1970.
*Salfeld, Siegmund*, Das Martyrologium des Nürnberger Memorbuches, edited by Siegmund Salfeld. Berlin 1898.
*Schatzker, Chaim*, The Jewish Youth Movement in Germany. Jerusalem 1969.
*Schiffmann, Sara*, Heinrich IV und die Bischöfe in ihrem Verhalten zu den deutschen Juden zur Zeit des ersten Kreuzzuges. (Doctoral thesis) Berlin 1931.
*Schnee, Heinrich*, Die Hoffinanz und der moderne Staat. Geschichte und System der Hoffaktoren an deutschen Fürstenhöfen im Zeitalter des Absolutismus. 6 Volumes, Berlin 1953-1967.
*Schoeps, Hans J.*, Geschichte der jüdischen Religionsphilosophie i.d. Neuzeit. Berlin 1935.
— Jüdischer Glaube in dieser Zeit, Prolegomena zur Grundlegung einer systematischen Theologie des Judentums. Berlin 1930.
— Philosemitismus im Barock. Religions- und geistesgeschichtliche Untersuchungen. Tübingen 1952.
— Gumpertz Levison. Leben und Werk eines gelehrten Abenteurers des 18. Jahrhunderts. In: ZRGG IV, 1952.
— Salomon Ludwig Steinheim zum Gedenken. Ein Sammelband edited by Hans-Joachim Schoeps in connection with Heinz Moshe Graupe and Gerd-Hesse Goemann, Leiden 1966.
*Scholem, Gerschom*, Major Trends in Jewish Mysticism. 3rd edition, New York 1954.
— Sabatai Ṣevi, The Mystical Messiah, 1626-1676. London 1973.
— Wider den Mythos vom deutsch-jüdischen Gespräch. In: BLBI 7, 1964.
— Wissenschaft vom Judentum einst und jetzt. In: BLBI 3, 1960.
*Seligmann, Cäsar*, Geschichte der jüdischen Reformbewegung. Frankfurt 1922.
*Shohet, Azriel*, Im Ḥilufe Tekufot, Reshit Hahaskalah be-Yahadut German-iah, (Beginnings of the Haskalah among German Jewry). (Hebrew) Jerusalem 1960.
*Silberner, Edmund*, Moses Hess. Geschichte seines Lebens. London 1966.
— Moses Hess—Briefwechsel. Den Haag 1959.
— Sazialisten zur Judenfrage. Berlin 1962.
*Simon, Ernst*, Aufbau im Untergang. Tübingen 1959.
— Brücken. Gesammelte Aufsätze. Heidelberg 1965.
*Stein, Siegfried*, Liebliche Tefilloh—A Judeo-German Prayer-book printed in 1709. In: YLBI 15, 1970.
*Stern, Moritz*, Beiträge zur Geschichte der Jüdischen Gemeinde zu Berlin. Booklet 3: Die Anfänge von Hirschel Löbels Rabbinat, Berlin 1931. Booklet 5: Jugendunterricht in der Berliner Jüdischen Gemeinde

während des 18. Jahrhunderts, Berlin 1934. Booklet 6: David Friedländers Schrift 'Über die durch die neue Organisation der Judenschaften in den preußischen Staaten notwendig gewordenen Umbildungen etc.' 1812. Reprint with Appendix Berlin 1934.

*Stern, Selma*, Josel von Rosheim, Befehlshaber der Judenschaft im heiligen römischen Reich deutscher Nation. Stuttgart 1959.

— Der preußische Staat und die Juden. 7 volumes. Tübingen 1962-1971.

— The Court Jew. A Contribution to the History of the Period of Absolutism in Central Europe. Philadelphia, 1950.

— Jud Sueß, Ein Beitrag zur deutschen und jüdischen Geschichte. Berlin 1929, München 1973.

*Stobbe, Otto*, Die Juden in Deutschland während des Mittelalters in politischer, sozialer und rechtlicher Beziehung. (1866) 3rd edition, Berlin 1923.

*Strack, Hermann*, Einleitung in Talmud und Midrasch. Reprint of 5th edition, München 1961.

— Das Blut im Glauben und Aberglauben der Menschheit. München 1900.

*Straus, Raphael*, Die Juden in Wirtschaft und Gesellschaft, Untersuchungen zur Geschichte einer Minorität. Frankfurt 1964.

*Terlinden, R. F.*, Grundsätze des Judenrechts nach den Gesetzen für die preußischen Staaten. Halle 1804.

*Theilhaber, Felix A.*, Der Untergang der deutschen Juden. Eine volkswirtschaftliche Studie. München 1911.

*Toury, Jacob*, Die politischen Orientierungen der Juden in Deutschland von Jena bis Weimar. Tübingen 1966.

— Prolegomena to the Entrance of Jews into German Citizenry (Hebrew), Tel-Aviv 1971.

— Der Eintritt der Juden ins deutsche Bürgertum. Eine Dokumentation. Tel-Aviv 1972.

— Deutsche Juden im Vormärz. In: BLBI VIII, 1965.

*Wagenaar, H. A.*, Toldot Ya'abez. Jacob Hirschels (Emdens) Leben und Schriften (Hebrew). Amsterdam 1868.

*Weinryb, Bernard D.*, The Jews of Poland. A Social and Economic History of the Jewish Community in Poland from 1100 to 1800. Philadelphia, 1976.

*Wiener, Max*, Jüdische Religion im Zeitalter der Emanzipation. Berlin 1933.

*Wilhelm, Kurt*, (Editor) Wissenschaft des Judentums im deutschen Sprachbereich. Ein Querschnitt, 2 volumes. Tübingen 1967.

*Zechlin, Egmont*, Die deutsche Politik und die Juden im Ersten Weltkrieg. Göttingen 1969.

# Bibliography II

A select bibliography of the main thinkers and authors treated in this book whose works are available in English translation.

Aḥad Ha-am, Selected Essays of, translated from the Hebrew and introduced by Leon Simon. Atheneum, New York 1970.

Leo Baeck, The Essence of Judaism, translated by Victor Grubenwieser and Leonard Pearl. Macmillan, London 1936 and Schocken, New York 1961.

— Judaism and Christianity, translated and introduced by Walter Kaufmann. (This contains 'The Faith of Paul' and three of the essays in: Aus drei Jahrtausenden), Harper & Row, London and Harper Torchbooks, New York 1966.

— The Pharisees and other Essays (contains four of the essays in: Aus drei Jahrtausenden), translated and introduced by Krister Stendahl, Schocken, New York 1966.

— This People Israel: the Meaning of Jewish Existence, translated with introductory essay by Albert A. Friedlander. W. H. Allen, London and Jewish Pub. Soc., Philadelphia, 1965. (This comprises the two separately published German volumes Dieses Volk, Frankfurt 1955, 1957).

— Theology and History, translated by Michael M. Mayer, Judaism, Summer 1964.

— Leo Baeck. Teacher of Theresienstadt, by Albert A. Friedlander, Holt, Rinehart & Winston, New York 1968, and Routledge & Kegan Paul, London 1973.

Martin Buber, Tales of the Hasidim, 2 volumes, translated by Olga Marx, Thames & Hudson, London 1956, and Schocken, New York 1961.

— Hasidism and Modern Man, edited and translated by Maurice Friedman, Horizon, New York 1958.

— The Origin and Meaning of Hasidism, translated by M. Friedman, Horizon, New York 1960.

— The Legend of the Baal Shem, translated by M. Friedman, Schocken, New York 1969.
— I and Thou, translated by Ronald Gregor Smith, T. & T. Clark, Edinburgh and Scribner's, New York 1960. See also new translation (same publishers) by Walter Kaufmann, 1970.
— Two Types of Faith, translated by N. P. Goldhawk, Routledge & Kegan Paul, London and Harper, New York 1961.
— On Judaism (The Early Addresses of Reden ueber das Judentum) translated by Eva Jospe, Schocken, New York 1967.
— Martin Buber, in Library of Living Philosophers, edited by Paul A. Schilpp and Maurice Friedman, Evanston, Illinois. (Page-quoting according to the German edition, Stuttgart 1963).

Hermann Cohen, The Religion of Reason, translated by Simon Kaplan, Ungar Pub. Co., New York 1972.
— Reason & Hope (Selections from the Jewish Writings of Hermann Cohen) translated and introduced by Eva Jospe, Norton & Co., New York 1971, subsequently by Viking Press, New York.

Simon Dubnow, Nationalism and History. Essays on Old and New Judaism, edited and introduced by Koppel S. Pinson, Atheneum, New York 1970.
— Jewish History, translated by Henrietta Szold, Philadelphia, (1903) 1927, Books for Libraries Press, Freeport, New York 1972.
— World History of the Jewish People, translated by M. Spiegel, New York 1967 ff.

Glückel of Hameln 1696-1724, The Life of, translated by Bath-Zion Abrahams, East and West Library, London 1962.

Heinrich Graetz, History of the Jews, translated by Bella Loewy, 6 volumes, Jewish Pub. Soc., Philadelphia.

Judah Halevi, The Kuzari, translated by H. Hirschfeld. London (1906), 1931, reprinted Schocken, New York 1964.
— dto. abridged translation by I. Heinemann (1947) Oxford and Schocken, New York 1961.

Theodor Herzl, The Jewish State, translated by Sylvie D'Avigdor, 6th edition, London 1972. Also newly translated by Harry Zohn, Herzl Press, New York 1970.
— Old-New Land, translated with revised notes by Lotta Levenson with new preface by E. Newman, Bloch Pub. Co. and Herzl Press, New York 1960. Also translated by Paula Arnold with illustrations, Haifa Pub. Co., Israel 1960.
— The Complete Diaries of Theodor Herzl, translated by Harry Zohn, Herzl Press, New York 1960 and London.
— Theodor Herzl, by Alex Bein, Harper & Row, London and Harper Torchbooks, New York 1966.

Moses Hess, Rome and Jerusalem, translated by M. Waxman. New York
  1943.
— The Life and Opinions of Moses Hess, by Sir Isaiah Berlin, Heffer,
  Cambridge, England 1959.
Samson Raphael Hirsch, The Nineteen Letters on Judaism, translated by
  Rabbi Bernard Drachmann with preface by Jacob Breuer, Philipp
  Feldheim, New York 1960. Also in Torah Classics Library, New York.
— Horeb—Essays on Israel's Duties in the Diaspora, translated and edited
  by I. Grunfeld, London 1962.
Immanuel Kant, Critique of Pure Reason, translated by Norman Kemp
  Smith, Macmillan, London and New York 1933.
— Religion within the Limits of Reason alone, translated and introduced
  by Theodore M. Greene and Hoyt H. Hudson, with a new essay on
  The Ethical Significance of Kant's Religion by John R. Silber, Harper
  Torchbooks, New York 1960.
— Critique of Practical Reason, translated by L. W. Beck, Library of Lib-
  eral Arts, Indianapolis 1956.
— Critique of Judgement, translated by Meredith, Oxford, Clarendon
  Press (1911) 1964.
Moritz Lazarus, The Ethics of Judaism, translated by Henrietta Szold. Phila-
  delphia, 1901, 1902.
Moses Maimonides, Guide for the Perplexed, translated by S. Pines. London
  & University of Chicago Press, 1963.
— dto. translated from the original Arabic text by Michael Friedlaender.
  London (1881) 1904, reprinted by Dover Publications, New York 1956.
Moses Mendelssohn, Jerusalem and other Jewish Writings, translated by
  Alfred Jospe, Schocken, New York 1969.
— Moses Mendelssohn. A Biographical Study, by Alexander Altmann,
  Routledge & Kegan Paul, London and The Jewish Pub. Society, Phila-
  delphia 1973.
Rashi, The Pentateuch and Rashi's Commentary, translated by Abr. ben
  Isaiah and B. Sharfman, 5 volumes, Brooklyn, N.Y. 1949.
— dto. translated by M. Rosenbaum and A. M. Silbermann, 5 volumes.
  London 1924-1934.
Franz Rosenzweig, The Star of Redemption, translated by William W. Hallo,
  Routledge & Kegan Paul, London, and Holt, Rinehart & Winston,
  New York 1971.
— On Jewish Learning (three essays from Kleinere Schriften), edited and
  introduced by N. N. Glatzer and translated by William Wolf, Schocken,
  New York 1955.
— Franz Rosenzweig. His Life and Thought, by N. N. Glatzer, Schocken,
  New York 1961.

Gershom G. Scholem, Major Trends in Jewish Mysticism, Schocken, New
     York (1941) 3rd edition 1956, Paperback 1961.
  — Sabbatai Ṣevi. The Mystical Messiah 1626-1676, translated from Hebrew
     by R. J. Zwi Werblowsky, Routledge & Kegan Paul, London and
     Princeton Univ. Press, Princeton, N.J. 1973.
Chaim Weizmann, Trial and Error, Autobiography, Schocken, New York
     1961.
  — Chaim Weizmann, by Isaiah Berlin, Weidenfeld & Nicolson, London
     1958.

# Index

This index gives only the more important names and subjects relevant to the theme. It omits the names in Chapter 17—'Participation in General Cultural Life'—including names dealt with or referred to in other chapters. To list them here would give the book an undesired apologetic slant.

*non-Jews
†baptized Jews